HIT

数论经典著作系列

闵嗣鹤文集

The Symposium of Min Sihe

HITP
哈尔滨工业大学出版社
HARBIN INSTITUTE OF TECHNOLOGY PRESS

内容提要

闵嗣鹤教授是我国已故著名数学家，他的研究工作涉及许多数学分支，特别是对指数和估计、Riemann Zeta 函数论、数论在近似计算中的应用以及数字石油勘探中的数学方法等方面作出了卓越的贡献. 本文集精选了闵嗣鹤教授在这几方面的具有代表性的重要论文二十篇，这些论文至今仍有基本的理论价值和重大的实用价值. 本文集还收录了北京大学数学分析教研组第一次全系性试教等三篇附录以及闵嗣鹤教授几张珍贵的照片及手稿. 本文集对于从事研究解析数论、分析函数论及它们的应用的科技工作者、研究生是十分宝贵的重要资料，对从事中国近现代数学及研究的研究人员有重要的文献价值.

本书读者对象是从事数学研究的人员，以及大学数学专业高年级学生、研究生、教师及有关的科技工作者.

图书在版编目(CIP)数据

闵嗣鹤文集/闵嗣鹤著. —哈尔滨：哈尔滨工业大学出版社，2011.3

ISBN 978-7-5603-3216-1

Ⅰ.①闵…　Ⅱ.①闵…　Ⅲ.①数学—文集　Ⅳ.①01-53

中国版本图书馆 CIP 数据核字(2011)第 038414 号

策划编辑　刘培杰　张永芹
责任编辑　李广鑫
封面设计　孙茵艾
出版发行　哈尔滨工业大学出版社
社　　址　哈尔滨市南岗区复华四道街 10 号　邮编 150006
传　　真　0451－86414749
网　　址　http://hitpress.hit.edu.cn
印　　刷　哈尔滨市石桥印务有限公司
开　　本　787mm×1092mm　1/16　印张 17.25　插页 12　字数 350 千字
版　　次　2011 年 3 月第 1 版　2011 年 3 月第 1 次印刷
书　　号　ISBN 978-7-5603-3216-1
定　　价　98.00 元

谦和風采惭吾侪
廿年教泽啟人文

纪念
闵嗣鶴教授

江泽涵敬题
一九八八年四月

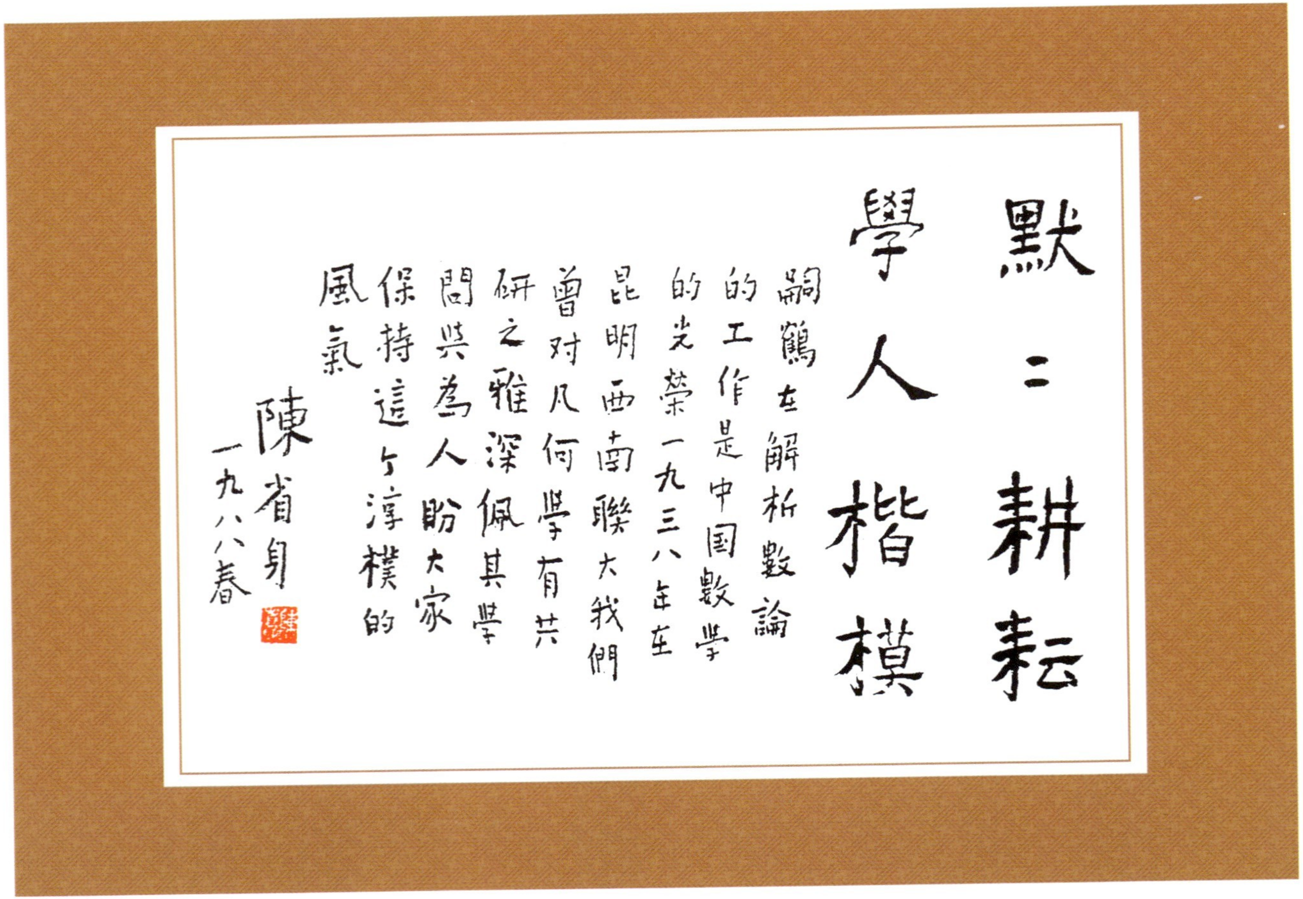
默默耕耘
學人楷模
嗣鶴在解析數論
的工作是中国數學
的光榮一九三八年在
昆明西南聯大我們
曾对凡何學有共
研之雅深佩其學
問與為人盼大家
保持這个淳樸的
風氣
陳省身
一九八八春

忆嗣鹤兄

一九二五曾同班
七三九月犹交谈
风风雨雨半世纪
深厚友谊记心间
好学不厌精数论
石油勘探闢新田
诲人不倦善培育
受业泉城齐怀念

段学夏 1988.3

怀念闵嗣鹤教授

您是虔诚的园丁，悉心培植着数学园地，从艰难深奥的数学理论到趣味盎然的数学小品。

您是虔诚的园丁，悉心培植着数学人才，从数学专业突出的研究生到一般的数学爱好者。

忆往昔桃李芬芳，弦歌不辍。看今朝硕果累累，人才辈出。总难忘您的业绩。

程民德谨题 一九八八年六月于北京大学

回忆老友闵嗣鹤先生

闵嗣鹤先生是一位有才华责任心很强的数学家。自从一九五二年院系调整以来，我和他就共事于北京大学数学系。经过多年相处，我深深感到他善于处理问题的能力和数学才干。承担任务的周到之，凡是请他担任的工作，无论是教学、科研，或研究院所用有求做课题或其它，例如审稿、数学竞赛命题等等，他总是应诺下来，作出精密计划，然后运用智慧胜利完成。可惜他积劳成疾，过早地离开了我们，未能将他的才能充分发挥出来。这是我国数学界的一大损失。他的业绩将不会被他的同事们和学生们忘记的。

江泽涵 一九八二年三月

深沉博學

數論專家

聰穎勤奮

應用英才

纪念闵嗣鹤教授

逝世十五周年

徐献瑜

一九八八年八月

能受苦方為志士
肯吃虧不是痴人

彥群兄嘗以此語勸我十九年來拳拳未敢忘今錄之以奉其遺著出版之賀

學弟趙慈庚題 一九八八 三月

闵嗣鹤教授治学严谨
诲人不倦教学科研均臻
上乘为后人楷模

孙树年题
八八年
三月

闵先生晚年与我交甚厚，我以师事之。先生持己以谨，待人以诚，治学以严，执教以虔，处事以正。憾其早逝，愿后来同行继其德业而光大之。

冷生明敬题 一九八八年八月

闵嗣鹤（1913—1973年）

家父在西南联大时留影*

20世纪60年代全家在颐和园留影

家父与长子在香山公园合影

1933年数学学会欢送本届毕业会员摄影
(后排左二为家父)

*本书中所有照片、书信、手稿及说明文字均由闵嗣鹤的子女提供。

数学家们在棉纺织厂前留影
（前排左四为家父，左一为吴光磊，
左二为江泽涵）

数学家们会后留影
（左一为家父，左四为华罗庚，
左六为庄圻泰）

晚年在斗室之前留影

惠泉：

8.15来信收到。那孩子的名字是史丰收。他能心算13位乘13位的数。六位乘六位差不多立刻写出结果。八位乘八位约用30—50秒。除法更快，开方也可以。此次本来有意留他，给他做系统，但是他的思路与方式可能比不上他的心算。现在系统计算已做出，今天有一位同[redacted]来送他回陕西去。明天我们要出谈一次，讨论系统的情况。

这件事比较容易招谣，最好不要"广为宣传"。他的心算是以一位数乘多位数做基础。最简单的是用2乘。例如用2乘6917，写作06917。从左到右写出得数，见0:6写0，后面过5加1，即第一位是1。其次见6:9写2（6-5=1，1×2=2），后面过5，加1得3，即第二位是3。再看9:1，见9写8（9-5=4，4×2=8），后面不到5不加，因此第三位是8。再看1:7，见1写2，后过5写加1，即得3。再看7:0，见7写4（7-5=2，2×2=4），即最后一位是4。于是

6917×2=13834。

对于2的口诀是"看见小于5的加倍，大于5的要减5后加倍，下面过5（即≥5）再加1。"这样法就可以很快从左到右写出得数。

用4，8，5乘有同样类似口诀。用3，6，9乘口诀较难。用7乘口诀更难。

闵嗣鹤给其子惠泉书信

最近我在301看心脏病，疗效还好。仍然在200号工作（拿回家来做），不久要开这方面的会。

三姑来过一次，打算秋天把奶奶的骨灰迁移到爷爷葬的墓地去。如果你能回来，一起也更好。听说，你秋天不能回来，最好在什么时候能回来一次。

被褥子带给你了，还能用吗？再等些时候，打算再给你买新的。你的布票还没有换，原因是比太提麻烦，不要给开介绍信，免不得去拿一次。

零零碎碎写了这封信。再谈吧！祝

进步

爸 72.8.20

北京大栅栏印刷厂出品 71.2 (1510)

闵嗣鹤给其子惠泉书信

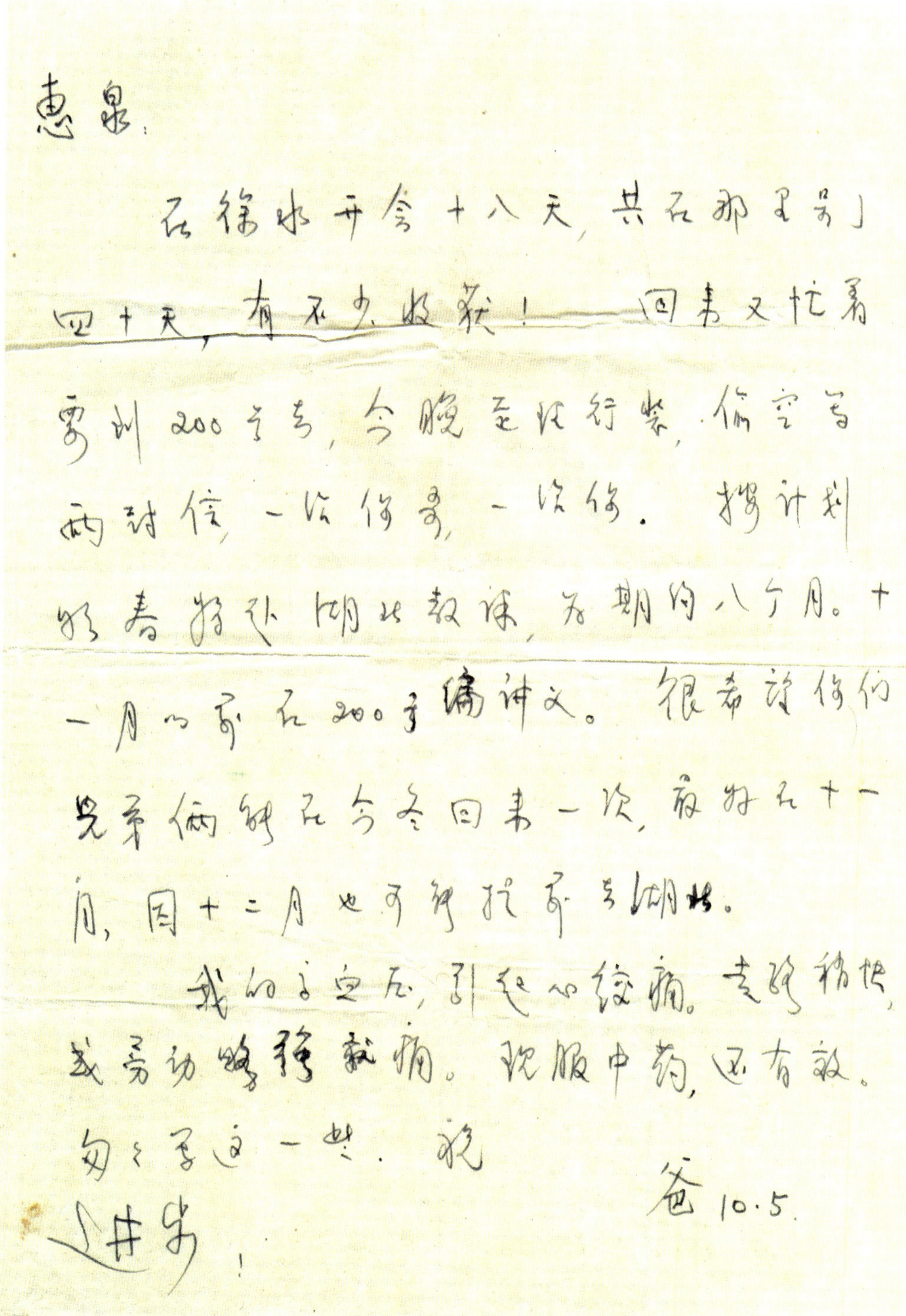

惠泉：

在徐州开会十八天，共在那里呆了四十天，有不少收获！——回来又忙着要到200号去，今晚在收行装，偷空写两封信，一给你哥，一给你。据计划明春将赴湖北教课，为期约八个月。十一月以前在200号编讲义。很希望你们兄弟俩能在今冬回来一次，最好在十一月，因十二月也可能提前去湖北。

我的[illegible]，引起心绞痛。走路稍快，或劳动略猛就痛。现服中药，还有效。

匆匆写这一些。祝

进步！

爸 10.5

闵嗣鹤给其子惠泉书信

$Q_s = p_1 p_2 \cdots p_s, \qquad (p_1, p_2, \cdots) = (3, 5, \cdots)$

可取 $p_s \leq x^{1/3}$ 或更大些. 设 $u \mid Q_s$ 时

$$\sum_{d \mid u} \rho_d \begin{cases} = 1 & u = 1, \\ \leq 0 & u > 1, \end{cases}$$

则

$$\sum_{\substack{n \leq x \\ (x-n, Q_s)=1}} \Lambda(n) \geq \sum_{n \leq x} \Lambda(n) \sum_{\substack{d \mid Q_s \\ d \mid x-n}} \rho_d$$

$$= \sum_{d \mid Q_s} \rho_d \sum_{\substack{n \leq x \\ n \equiv x\ (d)}} \Lambda(n)$$

$$= \sum_{d \mid Q_s} \rho_d\, \psi(x, x, d) \quad \text{Gallagher 的估计}$$

$$= x \sum_{d \mid Q_s} \frac{\rho_d}{\varphi(d)} + \sum_{d \mid Q_s} \rho_d \left| \psi(x, x, d) - \frac{x}{\varphi(d)} \right|$$

取

$$\rho_d = \mu(d, y), \qquad y = x^{1/2} / \log^{B} x,$$

则

$$\sum_{\substack{n \leq x \\ (x-n, Q_s)=1}} \Lambda(n) \geq x \sum_{d \mid Q_s} \frac{\mu(d, y)}{\varphi(d)} + O(x / \log^{A} x).$$

(A, B 意义见 Gallagher)

$B = 16A + 103$

或 $2A + 23$

闵嗣鹤1973年有关哥德巴赫猜想研究手稿

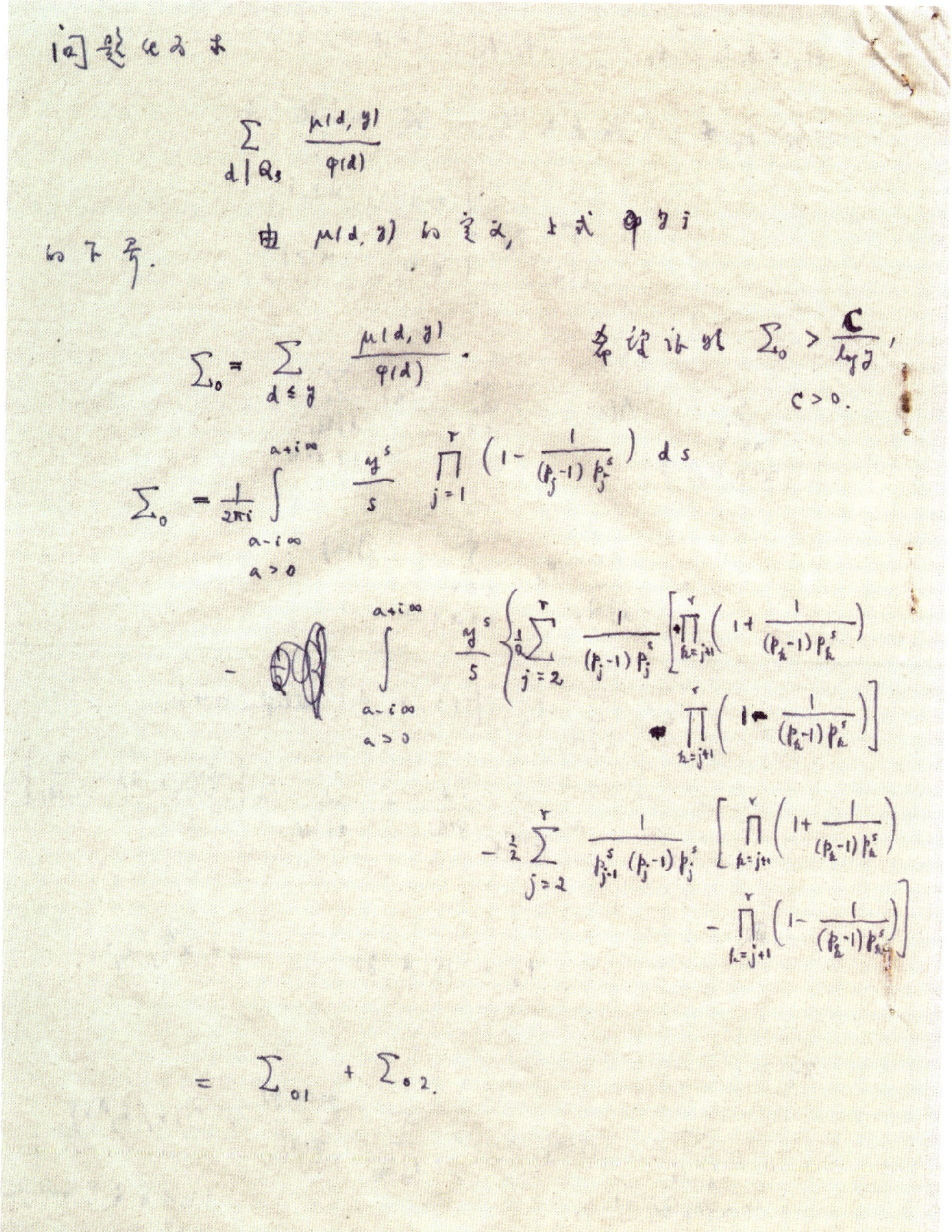

问题化为求

$$\sum_{d\mid Q_y}\frac{\mu(d,y)}{\varphi(d)}$$

的下界. 由 $\mu(d,y)$ 的定义, 上式即为:

$$\sum\nolimits_0=\sum_{d\le y}\frac{\mu(d,y)}{\varphi(d)}.$$

希望证明 $\sum_0>\frac{C}{\log y}$, $C>0$.

$$\sum\nolimits_0=\frac{1}{2\pi i}\int_{a-i\infty}^{a+i\infty}\frac{y^s}{s}\prod_{j=1}^{r}\left(1-\frac{1}{(p_j-1)p_j^s}\right)ds,\quad a>0$$

$$-\int_{a-i\infty}^{a+i\infty}\frac{y^s}{s}\Bigg\{\frac{1}{2}\sum_{j=2}^{r}\frac{1}{(p_j-1)p_j^s}\left[\prod_{k=j+1}^{r}\left(1+\frac{1}{(p_k-1)p_k^s}\right)+\prod_{k=j+1}^{r}\left(1-\frac{1}{(p_k-1)p_k^s}\right)\right]$$

$$-\frac{1}{2}\sum_{j=2}^{r}\frac{1}{p_{j-1}^s(p_j-1)p_j^s}\left[\prod_{k=j+1}^{r}\left(1+\frac{1}{(p_k-1)p_k^s}\right)-\prod_{k=j+1}^{r}\left(1-\frac{1}{(p_k-1)p_k^s}\right)\right],\quad a>0$$

$$=\sum\nolimits_{01}+\sum\nolimits_{02}.$$

闵嗣鹤1973年有关哥德巴赫猜想研究手稿

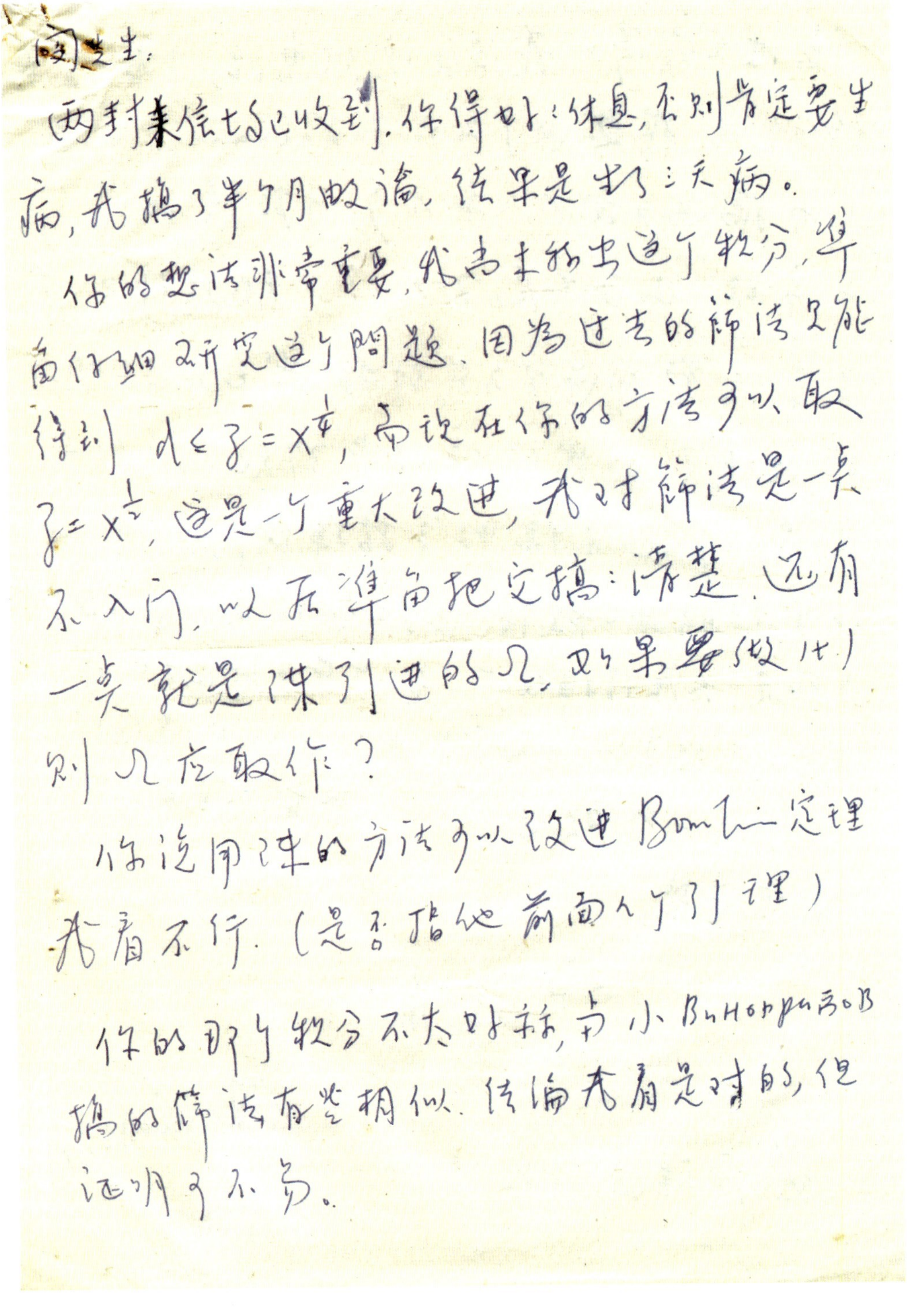

闵先生：

两封来信均已收到。你得好好休息，否则肯定要生病，我搞了半个月数论，结果是生了三天病。

你的想法非常重要，我尚未补出这个积分，准备仔细研究这个问题。因为过去的筛法只能得到 $d \le z = x^{\frac{1}{4}}$，而现在你的方法可以取 $z = x^{\frac{1}{2}}$，这是一个重大改进，我对筛法是一点不入门，以后准备把它搞搞清楚。还有一点就是陈景润的 λ，如果要(做1,1)则 λ 应取何？

你说用陈的方法可以改进Bombieri定理我看不行。（是否指他前面几个引理）

你的那个积分不太好补，与小Виноградов搞的筛法有些相似。结论我看是对的，但证明可不易。

潘承洞给闵嗣鹤的信

滤波公式寄上。我没有说什么话，只有一个具体计算，我想这个公式与Kalman不同，且国内搞这方面的人亦不少。可能给他们作一参考，山西太原748二厂（搞指挥仪）前天来信想用这个公式计算，我已把证明寄给他们了。而我们搞的是37炮，中央的意见是37炮不搞数字指挥仪，所以我们这里暂时告一段落。这个公式特点是简单、因存少，且稳定。太原指挥仪厂（是一个中国科技大学的毕业生在搞）他们的意见也是这样。我请他们多计算一些航道，总结一些取(ε,δ)的经验。

就写这些。

祝 健康

承洞
73.7.9.

必须注意休息！！

潘承洞给闵嗣鹤的信

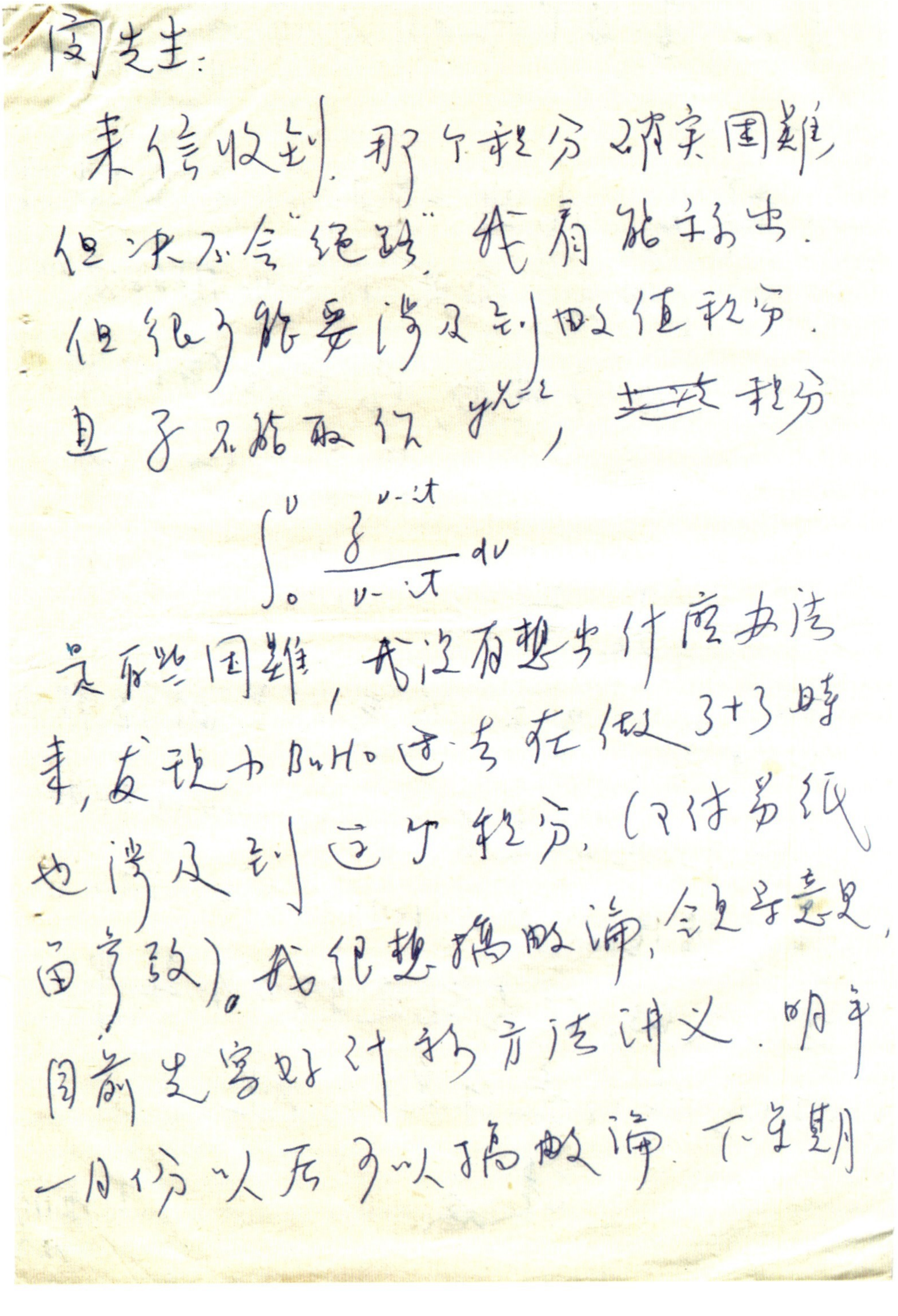

闵先生：

来信收到，那个积分确实困难，但决不会"绝路"，我看能算出，但很可能要涉及到数值积分，且可不能取值 ½，积分

$$\int_0^{\nu} \frac{\xi^{\nu-i\tau}}{\nu-i\tau}\,d\nu$$

是有些困难，我没有想出什么办法。未，发现 Bu Ho 还在在做 3+3 时也涉及到这个积分（下付另纸面致）。我很想搞数论，这是我的意见，目前先写好计算方法讲义，明年一月份以后可以搞数论。下星期

潘承洞给闵嗣鹤的信

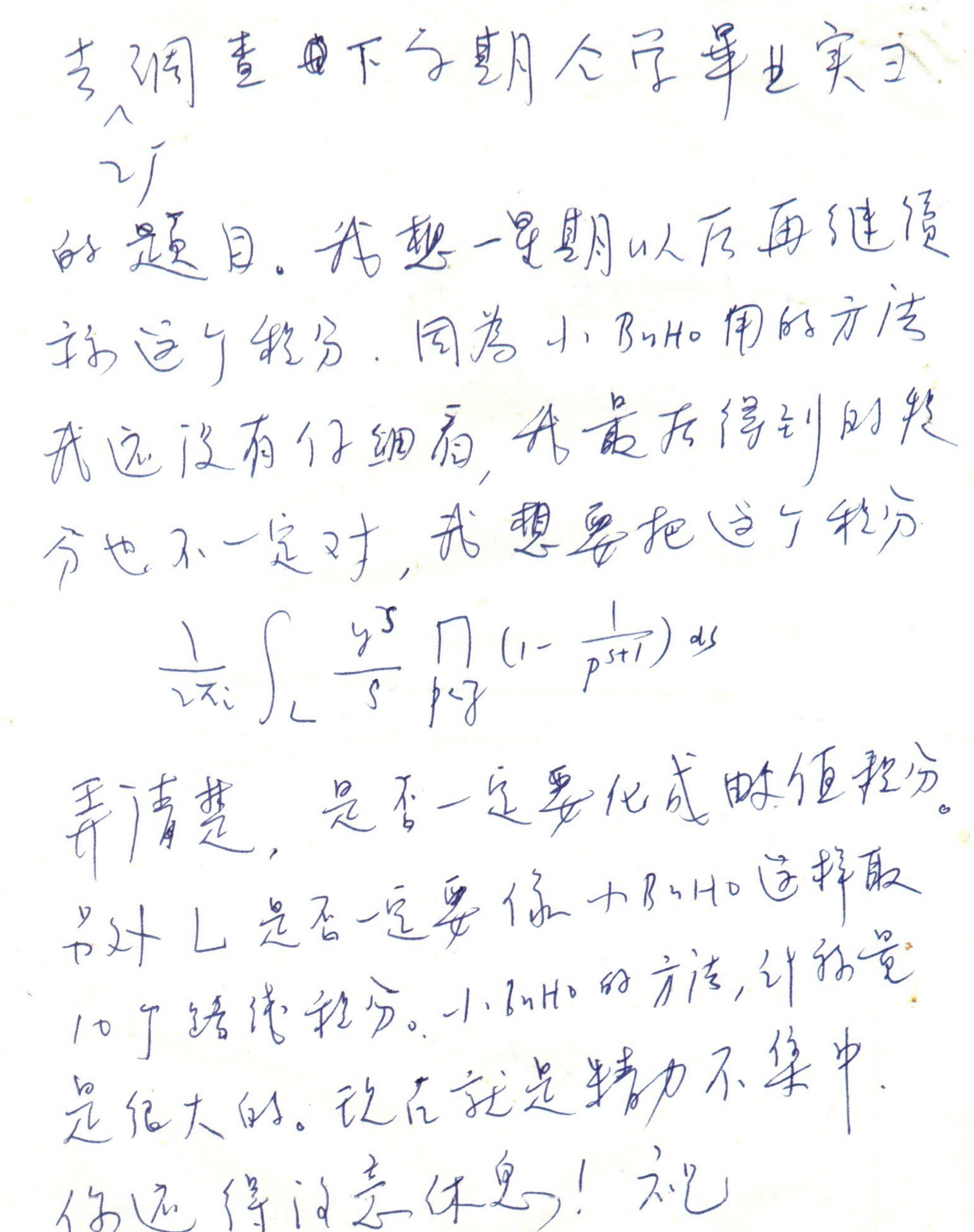
去21厂调查下学期全学年生实习的题目。我想一星期以后再继续计这个积分。因为小BuHo用的方法我还没有仔细看，我最后得到的积分也不一定对，我想要把这个积分

$$\frac{1}{2\pi i}\int_L \frac{y^s}{s}\prod_{p\le y}\left(1-\frac{1}{p^{s+1}}\right)ds$$

弄清楚，是否一定要化成数值积分。另外对L是否一定要像小BuHo选择取10个路线积分。小BuHo的方法，计算量是很大的。现在就是精力不集中。

你还得注意休息！祝

健康

承洞

73.7.14

潘承洞给闵嗣鹤的信

⊙序

今年是闵嗣鹤先生逝世十五周年，大家纪念他、出版他的文集，以表达对闵先生的敬意与深切怀念之情，这对于逝者的在天之灵也是莫大的宽慰.

我和闵先生从西南联大开始，在抗战胜利之后在清华和北大同事多年. 特别是在1946年夏我到英国牛津大学作短期访问时，我们有机会对当时的一些问题交换了看法，彼此有了深入的了解，建立了友谊. 一九七三年十月十日，闵先生在校医院溘然逝世，六十作古，令人深感痛心和惋惜.

闵先生是我国著名的数学家、优秀的教育家，他热爱社会主义祖国、热爱科学，将一生奉献给了理想与事业. 新中国成立前，他怀着一颗赤子之心回到祖国，报效人民. 他先后任清华大学数学系教授、北京大学数力系教授、中国科学院数学研究所专门委员、北京师范大学数学系兼职教授、北京数学会理事和《数学通报》编委等职.

闵先生谦虚朴实、平易近人，待人豁达开明、治学有方，当年在他席前的学生与受到他教益的数学工作者现在有些已经成为我国数学界的栋梁，有些已是国际上知名的数学家. 这些都是中国数学界的光荣，这里也浸透着闵先生的心血.

闵先生思路敏捷、创造性强、学识渊博、兴趣广泛，几十年来他在许多数学分支上均有建树，特别是在解析数论领域作出了重要贡献.他在生前的最后四年,主要致力于研究与生产实践相关的数学问题,为我国数字地质勘探事业作出了积极的贡献.

闵先生一生所走过的道路是比较曲折、坎坷的.他在旧社会经历过许多苦难与困扰,在新中国成立后也多次受到各种干扰,特别是十年浩劫中的冲击.这些使他未能发挥出更大的作用.然而闵先生始终不失做人的质朴,始终怀有对科学真理、对数学强烈而执著追求的高尚精神,他长期带病坚持工作,直到生命的最后一刻.他一生作出了许多显著的成就,这是非常难能可贵的.

“人事有代谢,往来成古今.”今天的人们,特别是年轻的一代是幸运多了.社会已经形成了一种“尊重知识,尊重人才”的环境和气氛,这是十分令人欣慰的.我们不仅要培养造就出更多更优秀的杰出人才,而且要百倍地珍惜和爱护他们,让他们在和谐的社会环境与自由的学术天地里发出更多的光彩.

这本文集收录了闵先生一生中几个时期的一些代表作以及他的学生们所撰写的一篇生平记事.从他一生对数学作出的重大贡献和积极地应用数学理论直接为社会主义经济建设服务的光辉范例就可以看出,闵先生是知识界的典范,是我们大家学习的榜样.我相信,这本文集的刊行一定会进一步激发人们为发展教育与科学事业、赶超世界先进水平、振兴中华作出应有的贡献.

周培源

一九八八年七月一日

闵嗣鹤教授生平

我们怀着无比怀念与崇敬的心情，回忆我们敬爱的老师闵嗣鹤教授平凡而又光荣的一生.

先生字彦群，1913 年 3 月 8 日生于北京，祖籍江西奉新. 他祖父是位前清进士，定居北京，对他十分钟爱，竟不让他上小学，亲自教他识字读书，学习古文，希望他以后学文学. 他极为好学，自学了小学课程，并在解算术难题上显露了才华. 1925 年考入北师大附中，此时他的学习兴趣已倾向于数学了. 1929 年夏，同时考取了北大和北师大理预科，考虑到学费低离家近他选择了后者. 1931 年升入数学系. 1935 年以优异成绩毕业. 在校学习期间就发表了四篇论文[1,2,3,4]①，并积极参加学术活动，曾负责编辑过北师大的《数学季刊》. 由于家境困难，从十七岁开始，便一直在中学兼课. 大学毕业后由老师傅种孙教授介绍到北师大附中任教. 在这期间他写出了后来获奖的论文《相合式解数之渐近公式及应用此理以讨论奇异级数》[5]，清华大学杨武之教授发现了这一位有才华的青年，立即于 1937 年 6 月聘请他去清华算学系当助教. 从此他把自己的一生都奉献给了祖国的数学事业，踏上了一条成功而又艰难之路.

先生接到清华聘书未满一月，尚未去工作，就爆发了“卢沟桥事变”，清华南迁，与北大、南开先在长沙组成临时大学，最后在昆明成立西南联大. 先生在北京安葬了祖父母及父亲的灵柩后，和母亲及三个妹妹与傅种孙先生一齐离开了北平. 他随清华先到长沙后到昆明. 他在西南联大曾为陈省身先生辅导黎曼几何；参加华罗庚先生的数论讨论班，并与华罗庚先生合作发表了数篇重要论文[6,7,8,9,15]. 华罗庚先生在他们合作的论文[6]底稿扉页上写着：“闵君之工作，占非常重要之地位.”对其工作作了很高的评价.

1945 年先生考取了公费留学，10 月到英国，在牛津大学由 E. C. Titchmarsh 指导研究解析数论，由于在 Riemann Zeta 函数的阶估计等著名问题上得到了优异的结果[18]，1947 年获博士学位. 随后赴美国普林斯顿高等研究院进行研究工作，并参加了数学大师 H. Weyl 的讨论班. 他在美国仅工作了一年，尽管有 Weyl 的真诚挽留，导师 Titchmarsh 热情邀请他再赴英伦，但爱国之心，思母之情促使他急于返回祖国. 1948 年秋回国后，再次在清华大学数学系执教，任副教授，1950 年晋升教授. 1952 年起任北京大学数学力学系教授. 他曾任中国科学院数学研究所专门委员，北京数学会理事等职.

---

① 所有引文均见“闵嗣鹤主要论著目录”.

1950 年与朱敬一女士结婚，有两子三女. 夫妻之间互敬互爱、风雨同舟，先生在学术上取得重大成就与夫人的支持协助是分不开的.

先生对数学的许多分支都有研究，他的工作涉及数论、几何、调和分析、微分方程、复变函数、多重积分的近似计算及广义解析函数等许多方面，但他最主要的贡献是在解析数论，特别是在三角和估计与 Riemann Zeta 函数理论. 诚如陈省身先生所指出的："嗣鹤在解析数论的工作是中国数学的光荣." 下面我们来简单谈一谈他的学术成就：

各种形式的三角和估计是解析数论中最重要的研究课题之一. 先生在大学毕业后，第一个重要的工作，就是得到了如下形式的完整三角和的均值估计[5]：

$$\sum_{a=1}^{p-1}\left|\sum_{x=1}^{p} e\left(\frac{af(x)}{p}\right)\right|^{s} \ll p^{s-1-(s-n-1)/(n-1)} \tag{1}$$

其中 p 为素数，$e(\theta) = e^{2\pi i\theta}$，$n > 2$，$2 \leqslant s \leqslant 2n$，以及整系数多项式

$$f(x) = a_n x^n + \cdots + a_1 x,\ (p, a_n, \cdots, a_1) = 1$$

由此，他进而证明：对任意整数 m 及 $2 < s \leqslant 2n$，同余方程

$$f(x_1) + \cdots + f(x_s) \equiv m \pmod p$$

的解数 $\phi(f(x), s)$ 有渐近公式

$$\phi(f(x), s) = p^{s-1} + O(p^{s-1-(s-2)/(n-1)})$$

这一结果优于由莫德尔(Mordell)的著名估计

$$\sum_{x=1}^{p} e\left(\frac{f(x)}{p}\right) \ll p^{1-1/n} \tag{2}$$

所能直接推出的渐近公式. 他的这一公式在多项式华林(Waring)问题中有重要应用. 他的这篇论文获得了当时为纪念高君韦女士有奖征文第一名.

如何把莫德尔著名估计(2)推广到 k 个变数的情形是一个重要问题. 他与华罗庚先生合作解决了 $k = 2$ 的情形[7,15]，然后他又独自解决了对任意的 k 的情形[16].

1947 年，先生研究 ζ 函数论中的著名问题：$\zeta(1/2 + it)$ 的估计. 通过改进某种形式的二维 Weyl 指数和

$$\sum_{m}\sum_{n} e(f(m, n)) \tag{3}$$

的估计，他证明了当时最好的结果[18]：对任何 $\varepsilon > 0$ 有

$$\zeta(1/2 + it) \ll (l + |t|)^{15/92+\varepsilon}$$

后来，先后指导他的研究生迟宗陶、尹文霖进一步利用他估计指数和(3)的方法，在除数问题，$\zeta(1/2 + it)$ 的阶估计等著名问题中得到了当时领先的结果.

数学中最著名的猜想之一是：Riemann Zeta 函数 $\zeta(s)$ 的全部复零点均位于直线 $1/2 + it(-\infty < t < \infty)$ 上，这就是所谓 Riemann 猜想，至今未获解决.

设 $s = \sigma + it$，$N(T)$ 表 $\zeta(s)$ 在区域

$$0 \leqslant t \leqslant T, \quad 1/2 \leqslant \sigma \leqslant 1$$

中的零点个数,$N_0(T)$ 表在直线

$$0 \leqslant t \leqslant T, \quad \sigma = 1/2$$

上的零点个数. Riemann 猜想就是要证明

$$N_0(T) > N(T)$$

ζ 函数论中的一个著名问题是定出尽可能好的常数 A,使得

$$N_0(T) > AN(T)$$

先生[30] 首先定出了 A 的值 $\geqslant (60\,000)^{-1}$. 这一结果直到 1974 年才被莱文森(N. Levinson) 改进.

在20 世纪50 年代中、后期,先生系统研究了 Riemann Zeta 函数的一种重要推广:

$$Z_{n,k}(s) = \sum_{\substack{x_1=-\infty \\ |x_1|+\cdots+|x_k|\neq 0}}^{\infty} \cdots \sum_{x_k=-\infty}^{\infty} \frac{1}{(x_1^n + \cdots + x_h^n)^s}$$

其中 n 是正偶数,他建立了这种函数的基本理论,其中一部分工作是与其学生尹文霖合作完成的[25,27,28,38,39].

在 1960 年前后,先生从事广义解析函数方面的研究[41],并在利用数论方法研究多重积分的近似计算方面也作了一些工作[35,36,37].

先生毕生热心于数学教育事业,热情培养年轻人,是一位优秀的教育家. 他讲授过数学分析、复变函数、初等数论等基础课,解析数论等专门化课程. 无论新课老课,他都认真备课,讲课十分生动,深入浅出,循循善诱,学生非常欢迎. 大家知道,数学分析教学中最重要的也是最困难的部分就是极限理论. 1953 年 5 月,北大数力系组织了全系观摩教学,由他主讲《有序变量与无穷小量》. 他利用亲自制作的玻璃教具,直观地演示了 ε 与 δ 的依赖关系,讲得通俗易懂,十分精彩. 听讲的学生在过了三十多年后,还清楚地记得当时的情景,听课就好像看电影,使这高等数学中最难学懂的部分,理解得既快又清楚. 当月的《数学通报》刊登了讲稿的部分内容[21]. 这对北大数力系以至全国高校当时的数学教学都起了很好的示范推动作用. 这一点是值得我们现在的教师特别是青年教师学习的. 1957 年他与严士健合作写了《初等数论》[32],这至今仍是一本初等数论的好教材. 他为解析数论研究生讲课的讲稿,经整理后分别于 1958 年和 1981 年出版了《数论的方法》上、下册[34,54],这是一本很有特色今天仍有价值的解析数论入门教材. 他另有一部《高等微积分》讲义未能出版.

先生在清华、北大招收了多届解析数论研究生,1960 年前后,他和庄圻泰先生在北大数力系一起领导了广义解析函数、拟保角映射及其应用的研究,为我国在这些分支方面的研究奠定了基础,为培养人才作出了贡献. 他一贯无私地指导、帮助与支持年青的数学工作者,今天,他所培养的这些学生已经成为我

国数学界的一支重要骨干力量. 这里特别值得一提的是被数学界传为佳话的他对陈景润的热情支持与指导. 1966 年春,《科学通报》第十七卷第九期(5 月 15 日出版)上发表了陈景润的著名论文——《大偶数表为一个素数及一个不超过二个素数乘积之和》——的简报,陈景润一拿到这期通报,首先想到的是他的闵老师,他在杂志的封面里恭恭敬敬地写上了:

"敬爱的闵老师:

非常感谢您对学生的长期指导,特别是对本文的详细指导.

学生

陈景润敬礼

1966. 5. 19"

并立即跑去送给最关心最支持他的老师. 他们之间的联系大约始于 1963 年,陈经常去先生家请教,热烈讨论问题,师生之间亲密无间,使陈获益匪浅. 尤其是先生正直的为人,严谨的学风,不分亲疏乐于助人的精神,使陈景润对他十分钦佩和无比信任. 陈景润不断地改进和简化他的定理的证明,于 1972 年寒假送去了他自己数年心血的结晶——厚厚的一叠原稿,请他最信任的老师审阅. 当时先生的身体已经很不好了,原来想好好休息一下,但他知道陈的论文是一项极重要的工作,如果对了,将是对解析数论的一个历史性的重大贡献. 因此,他放弃了休息,不顾劳累与经常发作的心脏病,逐步地细心校阅. 当他最后判定陈的证明是正确的时,高兴极了,他看到在激烈的竞争中,新中国自己培养出来的年青数学家,在解析数论的一个最重要的问题——Goldbach 猜想的研究上,终于又一次夺回了世界领先地位. 陈景润的著名文章终于在 1973 年的《中国科学》上全文发表了. 然而,先生又冷静而正确地指出:要最终解决 Goldbach 猜想还要走很长的一段路.

先生一生十分热心于中学数学教育和数学普及工作. 在西南联大期间,他经常为昆明龙渊中学学生开设数学讲座,有趣的数学知识受到中学生的热烈欢迎. 回国后,他是《数学通报》的编委,经常作科普报告,写通俗文章[23,25]. 他曾多次主持或参与我国高等院校入学考试的数学命题工作及中学生数学竞赛的命题工作[40,48]. 这些高质量的命题为我国选拔人才作出了贡献. 此外,他的著名的小册子《格点与面积》[47]生动地介绍了几何数论的一些重要而有趣的基本概念和知识,受到中学老师与学生的欢迎.

先生有很好的古典文学修养,喜爱书法与绘画,精通数门外语,这些是他在紧张的脑力劳动之余,借以休息的业余爱好. 他十分喜爱自己的孩子,在紧张的工作之间,总是抽空为他们画画,教他们读书,带着孩子们去公园游玩.

最后,我们怀着难以抑制的激动心情,回忆先生一生中令人难忘的最后四年. 在这我国历史上的异常时期,先生满腔热情地把全部精力投入了我国石油、地质勘探事业,应用数学知识为社会主义经济建设服务,取得了重大成就. 从1969年起,他先是与北大数力系同志一起到北京地质仪器厂与该厂共同研制当时急需的海上勘探设备——海洋重力仪. 由于西方国家对我们禁运,缺乏各种技术资料,困难很大. 先生为攻克该设备的理论关键——滤波问题作出了重要贡献. 他先后完成了《数字滤波的若干分析问题》等一系列研究,最后提出了《切比雪夫权系数的数字滤波方法》,从而保证了所设计的重力仪能成功地从五万倍强噪声背景中提取有用的微弱信号. 该仪器定名为"ZY-1"型海洋重力仪,其性能比日本用三次平均法制造的"东京 a-1 号"优越得多. 该仪器经五年海上实验于1975年通过国家鉴定,成为我国大面积普查的先进工具. 从1971年10月起先生又在石油部从事数字地震勘探工作. 他应用数学理论解决石油科技中的理论和实际问题,为祖国石油工业的大发展作出了一定的贡献. 当时他的身体已经很不好,患有严重的心脏病,经常发病,但是为了收集第一手资料他不顾个人安危深入生产第一线,亲赴海上勘探基地. 当他看到我国海洋石油勘探开发事业的壮观景象,高兴地忘掉了病痛欣然以"出海"为题赋诗一首,抒发自己的远大抱负和民族自豪感:

轻舟出海浪涛涛,听炮观涛兴致高.
鱼嫩菜香都味美,风和雨细胜篮摇.
东洋技术为我用,渤海方船更自豪.
一日往还学大庆,算法如今要赶超.

为了普及科学知识,他带病坚持为工人和技术人员讲课. 在各种地震勘探的学术会议和讨论班上,他作报告,介绍国外经验,提出自己的新看法与新成果,在他的指导、帮助和直接参与下,为我国数字石油勘探首创了一套数学方法,解决了一系列生产中的关键问题,培养了一批新生力量,使我国数字石油勘探事业取得了可喜的进展. 在这期间他写出了有关数值滤波与地震数字处理方面的研究论文[50,51,53,54],并主编了这方面的教材《地震勘探数字技术》[49,52]. 1973年9月起先生在北大为石油部开办数字地震勘探技术训练班,紧张、劳累、夜以继日地忘我工作,他终于病倒了. 最令人感动与终生难忘的是,在他生前的最后一天,还忍着病痛找来技术人员反复讨论、研究数字地震勘探技术中急需解决的数学关键问题,使问题终于获得解决. 临终前他还在病床上修改即将出版的《地震勘探数字技术》[52]书稿,并对劝他休息的爱人和子女说:"你们不要干扰我,我还有很多任务没有做完,心里总是不安宁."1973年10月10日终因劳累过度心脏病猝发,在北大校医院去世,永远离开了我们,终年仅六十岁. 先生过早地不幸去世是我国数学界和石油科技界的一大损失,他在数学与石油科技界的老师、同事和学生们都时刻深情地怀念他,他的无数动人事迹至今仍然深深留在人们的心中,为人传颂……

敬爱的闵老师离开我们已经十五年了,历史为他安排了一条坎坷而又充满希望的道路.他在数学园地上默默耕耘了四十余个春秋,奇花竞放,硕果累累.他把自己的一生献给了祖国与人民,献给了自己的理想与心爱的数学事业,他热爱党和社会主义,工作责任心很强,勇于承担和完成各种困难任务,他才华横溢,思维敏捷,学风严谨,一丝不苟;他数十年如一日埋头工作,任劳任怨,不争名利,不争地位;他为人谦虚朴实,温良敦厚,待人亲切热情,热心提携后进,他那双慈爱而又充满智慧的眼睛好像总是在亲切地鼓励他的学生奋发向上,勇于进取;他积极地应用数学理论直接为社会主义经济建设服务,为我们作出了榜样;他置个人安危于不顾,为了事业在自己的岗位上工作到生命的最后一刻.放心吧,亲爱的老师,我们一定学习您的精神与实践,像您一样为发展祖国的数学事业,促进数学为社会主义经济建设服务,献出我们的全部力量!

迟宗陶　严士健　潘承洞

邵品琮　李　忠　潘承彪

一九八八年八月

目录

相合式解数之渐近公式及应用此理以讨论奇异级数[①]

§1　问题之叙述

本文中 n 表一一定之整数，p 常表素数．又本文中所谓之常数乃依于 n 且仅依于 n 者．又用

$$f(x) = O\{\varphi(x)\}$$

表示当 x 趋于某定限时 $|f(x)| < A\varphi(x)$，此 A 为一常数，有时依于一无穷小数 ε．特如 $f(x) = O(1)$ 表此函数受囿．例如，当 $x \to +\infty$．

$$\sin x = O(1),\ (x+1)^2 = O(x^2),\ \log x = O(x^{\varepsilon})\ (\varepsilon > 0)$$

又本文中所用之字母除 e，i 及 π 外常代表整数．遇有特别声明时，不受此限．

命 $f(x)$ 表一已与 $n(n>2)$ 次之整系数多项式，其系数间无公因子．今之问题为相合式

$$f(x_1) + \cdots + f(x_s) \equiv m \pmod p,\quad 1 \leqslant x_v \leqslant p \qquad (1)$$

之解答之个数，以 $\varphi(f(x), s)$ 表之．

① 1939 年度纪念高君韦女士有奖征文中获选论文第一篇．原载：科学，1940，24(8)：591-607.

如由算术的方法入手以对付此问题，实非常艰难，几乎不知从何处下手．本文的方法乃导入指数函数和的观念，然后求出其答解（当p增大时）之渐近公式（asymptotic formula）．所根据者为次之极简的几何级数的公式：

$$\sum_{x=1}^{p}\exp\left\{\frac{2\pi i\alpha x}{p}\right\}\begin{cases}=p,\ \text{若}\ \alpha\ \text{是}\ p\ \text{的倍数}\\=0,\ \text{若}\ \alpha\ \text{非}\ p\ \text{的倍数}\end{cases}$$

导入此观念后（1）之解之个数等于

$$\frac{1}{p}\sum_{\alpha=1}^{p}\left(\sum_{x=1}^{p}\exp\left\{\frac{2\pi i\alpha}{p}f(x)\right\}\right)^{s}\exp\left\{\frac{2\pi i\alpha}{p}m\right\}$$

因此即等于

$$\frac{1}{p}\sum_{\alpha=1}^{p}\sum_{x_1=1}^{p}\cdots\sum_{x_s=1}^{p}\exp\left\{\frac{2\pi i\alpha}{p}(f(x_1)+\cdots+f(x_s)-m)\right\}=$$

$$\frac{1}{p}\sum_{x_1=1}^{p}\cdots\sum_{x_s=1}^{p}\sum_{\alpha=1}^{p}\exp\left\{\frac{2\pi i\alpha}{p}(f(x_1)+\cdots+f(x_s)-m)\right\}=$$

$$\sum_{x_1=1}^{p}\cdots\sum_{x_s=1}^{p}1=\varphi(f(x),s)$$

$$f(x_1)+\cdots+f(x_s)\equiv m(p)$$

故显然得

$$\varphi(f(x),s)=p^{s-1}+O\left(\frac{1}{p}\sum_{\alpha=1}^{p-1}\left|\sum_{x=1}^{p}\exp\left\{\frac{2\pi i\alpha}{p}f(x)\right\}\right|^{s}\right)$$

故求（1）之解之渐近公式之问题一变而为求

$$S(f,p)=\sum_{\alpha=1}^{p-1}\left|\sum_{x=1}^{p}\exp\left\{\frac{2\pi i\alpha}{p}f(x)\right\}\right|^{s}$$

之无穷大阶之问题.

上理又可应用之以讨论“奇异级数”（singular series）：

$$\sum_{q=1}^{\infty}\sum_{\substack{\alpha=1\\(\alpha,q)=1}}^{q}\left[\frac{\sum_{x=1}^{q}\exp\left\{\frac{2\pi i\alpha}{q}f(x)\right\}}{q}\right]^{s}\exp\left\{-\frac{2\pi i\alpha}{p}m\right\}\tag{2}$$

本文内特定s之一下限σ，使$s>\sigma$时，上级数为收敛．此级数之收敛性虽可直接讨论，但所得σ之值将嫌过大．本文中将证明于无穷乘积

$$\prod_{p}\left(1+\sum_{l=1}^{\infty}\left\{\sum_{\substack{\alpha=1\\p\times\alpha}}^{p^l}\left[\frac{\sum_{x=1}^{p^l}\exp\{2\pi i\alpha f(x)/p^l\}}{p^l}\right]^{s}\exp\{-2\pi i\alpha m/p^l\}\right\}\right)\tag{3}$$

（$\prod_{p}$表p经过一切素数），当[ ] 内各项换以绝对值后，为收敛时，即与（2）相等. 因而（2）之收敛问题遂化为

$$\prod_{p}\left(1+\sum_{l=1}^{\infty}\left|\sum_{\substack{\alpha=1\\ p\times\alpha}}^{p^l}\left[\frac{\sum_{x=1}^{p^l}\exp\{2\pi i\alpha f(x)/p^l\}}{p^l}\right]^s\right|\right) \tag{4}$$

之收敛问题，显然若所定 s 之值，能使[ ] 内之值为 $1+O(p^{-1-\varepsilon})$（其中 ε 为任意正数与 p 无关），则(4) 为收敛．故此问题复化为求

$$S(f,q)=\sum_{\substack{\alpha=1\\(\alpha,q)=1}}^{q}\left|\sum_{x=1}^{q}\exp\{2\pi i\alpha f(x)/q\}\right|^s$$

之无穷大阶之问题．用本文方法所定 σ 之值为 $n+1$.

§2　相合式之渐近公式

莫德尔氏曾证明：若 $f(x)$ 之数系不皆为 p 之倍数，则

$$\sum_{x=1}^{p}\exp\{2\pi i f(x)/p\}=O(p^{1-1/n}) \tag{5}$$

此式乃本节引 1 之一演理．由此结果立得

$$\varphi(f(x),s)=p^{s-1}+O(p^{s(1-1/n)})=p^{s-1}+O(p^{s-1-(s/n-1)}) \tag{6}$$

故当 $s\geqslant n+1$ 时得一渐近公式．

本文之旨趣在更求精(6) 中之舛误项．所用之原则是：以上所论之方法为“各个计算”而今后所用之方法为“求其中值”．

并不失其普遍性，吾人可设 $f(x)$ 之常数项为零．命

$$g(x)=a_nx^n+a_{n-1}x^{n-1}+\cdots+a_1x$$

作和式

$$\sum_{\alpha_1=1}^{p}\cdots\sum_{\alpha_n=1}^{p}\left|\sum_{x=1}^{p}\exp\{2\pi i g(x)/p\}\right|^{2n}$$

此即等于

$$\sum_{x_1=1}^{p}\cdots\sum_{x_n=1}^{p}\sum_{y_1=1}^{p}\cdots\sum_{y_n=1}^{p}\sum_{\alpha_1=1}^{p}\cdots\sum_{\alpha_n=1}^{p}\exp\left\{\frac{2\pi i}{p}[\alpha_n(x_1^n+\cdots+x_n^n-y_1^n-\cdots-y_n^n)+\cdots+\alpha_1(x_1+\cdots+x_n-y_1-\cdots-y_n)]\right\}=$$

$$\sum_{x_1=1}^{p}\cdots\sum_{x_n=1}^{p}\sum_{y_1=1}^{p}\cdots\sum_{y_n=1}^{p}p^n$$

$$x_1^n+\cdots+x_n^n\equiv y_1^n+\cdots+y_n^n\quad(p)$$

$$\cdots$$

$$x_1+\cdots+x_n\equiv y_1+\cdots+y_n\quad(p)$$

$$= p^n N$$

此 N 及

$$x_1^n + \cdots + x_n^n \equiv y_1^n + \cdots + y_n^n \pmod p$$

$$\cdots$$

$$x_1 + \cdots + x_n \equiv y_1 + \cdots + y_n \pmod p$$

之解之个数. 易见如 $y_1, \cdots, y_n$ 已定,则 $x_1, \cdots, x_n$,只为 $y_1, \cdots, y_n$ 之另一排列(因其所有之初等对称函数都相等),即

$$N \leqslant n!p^n$$

即已得

$$\sum_{\alpha_1=1}^{p} \cdots \sum_{\alpha_n=1}^{p} \left| \sum_{x=1}^{p} \exp\{2\pi i(\alpha_n x^n + \cdots + \alpha_1 x)/p\} \right|^{2n} \leqslant n!p^{2n} \tag{7}$$

今往检出此式之左端包有若干个与

$$\sum_{\alpha=1}^{p-1} \left| \sum_{x=1}^{p} \exp\{2\pi i\alpha f(x)/p\} \right|^{2n} \tag{8}$$

等值之和. 今设 $f(x)$ 之 x^n 之系数非 p 之倍数.

显然

$$\psi(\lambda, \mu) = \sum_{\alpha=1}^{p-1} \left| \sum_{x=1}^{p} \exp\left\{\frac{2\pi i\alpha\lambda^{-n}}{p}(f(\lambda x + \mu) - f(\mu))\right\} \right|^{2n}$$

$$\lambda = 1, \cdots, p-1;\ \mu = 1, \cdots, p \tag{9}$$

皆与(8)等值(因当 x 过一全剩余系,则 $\lambda x + \mu$ 亦过一全剩余系,mod p,而当 α 过一全剩余系 mod p,则 $\alpha\lambda^{-n}$ 亦然也).

命

$$g_{\alpha,\lambda,\mu}(x) = \alpha\lambda^{-n}(f(\lambda x + \mu) - f(\mu))$$

及

$$S(g_{\alpha,\lambda,\mu}(x), p) = \sum_{x=1}^{p} \exp\left\{\frac{2\pi i\alpha}{p} g_{\alpha,\lambda,\mu}(x)\right\}$$

今往定出于(9)中至少有若干个 $\psi(\lambda, \mu)$ 其中无二 g 相同者.

若 $\psi(\lambda, \mu)$ 与 $\psi(\lambda', \mu')$ 有一项相同,则 $\psi(\lambda', \mu')$ 必为 $\psi(\lambda, \mu)$ 之另一排列,盖如 $g_{\alpha,\lambda,\mu}(x)$ 与 $g_{\alpha',\lambda',\mu'}(x)$ 之相当系数相合 mod p,即

$$\alpha\lambda^{-n}(f(\lambda x + \mu) - f(\mu)) \equiv \alpha'\lambda^{1-n}(f(\lambda' x + \mu') - f(\mu')) \pmod p$$

则两端各乘以 $k(=1, \cdots, p-1)$ 必仍相合也.

由此可知"与一指定之 $\psi(\lambda_0, \mu_0)$ 有公共项之 $\psi(\lambda, \mu)$ 之数"即等于"与 $\psi(\lambda_0, \mu_0)$ 内一项 $g_{\alpha_0,\lambda_0,\mu_0}(x)$ 相合 mod p 之 $g_{\alpha,\lambda,\mu}(x)$ 之数",亦即等于"相合式

$$\alpha\lambda^{-n}(f(\lambda x + \mu) - f(\mu)) \equiv \alpha_0\lambda_0^{-n}(f(\lambda_0 x + \mu_0) - f(\mu_0)), \alpha q \not\equiv 0 \pmod p \tag{10}$$

之解(α,λ,μ)之数”.

设

$$f(x) = b_nx^n + \cdots + b_1x, \quad b_n \not\equiv 0,(p), p > n > 2$$

代入(10)而比较各项系数即得

$$\alpha b_n \equiv \alpha_0 b_n, \quad \alpha\alpha_0 \not\equiv 0 \pmod p \tag{11}$$

$$\alpha\lambda^{r-n}f^{(r)}(\mu) \equiv \alpha_0\lambda_0^{r-n}f^{(r)}(\mu_0), \quad r = 1,\cdots,n-1 \pmod p \tag{12}$$

由(11)及(12),

$$\alpha \equiv \alpha_0 \pmod p \tag{13}$$

$$\lambda^{r-n}f^{(r)}(\mu) \equiv \lambda_0^{r-n}f^{(r)}(\mu_0) \pmod p \tag{14}$$

$$r = 1,\cdots,n-1$$

第一情形. 设$f^{(n-1)}(\mu_0) \not\equiv 0(p)$,则由(14)得

$$\lambda \equiv \frac{\lambda_0 f^{(r-1)}(\mu)}{f^{(n-1)}(\mu_0)} \pmod p \tag{15}$$

$$f^{(r)}(\mu) \equiv f^{(r)}(\mu_0)\left(\frac{f^{(n-1)}(\mu)}{f^{(n-1)}(\mu_0)}\right)^{n-r}, r = 1,\cdots,n-1 \pmod p \tag{16}$$

如(16)中诸相合式之一非恒等式,则μ至多有n个值能适合该相合式,μ值定后,则α与λ可由(13)及(15)唯一地决定. 于是(11)及(12)至多有n解,故与$\psi(\lambda_0,\mu_0)$有公共项之后$\psi(\lambda,\mu)$之数至多有n个.

如(16)中尽为恒合式,则必得

$$f'(\mu) \equiv f'(\mu_0)\left(\frac{f^{(n-1)}(\mu)}{f^{(n-1)}(\mu_0)}\right)^{n-1}$$

一恒等式. 上式表明$f'(x)$可写成一一次因子$f^{(n-1)}(x)$之$n-1$次方幂与一常数之积. 故$f(x)$可书作下形

$$f(x) = A(x-\alpha)^n + B \tag{17}$$

其中A,B及α为常数.

第二情形. 设$f^{(n-1)}(\mu_0) \equiv O(p)$,则由(14)

$$\lambda^{-1}f^{(n-1)}(\mu) \equiv 0 \pmod p$$

即

$$f^{(n-1)}(\mu) \equiv 0 \pmod p \tag{18}$$

此式可决定μ之值.

如$f^{(s)}(\mu_0) \not\equiv O(p)(s < n-1)$,则由(14)

$$\lambda^{s-n}f^{(s)}(\mu) \equiv \lambda_0^{s-n}f^{(s)}(\mu_0) \tag{19}$$

此式至多有$n-1$个根. 由(13),(18)及(19)知(11)及(12)至多有$n-1 < n$解. 故与$\psi(\lambda_0,\mu_0)$有公共项之$\psi(\lambda_1,\mu_1)$之数必小于n.

如$f^{(s)}(\mu_0) \equiv O(p), s = 1,\cdots,n-2$,则$f(x)$可书作下形

$$f(x) = A(x - \mu_0)^n + B$$

由以上所讨论者,可知在 $f(x)$ 不能写成

$$A(x - \alpha)^n + B$$

之形式时,与任一指定之 $\psi(\lambda_0, \mu_0)$ 有公共项之 $\psi(\lambda, \mu)$ 之数必小于或等于 n. 故在式(9) 之中至少有

$$\frac{p(p-1)}{2n}$$

个 $\psi(\lambda, \mu)$,其中任意二者所含之项完全不同. 故得

$$\frac{p(p-1)}{2n} \sum_{\alpha=1}^{p-1} \left| \sum_{x=1}^{p} \exp\left\{\frac{2\pi \mathrm{i}\alpha}{p} f(x)\right\} \right|^{2n} \leqslant \sum_{a_1=1}^{p} \cdots \sum_{\alpha_n=1}^{p} \left| \sum_{x=1}^{p} \exp\left\{\frac{2\pi \mathrm{i}}{p} g(x)\right\} \right|^{2n}$$

故

$$\sum_{\alpha=1}^{p-1} \left| \sum_{x=1}^{p} \exp\left\{\frac{2\pi \mathrm{i}\alpha}{p} f(x)\right\} \right|^{2n} = O(p^{2n-2}) \tag{20}$$

在

$$f(x) = A(x - \alpha)^n + B$$

时,显然

$$\sum_{\alpha=1}^{p-1} \left| \sum_{x=1}^{p} \exp\left\{\frac{2\pi \mathrm{i}\alpha}{p} f(x)\right\} \right|^{2n} = \sum_{\alpha=1}^{p-1} \left| \sum_{x=1}^{p} \exp\left\{\frac{2\pi \mathrm{i}\alpha}{p} x^n\right\} \right|^{2n}$$

但

$$\sum_{\alpha=1}^{p} \left| \sum_{x=1}^{p} \exp\left\{\frac{2\pi \mathrm{i}\alpha}{p} x^n\right\} \right|^{2} = \sum_{\alpha=1}^{p} \sum_{x=1}^{p} \sum_{y=1}^{p} \exp\left\{\frac{2\pi \mathrm{i}\alpha}{p} (x^n - y^n)\right\} =$$

$$\sum_{\substack{x=1 \\ x^n \equiv y^n (p)}}^{p} \sum_{y=1}^{p} p = O(p^2) \tag{21}$$

今将检出式(21) 左端有若干项与

$$\left| \sum_{x=1}^{p} \exp\left\{\frac{2\pi \mathrm{i}}{p} b x^n\right\} \right|^2, \quad b \not\equiv O(p) \tag{22}$$

等值. 显然

$$\left| \sum_{x=1}^{p} \exp\left\{\frac{2\pi \mathrm{i}}{p} b \lambda^n x^n\right\} \right|^2, \quad \lambda = 1, \cdots, p-1 \tag{23}$$

均与(22) 等值. 又因 λ_0 一定时

$$\lambda^n \equiv \lambda_0^n$$

至多有 n 个根,故在(23) 内至少有 $\frac{p-1}{n}$ 项相异. 故

$$\frac{p-1}{n} \left| \sum_{x=1}^{p} \exp\left\{\frac{2\pi \mathrm{i}}{p} b x^n\right\} \right|^2 \leqslant \sum_{\alpha=1}^{p} \left| \sum_{x=1}^{p} \exp\left\{\frac{2\pi \mathrm{i}}{p} \alpha x^n\right\} \right|^2$$

故
$$\left|\sum_{x=1}^{p}\exp\left\{\frac{2\pi\mathrm{i}}{p}bx^{n}\right\}\right|^{2}=O(p)$$
故若 $n>2$,则
$$\sum_{\alpha=1}^{p-1}\left|\sum_{x=1}^{p}\exp\left\{\frac{2\pi\mathrm{i}\alpha}{p}f(x)\right\}\right|^{2n}=O(p^{n+1})=O(p^{2n-2})\tag{24}$$
由(20)及(24),得

引理 1　若 $f(x)$ 为 $n(n>2)$ 次整系数多项式,则
$$\sum_{\alpha=1}^{p-1}\left|\sum_{x=1}^{p}\exp\left\{\frac{2\pi\mathrm{i}\alpha}{p}f(x)\right\}\right|^{2n}=O(p^{2n-2})$$
莫德尔氏定理可由此引推得之(除去 $\sum\limits_{\alpha=1}^{p-1}$,再两端开 $2n$ 次方). 由上引理即得次之

定理 1　相合式$(n>2)$
$$f(x_1)+\cdots+f(x_n)+f(y_1)+\cdots+f(y_n)\equiv m\pmod p$$
之解之个数为
$$\varphi(f(x),2n)\equiv p^{2n-1}+O(p^{2n-3})$$
欲求 $2<s<2n$ 时 $\varphi(f(x),2s)$ 之渐近公式,尚须证两简单引理:

引理 2
$$\sum_{\alpha=1}^{p-1}\left|\sum_{x=1}^{p}\exp\left\{\frac{2\pi\mathrm{i}\alpha}{p}f(x)\right\}\right|^{2}=O(p^{2})$$
证
$$\sum_{\alpha=1}^{p-1}\left|\sum_{x=1}^{p}\exp\left\{\frac{2\pi\mathrm{i}\alpha}{p}f(x)\right\}\right|^{2}=\sum_{x=1}^{p}\sum_{y=1}^{p}\sum_{\alpha=1}^{p}\exp\left\{\frac{2\pi\mathrm{i}\alpha}{p}(f(x)-f(y))\right\}-p^{2}=$$
$$\sum_{x=1}^{p}\sum_{y=1}^{p}p-p^{2}=O(p^{2})$$
$$f(x)\equiv f(y)\,(p)$$
引理 3　若 $2\leqslant s<2n$,
$$\sum_{\alpha=1}^{p-1}\left|\sum_{x=1}^{p}\exp\left\{\frac{2\pi\mathrm{i}\alpha}{p}f(x)\right\}\right|^{s}=O\left(p^{s-1-\frac{s-n-1}{n-1}}\right)$$
证
$$\sum_{\alpha=1}^{p-1}\left|\sum_{x=1}^{p}\exp\left\{\frac{2\pi\mathrm{i}\alpha}{p}f(x)\right\}\right|^{s}=\sum_{\alpha=1}^{p-1}\left|\sum_{x=1}^{p}\exp\left\{\frac{2\pi\mathrm{i}\alpha}{p}f(x)\right\}\right|^{2n\frac{s-2}{2n-2}+2\frac{2n-s}{2n-2}}$$
由赫德尔(Hölder)氏不等式,知上式右边
$$\leqslant\left(\sum_{\alpha=1}^{p-1}\left|\sum_{x=1}^{p}\exp\left\{\frac{2\pi\mathrm{i}\alpha}{p}f(x)\right\}\right|^{2n}\right)^{\frac{s-2}{2n-2}}\left(\sum_{\alpha=1}^{p-1}\left|\sum_{x=1}^{p}\exp\left\{\frac{2\pi\mathrm{i}\alpha}{p}f(x)\right\}\right|^{2}\right)^{\frac{2n-s}{2n-2}}$$
由引理 1 及引理 2,知上式

$$= O(p^{(2n-2)\frac{s-2}{2n-2}+2\frac{2n-s}{2n-2}}) = O(p^{s-1-\frac{s-n+1}{n-1}})$$

由定理 1 及引理 3 立得

定理 2 相合式($n > 2$)

$$f(x_1) + \cdots + f(x_s) \equiv m \pmod p$$

之解之个数为

$$\varphi(f(x),s)\begin{cases} = p^{s-1} + O(p^{s-1-\frac{s-2}{n-1}}), & 2 < s < 2n \\ = p^{2n-1} + O(p^{2n-3}), & s = 2n \end{cases}$$

§3 华氏定理

莫德尔氏定理中之 p 限于素数,近华罗庚先生证明

$$\sum_{x=1}^{q} \exp\left\{\frac{2\pi i}{q}f(x)\right\} = O(q^{(1-1/k)+\varepsilon}) \tag{25}$$

其中 q 为任意整数,ε 为任意正数.

兹先证数引理:

引理 1 设 C 大于 0 之一定实数,q 为正整数,则

$$C^{v(q)} = O(q^{\varepsilon})$$

其中 $v(q)$ 表 q 之不同之素因数之个数,而 ε 为任意正数.

证 设 $q = p_1^{\alpha_1}\cdots p_j^{\alpha_j}$ 而 $p_1,\cdots,p_j$ 为相异素数,则

$$\frac{C^{v(q)}}{q^{\varepsilon}} \leqslant \frac{C^j}{p_1^{\varepsilon}\cdots p_j^{\varepsilon}}$$

任与一 $\varepsilon > 0$,则可得一正数 $N = C^{\frac{1}{\varepsilon}}$. 如小于 N 之素数之个数为 k,则易见

$$\frac{C^{v(q)}}{q^{\varepsilon}} \leqslant C^k$$

即

$$C^{v(q)} = O(q^{\varepsilon})$$

引理 2 若 $q = q_1q_2$,而 $(q_1,q_2) = 1$,则

$$\sum_{x=1}^{p} \exp\{2\pi i f(x)/q\} = \sum_{x=1}^{q_1} \exp\{2\pi i f_1(x)/q_1\} \sum_{x=1}^{q_2} \exp\{2\pi i f_2(x)/q_2\}$$

其中 $f(x)$ 为无常数项之整系数多项式,而

$$f_1(x) = \frac{f(q_2x)}{q_2}, \quad f_2(x) = \frac{f(q_1x)}{q_1}$$

证 命 $x = yq_1 + zq_2$,则当 y 经过全剩余系 mod q_2 而 z 经过全剩余系 mod q_1 时,x 必经过全剩余系 mod q. 故

$$\sum_{x=1}^{p}\exp\{2\pi i f(x)/q\} = \sum_{z=1}^{q_1}\sum_{y=1}^{q_2}\exp\{2\pi i f(yq_1+zq_2)/q\} =$$
$$\sum_{z=1}^{q_1}\sum_{y=1}^{q_2}\exp\{2\pi i(f(yq_1)+f(zq_2))/q\} =$$
$$\sum_{x=1}^{q_1}\exp\{2\pi i f_1(x)/q_1)\}\sum_{x=1}^{q_2}\exp\{2\pi i f_2(x)/q_2\}$$

由此引理可推出

引理3 若 $q = p_1^{l_1}\cdots p_r^{l_r}$,而 $p_1,\cdots p_r$ 为相异素数,则

$$\sum_{x=1}^{p}\exp\{2\pi i f(x)/q\} = \prod_{j=1}^{v}\Big(\sum_{x=1}^{p^{l_j}} e^{\frac{2\pi i}{p^{l_j}}f_j(x)}\Big)$$

其中 $f(x)$,$f_j(x)$ 均为无常数项之整系数多项式.

由引理1及引理3,可知欲证(25)只须证

$$\sum_{x=1}^{p^l}\exp\{2\pi i f(x)/p^l\} \leqslant Cp^{l(1-\frac{1}{n})} \tag{26}$$

(其中 C 只与 n 有关)便得. 今先引入多项式 $f(x)$ 之级(index)之观念.

定义 设

$$f(x) = \alpha_n x^n + \cdots + \alpha_1 x$$

$p^{lv} \| v\alpha v, t = \min(l_1,\cdots,l_m), t \geqslant 0$. 设 s 为最大正整数. 能合 $p^l \| s\alpha_s$ 者,则 s 称为 $f(x)$ 之级. 以式表之为

$$S = \operatorname{ind} f(x)$$

引理4 $\operatorname{ind} f(x) = \operatorname{ind} f(x+\lambda)$.

引理5 $\operatorname{ind} f(x) \geqslant \operatorname{ind} f(px)$.

引理6 若 $\operatorname{ind} f(x) = \operatorname{ind} f(px)$,则

$$f'(x) \equiv O \pmod{p^{t+1}}$$

时,必得 $p \mid x$.

引理4与引理5甚明显. 今证引理6如下:

引理6之证 由定义,对任何 $v \neq s$ 必得

$$l_s \leqslant l_v \text{ 及 } l_s + s \leqslant l_v + v$$

吾谓

$$l_s < l_v$$

盖如 $s < v$,则上式可由定义立即知之;又如 $s > v$,则

$$l_s \leqslant l_v + v - s < l_v$$

故若 $f'(x) \equiv O(\bmod p^{t+1})$,则必得

$$s\alpha_s x^{s-1} \equiv O(p^{t+1}), \text{即 } p \mid x$$

定理 3

$$\left|\sum_{x=1}^{p^l}\exp\{2\pi i f(x)/p^l\}\right|\leqslant n^{2n}p^{l(1-1/n)}\quad (p\nmid f(x))$$

证　设 $\lambda_1,\cdots,\lambda_e$ 为

$$f'(x)\equiv 0\pmod{p^{t+1}}$$

之相异根(式中之 t 见前之定义). 显然 $e\leqslant p^t n\leqslant n^2$.

若 $l\leqslant t+1(t>0)$,则 $n\geqslant p^t\geqslant p^{l-1}$,故

$$\sum_{x=1}^{p^l}\exp\{2\pi i f(x)/p^l\}\ |\leqslant p^l = n^2 \tag{27}$$

今设 $l>t+1$,若 k 异于各 λ,则

$$\sum_{\substack{x=1\\ x\equiv k(p^{t+1})}}^{p^l}\exp\{2\pi i f(x)/p\} = \sum_{\substack{y=1\\ y\equiv k(p^{t+1})}}^{p^{l-t-1}}\sum_{z=1}^{p^{t+1}}\exp\{2\pi i(f(y)+p^{l-t-1}f'(y)z)\}$$

盖 p^t 必除尽 $f''(y),f'''(y),\cdots$ 之各系数,故(　)内其余各项均可略去也. 因 $f'(y)$ 不为 0 故上式为 0,于是

$$\left|\sum_{x=1}^{p^l}\exp\{2\pi i f(x)/p^l\}\right| = \left|\sum_{j=1}^{e}\sum_{\substack{x=1\\ x\equiv\lambda_i,(p^{t+1})}}^{p^l}\exp\{2\pi i f(x)/p^l\}\right|\leqslant$$

$$e\max_{1\leqslant j\leqslant e}\left|\sum_{y=1}^{p^{l-t-1}}\exp\{2\pi i f(\lambda_j+p^{t+1}+y)/p^l\}\right| =$$

$$e\max_{1\leqslant j\leqslant e}\left|\sum_{y=1}^{p^{l-t-1}}\exp\{2\pi i(f(\lambda_j+p^{t+1}y)-f(\lambda_j))/p^l\}\right| =$$

$$e\max_{1\leqslant j\leqslant e}\left|\sum_{y=1}^{p^{l-t-1}}\exp\left\{\frac{2\pi i}{p^{l}-\mu_j}g_j(x)\right\}\right|$$

其中

$$g_j(x) = (f(\lambda_j+p^{t+1}y)-f(\lambda_j))/p^{\mu_j}$$

而 p^{μ_j} 为 p 之最大方幂之能除尽

$$f(\lambda_j+p^{t+1}y)-f(\lambda_j)$$

之各系数者. 故

$$\left|\sum_{x=1}^{p^l}\exp\left\{\frac{2\pi i}{p^l}f(x)\right\}\right|\leqslant e\max_{1\leqslant j\leqslant l}p^{\mu_j-t-1}\left|\sum_{x=1}^{p^l-\mu_j}\exp\left\{\frac{2\pi i}{p^l-\mu_j}g_j(x)\right\}\right|$$

即

$$\left|\sum_{x=1}^{p^l}\exp\left\{\frac{2\pi i}{p^l}f(x)\right\}\right|\leqslant e\max_{1\leqslant j\leqslant e}p^{\mu_j(1-1/n)}\left|\sum_{x=1}^{p^l-\mu_j}\exp\left\{\frac{2\pi i}{p^l-\mu_j}g_j(x)\right\}\right| \tag{28}$$

因 $\mu_j\leqslant n(1+t)$ 故也.

式(28)之中 μ_j 显然永异于 0,故确为一化简公式. 若

$$\operatorname{ind} f(x) = \operatorname{ind} g_j(x)$$

则由引理3知$e = 1$. 否则$e \leqslant n^2$. 连用此种方法,则至多k次各添一因子k^2,其余则仅添1而已. 有时至最后一步,彼时之l已小于彼时之$t+1$,上法虽不能再用,但可用(27),亦仅添因子n^2而已.

此定理为最佳者(best possible),盖在k/l时易证

$$\sum_{x=1}^{p^l} \exp\left\{\frac{2\pi i}{p^l} x^k\right\} = p^{l(1-1/k)}$$

由引理3,引理1及上定理即得

定理4 (华氏定理)

$$\sum_{x=1}^{q} \exp\left\{\frac{2\pi i}{p^l} f(x)\right\} = O(q^{1-\frac{1}{n}+\varepsilon})$$

其中$f(x)$为任意n次整系数多项式,而ε为任意正数.

§4 奇异级数之研究

本节将应用以前诸节所得结果以讨论奇异级数.

命

$$A(q) = \sum_{\substack{\alpha=1 \\ (\alpha,q)=1}}^{q} \left[\frac{\sum_{x=1}^{q} \exp\{2\pi i\alpha f(x)/q\}}{q}\right]^s \exp\{-2\pi i\alpha m/q\}$$

则奇异级数可书为

$$\sum_{q=1}^{\infty} A(q)$$

引理1① 高$F(n)$可乘(multiplicative)②,则

$$\sum_{n=1}^{\infty} F(n) = \prod_{p} (1 + F(p) + F(p^2) + \cdots)$$

之成立,但须任一边,当F换成$|F|$后,为收敛即可;而在此时另一边必有同样性质.

证 $F(1) = 1$.(因$F(n)$可乘,故$F(1) = 1$或0,但如$F(1) = 0$,则$F(n) = 0$.)

(i) 今先设

① 此引理及其证,本人系得之于华罗庚先生,而华先生则得之于英国人 Ingraham 之口授.

② 即当$(a,b) = 1$时,$f(a)f(b) = f(ab)$.

$$\sum_{n=1}^{\infty} |F(n)| = \bar{S}$$

命

$$P(x) = \prod_{p \leqslant x} (1 + F(p) + F(p^2) + \cdots), x \geqslant 2$$

对每 p, $\sum_{l=0}^{\infty} |F(p^l)|$ 必为收敛. 故 $p(x)$ 为有限个绝对收敛级数之积. 于是

$$P(x) = \sum{}' F(n)$$

其中 $\sum{}'$ 表经过一切 n 之"无大于 x 之素因数"者.

命

$$S = \sum_{1}^{\infty} F(n)$$

即

$$P(x) - S = - \sum{}'' F(n)$$

其中 $\sum{}''$ 表经过一切 n 之"至少含一大于 x 之素因数"者.

但

$$|P(x) - S| \leqslant \sum_{n > s} |F(n)|$$

今由假设,右端在 $x \to \infty$ 时趋于0,故在 $x \to \infty$ 时

$$P(x) \to S$$

即

$$\prod_{p} (1 + F(p) + F(p^2) + \cdots) = S$$

又将上理用于 $|F(n)|$,即得

$$\prod_{p} (1 + |F(p)| + |F(p^2)| + \cdots) = \bar{S}$$

(ii) 兹再设

$$\prod_{p} (1 + |F(p)| + \cdots) = \bar{p}$$

命

$$\bar{P}(x) = \prod_{p \leqslant x} (1 + |F(p)| + \cdots)$$

则

$$\bar{P}(x) = \sum{}' |F(n)|$$

其中 $\sum{}'$ 表经过一切 n 之"无大于 x 之素因子"者.

因

$$\overline{P}(x) \geqslant \sum_{n \leqslant x} |F(n)|$$

故

$$\sum_{n=1}^{\infty} |F(n)|$$

为收敛. 此正合乎(i) 内之假设,故得

$$\sum_{n=1}^{\infty} F(n) = \prod_{p} (1 + F(p) + \cdots)$$

引理 2　若 $q = q_1q_2$,而 $(q_1q_2) = 1$,则

$$A(q) = A(q_1)A(q_2)$$

证　命 $x = q_1y_1 + q_2y_2$,则当 y_1 经过一全剩余 mod q_2 与 y_2 经过一全剩余系 mod q_1 时,x 即经过一全剩余系mod q. 于是

$$A(q) = \sum_{\substack{q=1\\(\alpha,q)=1}}^{q} \left[\frac{\sum_{y_1=1}^{q_2}\sum_{y_2=1}^{q_2} \exp\{2\pi i\alpha f(q_1y_1 + q_2y_2)/(q_1q_2)\}}{q_1q_2}\right]^s \exp\{-2\pi i\alpha m/(q_1q_2)\} =$$

$$\sum_{\substack{\alpha=1\\(\alpha,q)=1}}^{q} \left[\frac{\sum_{y_1=1}^{q_2} \exp\{2\pi i\alpha f(q_1y_1)/(q_1q_2)\}}{q_2}\right]^s \left[\frac{\sum_{y_2=1}^{q_1} \exp\{2\pi i\alpha f(q_2y_2)/(q_1q_2)\}}{q_1}\right]^s \times$$
$$\exp\{-2\pi i\alpha m/(q_1q_2)\}$$

命 $\alpha = q_1\alpha_1 + q_2\alpha_2$,则当 α_1 经过一约全剩余系(reduced complete system of residues)mod q_2 及 α_2 经过一约全剩余系 mod q_1 时,α 即经过一约全剩余系 mod q. 因此

$$A(q) = \sum_{\substack{\alpha_1=1\\(\alpha_1,q_2)=1}}^{q_2} \sum_{\substack{\alpha_2=1\\(\alpha_2,q_1)=1}}^{q_1} \left[\frac{\sum_{y_1=1}^{q_2} \exp\left\{\frac{2\pi i\alpha_1 f(q_1y_1)}{q_2}\right\}}{q_2}\right]^s \left[\frac{\sum_{y_2=1}^{q_1} \exp\left\{\frac{2\pi i\alpha_2 f(q_2y_2)}{q_1}\right\}}{q_1}\right]^s \times$$
$$\exp\left\{-\frac{2\pi i\alpha_2 m}{q_2} - \frac{2\pi i\alpha_1 m}{q_1}\right\} = A(q_1)A(q_2)$$

引理 3　若 $n > 2, s = n + 1 + \varepsilon(\varepsilon > 0)$,则

$$\sum_{l=1}^{\infty} |A(p^l)| = O(p^{-1-\frac{\varepsilon}{n}})$$

证　由 §2 引理3

$$|A(p)| \leqslant \sum_{\alpha=1}^{p-1} p^{-s} \left|\sum_{x=1}^{p} \exp\left\{\frac{2\pi i\alpha}{p} f(x)\right\}\right|^s =$$
$$O(p^{-s}p^{s-1-\frac{s-n-1}{n-1}}) = O(p^{-1-\varepsilon/(n-1)}) \tag{29}$$

又由定理3

$$|A(p^l)| = O(p^l p^{-ls/n}) = O(p^{l(1-s/n)}) = O(p^{-\frac{1}{n}-\frac{\varepsilon}{n}})$$

故

$$\sum_{l=n}^{\infty} |A(p^l)| = O(p^{-1-\varepsilon/n}) \tag{30}$$

尚待定者乃 $l=2,\cdots,n-1$ 时 $A(p^l)$ 之阶. 因

$$\sum_{x=1}^{p_l} \exp\left\{\frac{2\pi i\alpha}{p^l}f(x)\right\} = \sum_{y=1}^{p^{l-1}} \sum_{z=1}^{p} \exp\left\{\frac{2\pi i\alpha}{p^l}f(y+zp^{l-1})\right\} =$$

$$\sum_{x=1}^{p^{l-1}} \sum_{z=1}^{p} \exp\left\{\frac{2\pi i\alpha}{p^l}[f(y)+f'(y)zp^{l-1}]\right\}$$

若 $p>n$,则 $p \times f'(y)$,故 $f'(y) \equiv 0, \bmod p, 1 \leqslant y \leqslant p^{l-1}$ 至多有 np^{l-2} 根,于是

$$\left|\sum_{x=1}^{p^l} \exp\left\{\frac{2\pi i\alpha}{p^l}f(x)\right\}\right| \leqslant np^{l-1}$$

故在 $2 \leqslant l \leqslant n-1$ 时

$$|A(p^l)| = O(p^{i}p^{-s}) = O(p^{-(n+1-l+\varepsilon)})$$

但 $n+1-l>2$,故

$$|A(p^l)| = O(p^{-2-\varepsilon}) \tag{31}$$

由(29),(30)及(31),知

$$\sum_{l=1}^{\infty} |A(p^l)| = O(p^{-1-\varepsilon/n})$$

定理4 在 $s=n+1+\varepsilon(n>2,\varepsilon>0)$ 时,奇异级数

$$\sum_{q=1}^{\infty} A(q)$$

为绝对收敛.

证 由引理3,

$$\sum_{p}\left(\sum_{l=1}^{\infty} |A(p^l)|\right)$$

为收敛,故

$$\prod_{p}(1+|A(p)|+|A(p^2)|+\cdots)$$

为收敛. 再用引理2及引理1,即得本定理.

AN ANALOGUE OF TARRY'S PROBLEM①

The object of this note is to find an asymptotic formula of the number of solutions of the following system of congruences

$$x_1^h + \cdots + x_s^h \equiv y_1^h + \cdots + y_s^h, 1 \leqslant h \leqslant k \quad (\mathrm{mod}\, p^l) \quad (1)$$

where p is a prime $> k$, all other letters (and hereafter except e, π, i) denote integers and $s \geqslant k \geqslant 2$, $l \geqslant k^2$. This is an analogue of Tarry's problem which is still unsolved and the corresponding asmptotic formula is found only when $s \geqslant ck^3 \log k$, where c is an absolute constant[1].

Evidently the number of solutions of (1) is equal to $p^{-kl}S$, where

$$S = \sum_{a_k=1}^{p^l} \cdots \sum_{a_1=1}^{p^l} \left| \sum_{x=1}^{p^l} e^{2\pi i(a_k x^k + \cdots + a_1 x)/p^l} \right|^{2s}$$

The problem in thus reduced to estimate the sums S.

Let

$$f(x) = a_k x^k + \cdots + a_1 x$$

be a primitive polynomial, i. e. not all the coeffcients of it are divisible by p.

If

$$p \mid (a_k, \cdots, a_{k+1}), p \nmid a_k, \quad k \geqslant 1$$

① 原载:Science Record, 1942, 1(1-2): 26-29. 合作者:华罗庚.

then $f(x)$ is said to be of index k. The roots of the congruences

$$f'(x) \equiv 0 \quad (p), \quad 0 \leqslant x \leqslant p-1$$

are called the *characteristic roots of the first order* of $f(x)$. Let λ be one of them If

$$p^{\mu} \parallel f(\lambda + py) - f(\lambda)^{[2]}$$

then μ is called the *rank of the first order* of $f(x)$ *with respect to* λ, and we write

$$f_{\lambda}(y) = p^{-\mu}(f(\lambda + py) - f(\lambda))$$

The characteristic roots and ranks of the first order of $f(x)$ are defined to the *characteristic roots and ranks of the second order of* $f(x)$ respectively. The characteristic roots and ranks of $f(x)$ defined successively from *sequences of characteristic roots and ranks.* If $f(x)$ has a sequence of ranks $\mu, \mu_1, \cdots, \mu_{\rho-1}$, such that

$$\mu + \mu_1 + \cdots + \mu_{\rho-2} \leqslant l - 2$$
$$\mu + \mu_1 + \cdots + \mu_{\rho-1} \geqslant l - 1$$

then the sequence (and the corresponding sequence of ranks) is said *to be complete*, and the numbers ρ and

$$\omega = \mu + \mu_1 + \cdots + \mu_{\rho-1}$$

are called the *order* and the *weight* of the sequence respectively. The smallest (the greatest) of the orders (weights) of all complete sequences of ranks of $f(x)$ is called the *order* (*weight*) *of* $f(x)$.

The greatest of the indices of $f_{\lambda\lambda_1\cdots\lambda_{\rho-1}}(x)$ for various sequences $\lambda, \lambda_1, \cdots, \lambda_{\rho-1}$ is called the last index of $f(x)$.

Adapting a method of Hua,[1] we prove

Lemma A *Let* $f(x)$ *be a primitive polynomial of order* ρ *and weight* ω. *Let the index and the last index of* $f(x)$ *be* k *and* v *respectively. Then*

$$S = \left| \sum_{x=1}^{p^l} e^{2\pi i f(x)/p^l} \right| \leqslant \begin{cases} k!v!p^{l-\rho} & \text{if } \omega \geqslant l \\ k!v!p^{l-\rho-1/v} & \text{if } \omega = l-1 \end{cases}$$

When $f(x)$ *has a unique sequence of ranks of order* ρ *and a unique sequence of characterisic roots corresponding to it, we have*

$$S = \begin{cases} p^{l-\rho}(1 + k!v!p^{-1}/v) & \text{if } \omega \geqslant l \\ p^{l-\rho-1}(S_0 + k!v!) & \text{if } \omega = l-1 \end{cases}$$

where

$$S_0 = \left| \sum_{x=1}^{p} e^{2\pi i f_{\lambda\lambda_1\cdots\lambda_{\rho-1}}(x)/p} \right|$$

When $f(x)$ *has no complete sequence of ranks we have*

$$S = 0$$

From the definitions we have

Lemm AB *Necessary and sufficient conditions that the primitive polynomial $f(x)$ has the complete sequence of ranks*

$$\mu_0 = \mu, \mu_1, \cdots, \mu_{\rho-1}, \quad 2 \leqslant \mu_i \leqslant k$$

and the corresponding sequence of characteristic roots

$$\lambda_0 = \lambda, \lambda_1, \cdots, \lambda_{\rho-1}, \quad 0 \leqslant \lambda_i \leqslant p - 1$$

are that

$$p^{\mu+\mu_1+\cdots+\mu_r} \parallel (f^{(u_r)}(\lambda + \lambda_1 p + \cdots + \lambda_r p^r) p^{(r+1)\mu_r}, \cdots,$$
$$f^{(\mu_{r+1})}(\lambda + \lambda_1 p + \cdots + \lambda_r p^r) p^{(r+1)\mu_{r+1}}),$$
$$r = 0, 1, \cdots, \rho - 1$$

The second lemma furnishes a method to determine the number of polynomials having preassigned order and weight. By means of the two lemmas we can estimate S accurately. The essential difficulty lies in the determination of all those terms whose sum dominates S. After delicate analysis. We obtained the following:

Theorem *Let p be a prime $> k$, $l = rk - t \geqslant k^2, 0 \leqslant t < k$ and $s \geqslant k \geqslant 4$. Then the number ofsolutions of the system of congruences (1) is*

$$N(s,k) = \begin{cases} p^{(2s-k)}(1 + O(p^{-1/k})), & s > \frac{1}{4}(k^2 + k + 2) \\ \lambda p^{(2s-k)}(1 + O(p^{-1/k})), & s = \frac{1}{4}(k^2 + k + 2) \\ p^{2sl+\frac{1}{2}l-\alpha(r)}(1 + O(p^{-1/k})), & \\ \qquad \frac{1}{4}(k^2 - k + 2) < s < \frac{1}{4}(k^2 + k + 2), t < b & \\ \lambda_1 p^{(2s+\frac{1}{2})(l-k+t)-k(k-1)-\alpha(k-t)(r-1)}(1 + O(p^{-1/k})), & \\ \qquad \frac{1}{4}(k^2 - k + 2) < s < \frac{1}{4}(k^2 + k + 2), t \geqslant b & \\ \lambda_2 p^{2sl+\frac{1}{2}l-\alpha(\rho_0)}(1 + O(p^{-1/k})), & \\ \qquad \frac{1}{2}(\mu_0^2 - \mu_0) < 2s - 1 < \frac{1}{2}(\mu_0^2 + \mu_0) & \\ \lambda_3 p^{2sl+\frac{1}{2}l-\alpha(\rho_1)}(1 + O(p^{-1/k})), 2s - 1 = \frac{1}{2}(\mu_0^2 - \mu_0) & \end{cases}$$

where λ's and ρ's are well-defined constants,

$$\alpha(r) = (2s-1)r + \frac{1}{2}(rk^2 - 2tk + t)$$

$$\alpha^{(k-t)}(r-1) = (2s-1)(r-1) + \frac{1}{2}(r-1)k^2$$

$$b = \frac{1}{2}(k^2 + k) - 2s + 1$$

and μ_0 *is a positive integer* $\leqslant k$.

The asymptotic formula can be also obtained for $k = 2$ and 3.

References

[1] Hua, *Quart Jour. of Math.*, Oxford series 9(1933),315-320.

[2] $p^\mu \parallel\!\!\!\mid \alpha_k x^k + \cdots + \alpha_1 x$ is meant $p^\mu \parallel (\alpha_k, \cdots, \alpha_1)$.

[3] Hua, *Comptes Rendus*, 210(1940), 520-523,

NON-ANALYTIC FUNCTIONS①

The triumph of the theory of analytic functions lies in the fact that it has wide applications not only in other branches of mathematics but also in many physical investigations. In regard to the latter, it is possible merely because many physical quantities are distributed like the values of a harmonic function, the real part of an analytic function. Since the likeness is actually approximate, we are compelled to ask the question whether such applications may not lead to serious mistakes and if not, what is the limit of the errors?

It is the purpose of this note to investigate non-analytic functions which are "approximately analytic" and find the necessary modifications for some fundamental theorems in the theory of analytic functions. This furnishes an indirect answer of the question suggested.

1. Functions of non-analyticity r

If $f(z) = X(x,y) + iY(x,y)$ is an analytic function of z in a region R, it has, at each point of R, a unique derivative

$$f'(z) = \lim_{\delta\to 0}\frac{f(z+\delta) - f(z)}{\delta}$$

The derivative will not exist if $f(z)$ is non-analytic. We have,

① 原载:Amer. Math Monthly, 1944,51(9): 510-516.

however, the following theorem.

Theorem 1 *Let $X(x,y)$ and $Y(x,y)$ be continuous and have continuous partial derivatives of the first order near $z_0 = x_0 + iy_0$ and let*

$$w(\lambda) = u(\lambda) + iv(\lambda) = \lim_{\delta\to 0}{}^{\lambda} \frac{f(z_0+\delta) - f(z_0)}{\delta}$$

where $\lim_{\delta\to 0}^{\lambda}$ denotes that $\delta \to 0$ along a line of slope λ. Then the point $w(\lambda)$ lies on the circle

$$\left[u - \frac{1}{2}(X_x^0 + Y_y^0)\right]^2 + \left[v - \frac{1}{2}(Y_x^0 - X_y^0)\right]^2 = r^2(z_0) \tag{1}$$

where

$$r(z_0) = \frac{1}{2}[(X_x^0 - Y_y^0)^2 + (Y_x^0 + X_y^0)^2]^{1/2}$$

and

$$X_x^0 \left[\frac{\partial}{\partial x} X(x,y)\right]_{x=x_0,\ y=y_0} \quad etc$$

Proof Let $\delta = h + ki$. Then, by law of the mean,

$$\frac{f(z_0+\delta) - f(z_0)}{\delta} =$$

$$\frac{X(x_0+h,\ y_0+k) - X(x_0,\ y_0) + i(Yx_0+h,\ y_0+k) - Y(x_0,\ y_0))}{h+ki} =$$

$$\frac{hX_x^\theta + kX_y^\theta + i(hY_x^{\theta'} + kY_y^{\theta'})}{h+ki}$$

where $0 < \theta < 1,\ 0 < \theta' < 1$ and

$$X_x^\theta = X_x(x_0+\theta h,\ y_0+\theta k),\ Y_x^{\theta'} = Y_x(x_0+\theta' h, y_0+\theta' k),\ etc.$$

Let $k/h = \lambda$, then

$$\frac{f(z_0+\delta) - f(z_0)}{\delta} = \frac{X_x^\theta + \lambda X_y^\theta + i(Y_x^{\theta'} + \lambda Y_y^{\theta'})}{1+\lambda i} =$$

$$\frac{1}{1+\lambda^2}[X_x^\theta + \lambda(X_y^\theta + Y_x^{\theta'}) + \lambda^2 Y_y^{\theta'}] +$$

$$\frac{i}{1+\lambda^2}[Y_x^{\theta'} + \lambda(Y_y^{\theta'} - X_x^\theta) - \lambda^2 X_y^\theta]$$

Since X_x, X_y, Y_x and Y_y are continuous near $(x_0,\ y_0)$ we have

$$u(\lambda) = \frac{1}{1+\lambda^2}[X_x^0 + \lambda(X_y^0 + Y_x^0) + \lambda^2 Y_y^0]$$

$$v(\lambda) = \frac{1}{1+\lambda^2}[Y_x^0 + \lambda(Y_y^0 - X_x^0) - \lambda^2 X_y^0]$$

The theorem follows by a direct computation.

We define (1) as the *derivative circle* and its center the *derivative* of $f(z)$ at $z = z_0$. We write

$$f'(z) = \frac{1}{2}(X_x + Y_y) + \frac{1}{2}i(Y_x - X_y)$$

It is interesting to note that if $r(z) = 0$, the Riemann – Cauchy differential equations are satisfied and the function $f(z)$ is analytic. Thus we may define $r(z_0)$ as the *non-analyticity* of $f(z)$ at $z = z_0$, and its least upper bound in R, the non-analyticity of $f(z)$ in R.

Theorem 2 *If $f(z)$ is of* non-analyticity $r \geqslant 0$ *at* $z = z_0$ *then for any given* $\varepsilon > 0$, *we can find* $\delta_0 > 0$ *such that*

$$\left|\frac{f(z) - f(z_0)}{z - z_0} - f'(z_0)\right| = r + \varepsilon\eta \tag{2}$$

provided that $0 < | z - z_0 | \leqslant \delta_0$, *where* $-1 \leqslant \eta \leqslant 1$.

proof As in the proof of Theorem 1,

$$\frac{f(z_0 + \delta) - f(z_0)}{\delta} = \frac{1}{1 + \lambda^2}[X_x^\theta + \lambda(X_y^\theta + Y_x^{\theta'}) + \lambda^2 Y_y^{\theta'}] + \frac{i}{1 + \lambda^2}[Y_x^{\theta'} + \lambda(Y_y^{\theta'} - X_x^\theta) - \lambda^2 X_y^\theta]$$

Since X_x, X_y, Y_x and Y_y are continuous, having given $\varepsilon > 0$ we can find $\delta_0 > 0$ such that

$$| X_x^\theta - X_x^0 | < \frac{\varepsilon}{4}, \text{ etc.}$$

provided that $| \delta | \leqslant \delta_0$. Using the notations $u(\lambda)$ and $v(\lambda)$ of theorem 1, we have, then,

$$\frac{f(z_0 + \delta) - f(z_0)}{\delta} = u(\lambda) + iv(\lambda) + \eta'\varepsilon$$

where $| \eta' | \leqslant \frac{1}{2}(1 + | \lambda |^2/(1 + \lambda^2) \leqslant 1$. Therefore

$$\frac{f(z_0 + \delta) - f(z_0)}{\delta} - f'(z_0) - \left[u(\lambda) - \frac{1}{2}(X_x^0 + Y_y^0)\right] + i\left[v(\lambda) - \frac{1}{2}(Y_x^0 - X_y^0)\right] + \eta'\varepsilon = \xi r + \eta'\varepsilon = \xi(r + \eta'\xi^{-1}\varepsilon)$$

where $| \xi | = 1$, by theorem 1.

The theorem follows immediately, since

$$r + \varepsilon \geqslant | r + \eta'\xi^{-1}\varepsilon | \geqslant r - \varepsilon$$

In the preceding treatment, we have assumed that $X(x,y)$ and $Y(x,y)$ have continuous partial derivatives of the first order. It is better to generalize our definitions as follows.

Definitions Let $f(z) = X(x,y) + iY(x,y)$ be continuous in the region R and $X(x,y)$ and $Y(x,y)$ have partial derivatives of the first order in R. Let

$$f'(z) = \frac{1}{2}(X_x + Y_y) + \frac{1}{2}i(Y_x - X_y) \qquad (3)$$

Let z_0 be a point in R. If for any $\varepsilon > 0$ we can find $\delta_0 > 0$, such that

$$|f(z_0 + \delta) - f(z_0) - \delta f'(z_0)| \leqslant |\delta|(s + \varepsilon), \ s \geqslant 0$$

provided that $|\delta| \leqslant \delta_0$, then $f(z)$ is called a function of *non-analyticity* $\leqslant s$ at z. The greatest lower bound of s is called the *non-analyticity* of $f(z)$ at $z = z_0$. We denote it by $r(z_0)$. The least upper bound of $r(z)$ in R called the non-analyticity of $f(z)$ in R.

Evidently we may put $s = r(z_0)$.

By the tow-dimensional form of the modified Heine-Borel theorem, ①we have

Theorem 3 *Let $f(z)$ be of non-analyticity r in a region containing the closed region R. Then given $\epsilon > 0$ we can divide R into a finite number of parts (squares with sides parallel to the axes and their interiors or portions of such squares which do not exist when R is a square) such that inside or on the boundary of any part there is one point z_0 such that the inequality*

$$|f(z) - f(z_0) - (z - z_0)f'(z_0)| \leqslant (r + \varepsilon)(z - z_0)$$

is satisfied by all points z inside or on the boundary of that part.

From the definitions we derive immediately the following rules

Theorem 4 *Let $f_x(z) = X_x + iY_x$, $f_y(z) = X_y + iY_y$, then*

(a) $$f'(z) = \frac{1}{2}(f_x - if_y)$$

(b) $$(f(z) + \phi(z))' = f'(z) + \phi'(z)$$

(c) $$(f(z)\phi(z))' = f(z)\phi'(z) + f'(z)\phi(z)$$

Theorem 5 *Let $f(z)$ and $\phi(z)$ be functions of non-analyticity r_1 and r_2 respectively at $z = z_0$ (in a region containing the closed region R). Then*

(a) *$f(z) + \phi(z)$ is of non-analyticity $\leqslant r_1 + r_2$ at z_0 (or in R)*

---

① See Whittaker and Watson, A Course of Modern Analysis, first edition. ξ3.6

(b) $\quad f(z)\phi(z)$ *is of non-analyticity* $\leqslant |f(z_0)| r_2 + |\phi(z_0)| r_1$ *at* z_0

$$(or \leqslant r_2 \max_{z in R} |f(z)| + r_1 \max_{z in R} |\phi(z)| \text{ in } R)$$

2. A generalization of Cauchy's fundamental theorem

Theorem 6 *If $f(z)$ is of non-analyticity r in a simply connected region R and if C is a rectifiable simple closed curve lying entirely within R, then*

$$\left|\int_c f(z)\,\mathrm{d}z\right| \leqslant 4\sqrt{2}\Omega r$$

where Ω is the area enclosed by C.

The proof of this theorem is a simple modification of the ordinary proof of Cauchy's fundamental theorem. It runs as follows.

proof Let us divide the whole plane into equal squares with sides of length d and parallel to the real and the imaginary axes respectively. Consequently the interior A of C is divided into a number of sub-regions. Let us re-divide each of the sub-regions in the manner of theorem 3. Then A is finally divided into a number of regions whose boundaries are squares $p_1, \cdots, p_M$ and regions whose boundaries $q_1, \cdots, q_N$ are portions of sides of squares and parts of C. Then

$$\int_C f(z)\,\mathrm{d}z = \sum_{i=1}^{M}\int_{p_i} f(z)\,\mathrm{d}z + \sum_{j=1}^{N}\int_{q_j} f(z)\,\mathrm{d}z \tag{4}$$

where the paths of integration are taken counter-clockwise. According to theorem 3, we can find a point u_i within p_i and a point v_j within q_j such that

$$f(z) - f(u_i) = f'(u_i)(z - u_i) + \eta_i(r+\varepsilon)(z - u_i), \quad |\eta_i| \leqslant 1, \text{ for } z \text{ on } p_i$$

$$f(z) - f(v_j) = f'(v_j)(z - v_j) + \zeta_j(r+\varepsilon)(z - u_j), \quad |\zeta_j| \leqslant 1, \text{ for } z \text{ on } q_j$$

where ε is a given positive number.

Then

$$\int_{p_i} f(z)\,\mathrm{d}z = f'(u_i)\int_{p_i}(z-u_i)\,\mathrm{d}z + (r+\varepsilon)\int_{p_i}\eta_i(z-u_i)\,\mathrm{d}z =$$

$$(r+\varepsilon)\int_{p_i}\eta_i(z-u_i)\,\mathrm{d}z$$

and

$$\left|\int_{p_i} f(z)\,\mathrm{d}z\right| \leqslant 4\sqrt{2}c_i^2(r+\varepsilon)$$

where c_i is the length of the sides of p_i. Similarly

$$\left|\int_{p_j} f(z)\,\mathrm{d}z\right| \leqslant (4d_j + l_j)\sqrt{2d_j}(r+\varepsilon)$$

where l_j is the length of the curved part of q_j and d_j is the side-length of the square consisting a part of q_i. By (4),

$$\left|\int_C f(z)\,\mathrm{d}z\right| \leqslant 4\sqrt{2}(r+\varepsilon)\left(\sum_{i=1}^{M} c_i^2 + \sum_{j=1}^{N} d_j^2 + ld\right)$$

where $l = \sum_{j=1}^{N} l_j$ is the length of C.

Let $d \to 0$, $\varepsilon \to 0$, then

$$\sum_{i=1}^{M} c_i^2 + \sum_{j=1}^{N} d_j^2 \to \Omega$$

and the theorem follows .

3. The approximation of a non-analytic function by an analytic function

It is well-known that a real continuous function can be approximated by a real continuous function, as accurately as we please. A non-analytic function of a complex variable, however, cannot be approximated by an an analytic function with arbitrary degree of accuracy. Before handling this problem, we have to generalize Cauchy's fundamental formula.

Theorem 7 *If $f(z)$ is of non-analyticity r in a simply connected region containing the rectifiable simple closed curve C, we have for any z inside C,*

$$f(z) = \frac{1}{2\pi\mathrm{i}}\int_C \frac{f(w)\,\mathrm{d}w}{w-z} + kr,\ k \leqslant 4\sqrt{2}\left(1+\frac{\Omega}{2\pi}\right)$$

where Ω is the area enclosed by C.

Proof 1) Suppose C lies within the unit circle about z. (A part or the whole of C may coincide with the circle.) Let us describe, within C, a small circle about z, and join c and C by a cut l so that the region S bounded by c, C and l is simply connected. Let Γ be the boundary . Then

$$\int_C \frac{f(w)-f(z)}{w-z}\mathrm{d}w = \int_\Gamma - \int_c = I_1 - I_2$$

say, where the paths of integration are taken counter-clockwise.

We may choose the radius δ of c so small that, on c,

$$f(w) - f(z) = (w-z)f'(z) + \eta(r+\varepsilon)(w-z), \qquad |\eta| \leqslant 1$$

Then

$$I_2 = \int_c f'(z)\,\mathrm{d}w + (r+\varepsilon)\int_c \eta\,\mathrm{d}w = (r+\varepsilon)\int_c \eta\,\mathrm{d}w$$

$$|I_2| \leqslant 2\pi\delta(r+\varepsilon)$$

By theorem 5, the non-analyticity of $(f(w)-(z))/(w-z)$ at any point within Γ is $\leqslant r/|w-z|$, since the non-analyticity of $(w-z)^{-1}$ within Γ is 0.

Dividing the interior S of Γ into any number of sub-regions with boundaries $c_1\cdots$, c_N, we have

$$I_1 = \sum_{t=1}^{N} \int_{c_i} \frac{f(w) - f(z)}{w - z} \mathrm{d}z$$

where the paths of integration are taken counter-clockwise. By theorem 6,

$$| I_1 | \leqslant 4\sqrt{2} \sum_{i=1}^{N} \Omega_i \delta_i r$$

where Ω_i is the area enclosed by c_i and δ_i is the least upper bound of $1/| w - z |$ within and on c_i. By the definition of double integral,

$$| I_1 | \leqslant 4\sqrt{2} r \iint_S \frac{\mathrm{d}x\mathrm{d}y}{\sqrt{(x - a)^2 + (y - b)^2}} \leqslant$$

$$4\sqrt{2} r \int_\delta^1 \mathrm{d}\rho \int_0^{2\pi} \mathrm{d}\phi \leqslant 8\sqrt{2}\pi r$$

where (a, b) are the coordinates of z

Making $\delta \to 0$, we have $\varepsilon \to 0$ and

$$\left| \int_C \frac{f(w) - f(z)}{w - z} \mathrm{d}w \right| \leqslant 8\sqrt{2}\pi r$$

2) Now consider the case that C does not lie entirely within the unit circle described about z. The arc of the circle, which lies within C, will divide the region enclosed by C into two parts. Let Γ_1 and Γ_2 be their boundaries. Let Γ_1 include z. By theorem 5, $(f(w) - f(z))/(w - z)$ is of non-analyticity $\leqslant r$ inside and on Γ_2. By 1) and theorem 6, we have

$$\left| \int_C \frac{f(w) - f(z)}{w - z} \mathrm{d}w \right| \leqslant \left| \int_{\Gamma_1} \right| + \left| \int_{\Gamma_2} \right| \leqslant 8\sqrt{2}\pi r + 4\sqrt{2}\Omega r$$

The theorem follows immediately.

The theorem gives an analytic approximation of $f(z)$, since the function $\int_C f(w)\mathrm{d}w/(w - z)$ is analytic within C. the error is kr which depends on the non-analyticity r of $f(z)$ and the area Ω of the domain of validity of the formula. From this theorem, we can deduce an approximate Taylor's expansion of $f(z)$ with the same error kr.

ON A SYSTEM OF CONGRUENCES[①]

The object of this paper is to find, by elementary methods, an asymptotic formula for the number of solutions of the system of congruences

$$\left.\begin{aligned} f(x_1)+f(x_2)+f(x_3) &\equiv f(y_1)+f(y_2)+f(y_3)\\ g(x_1)+g(x_2)+g(x_3) &\equiv g(y_1)+g(y_2)+g(y_3)\\ h(x_1)+h(x_2)+h(x_3) &\equiv h(y_1)+h(y_2)+h(y_3)\end{aligned}\right\}(\bmod p^l) \tag{1}$$

where p is a prime greater than 3, l is a positive integer, $f(x)$, $g(x)$, $h(x)$ are cubic polynomials with integer coefficients and $1, f(x), g(x), h(x)$ are linearly independent $(\bmod p)$, i. e., an identity of the form

$$af(x)+bg(x)+ch(x)+d\equiv 0 \quad (\bmod p)$$

implies that $a\equiv b\equiv c\equiv d\equiv 0\ (\bmod p)$[②].

We prove the following lemmas.

Lemma 1 *Let $N(\lambda,\mu)$ be the number of solutions of the system of congruences*

$$\left.\begin{aligned} u_1+u_2+u_3 &\equiv 0\\ u_1v_1+u_2v_2+u_3v_3 &\equiv 0\\ u_1(u_1^2+3v_1^2)+u_2(u_2^2+3v_2^2)+u_3(u_3^2+3v_3^2) &\equiv 0\end{aligned}\right\}(\bmod p^l) \tag{2}$$

① 原载:*J. London Math. Soc.*, 1947(22): 47-53.

② Throughout this paper all letters denote integers.

*with*①

$$p^{\lambda} \parallel u_1,\ p^{\lambda} \parallel u_2,\ p^{\mu} \parallel u_3,\quad l \geqslant \mu \geqslant \lambda \geqslant 0 \tag{3}$$

Then, for $p > 3$,

$$N(\lambda, \mu) = \begin{cases} p^{3l+[(l-\mu)/2]}(1 + O(p^{-1})), & \text{for } l \leqslant 2\lambda + \mu \\ 2p^{3l+\lambda}(1 + O(p^{-1})), & \text{for } l > 2\lambda + \mu \end{cases}$$

Proof For definiteness, we suppose that

$$1 \leqslant u_i \leqslant p^l,\quad 1 \leqslant v_i \leqslant p^l,\quad i = 1, 2, 3$$

Eliminating u_3 from (2), we have

$$\left.\begin{aligned} & u_1v_1 + u_2v_2 \equiv (u_1 + u_2)v_3 \quad (4) \\ & u_1v_1^2 + u_2v_2^2 - (u_1^2u_2 + u_2^2u_1) \equiv (u_1 + u_2)v_3^2 \quad (5) \end{aligned}\right\} (\bmod p^l)$$

Since $p^{\mu} \parallel u_3$ and $u_3 \equiv -u_1 - u_2 (\bmod p^l)$, we have, by (4),

$$u_1v_1 + u_2v_2 + (u_1 + u_2)v_3 \equiv 0 \quad (\bmod p^{\mu})$$

Therefore, by (4),

$$(u_1v_1 + u_2v_2)^2 - (u_1 + u_2)^2v_3^2 \equiv 0 \quad (\bmod p^{l+\mu}) \tag{6}$$

By (5) and (6),

$$(u_1v_1 + u_2v_2)^2 - (u_1 + u_2)[(u_1v_1^2 + u_2v_2^2) - (u_1^2u_2 + u_2^2u_1)] \equiv 0 \quad (\bmod p^{l+\mu})$$

or

$$u_1u_2((u_1 + u_2)^2 - (v_1 - v_2)^2) \equiv 0 \quad (\bmod p^{l+\mu})$$

Since $p^{\lambda} \parallel u_1$, $p^{\lambda} \parallel u_2$, we have

$$(u_1 + u_2)^2 - (v_1 - v_2)^2 \equiv 0 \quad (\bmod p^{l+\mu-2\lambda})$$

A moment's consideration shows that (2) with (3) is equivalent to

$$\begin{cases} u_3 \equiv -u_1 - u_2 & (\bmod p^l) \\ u_1v_1 + u_2v_2 \equiv (u_1 + u_2)v_3 & (\bmod p^l) \\ (v_1 - v_2)^2 - (u_1 + u_2)^2 \equiv 0 & (\bmod p^{l+\mu-2\lambda}) \end{cases} \tag{7}$$

with

$$p^{\lambda} \parallel u_1,\ p^{\lambda} \parallel u_2,\ p^{\mu} \parallel \mu_3,\quad l \geqslant \mu \geqslant \lambda \geqslant 0 \tag{8}$$

If $l \leqslant 2\lambda + \mu$, the last congruence of (7) can be written as

$$(v_1 - v_2)^2 \equiv 0 \quad (\bmod p^{l+\mu-2\lambda})$$

or

$$v_1 - v_2 \equiv 0 \quad (\bmod p^{v}) \tag{9}$$

where

$$v = \left[\frac{1}{2}(l + \mu - 2\lambda + 1)\right] \tag{10}$$

---

① $p^{\lambda} \parallel u^1$ means that p^{λ} divides but $p^{\lambda+1}$ does not divide u_1, etc.

If $l > 2\lambda + \mu$, then $l - 2\lambda > \mu$, and, by the last congruence of (7), we have

$$v_1 - v_2 \equiv u_1 + u_2 \equiv 0 \pmod{p^{\mu}}$$

since $p^{\mu} \parallel u_3$ and $u_3 \equiv -(u_1 + u_2) \pmod{p^l}$. Further, $p^{\mu+1}$ cannot divide both of

$$v_1 - v_2 \pm (u_1 + u_2)$$

since $p^{\mu} \parallel (u_1 + u_2)$. Therefore, by the last congruence of (7), one and only one of the congruences

$$v_1 - v_2 \pm (u_1 + u_2) \equiv 0 \pmod{p^{l-2\lambda}} \tag{11}$$

must be satisfied.

In the case $l \leqslant 2\lambda + \mu$, we have, by (9) and (8).

$$u_1 v_1 + u_2 v_2 = u_1(v_2 + \rho p^v) + u_2 v_2 =$$
$$(u_1 + u_2)v_2 + \rho u_1 p^v \equiv 0 \pmod{p^{\mu}}$$

where ρ is an integer. Thus the left-hand side is divisible by p^{μ}. The same is true for the case $l > 2\lambda + \mu$. Thus, in either case, when u_1, u_2, v_1 and v_2 are determined, the second cogruence of (7) gives p^{μ} solutions of v_3 since $p^{\mu} \parallel (u_1 + u_2)$.

Now u_1 can take $p^{l-\lambda}(1 - p^{-1})$ values by (8), u_2 can take $p^{l-\mu}(1 + O(p^{-1}))$ values by (8) and the first congruence of (7), and u_3 is uniquely determined by that congruence. Therefore in both cases the number of sets of values which u_1, u_2 and u_3 can take is

$$p^{(l-\lambda)+(l-\mu)}(1 + O(p^{-1})) = p^{2l-\lambda-\mu}(1 + O(p^{-1}))$$

In both cases, v_2 can take p^l values. In the first case, v_1 is determined by (9), and the number of values v_1 can take is p^{l-v}. Therefore, in the first case, the number of values which v_1, v_2 and v_3 can take is

$$p^{l+(l-v)+\mu} = p^{2l+\mu-v}$$

The total number of solutions of (7) is, then,

$$p^{2l-\lambda-\mu+2l+\mu-v}(1 + O(p^{-1})) = p^{4l-[\frac{1}{2}(l+\mu+1)]}(1 + O(p^{-1})) =$$
$$p^{3l+[\frac{1}{2}(l-\mu)]}(1 + O(p^{-1}))$$

In the second case, v_1 is determined by (11). The number of values which v_1 can take is $2p^{2\lambda}$, since the congruences (11) have no common solutions. Therefore, in the second case, the number of the sets of values which v_1, v_2 and v_3 can take is

$$2p^{2\lambda+l+\mu}$$

The total number of solutions of (8) is then,

$$2p^{2l-\lambda-\mu+l+2\lambda+\mu}(1+O(p^{-1})) = 2p^{3l+\lambda}(1+O(p^{-1}))$$

Thus the lemma is proved.

Lemma 2 *The number of solutions of the system of congrucnces*

$$\left.\begin{aligned} x_1+x_2+x_3 &\equiv y_1+y_2+y_3 \\ x_1^2+x_2^2+x_3^2 &\equiv y_1^2+y_2^2+y_3^2 \\ x_1^3+x_2^3+x_3^3 &\equiv y_1^3+y_2^3+y_3^3 \end{aligned}\right\} \pmod{p^l} \qquad (12)$$

*is*①, *for* $p > 3$,

$$\alpha p^{3l+[l/3]}(1+O(p^{-1}))$$

where $\alpha = 1, 6$ *or* 16 *according as* $l \equiv 0, 1$ *or* $2 \pmod 3$.

Proof Let

$$u_i = x_i - y_i, \quad v_i = x_i + y_i, \quad i = 1, 2, 3$$

Then (9) becomes

$$\left.\begin{aligned} u_1+u_2+u_3 &\equiv 0 \\ u_1v_1+u_2v_2+u_3v_3 &\equiv 0 \\ u_1(u_1^2+3v_1^2)+u_2(u_2^2+3v_2^2)+u_3(u_3^2+3v_3^2) &\equiv 0 \end{aligned}\right\} \pmod{p^l}$$

since $\quad x_i^3 - y_i^3 = (x_i - y_i)(x_i^2 + x_iy_i + y_i^2) = \frac{1}{4}u_i(u_i^2 + 3v_i^2)$

Using the notation of Lemma 1, we can express the number of solutions of (12) as

$$N = \sum_{\lambda=0}^{l} N(\lambda, \lambda) + 3\sum_{\substack{\lambda=0 \\ \lambda<\mu}}^{l}\sum_{\mu=0}^{l} N(\lambda, \mu) = S_1 + 3S_2, \text{ say} \qquad (13)$$

The factor of the second sum on the right is introduced because the relation (8) is not symmetrical with respect to u_1, u_2 and u_3 and we may permute them to obtain the three distinct sets of relations.

By Lemma 1, we have

$$S_1 = 2\sum_{\lambda=0}^{[(l-1)/3]} p^{3l+\lambda}(1+O(p^{-1})) + \sum_{\lambda=[(l-1)/3]+1}^{l} p^{3l+[(l-\lambda)/2]}(1+O(p^{-1})) =$$

$$p^{3l}\Big(2\sum_{\lambda=0}^{[(l-1)/3]} p^{\lambda} + \sum_{\lambda=[(l-1)/3]+1}^{l} p^{[(l-\lambda)/2]}\Big)(1+O(p^{-1})) =$$

$$p^{3l}(2p^{[(l-1)/3]} + p^{[(l-[(l-1)/3]-1)/2]} + p^{[(l-[(l-1)/3]-2)/2]})(1+O(p^{-1}))$$

since, for $b > a$,

$$\sum_{n=a}^{b} p^{n\delta} = \begin{cases} p^{a\delta}(1+O(p^{\delta})) & \text{for } \delta < 0 \\ p^{b\delta}(1+O(p^{-\delta})) & \text{for } \delta > 0 \end{cases} \qquad (14)$$

---

① Throughout this paper the constants implied by O's are absolute.

Therefore

$$S_1 = \begin{cases} p^{3l+[l/3]}(1 + O(p^{-1})) & \text{for } l \equiv 0 \pmod 3 \\ 3p^{3l+[l/3]}(1 + O(p^{-1})) & \text{for } l \equiv 1 \pmod 3 \\ 4p^{3l+[l/3]}(1 + O(p^{-1})) & \text{for } l \equiv 2 \pmod 3 \end{cases} \tag{15}$$

By Lemma 1, we have

$$S_2 = 2\sum_{\mu=1}^{l-1} \sum_{\lambda=0}^{\min(\mu-1,\ [(l-\mu-1)/2])} p^{3l+\lambda}(1 + O(p^{-1})) + \sum_{\lambda=1}^{l-1} \sum_{\mu=\max(\lambda+1,\ l-2\lambda)}^{l} p^{3l+[(1-\mu)/2]}(1 + O(p^{-1}))$$

By (14),

$$\begin{aligned} S_2 = {} & 2\sum_{\mu=1}^{l-1} p^{3l+\min(\mu-1,\ [(1-\mu-1)/2])}(1 + O(p^{-1})) + \\ & \sum_{\lambda=0}^{l-1} p^{3l+[(l-\max(\lambda+1,\ l-2\lambda))/2]} + (1 + O(p^{-1})) = \\ & 2p^{3l}\Big(\sum_{\mu=1}^{[l/3]} p^{\mu-1} + \sum_{\mu=[l/3]+1}^{l-1} p^{[(l-\mu-1)/2]}\Big)(1 + O(p^{-1})) + \\ & p^{3l}\Big(\sum_{\lambda=0}^{[(l-1)/3]} p^{\lambda} + \sum_{\lambda=[(l-1)/3]+1}^{l-1} p^{[(l-\mu-1)/2]}\Big)(1 + O(p^{-1})) = \\ & 2p^{3l}(p^{[l/3]-1} + p^{[(l-[l/3]-2)/2]} + p^{[(l-[l/3]-3)/2]})(1 + O(p^{-1})) + \\ & p^{3l}(p^{[(l-1)/3]} + p^{[(l-[(l-1)/3]-2)/2]} + p^{[(l-[(l-1)/3]-3)/2]})(1 + O(p^{-1})) \end{aligned}$$

Therefore

$$S_2 = \begin{cases} O(p^{3l+[l/3]-1}) & \text{for } l \equiv 0 \pmod 3 \\ p^{3l+[l/3]}(1 + O(p^{-1})) & \text{for } l \equiv 1 \pmod 3 \\ 4p^{3l+[l/3]}(1 + O(p^{-1})) & \text{for } l \equiv 2 \pmod 3 \end{cases} \tag{16}$$

By (13), (15) and (16),

$$N = \begin{cases} p^{3l+[l/3]}(1 + O(p^{-1})) & \text{for } l \equiv 0 \pmod 3 \\ 6p^{3l+[l/3]}(1 + O(p^{-1})) & \text{for } l \equiv 1 \pmod 3 \\ 16p^{3l+[l/3]}(1 + O(p^{-1})) & \text{for } l \equiv 2 \pmod 3 \end{cases}$$

Lemma 3 *The system of congruences* (1) *is equivalent to the system*

$$\left.\begin{aligned} x_1 + x_2 + x_3 &\equiv y_1 + y_2 + y_3 \\ x_1^2 + x_2^2 + x_3^2 &\equiv y_1^2 + y_2^2 + y_3^2 \\ x_1^3 + x_2^3 + x_3^3 &\equiv y_1^3 + y_2^3 + y_3^3 \end{aligned}\right\} \pmod{p^l} \tag{17}$$

Proof Evidently (17) implies (1). Let

$$f(x) = a_3x^3 + a_2x^2 + a_1x + a_0$$
$$g(x) = b_3x^3 + b_2x^2 + b_1x + b_0$$
$$h(x) = c_3x^3 + c_2x^2 + c_1x + c_0$$

Then

$$\begin{vmatrix} a_3 & a_2 & a_1 \\ b_3 & b_2 & b_1 \\ c_3 & c_2 & c_1 \end{vmatrix} \not\equiv 0 \pmod p$$

since $p > 3$. We can derive (17) from (1) without difficulty.

Theorem 1 *The number of solutions of* (1) *is*

$$ap^{3l+[l/3]}(1 + O(p^{-1}))$$

where $a = 1, 6$ *or* 16 *according as* $l \equiv 0, 1$ *or* $2 \pmod 3$.

Proof The theorem follows from Lemmas 2 and 3.

ON A GENERALIZED HYPERBOLIC GEOMETRY①②

1. Introduction

It is well known that any real non-singular quadric in an ordinary projective space defines in the space a hyperbolic geometry. The purpose of this paper is to show that a Riemannian metric can be defined when an arbitrary surface, not necessarily a quadric, is given in the space.

2. The Lie quadrics of a surface and the associated six-parameter family of frames of reference

We may take as a frame of reference (in French, "repère")③ in an ordinary projective space a set of four "analytic" points A, A_1, A_2, A_3 defined to within a transformation

$$\bar{A} = \lambda A, \bar{A}_1 = \lambda A_1, \bar{A}_2 = \lambda A_2, \bar{A}_3 = \lambda A_3 \qquad (1)$$

The method of the moving frame of reference in the projective theory of surfaces consists in attaching to each point of the

① 原载:*J. London Math. Soc.*, 1947(22): 153-160.

② I wish to express my thanks to Professor Shiing - shen Chern for his helpful suggestions.

③ *Cf.* E. Cartan, *Lecons sur la thèorie des espaces à connexion projective*, especially Chap. Ⅲ. This book will hereafter be cited as Cartan, *Connexion projective.*

surface a frame such that the equation of the surface referred to it will be in a simple form. If M is a point in space, we define the non-homogeneous coordinates x, y, z of M, referred to the frame $A\ A_1\ A_2\ A_3$, by the relation

$$M = A + xA_1 + yA_2 + zA_3 \tag{2}$$

The equation of the surface is then of the form

$$z = f(x, y) \tag{3}$$

We can choose the frame of reference such that the equation of the Lie quadric at A is

$$z = xy \tag{4}$$

We proceed to find the most general family of frames of reference having this property.

Since the surface has contact of the second order with its Lie quadric, the equation of the surface referred to $AA_1A_2A_3$ must be of the form

$$z = xy + \frac{1}{6}(\alpha x^3 + 3\beta x^2 y + 3\gamma xy^2 + \delta y^3) + \frac{1}{24}(ax^4 + 4bx^3y + 6cx^2y^2 + 4dxy^3 + ey^4) + \cdots \tag{5}$$

where the terms represented by dots are of the fifth or higher orders in x, y. To find the conditions that the Lie quadric have the equation (4), we must find the equation of the quadric when the surface is given by (5).

Following the method of Cartan①, we find that the equations of the first asymptotic curve through A are

$$\begin{cases} y = -\frac{1}{4}\alpha x^2 + \frac{1}{24}(5\alpha\beta - 2a)x^3 + \cdots \\ z = -\frac{1}{12}\alpha x^3 + \frac{1}{24}(2\alpha\beta - a)x^4 + \cdots \end{cases} \tag{6}$$

and those of the second asymptotic curve through A are

$$\begin{cases} x = -\frac{1}{4}\delta y^2 + \frac{1}{24}(5\gamma\delta - 2e)y^3 + \cdots \\ z = -\frac{1}{12}\delta y^3 + \frac{1}{24}(2\gamma\delta - e)y^4 + \cdots \end{cases} \tag{7}$$

The second asymptotic tangent at the point of abscissa x on the first asymptotic curve bas equations of the form

$$X = x + \lambda\rho,\ Y = y + \rho,\ Z = z + \mu\rho \tag{8}$$

① E. Cartan, *Connexion projective*, 137-139.

where y and z are functions of x given by (6) and ρ is the parameter defining the different points of the line. To find λ, μ it is necessary only to substitute the expressions X, Y, Z in the equation (5) of the surface and to equate to zero the coefficients of ρ, ρ^2. We find

$$\begin{cases} \lambda = -\frac{1}{2}\gamma x + \left(\frac{1}{2}\beta\gamma - \frac{1}{8}\alpha\delta + \frac{1}{4}c\right)x^2 + \cdots \\ \mu = x + \frac{1}{2}\beta x^2 + \cdots \end{cases} \tag{9}$$

Substituting these expressions into (8), we get

$$Z - XY = \frac{1}{2}\beta x^2 Y + \left\{\frac{1}{2}\gamma x - \left(\frac{1}{2}\beta\gamma - \frac{1}{8}\alpha\delta + \frac{1}{4}c\right)x^2\right\}Y^2 + \text{terms in } x^3$$

In order that the equation of the Lie quadric be given by (4) it is necessary and sufficient that

$$\beta = \gamma = 0,\ c = \frac{1}{2}\alpha\delta$$

Therefore *the most general frame of reference* $A\ A_1\ A_2\ A_3$ *with respect to which the Lie quadric has the equation* (4) *is one such that the equation of the surface takes the form*

$$\begin{cases} z = xy + \frac{1}{6}(\alpha x^3 + \delta y^3) + \frac{1}{24}(\alpha x^4 + 4bx^3 y + 6cx^2 y^2 + 4dxy^3 + ey^4) + \cdots \\ c = \frac{1}{2}\alpha\delta \end{cases} \tag{10}$$

Evidently, the family of frames of reference about a point that have this property depends on four parameters, and the whole family depends on six parameters.

Let

$$\begin{cases} dA = \bar{\omega}_0^0 A + \omega^1 A_1 + \omega^2 A_2 + \omega^3 A_3 \\ dA_1 = \omega_1^0 A + \bar{\omega}_1^1 A_1 + \omega_1^2 A_2 + \omega_1^3 A_3 \\ dA_2 = \omega_2^0 A + \omega_2^1 A_1 + \bar{\omega}_2^2 A_2 + \omega_2^3 A_3 \\ dA_3 = \omega_3^0 A + \omega_3^1 A_1 + \omega_3^2 A_2 + \bar{\omega}_3^3 A_3 \end{cases} \tag{11}$$

be the equations of an infinitesimal displacement of the frame of reference within the family. The conditions for the point M in (2) to be fixed are①

① Cartan, *Connexion projective*, 143.

$$\begin{cases} dx + \omega^1 + x\omega_1^1 + y\omega_2^1 + z\omega_3^1 - x^2\omega_1^0 - xy\omega_2^0 - xz\omega_3^0 = 0 \\ dy + \omega^2 + x\omega_1^2 + y\omega_2^2 + z\omega_3^2 - xy\omega_1^0 - y^2\omega_2^0 - yz\omega_3^0 = 0 \\ dz + \omega^3 + x\omega_1^3 + y\omega_2^3 + z\omega_3^3 - xz\omega_1^0 - yz\omega_2^0 - z^2\omega_3^0 = 0 \end{cases} \tag{12}$$

where

$$\omega_1^1 = \overline{\omega}_1^1 - \overline{\omega}_0^0 \tag{13}$$

By substituting the equation (10) into (12) and comparing the equations (12), we get

$$\begin{cases} \omega^3 = 0,\ \omega_1^3 = \omega^2,\ \omega_2^3 = \omega^1 \\ \omega_1^2 = -\frac{1}{2}\alpha\omega^1,\ \omega_3^3 = \omega_1^1 + \omega_2^2,\ \omega_2^1 = -\frac{1}{2}\delta\omega^2 \\ \omega_1^0 = \omega_3^2 + \frac{1}{2}b\omega^1,\ \omega_2^0 = \omega_3^1 + \frac{1}{2}d\omega^2 \\ \omega_3^0 = r\omega^1 + s\omega^2 \end{cases} \tag{14}$$

where r and s depend on the coefficients in (10). Hence the equations of infinitesimal displacement are

$$\begin{cases} dA = \overline{\omega}_0^0 A + \omega^1 A_1 + \omega^2 A_2 \\ dA_1 = \left(\omega_3^2 + \frac{1}{2}b\omega^1\right)A + \overline{\omega}_1^1 A_1 - \frac{1}{2}\alpha\omega^1 A_2 + \omega^2 A_3 \\ dA_2 = \left(\omega_3^1 + \frac{1}{2}d\omega^2\right)A - \frac{1}{2}\delta\omega^2 A_1 + \overline{\omega}_2^2 A_2 + \omega^1 A_3 \\ dA_3 = (r\omega^1 + s\omega^2)A + \omega_3^1 A_1 + \omega_3^2 A_2 + \overline{\omega}_3^3 A_3 \end{cases} \tag{15}$$

The independent relative components are ω^1, ω^2, ω_1^1, ω_2^2, ω_3^1, ω_3^2.

3. Definition of the Riemannian metric. The case of a quadric

To define the Riemannian metric we associate, in an arbitrary way, to every point in space a definite Lie quadric of the surface such that the element of arc at this point is defined to be the infinitesimal projective distance of this point from a neighbouring point with respect to the associated Lie quadric. Let u, v be the parameters on the surface. We take a two-parameter family of frames of reference $A\ A_1\ A_2\ A_3$ from the sixparameter family found above, such that at each point of the surface there is one frame of the family. To every geometrical point M in space there then correspond values u, v, k such that

$$M = A_3 + kA \tag{16}$$

Obviously, u, v, k can be taken as coordinates in the space. The equations of an infinitesimal displacement of the frame $A\ A_1\ A_2\ A_3$ within the family are given by

(15), the coefficients of $A\ A_1\ A_2\ A_3$ being now Pfaffian forms in u, v.

Referred to $A\ A_1\ A_2\ A_3$, the points M and dM have respectively the coordinates $(k, 0, 0, 1)$ and

$$(dk + k\overline{\omega}_0^0 + r\omega^1 + s\omega^2,\ \omega_3^1 + k\omega^1,\ \omega_3^2 + k\omega^2,\ \overline{\omega}_3^3) \tag{17}$$

while the Lie quadric has the equation

$$tz - xy = 0 \tag{18}$$

Therefore the element of arc is①

$$ds^2 = \frac{c^2}{k^2}\{(dk - k\omega_3^2 + r\omega^1 + s\omega^2)^2 + 4k(\omega_3^1 + k\omega^1)(\omega_3^2 + k\omega^2)\} \tag{19}$$

where c is a constant giving the unit of projective length.

The definition of ds^2 in (19) depends on the choice of the two-parameter family of frames of reference $A\ A_1\ A_2\ A_3(u, v)$, and is not intrinsically related to the surface. We want to show that *the ds^2 in (19) is independent of this choice if and only if the surface is a quadric.* This theorem is geometrically plausible and can be established analytically as follows.

Let

$$\begin{cases} w^1 = dk - k\omega_3^3 + r\omega^1 + s\omega^2 \\ w^2 = \omega_3^1 + k\omega^1 \\ w^3 = \omega_3^2 + k\omega^2 \end{cases} \tag{20}$$

The conditions for the point (16) to be fixed are

$$w^1 = w^2 = w^3 = 0 \tag{21}$$

From the equations of structure of the projective group in space② we find

$$\begin{cases} (w^1)' = -[w^1\omega_3^3] + \left[w^2\left(\frac{1}{2}b\omega^1 - 2k\omega^2\right)\right] + \left[w^3\left(\frac{1}{2}d\omega^2 - 2k\omega^1\right)\right] \\ (w^2)' = [w^1\omega^1] - [w^2\omega_2^2] - \frac{1}{2}\delta[w^3\omega^2] \\ (w^3)' = [\omega^1\omega^2] - \frac{1}{2}\alpha[w^2\omega^1] - [w^3\omega_1^1] \end{cases} \tag{22}$$

We introduce the operation δ which leaves the point M fixed, so that

$$w^1(\delta) = w^2(\delta) = w^3(\delta) = 0$$

Put

$$w^i = w^i(d),\quad e^i = \omega^i(\delta),\quad e_j^i = \omega_j^i(\delta) \tag{23}$$

---

① F. Klein, "Über die sogenannte nicht-Euklidische Geometrie", *Math. Annalen*, 1871(4), or *Gesamm Abh.*, Bd. I, 298.

② Cartan, *Connexion projective*, 120-121.

Then we have, from (22)

$$\begin{cases}\delta w^1 = e_3^3 w^1 - \left(\frac{1}{2}be^1 - 2ke^2\right)w^2 - \left(\frac{1}{2}de^2 - 2ke^1\right)w^3 \\ \delta w^2 = -e^1\omega^1 + e_2^2 w^2 + \frac{1}{2}\delta e^2 w^3 \\ \delta w^3 = -e^2 w^1 + \frac{1}{2}\alpha e^1 w^2 + e_1^1 w^3\end{cases} \tag{24}$$

Applying these equatioins to ds^2, we get

$$\delta(ds^2) = \frac{c^2}{k^2}\left\{\frac{2}{k}(re^1 + se^2)(w^1)^2 + 2k\alpha e^1(w^2)^2 + 2k\delta e^2(w^3)^1 - be^1w^1w^2 - de^2w^1w^3 + 4(re^1 + se^3)w^2w^3\right\}$$

This shows that ds^2 is independent of the choice of the two-parameter family of frames of reference when and only when

$$\alpha = \delta = b = d = r = s = 0$$

and this holds only when the given surface is a quadric. Thus our theorem is proved.

To get a definition of ds^2 intrinsically related to the surface in the case of a non-ruled surface, we may take the family of frames of reference of the fourth order attached to the surface. The equations of infinitesimal displacement are then①

$$\begin{cases}dA = \omega_0^0 A + \omega^1 A_1 + \omega^2 A_2 \\ dA_1 = (D\omega^1 + F\omega^2)A + (\omega_0^0 + 2A\omega^1 + B\omega^2)A_1 + \omega^1 A_2 + \omega^2 A_3 \\ dA_2 = (E\omega^1 + C\omega^2)A + \omega^2 A_1 + (\omega_0^0 A\omega^1 + 2B\omega^2)A_2 + \omega^1 A_3 \\ dA_3 = (C\omega^1 + D\omega^2)A + (E\omega^1 + C\omega^2)A_1 + (D\omega^1 + F\omega^2)A_2 + \\ \quad (\omega_0^0 + 3A\omega^1 + 3B\omega^2)A_3\end{cases} \tag{25}$$

so that

$$\begin{cases}w^1 = dk + (C - 3Ak)\omega^1 + (D - 3Bk)\omega^2 \\ w^2 = (E + k)w^1 + C\omega^2 \\ w^3 = D\omega^1 + (F + k)\omega^2\end{cases} \tag{26}$$

and

$$ds^2 = \frac{c^2}{k^2}\{(w^1)^2 + 4kw^2w^3\} \tag{27}$$

---

① Cartan, *Connexion projective*, 147-149.

The functions A, B, C, D, E, F are the six fundamental invariants of the surface.

4. Parallelism of Levi-Civita and the curvature tensor

To define the parallelism of Levi-Civita from the Riemannian metric (27) we put

$$\theta = \frac{w^1}{k},\ \theta^2 = \frac{w^2}{\sqrt{k}},\ \theta^3 = \frac{w^3}{\sqrt{k}} \tag{28}$$

so that

$$ds^2 = c^2\{(\theta^1)^2 + 4\theta^2\theta^3\} \tag{29}$$

At each point of the space we choose a trihedral $Mx_1\ x_2\ x_3$ (Euclidean frame) such that

$$\begin{cases} x_1^2 = c^2,\ x_2x_3 = 2c^2 \\ x_2^2 = x_3^2 = x_1x_3 = x_1x_2 = 0 \end{cases} \tag{30}$$

and such that the equations of an infinitesimal displacement are

$$\begin{cases} dM = \theta^1 x_1 + \theta^2 x_2 + \theta^2 x_3 \\ dx_1 = \phi^1 x_2 + \phi^2 x_3 \\ dx_2 = -2\phi^2 x_1 + \phi x_2 \\ dx_3 = -2\phi^1 x_1 - \phi x_3 \end{cases} \tag{31}$$

The parallelism of Levi-Civita defined for a Riemannian metric is the infinitesimal displacement characterized by the condition that the torsion should be zero:

$$d\delta M - \delta dM = 0$$

From (31) we find that the Pfaffian forms ϕ, ϕ^1, ϕ^2 are to be determined by the equations

$$\begin{cases} 2[\phi^2\theta^2] + 2[\phi^1\theta^3] = (\theta^1)' \\ -[\phi^1\theta^1] - [\phi\theta^2] = (\theta^2)' \\ -[\phi^2\theta^1] + [\phi\theta^3] = (\theta^3)' \end{cases} \tag{32}$$

The members on the right hand sides of these equations can be found from (22) and (28) and are quadratic exterior forms in θ^1, θ^2, θ^3. A calculation gives

$$
\begin{cases}
(\theta^1)' = -\dfrac{1}{\Delta\sqrt{k}}\{(CF - D^2 + Ck)[\theta^1\theta^2] + \\
\qquad (DE - C^2 + Dk)[\theta^1\theta^3]\} + 2\dfrac{F - E}{\Delta}k[\theta^2\theta^3] \\
(\theta^2)' = \left(-\dfrac{1}{2} + \dfrac{F}{\Delta}k + \dfrac{1}{\Delta}k^2\right)[\theta^1\theta^2] - \dfrac{C}{\Delta}k[\theta^1\theta^3] - \\
\qquad \dfrac{1}{2\Delta\sqrt{k}}\{DE - C^2 + (AC + BE - D)k + Bk^2\}[\theta^2\theta^3] \\
(\theta^3)' = -\dfrac{D}{\Delta}k[\theta^1\theta^2] + \left\{-\dfrac{1}{2} + \dfrac{E}{\Delta}k + \dfrac{1}{\Delta}k^2\right\}[\theta^1\theta^3] + \\
\qquad \dfrac{1}{2\Delta\sqrt{k}}\{CF - D^2 + (AF + BD - C)k + Ak^2\}[\theta^2\theta^3]
\end{cases}
\tag{33}
$$

where

$$
\Delta = EF + CD + (E + F)k + k^2 \tag{34}
$$

Substituting these expressions in (32) we find one and only one set of Pfaffian forms ϕ, ϕ^1, ϕ^2 satisfying (32), and these are

$$
\begin{cases}
\phi = \lambda_1\theta^1 + \lambda_2\theta^2 + \lambda_3\theta^3 \\
\phi^1 = \mu_1\theta^1 + \mu_2\theta^2 + \mu_3\theta^3 \\
\phi^2 = v_1\theta^1 + v_2\theta^2 + v_3\theta^3
\end{cases}
\tag{35}
$$

where

$$
\begin{cases}
\lambda_1 = 0,\ \lambda_2 = \dfrac{1}{2\Delta\sqrt{k}}\{CF - D^2 + (AF + BD - C)k + Ak^2\} \\
\lambda_3 = -\dfrac{1}{2\Delta\sqrt{k}}\{DE - C^2 + (AC + BE - D)k + Bk^2\} \\
\mu_1 = -\dfrac{1}{2\Delta\sqrt{k}}(DE - C^2 + Dk) \\
\mu_2 = -\dfrac{1}{2} + \dfrac{F}{\Delta}k + \dfrac{1}{\Delta}k^2,\ \mu_3 = -\dfrac{C}{\Delta}k \\
v_1 = -\dfrac{1}{2\Delta\sqrt{k}}(CF - D^2 + Ck),\ v_2 = -\dfrac{D}{\Delta}k \\
v_3 = -\dfrac{1}{2} + \dfrac{E}{\Delta}k + \dfrac{1}{\Delta}k^2
\end{cases}
\tag{36}
$$

The equations (31), with ϕ^1, ϕ^2 given by (35), are the equations for the parallelism of Levi-Civita.

The curvature of the space is then given by the exterior forms Φ, Φ^1, Φ^2 determined by the equations

$$
\begin{cases}
\Phi = (\phi)' - 2[\phi^1\phi^2] \\
\Phi^1 = (\phi^1)' + [\phi\phi^1] \\
\Phi^2 = (\phi^2)' - [\phi\phi^2]
\end{cases}
\tag{37}
$$

ON A DOUBLE EXPONENTIAL SUM①

Abstract

Let κ be a finite field with p^m elements. Let $f(x,y)$ by a polynomial of the n-th degree in κ, not equivalent to a polynomial of a single variable. let $S[a]$ denote the trace of the element a in κ. Then

$$\sum_{x,y\in\kappa} \exp\{2\pi i S[f(x,y)]/p\} = O(p^{m(2-2/n)})$$

where x and y run over all elements in κ and the constant implied by O depends only on n. In particular, for $n = s$, we have a more precise result

$$\sum_{x\in\kappa} \exp\{2\pi i S[f(x,y)]/p\} = O(p^{3m/4})$$

It is rather difficult to indicate the proof of the result here, but the authors should like to remark that they use a great number of results concerning the solutions of differential equations in a finite field.

Throughout the paper we consider a finite field κ with p^m elements where p is a prime and m is a positive integer.

The object of the paper is to prove the following theorem:

---

① 原载:The Science Reports of National Tsing Hua University, Ser. A, 1947,4(4-6): 484-518. 合作者华罗庚.

Let $f(x,y)$ be a polynomial of degree $n \geqslant 4$, which can not be expressed as a polynomial of the n-th degree of a single variable in κ. Then

$$\sum_{\xi,\eta} \exp\{2\pi i S[f(\xi,\eta)]/p\} = O(p^{m(2-2/n)})$$

where ξ, η run over independetly all the elements of the field κ and where the constant implied by the symbol O depends only on n.

In particular, when we take κ to be the field formed by the residue classes, mod p, we have then

$$\sum_{\xi=1}^{p}\sum_{\eta=1}^{p} \exp\{2\pi i f(\xi,\eta)/p\} = O(p^{2-2/n})$$

Definition *Let*

$$f_1(x_1,\cdots,x_n),\ \cdots,\ f_n(x_1,\cdots,x_n)$$

be n polynomials in κ. Let

$$J = J(f_1,\cdots,f_n) = \frac{D(f_1,\cdots,f_n)}{D(x_1,\cdots,x_n)}$$

denote the Jacobian of $f_1,\cdots,f_n$. The solutions of

$$f_1(x_1,\cdots,x_n) = 0,\ i = 1,\cdots,n$$

for which $J \neq 0$ are called non-singular solutions and those for which $J = 0$ are called singular solutions.

Lemma 1 *The number of non-singular solutions of*

$$f_i(x_1,\cdots,x_n) = 0,\ i = 1,\cdots,n \tag{1}$$

is $O(1)$.

Proof The theorem is evident for $n = 1$. Suppose that the theorem is true for $n-1$ variables and $n-1$ equations. Let us prove the theorem for n variables and n equations.

If $f_1,\cdots,f_n$ do not involve x_n, the theorem is true, for, in this case, $J(f_1,\cdots,f_n) = 0$ identically and (1) has no non-singular solutions. If one of them contains x_n the theorem is also true, for if f_n contains x_n and $(x_1^{(0)},\cdots,x_n^{(0)})$ is a non-singular solution of (1), then we have

$$J(f_1,\cdots,f_n) = \frac{\partial f_n}{\partial x_n} J(f_1,\cdots,f_{n-1}) \neq 0, \quad \text{at } x_v = x_v^{(0)}$$

which shows that $(x_1^{(0)},\cdots,x_{n-1}^{(0)})$ is a non-singular solution of $f_1 = 0,\cdots,f_{n-1} = 0$ and that $f_n(x_1^{(0)},\cdots,x_{n-1}^{(0)},x)$ is not identically zero.

Let the degree of f_i with respect to x_n be λ_i. Then the theorem is true when $\lambda_1 + \cdots + \lambda_r \leqslant 1$. For in this case, at most one of the equations (1) involves x_n. Now suppose that the theorem is true for $\lambda_1 + \cdots + \lambda_n \leqslant \gamma$. Let us prove the theorem for $\lambda_1 + \cdots + \lambda_n \leqslant \gamma + 1$.

Without loss of generality we assume that

$$f_1 = f_{10}x_n^{\lambda_1} + \cdots + f_{1\lambda_1}$$
$$f_2 = f_{20}x_n^{\lambda_2} + \cdots + f_{2\lambda_2} \tag{2}$$

where $\lambda_1 \geqslant \lambda_2 > 1$ and f_{1i}, f_{2i} are polynomials in $x_1, \cdots, x_{n-1}$.

Consider the system of equations

$$f'_1 = f_{20}f_1 - f_{10}x_n^{\lambda_1-\lambda_2}f_2 = 0①, f_i = 0, i = 2, \cdots, n$$

Evidently every solution of (1) is a solution of (2). We shall prove that each non-singular solution $(x_1^{(0)}, \cdots, x_n^{(0)})$ of (1), for which $f_{20} \neq 0$ is a non-singular solution of (2).

By differentiating the first equation in (2) with respect to x_i, $i = 1, \cdots, n$ we have

$$\frac{\partial f'_1}{\partial x_i} = f_{20}\frac{\partial f_1}{\partial x_i} - f_{10}x_n^{\lambda_1-\lambda_2}\frac{\partial f_2}{\partial x_i} + \frac{\partial f_{20}}{\partial x_i}f_1 - \frac{\partial f_{10}}{\partial x_i}x_n^{\lambda_1-\lambda_2}f_2$$
$$\left(= f_{20}\frac{\partial f_1}{\partial x_i} - f_{10}x_n^{\lambda_1-\lambda_2}\frac{\partial f_2}{\partial x_i} \text{ at } x_v = x_v^{(0)}\right), i = 1, \cdots, n-1 \tag{3}$$
$$\frac{\partial f'_1}{\partial x_n} = f_{20}\frac{\partial f_1}{\partial x_n} - f_{10}x_n^{\lambda_1-\lambda_2}\frac{\partial f_2}{\partial x_n} + \frac{\partial f_{20}}{\partial x_n}f_1 - \frac{\partial f_{10}}{\partial x_n}x_n^{\lambda_1-\lambda_2}f_2 - (\lambda_1 - \lambda_2)f_{10}x_n^{\lambda_1-\lambda_2-1}f_2$$
$$\left(= f_{20}\frac{\partial f_1}{\partial x_n} - f_{10}x^{\lambda_1-\lambda_2}\frac{\partial f_2}{\partial x_n} \text{ at } x_v = x_v^{(0)}\right)$$

Therefore

$$J(f'_1, f_2, \cdots, f_n) = f_{20}J(f_1, f_2, \cdots, f_n) \neq 0 \text{ at } x_v = x_v^{(0)}$$

Now suppose that $(x_1^{(0)}, \cdots, x_v^{(0)})$ is a non-singular solution of (1), for which $f_{20} = 0$. Then the solution satisfies both

$$f_1 = 0, \quad f'_2 = f_2 - f_{20}x_n^{\lambda_2} = 0, \quad f_i = 0, \quad i = 3, \cdots, n \tag{4}$$

and

$$f_1 = 0, \quad f_{20} = 0, \quad f_i = 0, \quad i = 3, \cdots, n \tag{5}$$

By (4)

$$\frac{\partial f'_2}{\partial x_i} = \frac{\partial f_2}{\partial x_i} - \frac{\partial f_{20}}{\partial x_i}x_n^{\lambda_2}, \quad i = 1, \cdots, n-1 \tag{6}$$
$$\frac{\partial f'_2}{\partial x_n} = \frac{\partial f_2}{\partial x_n} - \lambda_2 f_{20}x_n^{\lambda_2-1}\left(= \frac{\partial f_2}{\partial x_n} \text{ at } x_v = x_v^{(0)}\right)$$

Hence

① This equation may be an identity and hence (2) may have no non-singular solutions.

$$0 \neq J(f_1, \cdots, f_n) = J(f_1, f'_2, f_3, \cdots, f_n) + x_n^{\lambda_2} J(f_1, f_{20}, f_3, \cdots, f_n) \text{ at } x_v = x_v^{(0)}$$

which shows that $J(f_1, f'_2, f_3, \cdots, f_n)$ and $J(f_1, f_{20}, f_3, \cdots, f_n)$ can not be both zero.

Therefore each non-singular solution of (1) must be a non-singular solution of one of the systems (2), (4) and (5). Since the sum of the degrees with respect to x_n of each of these systems is $\leqslant r$, the number of non-singular solutions of each of them is $O(1)$. Therefore (1) has only $O(1)$ non-singular solutions.

Lemma 2 *Let $f(x_1, \cdots, x_n)$ be a polynomial $\neq 0$ in k, then the number of solutions of*

$$f(x_1, \cdots, x_n) = 0 \tag{7}$$

is $O(p^{m(n-1)})$.

Proof The theorem is evident for $n = 1$. Suppose that the lemma is true for $n = s - 1$.

Let

$$f(x_1, \cdots, x_s) = g_0(x_1, \cdots, x_{s-1})x_s^k + \cdots + g_k(x_1, \cdots, x_{s-1})$$

where g_i are polynomials and $g_0 \neq 0$. The number of solutions of

$$f(x_1, \cdots, x_s) = 0, \quad g_0(x_1, \cdots, x_{s-1}) \neq 0$$

is evidently $O(p^{m(s-1)})$, and that of

$$f(x_1, \cdots, x_s) = 0, \quad g_0(x_1, \cdots, x_{s-1}) = 0$$

is $O(p^{m(s-2)}p^m) = O(p^{m(s-1)})$, by our supposition. Therefore the number of solutions of

$$f(x_1, \cdots, x_s) = 0$$

is $O(p^{m(s-1)})$. Hence the lemma is true.

Lemma 3 *Let $g(u)$ be a polynomial of degree $s < p$ satisfying*

$$A(u)g'(u) + B(u)g(u) = 0 \tag{8}$$

where $A(u)$, $B(u)$ are polynomials. Then each irreducible factor of $g(u)$ is a factor of $A(u)$.

Proof Let $h(u)$ be an irreducible factor of $g(u)$, and suppose that

$$(h(\mu))^v \parallel g(u)①$$

Then, since $v < p$

$$(h(u))^{v-1} \parallel g'(u)$$

By (8)

$$h(u) \mid A(u)$$

① $(h(u))^v \parallel g(u)$ means that $(h(u))^v \mid g(u)$ and $(h(u))^{v+1} \nmid g(u)$.

Lemma 4 *Let $A(u)$, $B(u)$, $C(u)$ and $D(u)$ be polynomials and*

$$(A(u), A'(u)B(u)) = 1$$

Suppose that $g(u)$ is a polynomial of degree $s < p$ satisfying

$$A(u)B(u)g'(u) - \left[A(u)C(u) + \frac{h}{k}A'(u)B(u)\right]g(u) + (A(u))^{\mu}D(u) = 0 \tag{9}$$

where h, k are integers and $h < p$, $\mu < \frac{h}{k} + 1$. Then

$$(A(u))^{\mu} \mid g(u)$$

Proof Suppose that

$$g(u) = (A(u))^{\mu\theta}h(u),\ A(u) \nmid h(u),\ 0 \leqslant \mu' \leqslant \mu - 1$$

Substituting this into (9) and removing the factor $(A(u))^{\mu'}$, we have

$$A(u)B(u)h'(u) - \left[A(u)C(u) + \frac{h - k\mu'}{k}A'(u)B(u)\right]h(u) +$$

$$(A(u))^{\mu-\mu'}D(u) = 0$$

Since $0 < h - k\mu' < p$, we have

$$A(u) \mid h(u)$$

which is contrary to our supposition. Therefore

$$(A(u))^{\mu} \mid g(u)$$

Lemma 5 *Let β be a constant $\neq 0$, and let λ and s be integers satisfying $3 \leqslant \lambda < p$, $4 \leqslant s < p$. Let*

$$c_i = c_i(\alpha) = c_i^{(0)} + c_i^{(1)}\alpha + \cdots,\ i = 0, 1, \cdots, 5$$

be polynomials in α not all zero. Suppose that $g(u)$ is a polynomial of degrees which is independent of α and satisfies the equation

$$(c_0u^2 + c_1u + c_2)g'(u) + (c_3u + c_4)g(u) = c_5(\beta u - \alpha)^{\lambda} \tag{10}$$

for all value of α. Then each irreducible factor of $g(u)$ is a factor of $c_0u^2 + c_1u + c_2$.

Proof If $c_5 = 0$, the theorem follows from lemma 3. Suppose that $c_5 \neq 0$ and let

$$c_5 = c_5^{(0)} + \cdots + c_5^{(k)}\alpha^k,\ c_5^{(k)} \neq 0,\ c_5^{(\lambda)} = 0 \text{ for } \lambda < 0$$

Equating the coefficients of $\alpha^{\lambda+k-j}$, $j = 0, 1, 2, 3$, on both sides of (10), we have

$$(c_0^{(\lambda+k)}u^2 + c_1^{(\lambda+k)}u + c_2^{(\lambda+k)})g'(u) + (c_3^{(\lambda+k)}u + c_4^{(\lambda+k)})g(u) = (-1)^{\lambda}c_5^{(k)} \tag{11}$$

$$\begin{aligned}(c_0^{(\lambda+k-1)}u^2 + c_1^{(\lambda+k-1)}u + c_2^{(\lambda+k-1)})g'(u) + (c_3^{(\lambda+k-1)}u + c_4^{(\lambda+k-1)})g(u) = \\ (-1)^{\lambda-1}\lambda\beta c_5^{(k)}u + (-1)^{\lambda}c_5^{(k-1)}\end{aligned} \tag{12}$$

$$(c_0^{(\lambda+k-2)}u^2 + c_1^{(\lambda+k-2)}u + c_2^{(\lambda+k-2)})g'(u) + (c_3^{(\lambda+k-2)}u + c_4^{(\lambda+k-2)})g(u) = (-1)^{\lambda-2}\binom{\lambda}{2}\beta^2 c_5^{(k)}u^2 + (-1)^{\lambda-1}\lambda\beta c_5^{(k-1)}u + (-1)^{\lambda}c_5^{(k-2)} \tag{13}$$

$$(c_0^{(\lambda+k-3)}u^2 + c_1^{(\lambda+k-3)}u + c_2^{(\lambda+k-3)})g'(u) + (c_3^{(\lambda+k-3)}u + c_4^{(\lambda+k-3)})g(u) = (-1)^{\lambda-3}\binom{\lambda}{3}\beta^3 c_5^{(k)}u^3 + (-1)^{\lambda-2}\binom{\lambda}{2}\beta^2 c_5^{(k-1)}u^2 + (-1)^{\lambda-1}\lambda\beta c^{(k-2)}u + (-1)^{\lambda}c_5^{(k-3)} \tag{14}$$

Evidently $c_0^{(\lambda+k)}$, $c_1^{(\lambda+k)}$, $c_2^{(\lambda+k)}$ can not be all zero. Let the first of them, which is different from zero be $c_i^{(\lambda+k)}$, $0 \leqslant i \leqslant 2$, Multiplying (11) by

$$\left((-1)^{\lambda-i-1}\binom{\lambda}{i+1}c_5^{(k)}\beta^{i+1}u^{i+1} + (-1)^{\lambda-i}\binom{\lambda}{i}c_5^{(k-1)}\beta^i u^i + \cdots + (-1)^{\lambda}c_5^{(k-i-1)}\right)/(-1)^i c_5^{(k)}$$

and substracting the resulting equation from $(12+i)$, we obtain an equation of the form

$$P(u)g'(u) + Q(u)g(u) = 0$$

where $P(u)$ is a polynomial of the third degree in which the coefficient of u^3 is $(-1)^i\binom{\lambda}{i+1} \times \beta^{i+1}c_i^{(\lambda+k)} \neq 0$. Since $g(u)$ is of degree $\geqslant 4$, $g(u)$ and $g'(u)$ must have a ommon factor different from a constant. Since the common factor is independent of α, we must have $c_5 = 0$. This is contrary to our supposition.

Lemma 6 *Let β be a constant $\neq 0$, and let λ, μ, h, k be integers satisfying*

$$h < p,\ 2 \leqslant \mu < \frac{h}{k} + 1,\ \mu - 1 \leqslant \lambda < p$$

Let $C = C(\alpha)$, $K = K(\alpha)$ be polynomials in α and let $Q(u) = Q(u, \alpha)$ be a polynomial in u and α. Suppose that $g(u)$ is a polynomial of degree $s < p$ satisfying

$$C\left(ug'(u) - \frac{h}{k}g(u)\right) + u^{\mu}Q(u) = (\beta u - \alpha)\lambda K \tag{15}$$

for all values of α. Then $K = 0$ and $u^{\mu} \mid g(u)$.

Proof Let

$$ug'(u) - \frac{h}{k}g(u) = u^{\mu}q(u) + C_1 u^{\mu-1} + \cdots + C_{\mu}$$

where $q(u)$ is a polynomial in u and $C'_i s$ are independent of u and α. By (15)

$$C(C_1u^{\mu-1} + \cdots + C_{\mu}) = (-1)^{\lambda}K\left[(-1)^{\mu-1}\binom{\lambda}{\mu-1}\alpha^{\lambda-\mu+1}\beta^{\mu-1}u^{\mu-1} + \cdots + \alpha^{\lambda}\right]$$

Therefore

$$CC_i = (-1)^{\lambda+\mu-i}K\binom{\lambda}{\mu-i}\beta^{\mu-i}\alpha^{\lambda-\mu+i}, \quad i = 1, \cdots, \mu$$

If $K \neq 0$, then $C_i \neq 0$, $i = 1, \cdots, \mu$. Therefore

$$CK^{-1} = (-1)^{\lambda+\mu-i}C_i^{-1}\binom{\lambda}{\mu-i}\beta^{\mu-i}\alpha^{\lambda-\mu+i}, \quad i = 1, \cdots, \mu$$

But these equations can not hold simultaneously. Therefore $K = 0$, and by lemma $u^\mu \mid g(u)$.

Lemma 7 *Let β be α constant $\neq 0$, and let h, λ, μ, be integers satisfying*

$$h < p, \quad 3 \leqslant \mu < h + 1, \quad 2 \leqslant \lambda < p$$

Let

$$Q(u) = Q(u, \alpha) = Q_0(u) + Q_1(u)\alpha + \cdots + Q_v(u)\alpha^v$$

where $Q_i(u)$, $i = 0, \cdots, v$ are polynomials in u. Let

$$C_i = C_i(\alpha) = C_i^{(0)} + C_i^{(1)}\alpha + \cdots, \; i = 0, 1, 2$$

be polynomials in α and $C_i \neq 0$. Suppose that $g(u)$ is a polynomial of degree $s < p$ which is indpendent of α and satisfies

$$(C_0 u + C_1)(ug'(u) - hg(u)) + u^\mu Q(u) = (\beta u - \alpha)^\lambda C_2 \tag{16}$$

for all values of α. Then $c_2 = 0$, and $u^\mu \mid g(u)$.

Proof If $c_2 = 0$, the lemma follows from lemma 4. Suppose that $c_2 \neq 0$, and let

$$c_2 = c_2^{(0)} + \cdots + c_2^{(l)}\alpha^l, \; c_2^{(l)} \neq 0$$

Equating the coefficients of $\alpha^{\lambda+l-j}$, $j = 0, 1, 2$ on both sides of (16) we have

$$(c_0^{(\lambda+l)}u + c_1^{(\lambda+l)})(ug'(u) - hg(u)) + u^\mu Q_{\lambda+l}(u) = (-1)^\lambda c_2^{(l)}$$

$$(c_0^{(\lambda+l-1)}u + c^{(\lambda+l-1)})(ug'(u) - hg(u)) + u^\mu Q_{\lambda+l-1}(u) =$$
$$(-1)^{\lambda-1}\lambda c_2^{(l)}\beta u + (-1)^\lambda c^{(l-1)}$$

$$(c_0^{(\lambda+l-2)}u + c_1^{(\lambda+l-2)})(ug'(u) - hg(u)) + u^\mu Q_{\lambda+l-2}(u) =$$
$$(-1)^{\lambda-2}\binom{\lambda}{2}c_2^{(l)}\beta^2u^2 + (-1)^{\lambda-1}\lambda c_2^{(l-1)}\beta u + (-1)^\lambda c^{(l-2)}$$

Obviously $c_0^{(\lambda+l)}$ and $c_1^{(\lambda+l)}$ can not be both zero. If the first is not zero, we multiply the first equation by $((-1)^{\lambda-1}\lambda c_2^{(l)}\beta u + (-1)^\lambda c_2^{(l-1)})/(-1)^\lambda c_2^{(l)}$ and substract it from the second, otherwise we multiply it by

$$((-1)^{\lambda-2}\binom{\lambda}{2}c_2^{(l)}\beta^2u^2 + (-1)^{\lambda-1}\lambda c_2^{(l-1)}\beta u + (-1)^\lambda c_2^{(l-2)})/(-1)^\lambda c_2^{(l)}$$

and substract it from the third. In either case, the resulting equation is of the form

$$P(u)(ug'(u) - hg(u)) + u^\mu R(u) = 0$$

where $P(u)$ is of the second degree. Hence, since $\mu \geqslant 3$

$$u \mid g(u)$$

By (16), $c_2 = 0$, which is contrary to our supposition.

Lemma 8 *Let β and τ be two constants different from zero. Let λ, μ, h be positive integers less than p. Let $C = C(\alpha)$, $K = k(\alpha)$ be two polynomials in α and $Q(u, \alpha)$ be a polynomial in u and α. Suppose that $g(u)$ is a polynomial of degree $s < p$ which is independent of α and satisfies*

$$c((u^2 + \tau)g'(u) - hug(u)) + (u^2 + \tau)^{\mu}Q(u) = (\beta u - \alpha)^{\lambda}K \quad (17)$$

for all values of α. Then $K = 0$ and, if $h \geqslant 2\mu$

$$(u^2 + \tau)^{\mu} \mid g(u)$$

Proof *Let*

$$-hu\, g(u) = (u^2 + \tau)q(u) + l_1 u + l_2 u \quad (18)$$

where $q(u)$ is a polynomial in u and l_1, l_2 are independent of α and u. Since

$$(\beta u - \alpha)^{\lambda} = -u\left(\sum_{i=0}^{[\frac{\lambda-1}{2}]}\binom{\lambda}{2i+1}\beta^{2i+1}\alpha^{\lambda-2i-1}u^{2i}\right) + \sum_{i=0}^{[\frac{\lambda}{2}]}\binom{\lambda}{2i}\beta^{2}\alpha^{\lambda i-2i}u^{2i}\text{①} =$$

$$-u\left(\sum_{i=0}^{[\frac{\lambda-1}{2}]}(-1)^{i}\binom{\lambda}{2i+1}\beta^{2i+1}\tau^{i}\alpha^{\lambda-2i-1}\right) +$$

$$\sum_{i=0}^{[\frac{\lambda}{2}]}\binom{\lambda}{2i}(-1)^{i}\beta^{2i}\tau^{i}\alpha^{\lambda-2i} + (u^2 + \tau)q_1(u)$$

where $q_1(u)$ is a polynomial in u, we have, by (17) and (18),

$$c(l_1 u + l_2) = \kappa\left\{-u\left(\sum_{i=0}^{[\frac{\lambda-1}{2}]}(-1)^{i}\binom{\lambda}{2i+1}\beta^{2i+1}\tau^{i}\alpha^{\lambda-2i-1}\right) + \sum_{i=0}^{[\frac{\lambda}{2}]}\binom{\lambda}{2i}(-1)^{i}\beta^{2i}\tau^{i}\alpha^{\lambda-2i}\right\}$$

If $K \neq 0$, then the above equation shows that

$$l_1 : l_2 = -\left(\sum_{i=0}^{[\frac{\lambda-1}{2}]}(-1)^{i}\binom{\lambda}{2i+2}\beta^{2i+1}\tau^{i}\alpha^{\lambda-2i-1}\right) : \sum_{i=0}^{[\frac{\lambda}{2}]}\binom{\lambda}{2i}(-1)^{i}\beta^{2i}\tau^{i}\alpha^{\lambda-2i}$$

which is impossible. Therefore $K = 0$ and, by lemma 4, $(u + \tau)^{\mu} \mid g(u)$.

Lemma 9 *Let $f(x,y)$ be a polynomial of degree n in κ where $4 \leqslant n \leqslant \sqrt{p}$, let*

$$F = f(\alpha t + \alpha', \beta t + \beta') = \sum_{i=0}^{n} A_i t^i$$

---

① $[\frac{\lambda-1}{2}]$ and $[\frac{\lambda}{2}]$ denote the integral parts of $\frac{\lambda-1}{2}$ and $\frac{\lambda}{2}$ respectively.

and let the matrix

$$\begin{pmatrix} A_{n\alpha} & \cdots & A_{1\alpha} \\ A_{n\beta} & \cdots & A_{1\beta} \\ A_{n\alpha'} & \cdots & A_{1\alpha'} \\ A_{n\beta'} & \cdots & A_{1\beta'} \end{pmatrix} \tag{19}$$

be of rand $\leqslant 3$. *Then* $f(x,y)$ *can be transformed by a liner non-singular transformation in* κ *to* $g(\xi, \eta)$ *which is either of degree* $\leqslant \frac{n}{2}$ *in* η *or a polynomial of* $\xi^2 + \tau\eta^2$.

Proof Since (19) is of rank $\leqslant 3$, we can find four polynomials A, A', B, B' of α, α', β, β', not all zero, such that

$$AA_{r\alpha} + A'A_{r\alpha'} + BA_{r\beta} + B'A_{r\beta'} = 0,\ r = 1, \cdots, n$$

Therefore

$$AF_{\alpha} + BF_{\beta} + A'F_{\alpha'} + B'F_{\beta'} = K$$

where K is a polynomial in α, α', β, β'. Since $F_{\alpha} = tF_{\alpha'}$, $F_{\beta} = tF_{\beta'}$, we have

$$(At + A')F_{\alpha'} + (Bt + B')F_{\beta'} = K \tag{20}$$

Let

$$f(x,y) = \sum_{i=0}^{n} f_i(x,y)$$

where f_i, $i = 0, \cdots, n$, are homogeneous polynomials of the *i-th* degree, Let

$$K = K_0 + K_1 + \cdots$$

$$A = A_0 + A_1 + \cdots + A_h,\quad A' = A'_0 + A'_1 + \cdots + A'_h$$

$$B = B_0 + B_1 + \cdots + B_h,\quad B = B'_0 + B'_1 + \cdots + B'_h$$

where K_i, A_i, A'_i, B_i, B'_i are homogeneous polynomials of α, α', β, β' of the *i-th* degree, and A_h, A'_h, B_h, B'_h, are not all zero.

Equating the terms of degree $n + h - 1$, $\cdots$, in α, α', β, β', respectively on both sides of (20), we have

$$\sum_{i=0}^{r} [(A_{h-r+i}t + A'_{h-r+i}) f_{n-i\alpha'}(\alpha t + \alpha', \beta t + \beta') + (B_{h-r+i}t + B'_{h-r+i}) \times f_{n-i\beta'}(\alpha t + \alpha', \beta t + \beta')] = K_{n+h-r-1},\ r = 0, \cdots, n-1 \tag{21}$$

where we define $A_j = B_j = A'_j = B'_j = 0$ for $j < 0$.

Let $\dfrac{\alpha t + \alpha'}{\beta t + \beta'} = u$, then $t = -\dfrac{\beta' u - \alpha'}{\beta u - \alpha}$, $\beta t + \beta' = \dfrac{\alpha'\beta - \alpha\beta'}{\beta u - \alpha}$. Therefore

$$f_{n-i}(\alpha t + \alpha', \beta t + \beta') = (\beta t + \beta')^{n-i} f_{n-i}(u)$$

where $f_{n-i}(u) = f_{n-i}(u, 1)$, and hence

$$f_{n-i\alpha'}(\alpha t+\alpha',\beta t+\beta')=(\beta t+\beta')^{n-i-1}f'_{n-i}(u)=\frac{(\alpha'\beta-\alpha\beta')^{n-i-1}}{(\beta u-\alpha)^{n-i-1}}f'_{n-i}(u)$$

$$\begin{aligned}f_{n-i}\beta'(\alpha t+\alpha',\beta t+\beta') &= -(\alpha t+\alpha')(\beta t+\beta')^{n-i-2}f'_{n-i}(u)+\\&\quad(n-i)(\beta t+\beta')^{n-i-1}f_{n-i}(u)=\\&\quad\frac{(\alpha'\beta-\alpha\beta')^{n-i-1}}{(\beta u-\alpha)^{n-i-1}}(-uf'_{n-i}(u)+(n-i)f_{n-i}(u))\end{aligned}$$

Substituting into (21) and multiplying by $(\beta u-\alpha)^n$. we have

$$\begin{aligned}&(\alpha'\beta-\alpha\beta')^{n-r-1}(\beta u-\alpha)^r\{[A'_h-B'_hu(\beta u-\alpha)-(A_h-B_hu)(\beta'u-\alpha')]\cdot\\&\quad f'_{n-r}(u)+(n-r)[B'_h(\beta u-\alpha)-B_h(\beta'_u-\alpha')]f_{n-r}(u)\}+\\&\quad L_r(f_n(u),f'_n(n),\cdots,f_{n-r+1}(u),f'_{n-r-1}(u))-\\&\quad(\beta u-\alpha)^nK_{n+h-r-1}=0,\ r=0,\cdots,n-1\end{aligned}\tag{22}$$

where L_r is a linear combination of $f_n(u)$, $\cdots$, $f'_{n-r+1}(u)$, whose coefficients are polynomials in α, α', β, β' and u. The equation (22) is an identity in α, α', β, β' and u. In fact, for any set of values of α, α', β, β' satistying $\alpha'\beta-\alpha\beta'\neq 0$, (22) is satisfied by all values of u except possibly $-\alpha/\beta$. Since $mp>n+1$, the left-hand side of (22) multiplied by $\alpha'\beta-\alpha\beta'$ is equal to zero identically. Since $\alpha'\beta-\alpha\beta'$ is not identically equal to zero, (22) must be an identity.

Since the greatest common divisor $(f_n(u),\cdots,f'_{n-r+1}(u))$ is independent of α and β, we may divide (22) throughout by $(\beta u-\alpha)^r$ and obtain an equation of the form

$$\begin{aligned}&(c_0u^2+c_1u+c_2)f'_{n-r}(u)-(n-r)(c_0u+c_3)f_{n-r}(u)+(f_n(n),\cdots,\\&\qquad f'_{n-r+1}(u))Q_r(u)=(\beta u-\alpha)^{n-r}K_{n+h-r-1}\end{aligned}\tag{23}$$

where c'_is are polynomials in α, α', β, β' and $Q_r(u)$ is a polynomial in u and α, α', β, β'.

When $r=0$, we have

$$(c_0u^2+c_1u+c_2)f'_n(u)-n(c_0u+c_3)f_n(u)=(\beta u-\alpha)^nK_{n+h-1}\tag{24}$$

Without loss of generality, we may assume that $f_n(u)=f_n(u,1)$ is of the *n-th* degree. Then, by lemma 5, there are three cases:

1) $f_n(x,y)=\rho(\lambda_1x+\mu_1y)^k(\lambda_2x+\mu_2y)^{n-k}$, $\frac{n}{2}<k<n$.

2) $f_n(x,y)=\rho(\lambda_1x+\mu_1y)^n$.

3) $f_n(x,y)=\rho(\lambda x^2+\mu xy+vy^2)^{n/2}$①.

Without loss of generality we may assume that $\rho=1$, $\lambda=1$. In the first two cases

---

① $\lambda x^2+\mu xy+vy^2$ may be irreducible or reducible.

we make the transformation $\xi = \lambda_1 x + \mu_1 y$, $\eta = \lambda_2 x + \mu_2 y$ and in the last case the transformation $\xi = x + \mu/2$, $\eta = y$, then we can reduce $f_n(x,y)$ to one of the forms $\xi^k \eta^{n-k}$, ξ^n and $(\xi^2 + \tau\eta^2)^{n/2}$ respectively. Hence without loss of generality we assume that $f_n(x,y)$ is of one of the following forms:

1) $f_n(x,y) = x^k y^{n-k}$, $n/2 < k < n$.

2) $f_n(x,y) = x^n$.

3) $f_n(x,y) = (x^2 + \tau y^2)^{n/2}$, $\tau \neq 0$.

Let us consider these cases separately.

Gase 1 $f_n(u) = u^k$, $n/2 < k < n$. By (24)

$$k(c_0 u^2 + c_1 u + c_2) = n(c_0 u + c_3) u$$

Therefore $c_0 = 0$ and

$$c_0 u^2 + c_1 u + c_2 = \frac{n}{k} c_3 u$$

Substituting into (23), we obtain

$$\frac{n}{k} c_3 \left(u f'_{n-r}(u) - \frac{k(n-r)}{n} f_{n-r}(u) \right) + (f_n(u), \cdots, f'_{n-r+1}(u)) Q_r(u) = (\beta u - \alpha)^{n-r} K_{n+h-r-1} \tag{25}$$

When $r = 1$, we have

$$u^{k-1} \mid (f_n(u), \cdots, f'_{n-r+1}(u))$$

Since $k(n-1) < n^2 < p$, $2 \leqslant k - 1 < \frac{n-1}{n} k + 1$, $k - 2 < n - 1 < p$, we have, by lemma 6, $K_{n+h-2} = 0$ and

$$u^{k-1} \mid f_{n-1}(u)$$

Let $f_n^*(u) = f_n(1,u)$, $f_{n-1}^*(u) = f_{n-1}^*(1,u)$, then we obtain, analogously, an equation of the form

$$\frac{n}{n-k} c_3^* \left(u f_{n-1}^{*\prime}(u) - (n-k) \frac{n-1}{n} f_{n-1}^*(u) \right) + (f_n^*(u), f_n^{*\prime}(u)) Q_1^*(u) = (\beta u - \alpha)^{n-1} K_{n+h-2}$$

Since $K_{n+h-2} = 0$, and $u^{n-k-1} \mid (f_n^*(u), f_n^{*\prime}(u))$, we have by lemma 4,

$$u^{n-k-1} \mid f_{n-1}^*(u)$$

Therefore

$$f_{n-1}(x,y) = x^{k-1} y^{n-k-1} (\rho x + \sigma y)$$

By the transformation $x = \xi - \frac{\sigma}{k}$, $y = \eta - \frac{\rho}{n-k}$, we can transform $f(x,y)$ to $g(\xi, \eta)$ which does not contain terms of degree $n - 1$. Therefore, without loss of generality, we can assume that $f_{n-1}(u) = 0$.

Now assume that

$$u^{k-s+1} \mid f_{n-s}(u), \ s = 1, \cdots, r-1, \ r < \frac{n}{2}$$

then

$$u^{h-r+1} \mid f_n(u), \cdots, f'_{n-r+1}(n))$$

Since $k(n-r) < n^2 < p$, $2 \leqslant k - r + 1 < \frac{n-r}{n}k + 1$, $k - r < n - r < p$, we can apply lemma 6 to (25) and obtain

$$u^{k-r+1} \mid f_{n-r}(u)$$

or

$$u^{k-r+1} \mid f_{n-r}(x,y)$$

Therefore $f_{n-r}(x,y)$ is of degree $< \frac{n}{2}$ in y, when $r < \frac{n}{2}$. Hence $f(x,y)$ is of degree $\leqslant \frac{n}{2}$ in y.

Gase 2 $f_n(u) = u^n$. By (24)

$$c_0u^2 + c_1u + c_2 = (c_0u + c_3)u$$

Hence (23) becomes

$$(c_0u + c_3)(uf'_{n-r}(u) - (n-r)f_{n-r}(u)) + (f_n(u), \cdots, f'_{n-r+1}(u))Q_r(u) = (\beta u - \alpha)^{n-r}K_{n+h-r-1} \tag{26}$$

First, suppose that $c_3 \neq 0$. Assume that

$$u^{n-s} \mid f_{n-s}(u), \ s = 0, \cdots, r-1, \ r < \frac{n}{2}$$

then

$$u^{n-r} \mid f_n(u), \cdots, f'_{n-r+1}(u)$$

Since $n - r < p$, $3 \leqslant n - r < n - r + 1$, $2 < n - r < p$, we have by lemma 7,

$$x^{n-r} \mid f_{n-r}(u)$$

or

$$u^{n-r} \mid f_{n-r}(x,y), \ r < \frac{n}{2}$$

Therefore $f(x,y)$ is of degree $\leqslant \frac{n}{2}$ in y.

Secondly, suppose that $c_3 = 0$. Assume that

$$u^{n-2s} \mid f_{n-s}(u), \ s = 0, \cdots, r-1$$

Then

$$u^{n-2r+1} \mid (f_n(u), \cdots, f'_{n-r+1}(u))$$

If $r \leqslant \frac{n}{2}$, then by (26), $K_{n+h-r-1} = 0$. By lemma 4,

$$u^{n-2r} \mid f_{n-r}(u)$$

Therefore $f_{n-r}(x,y)$ is of degree $\leqslant \frac{n}{2}$ in y.

Gase 3 $f_n(u) = (u^2 + \tau)^{n/2}$. By (24),

$$nu(c_0u^2 + c_1u + c_2) = n(u^2 + \tau)(c_0u + c_3)$$

Therefore we can find a constant c depending on $\alpha, \alpha', \beta, \beta'$, such that

$$c_0u^2 + c_1u + c_2 = c(u^2 + \tau),\ c_0u + c_3 = cu$$

Substituting into (23) we have

$$c((u^2 + \tau)f'_{n-r}(u) - (n - r)f_{n-r}(u)) + (f_n(u), \cdots, f'_{n-r+1}(u))Q_r(u) = (\beta u - \alpha)^{n-r}K_{n+h-r-1} \quad (27)$$

When $r = 1$, we have

$$(u^2 + \tau)^{n/2-1} \mid (f_n(u), \cdots, f'_{n-r+1}(u))$$

Since $n - 1 > 1$, $n - 1 > 2\left(\frac{n}{2} - 1\right)$ we have, by lemma 8,

$$(u^2 + \tau)^{n/2-1} \mid f_{n-1}(u)$$

Therefore

$$f_{n-1}(x,y) = (x^2 + \tau y^2)^{n/2-1}(\rho x + \sigma y)$$

By means of the transformation $x = \xi + \rho/2$, $y = \eta + \sigma/2$, we can reduce $f(x,y)$ to $g(\xi,\eta)$ which does not contain the terms of degree $n - 1$ in ξ, η. Therefore we may assume, without loss of generality, that $f_{n-1}(u) = 0$.

When $r = 2$, we have, since $f_n(u) = (u^2 + \tau)^{n/2}$, $f_{n-1}(u) = 0$,

$$(u^2 + \tau)^{n/2-1} \mid (f_n(u), f'_n(u), \cdots, f_{n-1}(u), f'_{n-1}(u))$$

Since $n - 2 > 1$, $n - 2 = 2\left(\frac{n}{2} - 1\right)$, we have, by lemma 8,

$$(u^2 + \tau)^{n/2-1} \mid f_{n-2}(u)$$

Therefore

$$f_{n-2}(x,y) - l(u^2 + \tau)^{n/2-1}$$

Substituting the expressions for $f_n(x,y)$, $f_{n-1}(x,y)$, $f_{n-2}(x,y)$ into (20) and equating the coefficients t^n, t^{n-1}, t^{n-2} on both sides, we have

$$nA(\alpha^2 + \tau\beta^2)^{n/2-1}\alpha + n\beta\tau(\alpha^2 + \tau\beta^2)^{n/2-1}\beta = 0 \quad (28)$$

$$\begin{aligned} &nA[(\alpha'(\alpha^2 + \tau\beta^2)^{n/2-2}((\alpha^2 + \tau\beta^2) + (n - 2)\alpha^2) + \\ &\beta'(\alpha^2 + \tau\beta^2)^{n/2-2}(n - 2)\tau\alpha\beta] + \\ &nB[\cdots] + nA'(\alpha^2 + \tau\beta^2)^{n/2-1}\alpha + n\beta'\tau(\alpha^2 + \tau\beta^2)^{n/2-1}\beta = 0 \end{aligned} \quad (29)$$

$$A\Big[\frac{n}{2}\Big\{\alpha'^2\frac{\partial^2}{\partial\alpha^2}(\alpha^2+\tau\beta^2)^{n/2-1}\alpha+2\alpha'\beta'\frac{\partial^2}{\partial\alpha\partial\beta}(\alpha^2+\tau\beta^2)^{n/2-1}\alpha+$$

$$\beta'^2\frac{\partial^2}{\partial\beta^2}(\alpha^2+\tau\beta^2)^{n/2-1}\alpha\Big\}+(n-2)l(\alpha^2+\tau\beta^2)^{n/2-2}\alpha\Big]+$$

$$B\Big[\frac{n\tau}{2}\Big\{\alpha'^2\frac{\partial^2}{\partial\alpha^2}(\alpha^2+\tau\beta^2)^{n/2-1}\beta+2\alpha'\beta'\frac{\partial^2}{\partial\alpha\partial\beta}(\alpha^2+\tau\beta^2)^{n/2-1}\beta+$$

$$\beta'^2\frac{\partial^2}{\partial\beta^2}(\alpha^2+\tau\beta^2)^{n/2-1}\beta\Big\}+(n-2)l(\alpha^2+\tau\beta^2)^{n/2-2}\beta\Big]+$$

$$nA'[\alpha'(\alpha^2+\tau\beta^2)^{n/2-2}(\alpha^2+\tau\beta^2+(n-2)\alpha^2)+$$

$$\beta'(\alpha^2+\tau\beta^2)^{n/2-2}(n-2)\tau\alpha\beta]+nB'[\cdots]=0 \qquad (30)$$

What we need to notice is only that the first and the second equations are homogeneous in α, α', β, β', and by multiplying (28) by $\frac{n-2}{2}l(\alpha^2+\tau\beta^2)^{-1}$ and substracting it from (30), the resulting equation is also homogeneous in α, α', β, β'. Therefore A, A', B, B', are, apart from common factor D, equal to four homogeneous polynomials in α, α', β, β'. Since, by (20), the common factor D must divide K, there is no loss of generality to assume that $D=1$.

Therefore, in (21), we have to put

$$A_{h-r+i}=B_{h-r+i}=A'_{h-r+i}=B'_{h-r+i}=0,\ i<r$$

and hence, in (23), $Q_r(u)=0$. Then we have

$$c((u^2+\tau)f'_{n-r}(u)-(n-r)uf_{n-r}(u))=(\beta u-\alpha)^{n-r}K_{n+h-r-1}$$

If $n-r\geqslant 1$, we have by lemma 8, $K_{n+h-r-1}=0$. If $2\nmid n-r$ we have by lemma 4,

$$(u^2+\tau)^{(n-r)/2}\mid f_{n-r}(u)$$

since we can take $\mu=\frac{n-r}{2}$. If $2+n-r$, we have, by lemma 4,

$$(u^2+\tau)^{[(n-r)/2]+1}\mid f_{n-r}(u)$$

since we can take $\mu=\left[\frac{n-r}{2}\right]+1<\frac{n-r}{2}+1$. In the second case, $f_{n-r}(u)=0$. Therefore $f(x,y)$ is a polynomial in $x^2+\tau y^2$.

Lemma 10 *Let $f(x)=a_0+a_1x+\cdots+a_nx^n$ ($a_n\neq 0$) be a polynomial in κ, then*

$$\sum_x \exp\{2\pi i S[f(x)]/p\}=O(p^{m(1-1/n)}) \qquad (31)$$

where x runs over all elements in κ.

Proof Let θ be the generating element of κ with respect to the prime field Π. Then every element x of κ can be written an

$$x = \alpha_0 + \alpha_1\theta + \cdots + \alpha_{m-1}\theta^{m-1},\ \alpha_i \in \prod$$

Therefore

$$\sum_x \exp\{2\pi i S[ax]/p\} = \sum_{a_0=1}^{p}\cdots\sum_{a_{m-1}=1}^{p} \exp\{2\pi i(a_0 S[a] + \cdots + a_{m-1}S[a\theta^{m-1}])/p\} = \begin{cases} p^m, & \text{if } S[a\theta^k] = 0 \text{ for all } k \\ 0, & \text{otherwise} \end{cases}$$

Further $S[a\theta^k] = 0$ for all k implies $a = 0$. In fact, we have $S[ax] = 0$ for all $x \in \kappa$. If $a \neq 0$, then $S[x] = 0$ for all $x \in \kappa$. This is impossible.

Hence

$$\sum_{b_1\in\kappa}\cdots\sum_{b_n\in\kappa}\left|\sum_{x\in\kappa}\exp\{2\pi i S[b_1x + \cdots + b_nx^n]/p\}\right|^{2n} = \sum_{x_1\in\kappa}\cdots\sum_{x_n\in\kappa}\sum_{y_1\in\kappa}\cdots\sum_{\substack{y_n\in\kappa \\ x_1+\cdots+x_n=y_1+\cdots+y_n \\ \cdots \\ x_1^n+\cdots+x_n^n=y_1^n+\cdots+y_n^n}} p^{mn} = n!p^{2mn} \tag{32}$$

The transformations $x = \lambda x' + \mu(\lambda \in \kappa, \mu \in \kappa, \lambda \neq 0)$ transform (31) into at least $\frac{p^m(p^m-1)}{n}$ different terms in the sum (32). In fact, if

$$f(\lambda x + \mu) = f(x)$$

then

$$\lambda^n a_n = a_n$$

$$n\lambda^{n-1}\mu a_n + \lambda^{n-1}a_{n-1} = a_{n-1}$$

The first equation determines λ; it has, at most, n solutions. The second determines μ uniquely.

Thus the lemma is proved.

Theorem 1 *If $f(x,y)$ is a polynomial of degree $n \geqslant 4$ in κ and if $f(x,y)$ is not equivalent to a polynomial of the n-th degree in a single variable in κ, then*

$$\sum_x\sum_y \exp\{2\pi i S[f(x,y)]/p\} = O(p^{m(2-2/n)})$$

where x, y run over all the elements of κ independently.

Proof 1) Suppose that the Jacobian of any four of the coefficients of $f(\alpha t + \alpha', \beta t + \beta')$ is identically zero in α, α', β, β'. By lemma 9, $f(x,y)$ can be transformed by a non-singular linear transformation in κ to $g(\xi, \eta)$ which is either a polynomial of degree $\leqslant \frac{n}{2}$ in η or a polynomial of $\xi^2 + \tau\eta^2$.

In the first case, let $g(\xi, \eta) = g_k(\xi)\eta^k + g_{k-1}(\xi)\eta^{k-1} + \cdots$, $g_k(\xi) \neq 0$, $k \leqslant n/2$, then we have, by lemma 10,

$$\left|\sum_x \sum_y \exp\{2\pi i S[f(x,y)]/p\}\right| = \left|\sum_\xi \sum_\eta \exp\{2\pi i S[g(\xi, \eta)]/p\}\right| \leqslant$$

$$\left|\sum_{\substack{\xi \\ g_h(\xi)\neq 0}} \sum_\eta \exp\{2\pi i S[g(\xi, \eta)]/p\}\right| + \left|\sum_{\substack{\xi \\ g_k(\xi)=0}} \sum_\eta \exp\{2\pi i S[g(\xi, \eta)]/p\}\right| \leqslant$$

$$p^m \operatorname*{Max}_{g_k(\xi)\neq 0} \left|\sum_n \exp\{2\pi i S[g(\xi, \eta)]/p\}\right| + O(p^m) =$$

$$O(p^m p^{m(1-2/n)}) + O(p^m) =$$

$$O(p^{m(2-2/n)})$$

unless $g(\xi, \eta)$ does not contain η.

In the second case, we have

$$\left|\sum_x \sum_y \exp\{2\pi i S[f(x,y)]/p\}\right| = \left|\sum_\xi \sum_\eta \exp\{2\pi i S[g(\xi^2 + \tau\eta^2)]/p\}\right| \leqslant$$

$$\left|\sum_\xi \sum_\eta \exp\{2\pi i S[g(\xi + \tau\eta)]/p\}\right| + \left|\sum_\xi \sum_\eta \left(\frac{\xi}{\kappa}\right)\exp\{2\pi i S[g(\xi + \tau\eta)]/p\}\right| +$$

$$\left|\sum_\xi \sum_\eta \left(\frac{\eta}{\kappa}\right)\exp\{2\pi i S[g(\xi + \tau\eta)]/p\}\right| +$$

$$\left|\sum_\xi \sum_\eta \left(\frac{\xi}{\kappa}\right)\left(\frac{\eta}{\kappa}\right)\exp\{2\pi i S[g(\xi + \tau\eta)]/p\}\right|$$

where

$$\left(\frac{\xi}{\kappa}\right) = \begin{cases} 1, & \text{if } \xi \text{ is a square of an element in } \kappa \\ -1, & \text{otherwise} \end{cases}$$

As in the first case, we can prove that each of the first three terms is $O(p^{m(2-2/n)})$. Also

$$\left|\sum_\xi \sum_\eta \left(\frac{\xi}{\kappa}\right)\left(\frac{\eta}{\kappa}\right)\exp\{2\pi i S[g(\xi + \tau\eta)]/p\}\right| =$$

$$\left|\sum_\xi{}' \sum_\eta{}' \left(\frac{\xi}{\kappa}\right)\left(\frac{\xi\eta}{\kappa}\right)\exp\{2\pi i S[g(\xi(1 + \tau\eta)]/p\}\right| + O(p^m) =$$

$$\left|\sum_\xi{}' \sum_\eta{}' \left(\frac{\eta}{\kappa}\right)\exp\{2\pi i S[g(\xi(1 + \tau\eta)]/p\}\right| + O(p^m)\text{①} =$$

$$O(p^{m(2-2/n)})$$

where $\sum_t{}'$ denoties that t runs over all elements, except zero, in κ.

Therefore

---

① Since the elements besides zero, of a finite field form a cyclic group with respect to multiplication, it is easy to prove that $\left(\frac{\xi}{\kappa}\right)\left(\frac{\eta}{\kappa}\right) = \left(\frac{\xi\eta}{\kappa}\right)$, provided that $\xi\eta \neq 0$.

$$\left|\sum_x \sum_y \exp\{2\pi i S[f(x,y)]/p\}\right| = O(p^{m(2-2/n)})$$

2) Suppose that the Jacobian of certain four coefficients of $f(\alpha t + \alpha', \beta t + \beta') - f(\alpha', \beta')$ is not equal to zero identically. Let it be

$$J = J(\alpha, \alpha', \beta, \beta')$$

and let the coefficient of the highest term in β' be $J_0 = J_0(\alpha, \alpha', \beta)$.

It is evident that

$$((p^{3m} - O(p^{2m}))\left|\sum_x \sum_y \exp\{2\pi i S[f(x,y)]/p\}\right|^{2n} =$$

$$\sum_{\substack{\alpha \quad \alpha' \quad \beta \\ \alpha J_0 \neq 0,\, f_n(\alpha,\beta)\neq 0}} \sum \sum \left|\sum_x \sum_{\beta'} \exp\{2\pi i S[f(\alpha x + \alpha', \beta x + \beta')]/p\}\right|^{2n} (\text{by lemma } 2) =$$

①

$$\sum_{\substack{\alpha \quad \alpha' \quad \beta \\ \alpha J_0 \neq 0,\, f_n\neq 0}} \sum \sum \left|\sum_{\substack{\beta' \quad x \\ J\neq 0}} \sum \exp\{2\pi i S[f(\alpha x + \alpha', \beta x + \beta')]/p\} +\right.$$

$$\left.\sum_{\substack{\beta' \quad x \\ J=0}} \sum \exp\{2\pi i S[f(\alpha x + \alpha', \beta x + \beta')]/p\}\right|^{2n} \leqslant$$

$$2^{2n-1} \sum_{\substack{\alpha \quad \alpha' \quad \beta \\ \alpha J_0 \neq 0,\, f_n\neq 0}} \sum \sum \left|\sum_{\substack{\beta' \quad x \\ J\neq 0}} \sum \exp\{2\pi i S[f(\alpha x + \alpha', \beta x + \beta')]/p\}\right|^{2n} +$$

$$2^{2n-1} \sum_{\substack{\alpha \quad \alpha' \quad \beta \\ \alpha J_0 \neq 0,\, f_n\neq 0}} \sum \sum \left|\sum_{\substack{\beta' \quad x \\ J=0}} \sum \exp\{2\pi i S[f(\alpha x + \alpha', \beta x + \beta')]/p\}\right|^{2n} \leqslant$$

(by Hölder's inequality)

$$2^{2n-1}p^{m(2n-1)} \sum_{\substack{\alpha \quad \alpha' \quad \beta \quad \beta' \\ \alpha J_0 J\neq 0,\, f_n\neq 0}} \sum \sum \sum \left|\sum_x \exp\{2\pi i S[f(\alpha x + \alpha', \beta x + \beta')]/p\}\right|^{2n} +$$

$$O(p^{m(3+2n(1-1/n))}) =$$

(by applying Hölder's inequality and lemma 10 to the first and the second terms respectively)

$$p^{m(2n-1)} O\left(\sum_{A_n} \cdots \sum_{A_1} \left|\sum \exp\{2\pi i S[A_n x^n + \cdots + A_1 x]/p\}\right|^{2n}\right) + O(p^{m(2n+1)}) =$$

(by lemma 1)

$O(p^{m(4n-1)})$ (by (32))

Therefore

$$\left|\sum_x \sum_y \exp\{2\pi i S[f(x,y)]/p\}\right|^{2n} = O(p^{m(4n-4)})$$

and hence

$$\sum_x \sum_y \exp\{2\pi i S[f(x,y)]/p\} = O(p^{m(2-2/n)})$$

---

① $f_n(x,y)$ is the sum of those terms of degree n in $f(x,y)$.

Appendix

The previous results hold under the condition that $n \geqslant 4$. In the appendix, we shall prove that the result holds also for $n = 2$ and 3. Even we have a sharper result, namely.

Theorem 2 *Let $f(x,y)$ be a cubic polynomial in κ, not equivalent to a cubic polynomial of a single variable. Then*

$$\sum_x \sum_y \exp\{2\pi i S[f(x,y)]/p\} = O(p^{m(2-3/4)})$$

The theorem suggests that some further improvements of the results obtained and stil possible.

Lemma 11 *Let $\phi = \sum_{i=1}^{r} \sum_{j=1}^{r} a_{ij} x_i x_j (a_{ij} = a_{ji})$ be quadratic form with integer coefficients. Let $p \nmid \Delta$, $\Delta = | a_{ij} |$. Then*

$$S = \sum_{x_1=1}^{p} \cdots \sum_{x_r=1}^{p} \exp\left\{\frac{2\pi i}{p}\phi\right\} = i^{r((p-1)/2)^2} p^{r/2} \left(\frac{\Delta}{p}\right)$$

Proof Consider the field $\prod$ formed by the residue classes, mod p. It is well-known that there exists a non-singular transformation in $\prod$:

$$x_i = \sum_{i=1}^{r} c_{ij} y_j, \quad i = 1, \cdots, r$$

which transforms ϕ to the canonical form $\sum_{i=1}^{r} \lambda_i y_i^2$. Since

$$| c_{ij} | \not\equiv 0(p)$$

it is clear that as x_i, $i_i = 1, \cdots, r$, run, each, over a complete residue class, mod p, independently, so do y_i, $i = 1, \cdots, r$. Therefore

$$S = \sum_{y_1=1}^{p} \cdots \sum_{y_r=1}^{p} \exp\left\{\frac{2\pi i}{p}(\lambda_1 y_1^2 + \cdots + \lambda_r y_r^2)\right\} =$$

$$\sum_{y_1=1}^{p} \exp\left\{\frac{2\pi i}{p}\lambda_1 y_1^2\right\} \cdots \sum_{y_r=1}^{p} \exp\left\{\frac{2\pi i}{p}\lambda_r y_r^2\right\} =$$

$$i^{r((p-1)/2)^2} p^{r/2} \left(\frac{\lambda_1 \cdots \lambda_r}{p}\right)$$

Since $\lambda_1 \cdots \lambda_r = \Delta | c_{ij} |^2$, we have the lemma.

Lemma 12① *If a belongs to κ and $a \neq 0$, then*

---

① The formula is a consequence of a result due to Davenpart and Haese. Without referring to their result, we give, however, the proof in detail so that the paper is complete in itself.

$$\sum_x \exp\{2\pi i S[ax^2]/p\} = \varepsilon i^{m((p-1)/2)^2} p^{m/2}\left(\frac{\alpha}{\kappa}\right)$$

where $\left(\frac{\alpha}{\kappa}\right) = +1$ *or* -1 *according as* $x^2 = u$ *has or has not solutions in* κ, *and* $\varepsilon = \pm 1$, *the sign depending only on the field* κ.

Proof 1) Suppose that $\left(\frac{\alpha}{\kappa}\right) = 1$. Without loss of generality we may assume that $a = 1$. Since every element x belonging to κ can be written as

$$x = a_0 + a_1\theta + \cdots + a_{m-1}\theta^{m-1},\ a_i \in \prod$$

we have

$$\sum_x e^{2\pi i S[x^2]/p} = \sum_{a_0=1}^{p} \cdots \sum_{a_{m-1}=1}^{p} e_p\Big(\sum_{r=1}^{2(m-1)} \sum_{i+j=r} a_i a_j S[\theta^r]\Big)$$

where $e_p(u) = e^{2\pi i u/p}$.

The determinant of $\sum_{r=0}^{2(m-1)} \sum_{i+j=r} S[\theta^r] a_i a_j$ is

$$| S[\theta^{i+j-2}] | = \begin{vmatrix} m & s_1 & \cdots & s_{m-1} \\ s_1 & s_2 & \cdots & s_m \\ \vdots & \vdots & & \vdots \\ s_{m-1} & s_m & \cdots & s_{2(m-1)} \end{vmatrix}$$

where $s_v = \theta^v + \theta_1^v + \cdots + \theta_{m-1}^v (v = 1, \cdots, m-1)$, $\theta_1, \cdots, \theta_{m-1}$ being the conjugate elements of θ. Hence

$$S[\theta^{i+j-2}] | = \begin{vmatrix} 1 & 1 & \cdots & 1 \\ \theta & \theta_1 & \cdots & \theta_{m-1} \\ \vdots & \vdots & & \vdots \\ \theta^{m-1} & \theta_1^{m-1} & \cdots & \theta_{m-1}^{m-1} \end{vmatrix} \begin{vmatrix} 1 & \theta & \cdots & \theta^{m-1} \\ 1 & \theta_1 & \cdots & \theta^{m-1} \\ \vdots & \vdots & & \vdots \\ 1 & \theta_{m-1} & \cdots & \theta_{m-1}^{m-1} \end{vmatrix} =$$

$$\prod_{0<i<j\leqslant m-1} (\theta_i - \theta_j)^2 = A \neq 0$$

since $\theta, \theta_1, \cdots, \theta_{m-1}$ are distinct.

Since $p \nmid A$, we have, by lemma 11,

$$\sum_x e^{2\pi i S[x^2]/p^2} = i^{m((p-1)/2)^2} p^{m/2}\left(\frac{A}{p}\right)$$

i. e.

$$\sum_x e^{2\pi i S[\alpha x^2]/p} = \varepsilon i^{m(p-1)^2} p^{m/2}\left(\frac{a}{\kappa}\right)$$

where ε depends only on κ since the left-hand side and $i^{m[(p-1/2)]^2} p^{m/2}\left(\frac{a}{\kappa}\right)$ are independent of the choice of the generating element θ.

2) Now suppose that $\left(\frac{a}{\kappa}\right) = -1$. As x runs over all elements $\neq 0$ in κ, x^2 runs over all elements $\neq 0$ which are squares and ax^2 run over all elements $\neq 0$ which are not squares. Therefore

$$\sum_x e^{2\pi i S[\alpha x^2]/p} + \sum_x e^{2\pi i S[x^2]/p} = 2\sum_x e^{2\pi i S[x]/p} = 0$$

Hence

$$\sum_x e^{2\pi i S[\alpha x^2]/p} = -\sum_x e^{2\pi i S[x^2]} = \varepsilon i^{m[(p-1)/2]^2}\left(\frac{\alpha}{\kappa}\right)$$

Lemma 13 *Let*

$$\phi = ax^2 + 2hxy + by^2 + 2fx + 2gy + c$$

be a polynomial in κ *and let* $\Delta = h^2 - ab \neq 0$. *Then*

$$S = \sum_x \sum_y e^{2\pi i S[\phi]/p} = \left(\frac{\Delta}{\kappa}\right) p^m e_p\left(S\left[c + \frac{bf^2 + ag^2 - 2fgh}{\Delta}\right]\right)$$

where $e_p(u) = e^{2\pi i u/p}$.

Proof We assume that $a \neq 0$. Then, letting

$$X = x + \frac{h}{a}y + \frac{f}{a}, \quad Y = y - \frac{aq - hf}{\Delta}$$

we have, by lemma 12,

$$S = \sum_x \sum_y e_p\left(S\left[aX^2 - \frac{\Delta}{a}Y^2 + c + \frac{bf^2 + ag^2 - 2fgh}{\Delta}\right]\right) =$$

$$\varepsilon\left(\frac{a}{\kappa}\right) i^{m[(p-1)/2]^2} p^{m/2} \varepsilon\left(\frac{-\Delta/a}{\kappa}\right) i^{m[(p-1)/2]^2} p^{m/2} \times$$

$$e_p\left(S\left[c + \frac{bf^2 + ag^2 - 2fgh}{\Delta}\right]\right)$$

since

$$ax^2 + 2hxy + by^2 + 2fx + 2gy + c =$$

$$a\left(x + \frac{h}{a}y + \frac{f}{a}\right)^2 - \frac{\Delta}{a}\left(y - \frac{aq - hf}{\Delta}\right)^2 + c + \frac{bf^2 + aq^2 - 2fgh}{\Delta}$$

Since the elements of a finite field form a cyclic group with respect to multiplication, is easy to prove that

$$\left(\frac{\xi}{\kappa}\right)\left(\frac{\eta}{\kappa}\right) = \left(\frac{\xi\eta}{\kappa}\right), \left(\frac{-1}{\kappa}\right) = (-1)^{(p^m-1)/2} = (-1)^{m(p-1)/2}$$

Hence

$$s = \left(\frac{\Delta}{\kappa}\right) p^m e_p\left(S\left[c + \frac{bf^2 + ag^2 - 2fgh}{\Delta}\right]\right)$$

The same result holds for $b \neq 0$. How suppose that $a = 0$, $b = 0$. Then $h \neq 0$ and

$$s = \sum_x \sum_y e_p(S[2hxy + 2fx + 2gy + c]) =$$
$$\sum_y e_p(S[2gy + c]) \sum_x e_p(S[(2hy + 2f)x]) =$$
$$p^m \sum_{2hy+2f=0} e_p(S[2gy + c]) = p^m e_p\left(S\left[c - \frac{2gf}{h}\right]\right)$$

Proof of the theorem Let

$$S = \sum_x \sum_y e_p(S[f(x,y)])$$

and

$$f(x,y) = a_0x^3 + a_1x^2y + a_2xy^2 + a_3y^3 + b_0x^2 + b_1xy + b_2y^2 + c_0x + c_1y$$

First, suppose that $a_0x^3 + a_1x^2y + a_2xy^2 + a_3y^3$ is, apart from a constant factor, a perfect cube. Without loss of generality, we may assume that $a_1 = a_2 = a_3 = 0$, for otherwise, we can reduce $f(x,y)$ to this form by a simple transformation. Therefore

$$S = \sum_x \sum_y e_p(S[a_0x^3 + b_0x^2 + b_1xy + b_2y^2 + c_0x + c_1y])$$

If $b_2 = 0$, the b_1 and c_1 can not be both zero, and hence

$$S = \sum_{\substack{x \\ b_1x+c_1=0}} \sum_y e_p(S[a_0x^3 + b_0x^2 + c_0x + (b_1x + c_1)y]) =$$
$$\begin{cases} O(p^m), & \text{if } b_1 \neq 0 \\ 0, & \text{if } b_1 = 0 \end{cases}$$

If $b_2 = 0$, then without loss of generality, we may assume that $b_1 = 0$, for, if $b_1 \neq 0$, we can reduce $f(x,y)$ to a polynomial without the term in xy by the transformation $X = x, Y = b_1x + b_2y$. Hence, by lemma 10 and 12,

$$S = \sum_x e_p(S[a_0x^3 + b_0x^2 + e_0x]) \sum_y e_p(S[b_2y^2 + c_1y]) =$$
$$O(p^{m(1-1/3)})O(p^{m/2}) = O(p^{m(2-5/6)})O(p^{m(2-3/4)})$$

Secondly, suppose that $a_0x^3 + a_1x^2y + a_2xy^2 + a_3y^3$ is not a constant multiple of a perfect cube. Then

$$|S|^2 = \sum_{x_1} \sum_{x_2} \sum_{y_1} \sum_{y_2} e_p(S[a_0(x_1^3 - x_2^3) + a_1(x_1^2y_1 - x_2^2y_2) + a_2(x_1y_1^2 - x_2y_2^2) +$$
$$a_3(y_1^3 - y_2^3) + b_0(x_1^2 - x_2^2) + b_1(x_1y_1 - x_2y_2) + b_2(y_1^2 - y_2^2) +$$
$$c_0(x_1 - x_2) + c_1(y_1 - y_2)])$$

Let

$$x_1 - x_2 = 2\xi_1, \quad x_1 + x_2 = 2\xi_2$$
$$y_1 - y_2 = 2\eta_1, \quad y_1 + y_2 = 2\eta_2$$

then, since

$$x_1^3 - x_2^3 = 2\xi_1(2\xi_2^2 + \xi_1^2),\ x_1^2y_1 - x_2^2y_2 = 2\eta_1(\xi_1^2 + \xi_2^2) + 4\xi_1\xi_2\eta_2,\ \text{etc},$$

we have

$$|S|^2 = \sum_{\xi_1}\sum_{\eta_1}\sum_{\xi_2}\sum_{\eta_2} e_p(S[2a_0\xi_1(3\xi_2^2 + \xi_1^2) + 2a_1(\eta_1(\xi_1^2 + \xi_2^2) + 2\xi_1\xi_2\eta_2) + 2a_2(\xi_1(\eta_1^2 + \eta_2^2) + 2\eta_1\eta_2\xi_2) + 2a_3\eta_1(3\eta_2^2 + \eta_1^2) + 4b_0\xi_1\xi_2 + 2b_1(\xi_1\eta_2 + \xi_2\eta_1) + 4b_2\eta_1\eta_2 + 2c_0\xi_1 + 2c_1\eta_1]) = \sum_{\xi_1}\sum_{\eta_1}\sum_{\xi_2}\sum_{\eta_2} e_p(S[\phi]) \tag{33}$$

where

$$\phi = (6a_0\xi_1 + 2a_1\eta_1)\xi_2^2 + 2(2a_1\xi_1 + 2a_2\eta_1)\xi_2\eta_2 + (2a_2\xi_1 + 6a_3\eta_1)\eta_2^2 + 2(2b_0\xi_1 + b_1\eta_1)\xi_2 + 2(b_1\xi_1 + 2b_2\eta_1)\eta_2 + 2a_0\xi_1^3 + 2a_1\xi_1^2\eta_1 + 2a_2\xi_1\eta_1^2 + 2a_3\eta_1^3 + 2c_0\xi_1 + 2c_1\eta_1$$

Let

$$\Delta = \Delta(\xi, \eta) = (2a_1\xi_1 + 2a_2\eta_1)^2 - (6a_0\xi_1 + 2a_1\eta_1)(2a_2\xi + 6a_3\eta_1) = 4(a_1^2 - 3a_0a_2)\xi_1^2 + 4(a_1a_2 - 9a_0a_3)\xi_1\eta_1 + 4(a_2^2 - 3a_1a_3)\eta_1^2$$

Then $\Delta(\xi, \eta)$ is not identically zero. In fact, if otherwise, we must have

$$a_1^2 = 3a_0a_2, \quad a_1a_2 = 9a_0a_3, \quad a_2^2 = 3a_1a_3$$

If $a_0 = 0$, then $a_1 = 0$, $a_2 = 0$, and therefore $a_0x^3 + a_1x^2y + a_2y^2 + a_3y^3 = a_3y^3$, which is contrary to our supposition. if $a_0 \neq 0$, then

$$a_2 = \frac{a_1^2}{3a_0},\ a_3 = \frac{a_1a_2}{9a_0} = \frac{a_1^3}{27a_0^3}$$

and hence

$$a_0x^3 + a_1x^2y + a_2xy^2 + a_3y^3 = a\left(x + \frac{a_1}{3a_0}y\right)^3$$

which is also contrary to our supposition. It is, then, clear that

$$\Delta = \Delta(\xi, \eta) = 0$$

has $O(p^m)$ solutions.

By (33)

$$|S|^2 = \sum_{\xi_1}\sum_{\substack{\eta_1 \\ \Delta\neq 0}}\sum_{\xi_2}\sum_{\eta_2} e_p(S[\phi]) + \sum_{\xi_1}\sum_{\substack{\eta_1 \\ \Delta = 0}}\sum_{\xi_2}\sum_{\eta_2} e_p(S[\phi]) = S_1 + S_2,\ \text{say}.$$

By lemma 13,

$$S_1 = p^m \sum_{\xi_1}\sum_{\substack{\eta_1 \\ \Delta\neq 0}} \left(\frac{\Delta}{\kappa}\right) e_p\left(S\left[2a_0\xi_1^3\eta_1 + 2a_1\xi_1^2n_1 + 2a_2\xi_1\eta_1^2 + 2c_0\xi_1 + 2c_1\eta_1 + \frac{H(\xi_1, \eta_1)}{\Delta(\xi_1, \eta_1)}\right]\right) =$$

$$p^m \sum_{\xi_1}\sum_{\substack{\eta_1 \\ \xi_1\Delta\neq 0}} \left(\frac{\Delta}{\kappa}\right) e_p\left(S\left[2a_0\xi_1^3 + 2a_1\xi_1^2\eta_1 + 2a_2\xi_1\eta_1^2 + 2c_0\xi_1 + 2c_1\eta_1 + \frac{H(\xi_1, \eta_1)}{\Delta(\xi_1, \eta_1)}\right]\right) +$$

$$O(p^{2m})$$

where

$$H = H(\xi_1, \eta_1) = (2a_2\xi_1 + 6a_3\eta_1)(2b_0\xi_1 + b_1\eta_1)^2 + (6a_0\xi_1 + 2a_1\eta_1)(b_1\xi_1 + 2b_2\eta_1)^2 - 2(2b_0\xi_1 + b_1\eta_1)(b_1\xi_1 + 2b_2\eta_1)(2a_1\xi_1 + 2a_2\eta_1)$$

Putting $\xi_1 = \xi$, $\eta_1 = \xi\eta$, we have

$$S_1 = p^m \sum_{\xi} \sum_{\substack{\eta \\ \Delta(1,\eta)\neq 0}} \left(\frac{\Delta(1, \eta)}{\kappa}\right) e_p\left(S\left[(2a_0 + 2a_1\eta + 2a_2\eta^2 + 2a_3\eta^3)\xi^3 + \left(2c_0 + 2c_1\eta + \frac{H(1, \eta)}{\Delta(1, \eta)}\xi\right]\right) + O(p^{2m}) \tag{34}$$

since the sum of terms in which $\xi = 0$ is $O(p^{2m})$.

If $2c_0 + 2c_1\eta + \frac{H(1, \eta)}{\Delta(1, \eta)}$ is zero identically, we have

$$|S_1|^2 \leqslant 2p^{2m}p^m \sum_{\substack{\eta \\ \Delta(1,\eta)\neq 0}} \left|\sum_{\xi} e_p(S[(2a_0 + 2a_1\eta + 2a_2\eta^2 + 2a_3\eta^3)\xi^3])\right|^2 + O(p^{4m}) =$$
$$O(p^{3m} \sum_{\alpha} \left|\sum_{\xi} e_p(S[a\xi^3]\right|^2)) + O(p^{4m}) =$$
$$O(p^{3m} \sum_{\xi_1}\sum_{\xi_2}\sum_{\alpha} e_p(S[\alpha(\xi_1^3 - \xi_2^3)])) + O(p^{4m}) =$$
$$O(p^{3m} \sum_{\substack{\xi_1 \quad \xi_2 \\ \xi_1^3 = \xi_2^3}} p^m) + O(p^{4m}) =$$
$$O(p^{5m})$$

Therefore

$$S_1 = O(p^{5m/2}) \tag{35}$$

If $2c_0 + 2c_1\eta + \frac{H(1, \eta)}{\Delta(1, \eta)}$ is not zero identically, then the equations

$$c^3(2a_0 + 2a_1\eta + 2a_2\eta^2 + 2a_3\eta^3) = A$$
$$c\left(2c_0 + 2c_1\eta + \frac{H(1, \eta)}{\Delta(1, \eta)}\right) = B,\ B \neq 0 \tag{36}$$

has $O(1)$ solutions. In fact, by eliminating c, we have

$$B^3(2a_0 + 2a_1\eta + 2a_2\eta^2 + 2a_3\eta^3) = A\left(2c_0 + 2c_1\eta + \frac{H(1, \eta)}{\Delta(1, \eta)}\right)^3$$

Since $2a_0 + 2a_1\eta + 2a_2\eta^2 + 2a_3\eta^3$ is not a constant multiple of a perfact cube, the above equation is not an identity. It has therefore $O(1)$ solutions in η. But c is uniquely determined by the second equation in (36), therefore (36) has $O(1)$ solutions in η, c.

By (34),

$$S_1 = p^m \sum_{\substack{\xi \\ \Delta(1,\eta)\neq 0}} \sum_{\eta} \left(\frac{\Delta(1,\eta)}{\kappa}\right) e_p\Big(S\Big[(2a_0+2a_1\eta+2a_2\eta^2+2a_3\eta^3)\xi^3 +$$
$$\left(2c_0+2c_1\eta+\frac{H(1,\eta)}{\Delta(1,\eta)}\right)\xi\Big]\Big) + O(p^{2m})$$
$$2c_0+2c_1\eta+\frac{H(1,\eta)}{\Delta(1,\eta)} \neq 0$$

Therefore

$$|S_1|^4 \leqslant 8p^{4m+3m} \sum_{\substack{\eta \\ \Delta(1,\eta)\neq 0}} \left| \sum_{\xi} e_p\Big(S\Big[(2a_0+2a_1\eta+2a_2\eta^2+2a_3\eta^3)\xi^3 +\right.$$
$$\left.\left(2c_0+2c_1\eta+\frac{H(1,\eta)}{\Delta(1,\eta)}\right)\xi\Big]\Big)\right|^4 + O(p^{3m})$$
$$2c_0+2c_1\eta+\frac{H(1,\eta)}{\Delta(1,\eta)} \neq 0$$

Hence

$$(p^m-1)|S_1|^4 \leqslant 8p^{7m} \sum_{c} \sum_{\substack{\eta \\ c\neq 0,\ \Delta(1,\eta)\neq 0}} \left| \sum_{\xi} e_p\Big(S\Big[c^3(2a_0+2a_1\eta+2a_2\eta^2+2a_3\eta^3)\xi^3 +\right.$$
$$\left. c\left(2c_0+2c_1\eta+\frac{H(1,\eta)}{\Delta(1,\eta)}\right)\xi\Big]\Big)\right|^4 + O(p^{9m})\left(2c_0+2c_1\eta+\frac{H(1,\eta)}{\Delta(1,\eta)}\neq 0\right) =$$
$$O(p^{7m}\sum_{A}\sum_{B} | e_p(S[A\xi^3+B\xi])|^4) + O(p^{9m}) =$$
$$O(p^{7m}p^{4m}) = O(p^{11m})$$

by lemma 11. Therefore

$$S_1 = O(p^{5m/2}) \qquad (37)$$

Now let us estimate S_2. Since $\Delta(\xi,\eta)=0$ has $O(p^m)$ solutions we have

$$S_2 = O(p^m \operatorname*{Max}_{\substack{\Delta(\xi_1,\eta_1)=0 \\ \xi_1\neq 0 \text{ or } \eta_1\neq 0}}) \sum_{\eta_2}\sum_{\eta_2} e_p(S[\phi]) + p^{2m})$$

Since $a_0+a_1\eta+a_2\eta^2+a_3\eta^3$ is not a constant multiple of a perfect cube, the coefficients of ξ_2^2, $\xi_2\eta_2$, η_2^2 in ϕ can not vanish simultaneously unless $\xi_1=\eta_1=0$, Since $\Delta=0$, the coefficients of ξ_2^2 and η_2^2 can not be both zero. Hence lemma 12,

$$S_2 = O(p^m p^m p^{m/2}) = O(p^{5m/2}) \qquad (38)$$

By (35) (or (37)) and (38), we have

$$|S|^2 = S_1 + S_2 = O(p^{5m/2})$$

Therefore

$$S = O(p^{5m/4}) = O(p^{m(2-(3/4))})$$

ON SYSTEMS OF ALGEBRAIC EQUATIONS AND CERTAIN MULTIPLE EXPONENTIAL SUMS①

1. Throughout the paper we use p to denote a prime. Let

$$f(x) = a_k x^k + \cdots + a_1 x, \quad k \geqslant 2$$

be a polynomial with integer coefficients. The exponential sum

$$S\{f(x)\} = \sum_{x=1}^{p} e^{2\pi i f(x)/p}$$

is called a *generalized Gaussian sum*. Mordell proved that, if a_k is not divisible by p, then, as p tends to ∞,

$$S\{f(x)\} = O(p^{1-1/k})$$

where the constant implied by O depends only on k.

The n-dimensional generalization of $S\{f(x)\}$ is the n-ple exponential sum

$$S\{f(x_1, \cdots, x_n)\} = \sum_{x_1=1}^{p} \cdots \sum_{x_n=1}^{p} \exp\left\{\frac{2\pi i}{p} f(x_1, \cdots, x_n)\right\}$$

where $f(x_1, \cdots, x_n)$ is a polynomial of degree k with integer coefficients. More generally we consider a field K containing p^m elements and suppose that $f(x_1, \cdots, x_n)$ is a polynomial of degree k in the field K. Construct the sum

① 原载:*Quart. J. Math. Oxford Ser.*, 1947, 18(71): 133-142.

$$S\{f(x_1,\cdots,x_n),K\} = \sum_{x_1}\cdots\sum_{x_n}\exp\left\{\frac{2\pi i}{p}S[f(x_1,\cdots,x_n)]\right\}$$

where $S[a]$ is the trace of a, and $x_1,\cdots,x_n$ run respectively over all elements in K.

Now let

$$f(\alpha_1 t+\beta_1,\cdots,\alpha_n t+\beta_n) = \sum_{r=0}^{k} F_r(\alpha_1,\cdots,\alpha_n;\beta_1,\cdots,\beta_n)t^r$$

and

$$M = \begin{pmatrix} \frac{\partial F_1}{\partial\alpha_1} & \cdots & \frac{\partial F_1}{\partial\alpha_n} & \frac{\partial F_1}{\partial\beta_1} & \cdots & \frac{\partial F_1}{\partial\beta_n} \\ \vdots & & \vdots & \vdots & & \vdots \\ \frac{\partial F_k}{\partial\alpha_1} & \cdots & \frac{\partial F_k}{\partial\alpha_n} & \frac{\partial F_k}{\partial\beta_1} & \cdots & \frac{\partial F_k}{\partial\beta_n} \end{pmatrix}$$

I shall prove that, if $k \geqslant 2n$ and M is of rank $2n$, i. e. if a certain $2n\times 2n$ minor is not identically zero, then, as p tends to infinity,

$$S\{f(x_1,\cdots,x_n),K\} = O(p^{mn(1-1/k)})$$

where the constant implied by O depends only on k and n.

When $m = n = 1$, M is of rank 2 unless $f(x_1)$ reduces to a linear function of x_1, so that the theorem includes Mordell's theorem as a special case. In fact, when $n = 1$, the minor determinant formed by the first two rows is

$$\frac{1}{2}\alpha_1^2[f'(\beta_1)f'''(\beta_1) - 2\{f''(\beta_1)\}^2]$$

This is identically zero only when $f(x_1)$ is a linear polynomial.

When $n = 2$, the theorem was established by Hua and me. We also proved by an elaborate method① that, if M is of rank $< 2n = 4$, $f(x_1,x_2)$ can be transformed by a linear non-singular transformation in K to $g(x,y)$ which is either of degree $\leqslant \frac{1}{2}k$ in y or is a polynomial in $x^2+\tau y^2$ $(\tau\in K)$. From this we deduced that the theorem holds unless② $f(x_1,x_2)$ is a polynomial in a single

---

① 'On a double exponential sum', *Science Report of Tsing-Hua Univ.* (in the press). A short sketch of the proof has been published in the *Science Record of Academia Sinica.* vol. i, Nos. 1-2. It is impossible, however, to give a sufficiently complete short sketch.

② The method of procedure where $f(x_1,x_2)$ is a polynomial in $x^2+\tau y^2$ may be outlined as follows (taking $m = 1$ for simplicity). The sum is the same as the corresponding sum with $x^2+\tau y^2$ replaced by $x+\tau y$, provided that each term is multiplied by

$$\{1+(x/p)\}\{1+(y/p)\}$$

This gives four sums; only the one containing (xy/p) presents difficulty. This is dealt with by putting $y = xz$, and applying Mordell's theorem to the resulting sum over x.

variable which is itself a linear function of x and y. It is very likely that a similar result exists in the general case, but this seems to be very difficult to establish. In the two-dimensional case I have obtained a still better result, which, roughly speaking, may be regarded as a two-dimensional analogue of a result due to Davenport①. I hope to publish it elsewhere.

2. In the theory of a system of linear equations the most important role is played by the matrix of the system. A natural generalization of this is the 'Jacobian matrix' of a system of algebraic equations.

Let

$$f_i(x_1,\cdots,x_n) = 0, \quad i = 1,\cdots,m \tag{1}$$

be a system of algebraic equations in a field F. We write the Jacobian matrix as

$$F(f_1,\cdots,f_m) = \begin{pmatrix} \frac{\partial f_1}{\partial x_1} & \cdots & \frac{\partial f_1}{\partial x_n} \\ \vdots & & \vdots \\ \frac{\partial f_m}{\partial x_1} & \cdots & \frac{\partial f_m}{\partial x_n} \end{pmatrix} \tag{2}$$

and, when $m = n$, denote its determinant by $J(f_1,\cdots,f_m)$.

Definition *A solution of* (1) *for which the matrix* $F(f_1,\cdots,f_m)$ *is of rank* r *is called a solution of rank* r. *If* $r = n$, *the solution is said to be non-singular; otherwise it is singular.*

The theorems to be proved hold both for fields of characteristic zero and those of characteristic p. We are interested in large primes p and polynomials of fixed degree.

Corresponding to the fact that a system of linear equations has only one solution if its determinant is different from zero, is the following

Theorem 1 *The number of non-singular solutions of* (1) *is* $O(1)$, *where the constant implied by* O *depends only on* n, m *and the degrees of* f_i $(i = 1,\cdots, m)$.

Proof Without loss of generality we may assume that $m = n$. The theorem is evident for $n = 1$. Suppose that the theorem is true for $n - 1$ variables and $n - 1$ equations. Let us prove the theorem for n variables and n equations.

① 'On certain exponential sums', *J. füy die reine und angew. Math.*, 169, Heft 1933(3): 158-76.

If $f_1, \cdots, f_n$ do not contain① x_n, the theorem is true, for in this case $J(f_1, \cdots, f_n) = 0$ identically and (1) has no non-singular solutions. If only one of them contains x_n the theorem is also true; for supposing that f_n contains x_n and that $(x_1^{(0)}, \cdots, x_{n-1}^{(0)}, x_n^{(0)})$ is a non-singular solution of (1), then we have

$$J(f_1, \cdots, f_n) = \frac{\partial f_n}{\partial x_n} J(f_1, \cdots, f_{n-1}) \neq 0 \quad \text{at } x_v = x_v^{(0)}$$

which shows that $(x_1^{(0)}, \cdots, x_{n-1}^{(0)})$ is a non-singular solution of $f_1 = 0, \cdots, f_{n-1} = 0$ and that $f_n(x_1^{(0)}, \cdots, x_{n-1}^{(0)}, x_n)$ is not identically zero. Let the degree of f_i with respect to x_n be λ_i. Then the theorem is true when $\lambda_1 + \cdots + \lambda_n \leqslant 1$. For, in this case, at most one of the equations (1) contains x_n. Now suppose that the theorem is true when

$$\lambda_1 + \cdots + \lambda_n \leqslant r$$

Let us prove the theorem when $\lambda_1 + \cdots + \lambda_n = r + 1$.

Without loss of generality we assume that

$$f_1 = f_{10} x_n^{\lambda_1} + \cdots + f_{1\lambda_1}, \; f_2 = f_{20} x_n^{\lambda_2} + \cdots + f_{2\lambda_2}$$

when $\lambda_1 \geqslant \lambda_2 \geqslant 1$ and f_{1i}, f_{2i} are polynomials in $x_1, \cdots, x_{n-1}$.

Consider the system of equations

$$f'_1 = f_{20} f_1 - f_{10} x_n^{\lambda_1 - \lambda_2} f_2 = 0②, \; f_i = 0, \quad i = 2, \cdots, n \tag{3}$$

Evidently, every solution of (1) is a solution of (3). I shall prove that each non-singular solution $(x_1^{(0)}, \cdots, x_n^{(0)})$ of (1), for which $f_{20} \neq 0$, is a non-singular solution of (3).

By differentiating the first equation in (3) with respect to $x_i (i = 1, \cdots, n)$, we have

$$\left.\begin{aligned}
\frac{\partial f'_1}{\partial x_i} &= f_{20} \frac{\partial f_1}{\partial x_i} - f_{10} x_n^{\lambda_1 - \lambda_2} \frac{\partial f_2}{\partial x_i} + \frac{\partial f_{20}}{\partial x_i} f_1 - \frac{\partial f_{10}}{\partial x_i} x_n^{\lambda_1 - \lambda_2} f_2 = \\
&\quad f_{20} \frac{\partial f_1}{\partial x_i} - f_{10} x_n^{\lambda_1 - \lambda_2} \frac{\partial f_2}{\partial x_i} \quad \text{at } x_v = x_v^{(0)}, \quad i = 1, \cdots, n-1 \\
\frac{\partial f'_1}{\partial x_n} &= f_{20} \frac{\partial f_1}{\partial x_n} - f_{10} x_n^{\lambda_1 - \lambda_2} \frac{\partial f_2}{\partial x_n} - (\lambda_1 - \lambda_2) f_{10} x_n^{\lambda_1 - \lambda_2 - 1} f_2 = \\
&\quad f_{20} \frac{\partial f_1}{\partial x_n} - f_{10} x_n^{\lambda_1 - \lambda_2} \frac{\partial f_2}{\partial x_n} \quad \text{at } x_v = x_v^{(0)}
\end{aligned}\right\} \tag{4}$$

---

① We consider $f_1, \cdots, f_n$ as polynomials in x_n whose coefficients are polynomials in $x_1, \cdots, x_{n-1}$. But f_1 may be of degree 0 in x_n. In this case we say, for convenience, that f_i does not contain x_n.

② In the case in which this equation becomes an identity, (3) has no non-singular solutions.

Therefore

$$J(f'_1, f_2, \cdots, f_n) = f_{20} J(f_1, \cdots, f_n) \neq 0 \text{ at } x_v = x_v^{(0)} \tag{5}$$

Now suppose that $(x_1^{(0)}, \cdots, x_n^{(0)})$ is a non-singular solution of (1), for which $f_{20} = 0$. Then the solution satisfies both

$$f_1 = 0, f'_2 = f_2 - f_{20} x_n^{\lambda_2} = 0, f_i = 0, \quad i = 3, \cdots, n \tag{6}$$

and

$$f_1 = 0, f_{20} = 0, f_i = 0, \quad i = 3, \cdots, n \tag{7}$$

By (6),

$$\frac{\partial f'_2}{\partial x_i} = \frac{\partial f_2}{\partial x_i} - \frac{\partial f_{20}}{\partial x_i} x_n^{\lambda_2}, \quad i = 1, \cdots, n-1$$

$$\frac{\partial f'_2}{\partial x_n} = \frac{\partial f_2}{\partial x_n} - \lambda_2 f_{20} x_n^{\lambda_2 - 1} = \frac{\partial f_2}{\partial x_n} \quad \text{at} \quad x_v = x_v^{(0)}$$

Hence

$$0 \neq J(f_1, \cdots, f_n) = J(f_1, f'_2, f_3, \cdots, f_n) + x_n^{\lambda_2} J(f_1, f_{20}, f_3, \cdots, f_n) \tag{8}$$

at $x_v = x_v^{(0)}$. *This shows that* $J(f_1, f'_2, f_3, \cdots, f_n)$ and $J(f_1, f_{20}, f_3, \cdots, f_n)$ can not both be zero.

Therefore, by (5) and (8), each non-singular solution of (1) must be a non-singular solution of one of the systems (3), (6), (7). Since the sum of the degrees (with respect to x_n) of each of the systems is less than or equal to r, the theorem follows by induction.

I shall establish three theorems which have some interest in themselves but are not required for the treatment of the exponential sums.

Theorem 2 *The number of solutions of* (1) *of rank* r *can be arranged in* $O(1)$ *sets*,① *each set being such that, if a certain* $n - r$ *of the variables are given, the remaining variables are determined with only* $O(1)$ *possibilities.*

Proof For a solution of rank r, at least one of the r-rowed minors in $F(f_1, \cdots, f_m)$ is not zero. Let it be the minor in the left upper corner, say M. By Theorem 1, if $x_{r+1}, \cdots, x_n$ are given, (1) has only $O(1)$ solutions for which $M \neq 0$. The theorem follows immediately.

3. Now let us consider homogeneous equations

$$g_i(x_1, \cdots, x_{n+1}) = 0, \quad i = 1, \cdots, m \tag{1}$$

where the $g_1, \cdots, g_m$ are homogeneous polynomials in $x_1, \cdots, x_{n+1}$, Consider the

① The constant implied by O in this theorem and Theorem 4 depends only on m, n and the degrees of the equations considered.

matrices

$$F(g_1,\cdots,g_m) = \begin{pmatrix} \frac{\partial g_1}{\partial x_1} & \cdots & \frac{\partial g_1}{\partial x_{n+1}} \\ \vdots & & \vdots \\ \frac{\partial g_m}{\partial x_1} & \cdots & \frac{\partial g_m}{\partial x_{n+1}} \end{pmatrix}$$

$$F_1(g_1,\cdots,g_m) = \begin{pmatrix} \frac{\partial g_1}{\partial x_1} & \cdots & \frac{\partial g_1}{\partial x_{j-1}} & \frac{\partial g_1}{\partial x_{j+1}} & \cdots & \frac{\partial g_1}{\partial x_{n+1}} \\ \vdots & & \vdots & \vdots & & \vdots \\ \frac{\partial g_m}{\partial x_1} & \cdots & \frac{\partial g_1}{\partial x_{j-1}} & \frac{\partial g_m}{\partial x_{j+1}} & \cdots & \frac{\partial g_m}{\partial x_{n+1}} \end{pmatrix}.$$

We have the following theorems.

Theorem 3 *There are no solutions for which*

$$\text{Rank of } F_j < \text{Rank of } F,\ j = 1,2,\cdots,n+1$$

except the trivial solutions

$$x_1 = 0,\cdots,x_{n+1} = 0$$

Proof If k_i is the degree of g_i and $x_v = x_v^{(0)}$ $(v = 1,\cdots,n+1)$ is a solution of (1), then

$$0 = k_i g_i = x_1 \frac{\partial g_i}{\partial x_1} + \cdots + x_{n+1} \frac{\partial g_i}{\partial x_{n+1}} \quad \text{at} \quad x_v = x_v^{(0)}$$

This shows that the rank of F is equal to that of F_j at $x_v = x_v^{(0)}$ unless $x_j^{(0)} = 0$. The theorem follows.

Theorem 4 *The number of non-equivalent solutions (proportional solutions being called 'equivalent') of rank r can be arranged in $O(1)$ sets, each set being such that, if a certain $n-r$ of the variables are given, the remaining variables are determined with only $O(1)$ possibilities.*

Proof Consider first the solutions with $x_j \neq 0$. There solutions satisfy also

$$x_j^{-k_i} g_i(x_1,\cdots,x_{n+1}) = g_i\left(\frac{x_1}{x_j},\cdots,\frac{x_{n+1}}{x_j}\right) = 0, \quad i = 1,\cdots,m \qquad (1')$$

where k_i is the degree of $g_i (1 \leqslant i \leqslant m)$. Let $X_i = x_i/x_j$ or x_{i+1}/x_j according as $i \leqslant j-1$ or $i \geqslant j$. Then (1′) can be written as

$$G_i(X_1,\cdots,X_n) = 0, \quad i = 1,\cdots,m \qquad (1'')$$

Plainly

$$\begin{pmatrix} \frac{\partial G_1}{\partial X_1} & \cdots & \frac{\partial G_1}{\partial X_n} \\ \vdots & & \vdots \\ \frac{\partial G_m}{\partial X_1} & \cdots & \frac{\partial G_m}{\partial X_n} \end{pmatrix} = x_j^{-k_i+1} \begin{pmatrix} \frac{\partial g_1}{\partial x_1} & \cdots & \frac{\partial g_1}{\partial x_{j-1}} & \frac{\partial g_1}{\partial x_{j+1}} & \cdots & \frac{\partial g_1}{\partial x_m} \\ \vdots & & \vdots & \vdots & & \vdots \\ \frac{\partial g_m}{\partial x_1} & \cdots & \frac{\partial g_m}{\partial x_{j-1}} & \frac{\partial g_m}{\partial x_{j+1}} & \cdots & \frac{\partial g_m}{\partial x_n} \end{pmatrix} = x_j^{-k_i+1} F_j$$

As shown in the proof of Theorem 3, for a solution with $x_j \neq 0$, the rank of F_j is equal to that of F. Hence, corresponding to a solution $(x_1, \cdots, x_{n+1})$ of (1) of rank r with $x_j \neq 0$, there is a solution $(X_1, \cdots, X_n)$ of (1″) of rank r. The theorem therefore follows from Theorem 2 if we consider only non-trivial solutions. But, since there is only one trivial solution, the proof is thus completed.

4. Before going on to prove the result stated in §1, I establish two lemmas. The con-stant implied by O in this section depends only on k and n.

Lemma 1 *Let K be a finite field containing p^m elements, where p is a prime and m a positive integer. Let*

$$f(x) = a_k x^k + \cdots + a_0,\ a_k \neq 0,\ a_i \in K$$

Then

$$\sum_x e^{2\pi i S[f(x)]/p} = O(p^{m(1-1/k)}) \tag{1}$$

*where $S[a]$ denotes the trace of a, and x runs over all elements of K*①.

Proof Let θ be the generating element of K with respect to the ground field π consisting of the residue classes to modulus p. Then every element x of K can be written as

$$x = \alpha_0 + \alpha_1\theta + \cdots + \alpha_{m-1}\theta^{m-1}, \alpha_i \in \pi$$

Since $S[x+y] = S[x] + S[y]$, we have, for $a \in K$,

$$\sum_x e^{2\pi i S[ax]/p} = \sum_{\alpha_0=1}^{p} \cdots \sum_{\alpha_{m-1}=1}^{p} e^{2\pi i(a\alpha_0 S[a] + \cdots + \alpha_{m-1}S[a\theta^{m-1}])/p} = \begin{cases} p^m, & \text{if } S[a\theta^k] = 0 \quad \text{for } k = 0, \cdots, m-1 \\ 0, & \text{otherwise} \end{cases}$$

Further, $S[a\theta^k] = 0$ for $k = 0, \cdots, m-1$ implies $a = 0$. In fact, we have $S[ax] = 0$ for all $x \in K$. If $a \neq 0$, we should have

① Setting $m = 1$ and $S[x] = x$ we get Mordell's theorem. In the proof we can simply put $\theta = 0$ and om it all unnecessary words.

$$0 = S[aa^{-1}] = 1$$

which is absurd. Hence①

$$\sum_{b_1}\cdots\sum_{b_k}\left|\sum_x e^{2\pi i S[b_1x+\cdots+b_kx^k]/p}\right|^{2k} =$$

$$\sum_{x_1}\cdots\sum_{x_k}\sum_{y_1}\cdots\sum_{y_k}\sum_{b_1}\cdots\sum_{b_k} e^{2\pi i S[b_1(x_1+\cdots+x_k-y_1-\cdots-y_k)+\cdots+b_k(x_1^k+\cdots-y_k^k)]/p} =$$

$$\sum_{\substack{x_1 \\ x_1+\cdots+x_k=y_1+\cdots+y_k \\ \cdots \\ x_1^k+\cdots+x_k^k=y_1^k+\cdots+y_k^k}}\cdots\sum_{x_k}\sum_{y_1}\cdots\sum_{y_k} p^{mk} = O(p^{2mk}). \quad (2)$$

If λ and μ are both in K and $\lambda = 0$, then

$$\sum_x e^{2\pi i S[f(\lambda x+\mu)]/p} = \sum_x e^{2\pi i S[f(x)]/p}$$

The transformatioin $x = \lambda x' + \mu(\lambda \in K, \mu \in K, \lambda \neq 0)$ transforms the sum in (1) into at least $p^m(p^m - 1)/k$ different terms in the sum (2). In fact, if $f(\lambda x + \mu) \equiv f(x)$②, *then*

$$\lambda^k a_k = a_k, \quad n\lambda^{k-1}\mu a_k + \lambda^{k-1}a_{k-1} = a_{k-1}$$

The first equation gives at most k values of λ and the second equation determines μ uniquely. Hence

$$\frac{p^m(p^m-1)}{k}\left|\sum_x e^{2\pi i S[f(x)]/p}\right|^{2k} = O(p^{2mk})$$

and

$$\sum_x e^{2\pi i S[f(x)]/p} = O(p^{m(1-1/k)})$$

Lemma 2 *Let $f(x_1, \cdots, x_n)$ be a polynomial not zero in K, then the number of solutions of*

$$f(x_1, \cdots, x_n) = 0 \quad (3)$$

is $O(p^{m(n-1)})$.

Proof The proof is evident for $n = 1$. Suppose that the lemma is true for $n - 1$ unknowns. Let $f(x_1, \cdots, x_n) = g_0x_n^k + \cdots + g_k$ where g_i are polynomials in $x_1, \cdots, x_{n-1}$ and $g_0 \not\equiv 0$. The number of solutions of $f = 0$, $g_0 \neq 0$ is evidently $O(p^{m(n-1)})$ and that of $f = 0$, $g_0 = 0$ is, by our supposition, $O(p^{m(n-2)}p^m) = O(p^{m(n-1)})$. Therefore the number of solutions of (3) is $O(p^{m(n-1)})$.

Now we can prove

Theorem 5 *Let $f(x_1, \cdots, x_n)$ be a polynomial of degree $k \geqslant 2n$ in the field*

---

① We consider $\alpha_1, \cdots, \alpha_k$ as fixed and $b_1, \cdots, b_k$ as variables that assume all values in K.

② This means that they are the same polynomial in K.

K containing p^m elements. Let

$$f(\alpha_1 t+\beta_1,\cdots,\alpha_n t+\beta_n)=\sum_{r=0}^{k}F_r(\alpha_1,\cdots,\alpha_n;\beta_1,\cdots,\beta_n)t^r$$

Suppose the matrix

$$M=\begin{pmatrix}\dfrac{\partial F_1}{\partial\alpha_1} & \cdots & \dfrac{\partial F_1}{\partial\beta_n}\\ \vdots & & \vdots\\ \dfrac{\partial F_k}{\partial\alpha_1} & \cdots & \dfrac{\partial F_k}{\partial\beta_n}\end{pmatrix}$$

is of rank $2n$, i. e. a certain $2n\times 2n$ minor is not identically zero. Then

$$\sum_{x_1}\cdots\sum_{x_n}e^{2\pi i S[f(x_1,\cdots,x_n)]/p}=O(p^{mn(1-1/k)})$$

Proof Let $J(\alpha_1,\cdots,\beta_n)$ be a minor which is not identically zero. We regard J as a polynomial in β_n and denote its leading coefficient① by $J'(\alpha_1,\cdots,\beta_{n-1})$. Then ragard J' as a polynomial in β_{n-1} and denote its leading coefficient by $J''(\alpha_1,\cdots,\beta_{n-1})$ and so on. Finally, we obtain a polynomial $J_0(\alpha_1,\cdots,\beta_1)$ such that, if $J_0(\alpha_1^{(0)},\cdots,\beta_1^{(0)})\neq 0$, the polynomial $J(\alpha_1^{(0)},\cdots,\beta_1^{(0)},\beta_2,\cdots,\beta_n)$ is not identically zero.

If $\alpha_1\neq 0$,

$$\sum_x\sum_{\beta_2}\cdots\sum_{\beta_n}e^{2\pi i S[f(\alpha_1 x+\beta_1,\cdots,\alpha_n x+\beta_n)]/p}=\sum_{x_1}\cdots\sum_{x_n}e^{2\pi i S[f(x_1,\cdots,x_n)]/p}$$

Since F_k depends only on $\alpha_1,\cdots,\alpha_n$, the number of solutions *of* $\alpha_1 J_0 F_k=0$ is $O(p^{mn})$ by Lemma 2, and hence the number of sets $(\alpha_1,\cdots,\alpha_n,\beta_1)$ for which $\alpha_1 J_0 F_k\neq 0$ is $p^{(n+1)m}-O(p^{mn})$. It follows that

$$\{p^{(n+1)m}-O(p^{mn})\}\left|\sum_{x_1}\cdots\sum_{x_n}e^{2\pi i S[f(x_1,\cdots,x_n)]/p}\right|^{2k}=$$

$$\sum_{\substack{\alpha_1\\ \alpha_1 J_0 F_k\neq 0}}\cdots\sum_{\alpha_n}\sum_{\beta_1}\left|\sum_x\sum_{\beta_2}\cdots\sum_{\beta_n}e^{2\pi i S[f(\alpha_1 x+\beta_1,\cdots,\alpha_n x+\beta_n)]/p}\right|^{2k}=$$

$$\sum_{\substack{\alpha_1\\ \alpha_1 J_0 F_k\neq 0}}\cdots\sum_{\alpha_n}\sum_{\beta_1}\left|\sum_x\sum_{\substack{\beta_2\\ J\neq 0}}\cdots\sum_{\beta_n}e^{2\pi i S[f(\alpha_1 x+\beta_1,\cdots,\alpha_n x+\beta_n)]/p}+\right.$$

$$\left.\sum_x\sum_{\substack{\beta_2\\ J=0}}\cdots\sum_{\beta_n}e^{2\pi i S[f(\alpha_1 x+\beta_1,\cdots,\alpha_n x+\beta_n)]/p}\right|^{2k}$$

By Hölder's inequality, this does not exceed

① That is, the coefficient of the highest power of β_n.

$$2^{2k-1}\sum_{\substack{\alpha_1\\ \alpha_1J_0F_k\neq 0}}\cdots\sum_{\alpha_n}\sum_{\beta_1}\left|\sum_{x}\sum_{\beta_2}\cdots\sum_{\beta_n}e^{2\pi iS[f(\alpha_1x+\beta_1,\cdots,\alpha_nx+\beta_n)]/p}\right|^{2k}+$$

$$2^{2k-1}\sum_{\substack{\alpha_1\\ \alpha_1J_0F_k\neq 0}}\cdots\sum_{\alpha_n}\sum_{\beta_1}\sum_{\beta_1}\left|\sum_{x}\sum_{\beta_2}\cdots\sum_{\substack{\beta_n\\ J\neq 0}}e^{2\pi iS[f(\alpha_1x+\beta_1,\cdots,\alpha_nx+\beta_n)]/p}\right|^{2k}=$$

$$\sum_1+\sum_2,\ \text{say}$$

By Lemmas 1 and 2,

$$\sum_2=O\Big(\sum_{\substack{\alpha_1\\ J_0\neq 0}}\cdots\sum_{\alpha_n}\sum_{\beta_1}\Big|\sum_{\beta_2}\cdots\sum_{\substack{\beta_n\\ J=0}}p^{m(1-1/k)}\Big|^{2k}\Big)=$$

$$O(p^{m[(n+1)+2k(n-2+1-1/k)]})=O(p^{m(2kn-2k+n-1)}) \qquad (4)$$

By Hölder's inequality,

$$\sum_1\leqslant 2^{2k-1}p^{m(n-1)(2k-1)}\sum_{\substack{\alpha_1\\ \alpha_1J_0F_kJ\neq 0}}\cdots\sum_{\alpha_n}\sum_{\beta_1}\cdots\sum_{\beta_n}\left|\sum_{x}e^{2\pi iS[f(\alpha_1x+\beta_1,\cdots,\alpha_nx+\beta_n)]/p}\right|^{2k}$$

Suppose that

$$f(\alpha_1x+\beta_1,\cdots,\alpha_nx+\beta_n)=F_kx^k+\cdots+F_1x+F_0$$

and that J is the Jacobian of $F_{r_1},\cdots,F_{r_{2n}}(1\leqslant r_1<\cdots<r_{2n}\leqslant k)$. Then the number of solutions of the system of equations

$$F_{ri}\equiv F_{ri}(\alpha_1,\cdots,\beta_n)=a_{ri},\quad i=1,\cdots,2n$$

in the $2n$ unknowns $\alpha_1,\cdots,\beta_n$ for which $J\neq 0$ is $O(1)$, by Theorem 1. It follows that

$$\sum_1=p^{m(n-1)(2k-1)}O\Big(\sum_{\alpha_k}\cdots\sum_{\alpha_1}\Big|\sum_{x}e^{2\pi iS[\alpha_k x^k+\cdots\alpha_1x]/p}\Big|^{2k}\Big)$$

Hence, by the inequality from which we deduced Lemma 1,

$$\sum_1=O(p^{m((n-1)(2k-1)}p^{2km})=O(p^{m(2kn-n+1)}) \qquad (5)$$

By (4) and (5)

$$\sum_{x_1}\cdots\sum_{x_n}e^{2\pi iS[f(x_1,\cdots,x_n)]/p}=O(p^{m[(2kn-n+1)-(n+1)]/2k})=O(p^{mn(1-1/k)})$$

the result required.

I wish to express my hearty thanks to the referees for their kind suggestions.

ON THE ORDER OF $\zeta(1/2 + it)$ ①②

Introduction. The problem of finding an upper bound for θ such that

$$\zeta(1/2 + \mathrm{i}t) = O(t^{\theta})$$

has been attacked by van der Corput and Koksma③, Walfisz④, Titchmarsh⑤, Phillips⑥, and Titchmarsh⑦. Their results obtained are, neglecting a factor involving $\log t$,

$$\theta \leqslant \frac{1}{6}, \frac{163}{988}, \frac{27}{164}, \frac{229}{1\ 392}, \text{ and } \frac{19}{116}$$

respectively. The object of the present paper is to prove that

$$\zeta(1/2 + \mathrm{i}t) = O(t^{15/92+\varepsilon}), \quad \varepsilon > 0$$

In this paper there are two main difficulties. The first is the vanishing of the Hessian $H(x,y)$ (see(6.7)below) along

① 原载:*Trans. of Amer. Math. Soc.*, 1949,65(3): 448-472.

② Scholar of the Sino – British Cultural and Educational Endonment Fund.

③ *Sur l'ordre de grandeur de la fonction $\zeta(s)$ de Riemann dans le bande critique*, Annales de Toulouse (3) vol. 1930,(22): 1-39.

④ *Zur Abschätzung von $\zeta(1/2 + it)$*, Göttingen Nachrichten, 1924: 155-158.

⑤ *On van der Corput's method and the zeta-function of Riemann* (Ⅱ), Quart. J. Math. Oxford Ser. vol. 1931,2: 313-320. This will be referred to as (Ⅱ).

⑥ *The zeta-function of Riemann; further developments of van der Corput's method*, Quart. J. Math. Oxford Ser. vol. 1933,4: 209-225. This will be referred to as P.

⑦ *On the order of $\zeta(1/2 + it)$*, Quart. J. Math. Oxford Ser. vol. 1942,13: 11-17. This will be referred to as loc. cit.

certain lines. This is solved by a suitable division of the domain of summation and by making use of a geometrical lemma (Lemma 10). The second difficulty is that if we use the straightforward way of choosing $\lambda' = \lambda'' = \lambda^2$ (see §9) we shall get, instead of (9.8), a result containing a negative power of a which will spoil the main idea. The fact that (9.8) contains no a indicates clearly that our method is a limiting case and we can get no more benefits by merely using more summations.

I wish to express my sincere thanks to my supervisor Professor E. C. Titchmarsh for his kindness in suggesting this problem to me, reading the drafts and giving invaluable criticism and encouragement.

1. Lemmas quoted

Lemma 1① *Let* $f(x)$ *be a real function with continuous derivatives* $f'(x)$, $f''(x)$ *and* $f'''(x)$. *Let* $f'(x)$ *be steadily decreasing*, $f'(b) = \alpha$, $f'(a) = \beta$ *and*②

$$\lambda_2 \leqslant | f''(x) | < A\lambda_2, \ | f'''(x) | < A\lambda_2$$

for $a \leqslant x < b$. *Let* n_v *be such that*

$$f'(n_v) = v, \quad \alpha \leqslant v \leqslant \beta$$

Then

$$\sum_{a \leqslant n \leqslant b} e^{2\pi i f(n)} = e^{-\pi i/4} \sum_{\alpha \leqslant n \leqslant \beta} \frac{e^{2\pi i [f(n_v) - v n_v]}}{| f''(n_v) |^{1/2}} + O(\lambda_2^{-1/2}) + O[\log\{2 + (b-a)\lambda_\alpha\}] + O[(b-a)\lambda_2^{1/5}\lambda_3^{1/5}]$$

Lemma 2③ *If* $F(n)$ *is a real function*, ρ, a *and* b *are integers and* $0 < \rho < b - a$, *then*

$$\left| \sum_{n=a}^{b} e^{2\pi i F(n)} \right| \leqslant \frac{1}{\rho}\{4(b-a)^2\rho + 4(b-a)\left| \sum_{r=1}^{\rho-1} (\rho - r) \sum_{m=a}^{b-r} e^{2\pi i \Phi(r,m)} \right|\}^{1/2}$$

where

$$\Phi(r,m) = F(m+r) - F(m) = \int_0^1 \frac{\partial}{\partial t} F(m+rt)\,dt$$

Lemma 3 *Let* $a_{\mu v}$ *be any numbers, real or complex, such that if* $S_{m,n} = \sum_{\mu=1}^{m}\sum_{v=1}^{n} a_{\mu_v}$ *then* $| S_{m,n} | \leqslant G(1 \leqslant m \leqslant M;\ 1 \leqslant n \leqslant N)$. *Let* $b_{m,n}$ *denote real*

---

① (Ⅱ), Theorem 4, 315.

② Throughout this paper we use A to denote a positive constant, not necessarily the same at each occurrence.

③ Titchmarsh, *On van der Corput's method and the zeta-function of Riemann*, Quart. J. Math. Oxford Ser. Vol. 1931,2: 166.

numbers, $0 \leqslant b_{m,n} \leqslant H$ *and let each of the expressions*

$$b_{m,n} - b_{m,n+1},\ b_{m,n} - b_{m+1,n},\ b_{m,n} - b_{m+1,n} - b_{m,n+1} + b_{m+1,n+1}$$

be of constant sign for values of m and n in question. Then

$$\left| \sum_{m=1}^{M} \sum_{n=1}^{N} a_{m,n} b_{m,n} \right| \leqslant 5GH$$

Lemma 4 *Let* $f(x,y)$ *be a real function of x and y, and*

$$S = \sum \sum e^{2\pi i f(m,n)}$$

the sum being taken over the lattice points of a region D included in the rectangle $a \leqslant x \leqslant b$, $\alpha \leqslant y \leqslant \beta$. *Let*

$$S' = \sum \sum e^{2\pi i \phi_1(m,n)},\ S'' = \sum \sum e^{2\pi i \phi_2(m,n)}$$

where

$$\phi_1(m,n) = f(m+\mu, n+v) - f(m,n) = \int_0^1 \frac{\partial}{\partial t} f(m+\mu t, n+vt)\,dt$$

$$\phi_2(m,n) = f(m+\mu, n-v) - f(m,n) = \int_0^1 \frac{\partial}{\partial t} f(m+\mu t, n-vt)\,dt$$

μ *and* v *are integers, and* S' *is taken over values of m and n such that both* (m,n) *and* $(m+\mu, n+v)$ *belong to D; and similarly for* S''. *Let* ρ *be a positive integer not greater than* $b-a$, *and let* ρ' *be a positive integer not greater than* $\beta-\alpha$. *Then*

$$S = O\left\{\frac{(b-a)(\beta-\alpha)}{(\rho\rho')^{1/2}}\right\} + O\left[\left\{\frac{(b-a)(\beta-\alpha)}{\rho\rho'} \sum_{\mu=1}^{\rho-1} \sum_{v=0}^{\rho'-1} |S'|\right\}^{1/2}\right] +$$
$$O\left[\left\{\frac{(b-a)(\beta-\alpha)}{\rho\rho'} \sum_{\mu=0}^{\rho-1} \sum_{v=0}^{\rho'-1} |S''|\right\}^{1/2}\right]$$

This lemma (as well as the next lemma) evidently remains true when ρ is not an integer but greater than 1. In that case $\sum_{\mu=1}^{\rho-1} \phi(\mu)$ is to be interpreted as $\sum_{1 \leqslant \mu \leqslant \rho-1} \phi(\mu)$, and so on. A similar interpretation should be made when ρ' is not an integer but greater than 1.

Lemma 5 *If* $0 < \rho \leqslant b-a$, *then*

$$S = O\left\{\frac{(b-a)(\beta-\alpha)}{\rho^{1/2}}\right\} + O\left[\left\{\frac{(b-a)(\beta-\alpha)}{\rho} \sum_{\mu=1}^{\rho-1} |S'''|\right\}^{1/2}\right]$$

where

$$S''' = \sum \sum e^{2\pi i \phi(m,n)}$$

with

$$\phi(m,n) = f(m+\mu, n) - f(m,n) = \int_0^1 \frac{\partial}{\partial t} f(m+\mu t, n)\,dt$$

the sum being taken over values of (m,n) such that (m,n) and $(m+\mu,n)$ belong to D.

Lemma 6 *Let $f(x,y)$ be a real differentiable function of x and y. Let $f_x(x,y)$ be a monotone function of x for each value of y considered, and $f_y(x,y)$ be a monotone function of y for each value of x considered. Let $|f_x| \leqslant 3/4$, $|f_y| \leqslant 3/4$, for $a \leqslant x \leqslant b, \alpha \leqslant y \leqslant \beta$ where $b-a \leqslant l$, $\beta - \alpha \leqslant l (l \geqslant 1)$. Let D be the rectangle $(a,b;\alpha,\beta)$ or part of the rectangle cut off by a continuous monotone curve. Then*

$$\sum_D\sum e^{2\pi i f(m,n)} = \iint_D e^{2\pi i f(x,y)} dxdy + O(l)$$

Lemmas 3,4,5,6 are either quotations or simple modifications of Lemmas $\alpha,\beta,\gamma,\delta$ of a paper by Titchmarsh.

2. Lemmas concerning double exponential integrals

In this section we give a refinement of a theorem due to Titchmarsh①.

Lemma 7 *Let D be the rectangle $(a,b;\alpha,\beta)$ and U be its longer side. let $f(x,y)$ be a real algebraic function satisfying the following conditions in D②.*

(1) $B \leqslant |f_{xx}| < AB$, $r^2B^{-1} \leqslant |f_{yy}| < AB$, $|f_{xy}| < AB$;

(2) $|f_{xx}f_{yy} - f_{xy}^2| > r^2$, $0 < r \leqslant B$;

(3) $|f_{xxx}| < AC$, $C < AB^{3/2}$, $CUr < AB^2$;

(4) $|f_{xx}^2 f_{xyy} - 2f_{xx}f_{xy}f_{xxy} + f_{xy}^2 f_{xxx}| < C_1B^2$, $B^{1/2}C_1 \leqslant r^2/2$;

and, for a positive integer k.

(5) $B^{k-1}C_1^{2k-1}U = O(r^{4k-3})$ *or* $B^{1/2-1/2k}C_1^{1-1/2k}U^{1/2k} = O(r^{2-3/2k})$.

Then

$$\int_a^b dx \int_\alpha^\beta e^{2\pi i f(x,y)} dy = O\left(\frac{1}{r}\right)$$

SProof We divide D into three regions, namely

D_1: $f_x \geqslant B^{1/2}$

D_2: $0 \leqslant f_x < B^{1/2}$

D_3: $f_x < 0$

ometimes we want to redivide D_1 into subregions. We denote by D_{11} the part of D_1 lying between the curves

---

① Proc. London Math. Soc. (2) vol. 1935,38: 96-115.

② The letters B,r,C and C_1 are used to denote positive constants.

$$f_y - f_x \frac{f_{xy}}{f_{xx}} = \pm \frac{r}{B^{1/2}}$$

and by D_{12} the remainder of D_1. Similarly we may divide D_2 into D_{21} and D_{22}.

1) Consider, first, D_1. Integration by parts gives

$$\iint_{D_1} e^{2\pi i f(x,y)} dxdy = \int \left[\frac{e^{2\pi i f(x,y)}}{2\pi i f_x} \right]_{\chi(y)}^{\omega(y)} dy + \frac{1}{2\pi i} \iint_{D_1} \frac{f_{xx}}{f_x^2} e^{2\pi i f(x,y)} dxdy = I_1 + I_2 \tag{2.1}$$

say, where $x = \omega(y)$ and $x = \chi(y)$ are boundaries of D_1.

① To estimate I_1, we conider, for example,

$$\int \frac{e^{2\pi i f(\chi(y),y)}}{2\pi i f_x(\chi(y),y)} dy$$

The function $\chi(y)$ is either the solution of $f_x = B^{1/2}$ or it is a constant.

In the former case we have

$$\frac{d}{dy} f(\chi(y),y) = f_y - f_x \frac{f_{xy}}{f_{xx}} = v$$

say. Hence

$$\int_{|v| \geqslant r/B^{1/2}} e^{2\pi i f(\chi(y),y)} dy = \int_{|v| \geqslant r/B^{1/2}} \frac{e^{2\pi i u} du}{v} = O\left(\frac{B^{1/2}}{r}\right)$$

and

$$\int_{|v| \geqslant r/B^{1/2}} \frac{e^{2\pi i f(\chi(y),y)} dy}{2\pi i f_x(\chi(y),y)} = O\left(\frac{1}{B^{1/2}} \frac{B^{1/2}}{r}\right) = O\left(\frac{1}{r}\right)$$

On the other hand,

$$\int_{|v| < r/B^{1/2}} \frac{e^{2\pi i f(\chi(y),y)}}{2\pi i f_x(\chi(y),y)} dy = O\left(\frac{1}{B^{1/2}} \int_{-r/B^{1/2}}^{r/B^{1/2}} \left|\frac{dy}{dv}\right| dv\right)$$

Here $f_x = B^{1/2}$, so

$$\frac{dv}{dy} = \frac{1}{f_{xx}} \left[f_{xx} f_{yy} - f_{xy}^2 - f_x \frac{f_{xx}^2 f_{xyy} - 2 f_{xx} f_{xy} f_{xxy} + f_{xy}^2 f_{xxx}}{f_{xx}^2} \right]$$

and, by (1), (2) and (4)

$$\left|\frac{dv}{dy}\right| > A \frac{r^2 - B^{1/2} C_1}{B} > A \frac{r^2}{B} \tag{2.2}$$

Hence

$$\int_{|v| < r/B^{1/2}} \frac{e^{2\pi i f(\chi(y),y)}}{2\pi i f_x(\chi(y),y)} dy = O\left(\frac{1}{B^{1/2}} \frac{r}{B^{1/2}} \frac{B}{r^2}\right) = O\left(\frac{1}{r}\right)$$

Secondly, if $\chi(y) = a$, a constant,

$$\int \frac{e^{2\pi i f(\chi(y),y)}}{2\pi i f_x(\chi(y),y)} dy = \int \frac{e^{2\pi i f(a,y)}}{2\pi i f_x(\chi(y),y)} dy$$

By (1) and a well known formula concerning exponential integrals①, this is

$$O\left(\frac{1}{B^{1/2}}\cdot\frac{1}{(r^2B^{-1})^{1/2}}\right)=O\left(\frac{1}{r}\right)$$

② Now consider I_2. We have

$$(2\pi i)^2 I_2=\int\left[\frac{f_{xx}}{f_x^3}e^{2\pi i f(x,y)}\right]_{\chi(y)}^{\omega(y)}dy-\int_{dy}\int\frac{f_{xxx}}{f_x^3}e^{2\pi i f(x,y)}dx+$$

$$3\iint\frac{f_{xx}^2}{f_x^4}e^{2\pi i f(x,y)}dxdy=I'_1+I'_2+I'_3$$

say. The first integral can be treated as I_1. So

$$I'_1=O(1/r)$$

We have

$$I'_2=\iint_{D_{12}}\frac{f_{xxx}}{f_x^3}e^{2\pi i f(x,y)}dxdy+\iint_{D_{11}}\frac{f_{xxx}}{f_x^3}e^{2\pi i f(x,y)}dxdy=$$

$$I'_{22}+I'_{21}$$

say. Let $x=\phi(y)\phi(y,u)$ be the solution of $f_x=u$. Then

$$\frac{\partial}{\partial y}f(\phi(y),y)=f_y-f_x\frac{f_{xy}}{f_{xx}}$$

In D_{12}, the absolute value of this expression is not less than $r/B^{1/2}$. Hence

$$I'_{22}=\int dy\int\frac{f_{xxx}}{f_x^3}e^{2\pi i f(x,y)}dx=\int dy\int\frac{f_{xxx}}{f_{xx}}e^{2\pi i f(x,y)}\frac{du}{u^3}=$$

$$\int\frac{du}{u^3}\int\frac{f_{xxx}}{f_{xx}}e^{2\pi i f(\phi(y,u),y)}dy=\int_{B^{1/2}}\frac{C}{B}O\left(\frac{B^{1/2}}{r}\right)\frac{du}{u^3}=$$

$$O\left(\frac{C}{rB^{3/2}}\right)=O\left(\frac{1}{r}\right)$$

by (3).

To estimate I'_{21}, we put $u=f_x$ and $v=f_y-f_xf_{xy}/f_{xx}$. Then

$$\frac{\partial(u,v)}{\partial(x,y)}=f_{xx}f_{yy}-f_{xy}^2-\frac{f_x}{f_{xx}^2}(f_{xx}^2f_{xyy}-2f_{xx}f_{xy}f_{xxy}+f_{xy}^2f_{xxx})\qquad(2.3)$$

The absolute value of this expression is greater than Ar^2 if

$$|f_x|<r^2C_1^{-1}/2$$

Denote by D'_{11} the part of D_{11} in which the inequality holds and by D''_{11} the remainder of D_{11}. Then

---

① If $f(x)$ is a real differentiable function with $|f''(x)|>\lambda$ in (c,d) then $\int_c^d e^{2\pi i j(x)}dx=O(1/\lambda^{1/2})$.

$$\left|\iint_{D'_{11}} \frac{f_{xxx}}{f_x^3} e^{2\pi i f(x,y)} dxdy\right| < AC\iint \frac{dxdy}{f_x^3} = AC\int_{B^{1/2}} \frac{du}{u^3}\int^{r/B^{1/2}} \frac{dv}{|\partial(u,v)/\partial(x,y)|} \leqslant$$

$$AC\frac{1}{(B^{1/2})^2}\cdot\frac{r}{B^{1/2}}\cdot\frac{1}{r^2} = \frac{AC}{B^{3/2}}\cdot\frac{1}{r} = O\left(\frac{1}{r}\right)$$

by (3). Also

$$\left|\iint_{D''_{11}} \frac{f_{xxx}}{f_x^3} e^{2\pi i f(x,y)} dxdy\right| < AC\iint \frac{dxdy}{f_x^3} = AC\int dy\int \frac{du}{|f_{xx}|u^3} =$$

$$O\left(\frac{C}{B}\cdot\frac{U}{(r^2C_1^{-1})^2}\right) = O\left(\frac{1}{r}\cdot\frac{CUr}{B^2}\cdot\frac{BC_1^2}{r^4}\right) = O\left(\frac{1}{r}\right)$$

by (3) and (4). Hence I'_{21} is also $O(1/r)$. Thus $I'_2 = O(1/r)$. It follows that

$$(2\pi i)^2 I_2 = O\left(\frac{1}{r}\right) + 3\iint_{D_1} \frac{f_{xx}^2}{f_x^4} e^{2\pi i f(x,y)} dxdy$$

Repeating this argument we find

$$I_2 = O\left(\frac{1}{r}\right) + O\left(\iint_{D_1} \frac{f_{xx}^k}{f_x^{2k}} e^{2\pi i f(x,y)} dxdy\right)$$

Denote the last double integral by J, then

$$J = \iint_{D_{12}} + \iint_{D_{11}} = J_2 + J_1$$

say. We have, as before①

$$I_2 = \int_{B^{1/2}} \frac{du}{u^{2k}}\int f_{xx}^{k-1} e^{2\pi i f(x,y)} dy = \int_{B^{1/2}} O\left(\frac{B^{1/2}}{r}\right)\cdot B^{k-1}\frac{du}{u^{2k}} =$$

$$O\left(\frac{1}{r}\frac{B^{k-1}B^{1/2}}{B^{(2k-1)/2}}\right) = O\left(\frac{1}{r}\right)$$

To estimate J_1, we write

$$J_1 = \iint_{D'_{11}} + \iint_{D''_{11}} = J'_1 + J''_1$$

As before②, by (1) and (2.3)

$$|J'_1| < AB^k\int_{B^{1/2}} \frac{du}{u^{2k}}\int^{r/B^{1/2}} \frac{dv}{|\partial(u,v)/\partial(x,y)|} =$$

$$O\left(B^k\frac{1}{B^{(2k-1)/2}}\cdot\frac{r}{B^{1/2}}\cdot\frac{1}{r^2}\right) = O\left(\frac{1}{r}\right)$$

$$|J''_1| < AB^{k-1}\iint_{D''_{11}} \frac{|f_{xx}|\,dxdy}{f_x^{2k}} < AB^{k-1}\iint \frac{dudy}{u^{2k}} =$$

---

① See the estimation of I'_{22} above (2.3).

② See the estimation of I'_{21}.

$$O\Big(\frac{B^{k-1}U}{(r^2C^{-1})^{2k-1}}\Big) = O\Big(\frac{1}{r}\frac{B^{k-1}C_1^{2k-1}U}{r^{4k-3}}\Big) = O\Big(\frac{1}{r}\Big)$$

by (5). Combining these results we find that J is $O(1/r)$. Hence I_2 is $O(1/r)$

2) Now consider the integral over D_2. Putting $f_x = u$, we have

$$\iint_{D_{22}} e^{2\pi i f(x,y)} \mathrm{d}x\mathrm{d}y = \int_0^{B^{1/2}} \mathrm{d}u \int \frac{e^{2\pi i f(x,y)}}{f_{xx}} \mathrm{d}y$$

As in (1.2), we have $\partial f(\phi(y,u),y)/\partial y \geqslant r/B^{1/2}$. Hence the inner integral is $O((1/B)\cdot(B^{1/2}/r)) = O(1/rB^{1/2})$. The result follows for this part.

Finally, by (2) and (4) we have, using (3) and the fact that $|f_x| < B^{1/2}$,

$$\Big|\iint_{D_{21}} e^{2\pi i f(x,y)} \mathrm{d}x\mathrm{d}y\Big| \leqslant \iint_{D_{21}} \mathrm{d}x\mathrm{d}y = \int_0^{B^{1/2}}\int_0^{r/B^{1/2}} \Big|\frac{\partial(x,y)}{\partial(u,v)}\Big| \mathrm{d}u\mathrm{d}v =$$

$$\int_0^{B^{1/2}}\int_0^{r/B^{1/2}} O\Big(\frac{1}{r^2-(B^{1/2}/B^2)\cdot C_1B^2}\Big)\mathrm{d}u\mathrm{d}v =$$

$$O\Big(B^{1/2}\cdot\frac{r}{B^{1/2}}\cdot\frac{1}{r^2}\Big) = O\Big(\frac{1}{r}\Big)$$

3) We have established the stated for $D_1 + D_2$, that is, the region $f_x \geqslant 0$. A similar proof can be applied to D_3.

Lemma 8 *Let D' be the part of D cut off by a curve (or several curves) whose equation is of the form $x = g(y)$ where $g(y)$ is an algebraic function satisfying*

(6) $\quad |Uf_{xx}g''(y)| < K_r$,

where K is a sufficiently small constant. Then if we replace the condition (1) in Lemma 7 by

(1′) $\quad B \leqslant |f_{xx}| < AB,\ |f_{xy}| < AB,\ |f_{yy}| < AB,\ f_{xx}f_{xy} > 0$

we have

$$\iint_{D'} e^{2\pi i f(x,y)} \mathrm{d}x\mathrm{d}y = O\Big(\frac{1+|\log B|+|\log U|}{r}\Big)$$

In particular, the curve may be a straight line $x = py + q$.

Proof If $|f_{yy}| \geqslant B/2$, the condition (1) holds if we replace B by $B/2$. Now suppose that $|f_{yy}| < B/2$. We put $x = \xi + \eta$, $y = \eta$. Then

$$\Big|\frac{\partial^2}{\partial\xi^2}f(x,y)\Big| = |f_{xx}| \geqslant B$$

$$\Big|\frac{\partial^2}{\partial\eta^2}f(x,y)\Big| = |f_{xx} + 2f_{xy} + f_{yy}| > \frac{B}{2}$$

Thus the condition (1) is restored. Conditions (2) and (3) remain true. So do (4) and (5) since the expression on the left-hand side of (4) is an invariant under our transformation. We may therefore assume that all these conditions are satisfied. We need only to consider integrals of the form

$$\int \frac{e^{2\pi i f(g(y),y)}}{f_x(g(y),y)}\mathrm{d}y \quad (|f_x| > B^{1/2})$$

We divide the interval of integration into three parts:

(1) $|f_x g'(y) + f_y| \geqslant r/B^{1/2}$.

(2) $|f_x g'(y) + f_y| < r/B^{1/2}$, $\quad |f_{xx} g'(y) + f_{xy}| \geqslant r/2$.

(3) $|f_x g'(y) + f_y| < r/B^{1/2}$, $\quad |f_{xx} g'(y) + f_{xy}| < r/2$.

In the first part,

$$\int \frac{e^{2\pi i f(g(y),y)}}{f_x(g(y),y)}\mathrm{d}y = \int \frac{e^{2\pi i \xi}\mathrm{d}\xi}{f_x(f_x g' + f_y)} = O\left(\frac{1}{r}\right)$$

In the second part,

$$\left|\int \frac{e^{2\pi i f(g(y),y)}}{f_x(g(y),y)}\mathrm{d}y\right| \leqslant \left|\int \frac{\mathrm{d}y}{f_x}\right| \leqslant \frac{2}{r}\left|\int \frac{f_{xx} g'(y) + f_{xy}}{f_x(g(y),y)}\mathrm{d}y\right| =$$

$$\frac{2}{r}\left|\left[\log f_x(g(y),y)\right]\right| = O\left(\frac{1+|\log B|+|\log U|}{r}\right)$$

In the third part, we put $u = f_x g' + f_y$, then

$$\frac{\mathrm{d}u}{\mathrm{d}y} = f_{xx} g'^2 + 2 f_{xy} g' + f_{yy} + f_x g'' =$$

$$f_{xx}^{-1}\left[(g' f_{xx} + f_{xy})^2 + f_{xx} f_{yy} - f_{xy}^2 + f_{xx} f_x g''\right]$$

If $|f_x| < Ur$, the theorem is true. If otherwise,

$$\left|\frac{\mathrm{d}u}{\mathrm{d}y}\right| > A\frac{r^2}{B}$$

Hence

$$\int \frac{f^{2\pi i f(g(y),y)}}{f_x(g(y),y)}\mathrm{d}y = O\left(\frac{1}{B^{1/2}}\int^{r/B^{1/2}}\left|\frac{\mathrm{d}y}{\mathrm{d}u}\right|\mathrm{d}u\right) = O\left(\frac{r}{(B^{1/2})^2}\cdot\frac{B}{r^2}\right) = O\left(\frac{1}{r}\right)$$

The lemma follows.

3. Lemmas concerning network

Suppose there is a network of which each cell is a rectangle S_0 of area U and with sides of lengths l and m. Suppose S is a rectangle with sides parallel to lines in the network and of lengths a and b respectively. Suppose L_1 and L_2 are parallel lines which bound with side of S a strip of area A. Let L be either of them and let the area of S under L be A_L.

Lemma 9 *The number of rectangles S_0 lying partially or entirely within S and entirely under L is*

$$N_L = \frac{A_L}{U} + O\left(\frac{a}{l} + \frac{b}{m} + 1\right)$$

The number of rectangles S_0 lying partially or entirely within S and partially or entirely under L is

$$N'_L = \frac{A_L}{U} + O\left(\frac{a}{l} + \frac{b}{m} + 1\right)$$

Proof (1) Without loss of generality, we may assume that the sides of S coincide with lines belonging to the network. For otherwise we may replace S by one with this kind of sides so that the variations of A_L and N_L are respectively

$$O\left[\left(\frac{a}{l} + \frac{b}{m} + 1\right)U\right] \text{ and } O\left[\frac{a}{l} + \frac{b}{m} + 1\right]$$

Without loss of generality we may assume that S_0 is a unit square so that $U = l = m = 1$. For, only the ratios of areas and lengths really matter. Without loss of generality we may also assume that L is of positive slope.

Now consider all the vertical lines of the network which are not entirely outside S. Let the line nearest the left-hand side of S be l_1 and the next l_2, and so on. Let the first of them which meets L inside S be l_k. Let the points of intersection of L with l_k, $l_{k+1} \cdots$ be P_k, P_{k+1}, $\cdots$.

We draw from $P_i (i = k, k+1, \cdots)$ a horizontal line toward the right until it reaches l_{i+1}. We denote the part of A_L which is below these horizontal linesegments by A_L^B and the remaining part by A_L^A. Then the first part of the lemma follows from the fact that $A_L^A = O(b)$, $0 \leqslant A_L^B - N_L = O(a)$.

(2) The second part of the lemma can be proved by drawing horizontal lines toward the left instead of the right.

Lemma 10 *The number of rectangles S_0 lying partially or entirely between L_1 and L_2 and partially or entirely within S is*

$$N = \frac{A}{U} + O\left(\frac{a}{l} + \frac{b}{m} + 1\right)$$

Proof We have $N = N_{L_1} - N'_{L_2}$ and the lemma follows from Lemma 9.

4. We have to consider sums of the form

$$S_1 = \sum_{n=a}^{d} n^{-it} = \sum_{n=a}^{b} \mathrm{e}^{-it\log n}, \quad a < b \leqslant 2a \tag{4.1}$$

By Lemma 2,

$$|S_1| \leqslant \frac{1}{\rho}\left\{4(b-a)^2\rho + 2(b-a)\left|\sum_{r=1}^{\rho-1}(\rho - r)\sum_{m=a}^{b-r} \mathrm{e}^{-it\log(m+r)/m}\right|\right\}^{1/2} \tag{4.2}$$

provided that

(C_1) $$0 < \rho < b - a$$

Let

$$S_2 = \sum_{r=1}^{\rho-1} (\rho - 1) \sum_{m=a}^{b-r} e^{-it\log(m+r)/m} \tag{4.3}$$

then, by Lemma 1,

$$S_2 = e^{-\pi i/4} \sum_{r=1}^{\rho-r} (\rho - r) \sum_{\alpha \leqslant v \leqslant \beta} \frac{e^{2\pi i \phi(r,v)}}{| f''(m_v) |^{1/2}} + O(\alpha^{3/2} t^{-1/2} \rho^{3/2}) + O(\rho^2 \log t) + O(\alpha^{-2/5} t^{2/5} \rho^{12/5}) \tag{4.4}$$

where

$$\begin{aligned} f(y) &= f(r,y) = -\frac{t}{2\pi} \log \frac{y+r}{y} \\ f'(m_v) &= v, \ \phi(v) = f(m_v) - v m_v \\ \alpha &= f'(b-r), \ \beta = f'(\alpha), \ b \leqslant 2a \end{aligned} \tag{4.5}$$

Let

(C_2) $$b = O(t^{1/2})$$

then

$$v = f'(m_v) = \frac{tr}{2\pi m_v (m_v + r)} > \frac{Atr}{m_v^2} > Ar$$

and

$$\rho = O(\beta) \tag{4.6}$$

Let

$$S_3 = \sum_{x=R+1}^{R'} \sum_{y=N+1}^{N'} e^{2\pi i \phi(x,y)}, \quad R < R' \leqslant 2R < \rho, \quad N < N' \leqslant 2N \leqslant \beta$$

Applying Lemma 5 twice and Lemma 4 once, we have

$$S_3 = O\left(\frac{RN}{\lambda^{1/2}}\right) + O\left(\frac{(RN)^{7/8}}{\lambda^{3/2}} \left\{ \sum_{y_1=1}^{\lambda-1} \left[\sum_{y_2=1}^{\lambda^2-1} \left(\sum_{x_3=1}^{\lambda'^2-1} \sum_{y_3=0}^{\lambda''^2-1} | S_4 | \right)^{1/2} \right]^{1/2} \right\}^{1/2} \right) + O\left(\frac{(RN)^{7/8}}{\lambda^{3/2}} \left\{ \sum_{y_1=1}^{\lambda-1} \left[\sum_{y_2=1}^{\lambda^2-1} \left(\sum_{x_3=1}^{\lambda'^2-1} \sum_{y_3=1}^{\lambda''^2-1} | S'_4 | \right)^{1/2} \right]^{1/2} \right\}^{1/2} \right) \tag{4.7}$$

where

$$S_4 = \sum_{x=R+1}^{R''} \sum_{y=N+1}^{N''} e^{2\pi i \psi(x,y)}, \quad R'' = R' - x_3, \quad N'' = N' - y_1 - y_2 - y_3 \tag{4.8}$$

with

$$\psi(x,y) = \iiint_0^1 \frac{\partial^3}{\partial t_1 \partial t_2 \partial t_3} \phi(x + x_3 t_3, y + y_1 t_1 + y_2 t_2 + y_3 t_3) \, dt_1 dt_2 dt_3 \tag{4.9}$$

and S'_4 is a similar sum. Here we assumed that

(C_3) $$1 \leqslant \lambda'^2 \leqslant R, \quad \lambda'^2 \leqslant \lambda''^2 \leqslant N, \quad \lambda'\lambda'' = \lambda^2$$

Since S'_4 can be estimated as S_4, we consider the latter only.

5. In this section we shall reduce $\psi(x,y)$ to a convenient form. We have

$$\psi(x,y) = y_1 y_2 \iiint_0^1 (x_3 \phi^*_{xy^2} + y_3 \phi^*_{y^3})\, dt_1 dt_2 dt_3 \tag{5.1}$$

where

$$\phi^*_{xy^2} = \frac{\partial^3}{\partial x^* \partial y^{*2}} \phi(x^*, y^*), \qquad \phi^*_{y^3} = \frac{\partial^3}{\partial y^{*3}} \phi(x^*, y^*)$$
$$x^* = x + x_3 t_3, \qquad y^* = y + y_1 t_1 + y_2 t_2 + y_3 t_3 \tag{5.2}$$

We have

$$f_x(x,y) = -\frac{t}{2\pi} \frac{1}{x+y}, \quad f_y(x,y) = -\frac{t}{2\pi}\left(\frac{1}{x+y} - \frac{1}{y}\right)$$

From $f_y(x, m_y(x)) = y$ we find, by choosing the proper sign,

$$m_y(x) = -\frac{x}{2} + \frac{x}{2}\left(1 + \frac{2t}{\pi x y}\right)^{1/2} \tag{5.3}$$

Since

$$\phi_x(x,y) = f_x(x, m_y(x)) + f_y(x, m_y(x)) \frac{\partial}{\partial x} m_y(x) - y \frac{\partial}{\partial x} m_y(x) = f_x(x, m_y(x))$$

$$\phi_y(x,y) = f_y(x, m_y(x)) \frac{\partial}{\partial y} m_y(x) - y \frac{\partial}{\partial y} m_y(x) - m_y(x) = -m_y(x))$$

we have, by (5.3)

$$\phi_x(x,y) = y\left(\frac{1}{2} - \frac{1}{2}\left(1 + \frac{2t}{\pi x y}\right)^{1/2}\right) =$$
$$\frac{y}{2} - \frac{1}{2}\left(\frac{2t}{\pi}\right)^{1/2} \frac{y^{1/2}}{x^{1/2}}\left[1 + \frac{1}{2}\frac{\pi x y}{2t} - \frac{1}{8}\left(\frac{\pi x y}{2t}\right)^2 + \cdots\right]$$
$$\phi_y(x,y) = x\left(\frac{1}{2} - \frac{1}{2}\left(1 + \frac{2t}{\pi x y}\right)^{1/2}\right) =$$
$$\frac{x}{2} - \frac{1}{2}\left(\frac{2t}{\pi}\right)^{1/2} \frac{x^{1/2}}{y^{1/2}}\left[1 + \frac{1}{2}\frac{\pi x y}{2t} - \frac{1}{8}\left(\frac{\pi x y}{2t}\right)^2 + \cdots\right] \tag{5.4}$$

Differentiation gives

$$\phi_{xyy}(x,y) = \frac{1}{8}\left(\frac{2t}{\pi}\right)^{1/2} x^{-1/2} y^{-3/2}\left[1 - \frac{3}{2}\frac{\pi x y}{2t} + \frac{15}{8}\left(\frac{\pi x y}{2t}\right)^2 + \cdots\right]$$
$$\phi_{yyy}(x,y) = -\frac{3}{8}\left(\frac{2t}{\pi}\right)^{1/2} x^{1/2} y^{-5/2}\left[1 - \frac{1}{6}\frac{\pi x y}{2t} - \frac{1}{8}\left(\frac{\pi x y}{2t}\right)^2 + \cdots\right] \tag{5.5}$$

Hence

$$\varphi(x,y) = \frac{1}{8}\left(\frac{2t}{\pi}\right)^{1/2} y_1 y_2 \iiint_0^1 x^{*-1/2} y^{*-5/2} (x_3, y^* - 3y_3 x^*)\, dt_1 dt_2 dt_3 - \frac{1}{16}\left(\frac{2t}{\pi}\right)^{1/2} y_1 y_2 \times \iiint_0^1 \frac{\pi x^* y^*}{2t} x^{*-1/2} y^{*-5/2} (3x_3 y^* - y_3 x^*)\, dt_1 dt_2 dt_3 + \cdots \tag{5.6}$$

6. In this section we consider the Hessian of $\psi(x,y)$, that is,

$$H(x,y) = \psi_{xx}\psi_{yy} - \psi_{xy}^2$$

We denote the first term on the right-hand side of (5.6) by $\psi^0(x,y)$ and write $\Phi(x,y) = x^{-1/2} \times y^{-5/2}(x_3 y - 3y_3 x)$. Then

$$\begin{aligned} \Phi_{xx}(x,y) &= 3x^{-5/2} y^{-5/2}(x_3 y + y_3 x)/4 \\ \Phi_{xy}(x,y) &= 3x^{-3/2} y^{-7/2}(x_3 y + 5y_3 x)/4 \\ \Phi_{yy}(x,y) &= 3x^{-1/2} y^{-9/2}(5x_3 y - 35y_3 x)/4 \end{aligned} \tag{6.1}$$

From this it is obvious that, for $R + 1 \leqslant x < 2R$, $N + 1 \leqslant y < 2N$,

$$\Phi_{xx} = O(R^{-5/2}N^{-5/2}Q),\ \Phi_{xy} = O(R^{-3/2}N^{-7/2}Q),\ \Phi_{yy} = O(R^{-1/2}N^{-9/2}Q) \tag{6.2}$$

where

$$Q = x_3 N + (y_3 + 1)R \tag{6.3}$$

Hence

$$\Phi_{x^4} = O(R^{-9/2}N^{-5/2}Q),\ \Phi_{x^3y} = O(R^{-7/2}N^{-7/2}Q),\ \Phi_{x^2y^2} = O(R^{-5/2}N^{-9/2}Q) \tag{6.4}$$

and so on.

Using the expansion

$$\begin{aligned} \Phi(x^*, y^*) = {} & \Phi(x,y) + x_3 t_3 \Phi_x(x,y) + (y_1 t_1 + y_2 t_2 + y_3 t_3)\Phi_y(x,y) + \\ & 2^{-1}[x_3^2 t_3^2 \Phi_{xx}(x,y) + 2x_3 t_3 (y_1 t_1 + y_2 t_2 + y_3 t_3)\Phi_{xy}(x,y) + \\ & (y_1 t_1 + y_2 t_2 + y_3 t_3)^2 \Phi_{yy}(x,y)] + \cdots \end{aligned}$$

we find that

$$\begin{aligned} \psi^0(x,y) = {} & \frac{1}{8}\left(\frac{2t}{\pi}\right)^{1/2} y_1 y_2 \Big[\Phi(x,y) + \frac{x_3}{2}\Phi_x(x,y) + \frac{y_1 + y_2 + y_3}{2}\Phi_y(x,y) + \\ & \frac{1}{2}\Big\{\frac{x_3^2}{3}\Phi_{xx}(x,y) + 2x_3\left(\frac{y_1 + y_2}{4} + \frac{y_3}{3}\right)\Phi_{xy}(x,y) + \\ & \left(\frac{y_1^2 + y_2^2 + y_3^2}{3} + \frac{y_1 y_2 + y_2 y_3 + y_3 y_1}{2}\right)\Phi_{yy}(x,y)\Big\} + \cdots\Big] = \\ & \frac{1}{8}\left(\frac{2t}{\pi}\right)^{1/2} y_1 y_2 \Big[\Phi(x', y') + \frac{1}{2}\Big\{\frac{x_3^2}{12}\Phi_{xx}(x,y) + \end{aligned}$$

$$\frac{x_3y_3}{6}\Phi_{xy}(x,y)+\frac{y_1^2+y_2^2+y_3^2}{12}\psi_{yy}(x,y)\Big\}+\cdots\Big]$$

where $x'=x+x_3/2$, $y'=y+(y_1+y_2+y_3)/2$.

Hence, by (6.4) and (C_3),

$$\psi_{xx}^0=\frac{1}{8}\left(\frac{2t}{\pi}\right)^{1/2}y_1y_2\left[\Phi_{xx}(x',y')+O\left(R^{-5/2}N^{-5/2}Q\left(\frac{Q_0}{RN}\right)^2\right)\right]$$

$$\psi_{xy}^0=\frac{1}{8}\left(\frac{2t}{\pi}\right)^{1/2}y_1y_2\left[\Phi_{xy}(x',y')+O\left(R^{-3/2}N^{-7/2}Q\left(\frac{Q_0}{RN}\right)^2\right)\right]$$

$$\psi_{yy}^0=\frac{1}{8}\left(\frac{2t}{\pi}\right)^{1/2}y_1y_2\left[\Phi_{yy}(x',y')+O\left(R^{-1/2}N^{-9/2}Q\left(\frac{Q_0}{RN}\right)^2\right)\right]$$

since $\lambda'^2/R+\lambda''^2/N=O(Q_0/RN)$ where $Q_0=\lambda'^2N+\lambda''^2R$.

Hence, by (5.6),

$$\begin{aligned}\psi_{xx}&=\frac{1}{8}\left(\frac{2t}{\pi}\right)^{1/2}y_1y_2\Phi_{xx}(x',y')+O\left(t^{1/2}y_1y_2R^{-5/2}N^{-5/2}Q\left(\frac{Q_0}{RN}\right)^2\right)+\\&\quad O(t^{-1/2}y_1y_2R^{-3/2}N^{-3/2}Q)\\\psi_{xy}&=\frac{1}{8}\left(\frac{2t}{\pi}\right)^{1/2}y_1y_2\Phi_{xy}(x',y')+O\left(t^{1/2}y_1y_2R^{-3/2}N^{-7/2}Q\left(\frac{Q_0}{RN}\right)^2\right)+\\&\quad O(t^{-1/2}y_1y_2R^{-1/2}N^{-5/2}Q)\\\psi_{yy}&=\frac{1}{8}\left(\frac{2t}{\pi}\right)^{1/2}y_1y_2\Phi_{yy}(x',y')+O\left(t^{1/2}y_1y_2R^{-1/2}N^{-9/2}Q\left(\frac{Q_0}{RN}\right)^2\right)+\\&\quad O(t^{-1/2}y_1y_2R^{-1/2}N^{-7/2}Q)\end{aligned}\tag{6.5}$$

We may omit the second error term from each of these relations provided that

(C_4) $$R^3N=O(t)$$

Hence, by (6.2) and (C_3),

$$\psi_{xx}=O(t^{-1/2}y_1y_2R^{-5/2}N^{-5/2}Q),\ \psi_{xy}=O(t^{1/2}y_1y_2R^{-3/2}N^{-7/2}Q)$$
$$\psi_{yy}=O(t^{1/2}y_1y_2R^{-1/2}N^{-9/2}Q)\tag{6.6}$$

Further, by (6.1),

$$\psi_{xx}\psi_{yy}-\psi_{xy}^2=\frac{9t}{128\pi}y_1^2y_2^2x'^{-3}y'^{-7}(x_3^2y'^2-10x_3y_3x'y'-15y_3^2x'^2)+$$
$$O\left(ty_1^2y_2^2R^{-3}N^{-7}Q^2\left(\frac{Q_0}{RN}\right)^2\right)$$

or

$$H(x,y)=\left(\frac{9t}{128\pi}\right)y_1^2y_2^2x'^{-3}y'^{-7}[x_3y'+(2(10)^{1/2}-5)x_3y']\times$$
$$[x_3y'-(2(10)^{1/2}+5)y_3x']+$$

$$O\left(ty_1^2y_2^2R^{-3}N^{-7}Q^2\left(\frac{Q_0}{RN}\right)^2\right) \tag{6.7}$$

Remarks The inequalities (6.5) to (6.7) obviously remain true if we replace $\psi(x,y)$ by a partial sum containing only the first $n(\geqslant 1)$ terms on the right-hand side of (5.6). Further, the general term is of the form

$$t^{1/2}y_1y_2\iiint_0^1\left(\frac{x^*y^*}{t}\right)^n x^{*-1/2}y^{*-5/2}(c_1x_3y^* + c_2y_3x^*)\,dt_1dt_2dt_3 =$$

$$t^{1/2}y_1y_2\iiint_0^1\left(\frac{xy}{t}\right)^n x^{-1/2}y^{-5/2}\left(1+\frac{x_3t}{x}\right)^{n-1/2} \times$$

$$\left(1+\frac{y_1t_1+y_2t_2+y_3t_3}{y}\right)^{n-5/2} \times$$

$$\left[c_1x_3y\left(1+\frac{y_1t_1+y_2t_2+y_3t_3}{y}\right)+c_2y_3x\left(1+\frac{x_3t_3}{x}\right)\right]dt_1dt_2dt_3 =$$

$$t^{1/2}y_1y_2x^{1/2}y^{3/2}\left[P(x^{-1},y^{-1})+O\left\{\left(\frac{x_3}{x}\right)^k\right\}+O\left\{\left(\frac{y_1+y_2+y_3}{y}\right)^h\right\}\right]$$

where $P(x^{-1},y^{-1})$ is a polynomial in x^{-1},y^{-1} (depending on y_1,y_3,y_3,x_3 and h). Now suppose that

(C_5) $\qquad \lambda'^2 < Rt^{-\varepsilon}, \quad \lambda''^2 < Nt^{-\varepsilon}, \quad (\varepsilon > 0)$①

When h is large enough, the inequalities (6.5) to (6.7) remain true if we neglect the terms which are

$$O\left[\left(\frac{x_3}{x}\right)^h\right]+O\left[\left(\frac{y_1+y_2+y_3}{y}\right)^h\right]$$

from each term on the right-hand side of (5.6). So we can write $\psi(x,y) = \psi_1(x,y)+\psi_2(x,y)$ where $\psi_1(x,y)$ is an algebraic function satisfying (6.5) to (6.7) and

$$\psi_2(x,y) = t^{1/2}y_1y_2x^{1/2}y^{-3/2}\left[O\left\{\left(\frac{x_3}{x}\right)^h\right\}+O\left\{\left(\frac{y_1+y_2+y_3}{y}\right)^h\right\}\right]$$

which can be made as small as we please by taking h sufficiently large. In fact, we can choose h so that, for a given positive δ, $\psi_2(x,y) = O(t^{-\varepsilon})$.

7. Now return to the sum S_4. Let

$$l_1 = c\frac{R^{5/2}N^{5/2}}{t^{1/2}y_1y_2Q}, \quad l_2 = c\frac{R^{3/2}N^{7/2}}{t^{1/2}y_1y_2Q} \tag{7.1}$$

① We use ε to denote a small positive number, which, like the symbol A, may or may not keep the same value.

where c is some positive constant.

By (4.6) we have

$$R = O(N), \quad l_1 = O(l_2) \tag{7.2}$$

We divide the region of summation of S_4, that is,

$$R+1 \leqslant x \leqslant R'', \quad N+1 \leqslant y \leqslant N''$$

into rectangles with sides parallel to the axes and of lengths l_1 and l_2 and parts of such rectangles. We may enumerate these subregions and denote them by Δ_p, $p=1,2,\cdots$. If c is small enough, the variations of ψ_x and ψ_y in each Δ_p will be less than 1/2. Hence to each Δ_p correspond integers μ and v such that if $\psi_p(x,y)=\varphi(x,y)-\mu x-vy$ the absolute value of the first derivatives of ψ_p is not greater than 3/4. So for each Δ_p we have, by Lemma 6,

$$\sum_{\Delta_p}\sum e^{2\pi i\psi(x,y)} = \sum_{\Delta_p}\sum e^{2\pi i\psi_p(x,y)} = \iint_{\Delta_p} e^{2\pi i\psi_p(x,y)}\mathrm{d}x\mathrm{d}y + O(l_2) \tag{7.3}$$

provided that

$$(\mathrm{C}_6) \qquad l_2 \geqslant 1$$

Hence

$$S_4 = \sum_p \left\{\iint_{\Delta_p} e^{2\pi i\psi_p(x,y)}\mathrm{d}x\mathrm{d}y + O(l_2)\right\}$$

The system of parallel lines

$$|x_3y-(2(10)^{1/2}+5)y_3x| = 4^m\xi, \quad m=0,1,\cdots,$$

divides each Δ_p into strips. Hence

$$S_4 = \sum_p \iint_{\Delta'_p} e^{2\pi i\psi_p(x,y)}\mathrm{d}x\mathrm{d}y + \sum_p\sum_{m=0}^{L-1}\iint_{\Delta_{p,m}} e^{2\pi i\psi_p(x,y)}\mathrm{d}x\mathrm{d}y +$$
$$\sum_p \iint_{\Delta''_p} e^{2\pi i\psi_p(x,y)}\mathrm{d}x\mathrm{d}y + \sum_p O(l_2) = J_0+J_1+J_2+J_3 \tag{7.4}$$

say, where

$$L = \left[\frac{\log(\xi^{-1}Q)}{\log 4}\right]$$

$\Delta_{p,m}$ denotes the part of Δ_p for which

$$4^m\xi < |x_3y-(2(10)^{1/2}+5)y_3x| < 4^{m+1}\xi, \quad m=0,1,\cdots,L-1 \tag{7.5}$$

Δ'_p denotes the part for which

$$|x_3y-(2(10)^{1/2}+5)y_3x| < \xi \tag{7.6}$$

and Δ''_p denotes the part for which

$$|x_3y-(2(10)^{1/2}+5)y_3x| > 4^L\xi(>AQ) \tag{7.7}$$

Evidently

$$|J_0| \leqslant \sum_p \iint_{\Delta'} dxdy = \int_{R+1}^{R''}\int_{N+1}^{N''}_{|x_3y-(2(10)^{1/2}-5)y_3x|<\xi} dxdy = O\left(\frac{R\xi}{x_3}\right) \tag{7.8}$$

In the next section we shall prove, under certain conditions, that

$$\iint_{\Delta_{p,m}} e^{2\pi i\psi_p(x,y)} dxdy = O\left(\frac{R^{3/2}N^{7/2}\log t}{t^{1/2}y_1y_2Q^{1/2}\cdot 2^m\xi^{1/2}}\right)$$

$$(C_7) \qquad \iint_{\Delta'_p} e^{2\pi i\psi_p(x,y)} dxdy = O\left(\frac{R^{3/2}N^{7/2}\log t}{t^{1/2}y_1y_2Q}\right)$$

On assuming this,

$$J_1 = O\left(\sum_{m=0}^{L-1}\sum_p^{(m)} \frac{R^{3/2}N^{7/2}\log t}{t^{1/2}y_1y_2Q^{1/2}\cdot 2^m\xi^{1/2}}\right)$$

where (m) denotes that the sum runs over only those p for which Δ_p lie partially or entirely in the strip (7.5). By Lemma 10, the number of such Δ_p is

$$O\left(\frac{4^m\xi R}{x_3l_1l_2}\right) + O\left(\frac{R}{l_1} + \frac{N}{l_2} + 1\right) = O\left(\frac{4^m\xi t y_1^2y_2^2Q^2}{x_3R^3N^6}\right) + O\left(\frac{t^{1/2}y_1y_2Q}{R^{3/2}N^{5/2}} + 1\right)$$

Therefore

$$J_1 = O\left[\log t\sum_{m=0}^{L-1}\left\{\frac{2^m\xi^{1/2}t^{1/2}y_1y_2Q^{3/2}}{x_3R^{3/2}N^{5/2}} + \frac{Q^{1/2}N}{2^m\xi^{1/2}} + \frac{R^{3/2}N^{7/2}}{t^{1/2}y_1y_2Q^{1/2}\cdot 2^m\xi^{1/2}}\right\}\right] =$$

$$O\left[\log t\left\{\frac{t^{1/2}y_1y_2Q^2}{x_3R^{3/2}N^{5/2}} + \frac{Q^{1/2}N}{\xi^{1/2}} + \frac{R^{3/2}N^{7/2}}{t^{1/2}y_1y_2Q^{1/2}\xi^{1/2}}\right\}\right] \tag{7.9}$$

Similarly

$$J_2 = O\left[\left(\frac{R}{l_1}+1\right)\left(\frac{N}{l_2}+1\right)\frac{R^{3/2}N^{7/2}\log t}{t^{1/2}y_1y_2Q}\right] =$$

$$O\left[\log t\left\{\frac{t^{1/2}y_1y_2Q}{R^{3/2}N^{3/2}} + \frac{R^{3/2}N^{7/2}}{t^{1/2}y_1y_2Q}\right\}\right] \tag{7.10}$$

since $R/l_1 = N/l_2$ and $(x+1)^2 = O(x^2+1)$. Finally,

$$J_3 = O\left[\left(\frac{R}{l_1}+1\right)\left(\frac{N}{l_2}+1\right)l_2\right] = O\left(\frac{RN}{l_1} + l_2\right) =$$

$$O\left(\frac{t^{1/2}y_1y_2Q}{R^{3/2}N^{3/2}}\right) + O\left(\frac{R^{3/2}N^{7/2}}{t^{1/2}y_1y_2Q}\right) \tag{7.11}$$

From (7.8) to (7.11)

$$S_4 = O\left(\frac{R\xi}{x_3}\right) + O\left[\log t\left\{\frac{t^{1/2}y_1y_2Q^2}{x_3R^{3/2}N^{5/2}} + \frac{Q^{1/2}N}{\xi^{1/2}} + \frac{R^{3/2}N^{7/2}}{t^{1/2}y_1y_2Q^{1/2}\xi^{1/2}}\right\}\right]$$

since $\xi < Q$ and $Q \geqslant x_3N$, by (6.3).

If we put $R\xi/x_3 = (Q^{1/2}N/\xi^{1/2})\log t$, we shall get $\xi = ((x_3NQ^{1/2}/R)\log t)^{2/3}$. But we take the bigger value

$$\xi = A\frac{Q}{R^{2/3}}\left(\frac{\lambda^2\lambda''^2}{y_1y_2(y_3+1)}\right)^{1/2}\log^{2/3}t, \quad A > 1 \tag{7.12}$$

The value is certainly bigger by (6.3). The reason for doing so will be seen in the following sections. We have

$$S_4 = O\left[\frac{R^{1/3}Q}{x_3}\left(\frac{\lambda^3\lambda''^2}{y_1y_2(y_3+1)}\right)^{1/2}\log^{2/3}t\right] + O\left[\frac{t^{1/2}y_1y_2Q^2}{x_3R^{3/2}N^{5/2}}\log t\right] + O\left[\frac{R^{11/6}N^{7/2}}{t^{1/2}y_1y_2Q\log^{1/3}t}\right] \tag{7.13}$$

Remarks If (C_6) is not true, the second term is not less than $O(RN)$. Hence (7.13) remains true.

8. Proof of (C_7) under certain conditions

We consider, for example, the first relation in (C_7) only. By the remarks at the end of §6, we can write $\psi_p = \psi_{p,1} + \psi_{p,2}$ where $\psi_{p,1}$ satisfies (6.5) to (6.7) and $\psi_{p,2} = O(t^{-\delta})$ where δ can be made as large as we please. Hence

$$\iint_{\Delta_{p,m}} e^{2\pi i\psi_p(x,y)}\,dxdy = \iint_{\Delta_{p,m}} e^{2\pi i\psi_{p,1}(x,y)}\,dxdy + \sum_{j=1}^{\infty} O\left[\iint_{\Delta_{p,m}} \frac{|\psi_{p,2}(x,y)|^j}{j!}dxdy\right] = \iint_{\Delta_{p,m}} e^{2\pi i\psi_{p,1}(x,y)}\,dxdy + O\left(\frac{R^{3/2}N^{7/2}}{t^{1/2}y_1y_2Q^{1/2}\cdot 2^m\xi^{1/2}}\right)$$

Write $\psi_{p,1} = \psi^*$. We need only to examine the conditions of Lemma 8. Let

$$B = At^{1/2}y_1y_2R^{-5/2}N^{-5/2}Q$$

then

$$t^{1/2}y_1y_2R^{-5/2}N^{-5/2}Q\left(\frac{Q_0}{RN}\right)^2 = O(Bt^{-2\varepsilon})$$

by (C_5). By the remarks at the end of §6, ψ^* satisfies (6.5) to (6.7). Hence, by (6.1),

$$B < \psi^*_{xx} < AB, \quad A < \psi^*_{xy} < A\frac{BR}{N}, \quad |\psi^*_{yy}| < A\frac{BR^2}{N^2} \tag{8.1}$$

Thus condition (1′) of Lemma 8 is satisfied. In condition (2), we may take, by (6.7), $r_0^2 = Aty_1^2y_2^2R^{-3}N^{-7}Q\cdot 4^m\xi$①, provided that $ty_1^2y_2^2R^{-3}N^{-7}Q^2(Q_0/RN)^2 < Kr_0^2$ for a sufficiently small K. By choosing the constant A in (7.12) sufficiently

---

① Here we write r_0 for the r in Lemma 8 to avoid confusion.

large, this can be achieved, provided that

(C_8) $$Q_0 = O(R^{2/3}N)$$

In condition (3), we take $C = ABR^{-1}$, $U = \min(N, l_2)$. Then we want $BR^{-1} < AB^{3/2}$ and $BR^{-1}Nr < AB^2$, that is, $R^{-2} < AB$ and $r_0N < ABR$. Since $2^m\xi^{1/2} < Q^{1/2}$, we have $r_0N < t^{1/2}y_1y_2R^{-3/2}N^{-5/2}Q < ABR$. The second condition is satisfied. Since $Q > x_3N$, we have $B > At^{1/2}R^{-5/2}N^{-3/2}$, and the first condition reduces to

(C_9) $$RN^3 = O(t)$$

By taking k sufficiently large, we can replace the conditions (4) and (5) by a stronger condition

$$B^{1/2}C_1 = O(r_0^2t^{-\varepsilon}) \qquad (8.2)$$

By differentiating ψ^*_{xy} with respect to y we get an extra factor N^{-1}. Hence $\psi^*_{xyy} = O(BRN^{-1})$. Similarly $\psi^*_{xxy} = O(BN^{-1})$, $\psi^*_{xxx} = O(BR^{-1})$. Therefore

$$|\psi^{*2}_{xx}\psi^*_{xyy} - 2\psi^*_{xx}\psi^*_{xy}\psi^*_{xxy} + \psi^{*2}_{xy}\psi^*_{xxx}| < B^3RN^{-2}$$

We now take $C_1 = BRN^{-2}$. Using (7.12) we find

$$r_0^2 > AB^2R^2N^{-2}Q^{-1}\xi > AB^2R^2N^{-2}R^{-2/3}\left(\frac{\lambda'^3\lambda''^2}{y_1y_2(y_3+1)}\right)^{1/2} \qquad (8.3)$$

The relation (8.2) becomes

$$R^{-1/3} = O\left[\left(B\frac{\lambda'^3\lambda''^2}{y_1y_2(y_3+1)}\right)^{1/2}t^{-\varepsilon}\right]$$

Since $Q > (y_3+1)R$, we have $B > At^{1/2}y_1y_2(y_3+1)R^{-3/2}N^{-5/2}$. So the last condition reduces to

(C_{10}) $$R^{-1/3} = O[(t^{1/2}\lambda'^3\lambda''^2R^{-3/2}N^{-5/2})^{1/2}t^{-\varepsilon}]$$

9. Now consider S_3. Since S'_4 can be estimated as S_4 we have, by (7.13) and (4.7),

$$S_3 = O\left(\frac{RN}{\lambda^{1/2}}\right) +$$
$$O\left(\frac{(RN)^{7/8}}{\lambda^{3/2}}\left\{\sum_{y_1=1}^{\lambda-1}\left[\sum_{y_2=1}^{\lambda^2-1}\left(\sum_{x_3=1}^{\lambda'^2-1}\sum_{y_3=1}^{\lambda''^2-1}\left\{\frac{R^{1/3}Q}{x_3}\frac{\lambda'^{3/2}\lambda''}{y_1^{1/2}y_2^{1/2}(y_3+1)^{1/2}}\log^{2/3}t+\right.\right.\right.\right.\right.$$
$$\left.\left.\left.\left.\left.\frac{t^{1/2}y_1y_2Q^2}{x_3R^{3/2}N^{5/2}}\log t+\frac{R^{11/6}N^{7/2}}{t^{1/2}y_1y_2Q\log^{1/3}t}\right\}\right)^{1/2}\right]^{1/2}\right\}^{1/2}\right) \qquad (9.1)$$

We choose λ' and λ'' such that $\lambda'^2N = \lambda''^2R$, then, since $\lambda'\lambda'' = \lambda^2$

$$\lambda'' = \left(\frac{N}{R}\right)^{1/4}\lambda, \quad \lambda' = \left(\frac{N}{R}\right)^{-1/4}\lambda \qquad (9.2)$$

This is possible provided that

(C_{11}) $$NR^{-1} \leqslant \lambda^4$$

Thus $Q = O(\lambda^{2}N) = O(\lambda^{2}R) = O(\lambda^2 N^{1/2}R^{1/2})$. Hence

$$S_3 = O\left(\frac{RN}{\lambda^{1/2}}\right) + O\left((RN)^{7/8}\left\{R^{1/3}N\log^{5/3}t + \frac{t^{1/2}\lambda^5}{RN}\log^2 t + \frac{R^{4/3}N^3}{t^{1/2}\lambda^5}\log t\right\}^{1/8}\right) =$$

$$O\left(\frac{RN}{\lambda^{1/2}}\right) + O(t^{1/16}R^{3/4}N^{3/4}\lambda^{5/8}\log^{1/4}t) \tag{9.3}$$

provided that

$$R^{1/3}N = O(t^{1/2}R^{-1}N^{-1}\lambda^5),\ t^{-1/2}\lambda^{-5}R^{4/3}N^3\log t = O(t^{1/2}R^{-1}N^{-1}\lambda^5) \tag{9.4}$$

Choose λ so that $RN\lambda^{-1/2} = t^{1/16}R^{3/4}N^{3/4}\lambda^{5/8}\log^{1/4}t$, then

$$\lambda = \left(\frac{R^{1/4}N^{1/4}}{t^{1/16}}\right)^{8/9}\log^{-2/9}t = \frac{R^{2/9}N^{2/9}}{t^{1/18}}\log^{-2/9}t \tag{9.5}$$

Inserting this value in (9.4), we find that the first relation is more stringent, It can be replaced by

(C_{12}) $$RN^4 = O(t^{-\varepsilon})$$

Inserting (9.5) into (9.3)

$$S_3 = O(t^{1/36}R^{8/9}N^{8/9}\log^{1/36}t) = O(t^{1/36+\varepsilon}R^{8/9}N^{8/9}) \tag{9.6}$$

We now return to (4.4). We observe that the above argument applies equally well if S_3 is over part of a rectangle cut off by either or both of the curves $v = \alpha$ and $v = \beta$. In fact, the equations of the two curves are, by (4.5)

$$v = -\frac{t}{2\pi}\left(\frac{1}{b} - \frac{1}{b-r}\right),\quad v = -\frac{t}{2\pi}\left(\frac{1}{a+r} - \frac{1}{a}\right)$$

Hence along these curves $\mathrm{d}^2r/\mathrm{d}v^2 = O(a^3/t^2)$. In Lemma 8 the condition (6) is satisfied if (see(C_7)) $|\psi_{pxx}l_2a^3t^{-2}| < Kr_0$ where ψ_p, l_2 and r_0 are given in §7 and §8 and K is sufficiently small. By cur choice of l_2, $|\psi_{pxx}l_2| < NR^{-1}$. By (6.3) and (7.12), $r_0 > At^{1/2}y_1y_2R^{-3/2}N^{-7/2}$. $Q^{1/2}\xi^{1/2} > At^{1/2}R^{-3/2}N^{-7/2}NR^{-1/3}$. Thus the condition reduces to $Kt^{1/2}R^{-11/6}N^{-9/2} > NR^{-1}a^3t^{-2}$ for a sufficiently small K. That is, $a^3R^{5/6}N^{7/2} < Kt^{5/2}$. Using the fact $N = O(Rt/a^2)$ or $N^{3/2} = O(R^{3/2}t^{3/2}/a^3)$, we reduced it to $R^{7/3}N^2 < Kt$. This is included in (C_{12}). Hence it is legitimate to use Lemma 8 in estimating S_4. We may also use Lemma 10 to get an upper bound for the number of rectangles (or parts of rectangles) $\Delta_{p,m}$ in a strip (7.5), since the domain of summation lies entirely within a rectangle of side-lengths R and N.

We observe that $|f_{yy}(r,y)| > Atra^{-3}$. Hence, by partial summations

$$S_2 = O(\rho(t\rho a^{-3})^{-1/2}t^{1/36+\varepsilon}\rho^{8/9}\beta^{8/9}) + O(a^{3/2}t^{-1/2}\rho^{3/2}) +$$
$$O(\rho^2\log t) + O(a^{-2/5}t^{2/5}\rho^{12/5}) =$$

$$O(t^{15/36+\varepsilon}a^{-5/18}\rho^{41/18}) + O(a^{3/2}t^{-1/2}\rho^{3/2}) + O(\rho^2\log t) + O(a^{-2/5}t^{2/5}\rho^{12/5})$$

since $\beta = O(t\rho a^{-2})$. Therefore, by (4.2)

$$S_1 = O(a\rho^{-1/2}) + O(t^{15/72+\varepsilon}a^{13/36}\rho^{5/36}) + O(a^{5/4}t^{-1/4}\rho^{-1/4}) + O(a^{1/2}\log^{1/2}t) + O(a^{3/10}t^{1/5}\rho^{1/5})$$

The first two terms are of the same order if

$$\rho = (t^{-15/72-\varepsilon}a^{23/36})^{36/23} = t^{-15/46-\varepsilon}a \tag{9.7}$$

This gives, for $a = O(t^{1/2})$,

$$S_1 = O(t^{15/92+\varepsilon}a^{1/2}) + O(t^{-31/184+\varepsilon}a) + O(a^{1/2}\log^{1/2}t) + O(t^{31/200}a^{1/2}) = O(t^{15/92+\varepsilon}a^{1/2})$$

Hence, by partial summation

$$\sum_{n=a}^{b}\frac{1}{n^{1/2+it}} = O(t^{15/92+\varepsilon}) \tag{9.8}$$

10. Let us examine the conditions we assumed

The conditions (C_1), (C_4) and (C_9) are included in (C_{12}). By (9.2), (C_3) is not stronger than (C_5). By the remarks at the end of §7 and by §8, the conditions (C_6) and (C_7) can be deleted. The conditions (C_2) is satisfied so far as we do not consider the case $a > At^{1/2}$. It remains, therefore, to consider (C_5), (C_8), (C_{10}), (C_{11}) and (C_{12}).

Since $Q_0 = O(\lambda'^2 N)$ and $\lambda'^2 N = \lambda''^2 R$, (C_5) and (C_8) can be replaced by $\lambda'^2 = O(R^{2/3}t^{-\varepsilon})$. By (9.2) and (9.5), this can be reduced to the trivial condition $R^5N^{-1} = O(t^{2-\varepsilon})$.

Using (9.2) and (9.5), (C_{10}) can be written as

$$R^{-1/3} = O\left[\left(t^{1/2}\frac{R^{10/9}N^{10/9}}{t^{5/18}}\left(\frac{N}{R}\right)^{1/2}R^{-3/2}N^{-5/2}\right)^{1/2}t^{-\varepsilon}\right]$$

which is actually equivalent to (C_{12}). Since $N = O(Rt/a^2)$ (use the relation above (4.6)), (C_{12}) is equivalent to $R^5t^{3+\varepsilon} = O(a^8)$. By (9.7), this reduces to $t^{-75/46}t^{3+\varepsilon} = O(a^3)$. That is

$$(\mathrm{C}) \qquad a > At^{21/46+\varepsilon}$$

Now consider (C_{11}). By (9.5), the condition is

$$NR^{-1} < t^{-2/9}R^{8/9}N^{8/9}\log^{2/9}t$$

or

$$(\mathrm{C}') \qquad t^2\log^2 t \leqslant AR^{17}N^{-1}$$

Using $N > ARta^{-2}$, this can be reduced to

(C'$_1$) $t^3\log^2 t = O(R^{16}a^2)$ or $R > A\left(\frac{t^3\log^2 t}{a^2}\right)^{1/16}$

11. If both (C) and (C') are satisfied we have nothing to justify. Now suppose that one of them is not true.

We shall not take the values for λ' and λ'' given in (9.2). We can, as did Professor Titchmarsh① in his paper, take $\lambda'' = \lambda^2$ and omit the x_3-summation. This amounts to using Lemma 5 three times.

We are compelled to examine the whole proof afresh, keeping to its original form as closely as possible §3 is now useless. In §4, we omit all the x_3-summations and put $x_3 = 0$, $\lambda' = 1$ whenever they occur elsewhere. In §5, we put $x_3 = 0$. In §6, we put $x_3 = \lambda' = 0$. Then, in (6.7), the first term on the right-hand side is now "positive definite".

Now §7 can be greatly simplified, for we have no need of redividing Δ_p. We may take Δ_p as Δ''_p there and put $J_0 = J = 0$. By arguing as before, we find

$$S_4 = J_2 + J_3 = O\left(\frac{RN}{l_1} + l_2\right)\log t = O\left[\frac{t^{1/2}y_1y_2y_3}{R^{1/2}N^{3/2}} + \frac{R^{1/2}N^{7/2}}{t^{1/2}y_1y_2y_3}\right]\log t$$

Inserting this result into (4.7) we obtain

$$S_3 = O(RN/\lambda^{1/2}) + O(R^{13/16}N^{11/16}t^{1/16}\lambda^{7/8}\log^{1/8}t) + O(R^{15/16}N^{21/16}t^{-1/16}\lambda^{-7/8}\log^{1/4}t) \tag{11.1}$$

The first two terms are of the same order if

$$\lambda = \left[\left(\frac{R^3N^5}{t\log^2 t}\right)^{1/22}\right] \tag{11.2}$$

This gives

$$S_3 = O(R^{41/44}N^{39/44}t^{1/44}\log^{1/22}t) \tag{11.3}$$

provided that the last term in (11.1) is negligible. This is true if $RN^5\log t = O(t\lambda^{14})$. Using (11.2) and the fact that $N < AtRa^{-2}$, we reduce this to

$$t^{16}R^{10}\log^{25}t = O(a^{40}) \tag{11.4}$$

First, suppose that (C) is true and (C') is false. Then (11.4) becomes $t^{16}(a^{-2}t^3\log^2 t)^{5/8}\cdot\log^{25}t = O(a^{40})$. This can be reduced to $a > t^{143/330}\log^{7/11}t$, a consequence of (C).

We expect that (11.3) implies (9.6). This is true of $R^{17}N^{-1} < t^{2+\varepsilon}$ which is weaker than the negation of (C'). Thus (9.6) is proved for this case.

---

① Loc. cit. p. 13.

Next, suppose that (C) is untrue. Then we have, as before,

$$S_2 = O(\rho^{51/22}t^{9/22}a^{-3/11}\log^{1/22}t) + O(a^{3/2}t^{-1/2}\rho^{3/2}) + O(\rho^2\log t) + O(a^{-2/5}t^{2/5}\rho^{12/5})$$

Hence

$$S_1 = O(a\rho^{-1/2}) + O(a^{4/11}\rho^{7/44}t^{9/44}\log^{1/44}t) + O(a^{5/4}\rho^{-1/4}t^{1/4}) + O(a^{1/2}\log^{1/2}t) + O(a^{3/10}\rho^{1/5}t^{1/5})$$

The first two terms are of the same order if

$$\rho = [(a^{28}t^{-9}\log^{-1}t)^{1/29}] \qquad (11.5)$$

This gives

$$\sum_{n=a}^{b} n^{-it} = O(a^{15/29}t^{9/58}\log^{1/58}t) + O(a^{117/116}t^{-5/29}\log^{1/116}t) + O(a^{1/2}\log^{1/2}t) + O(a^{143/290}t^{4/29})$$

It can be verified that the last three terms are negligible and all conditions except (11.4) can be removed. By partial summation,

$$\sum_{n=a} \frac{1}{n^{1/2+it}} = O(a^{1/58}t^{9/58}\log^{1/58}t) = O(t^{15/92}\log^{1/58}t)$$

since (C) is untrue and $(21/46) \times 1/58 + 9/58 = 15/92$. By (11.5) we may reduce (11.4) to

$$(C^*) \qquad a > t^{17/40}\log^{143/176}t$$

Thus we have proved (9.8) completely under the sole condition (C^*).

12. **Completing the proof**

We use, first, the inequality

$$\sum_{n=N}^{N'} \frac{1}{n^{1/2+it}} = O(N'^{5/82}t^{11/82}) + O(N^{-17/328}t^{61/328}), \quad N > t^{11/36}$$

For $N' < t^{17/40+\varepsilon}$, the first term is $O(t^{15/92+\varepsilon})$, for

$$\frac{17}{40}\cdot\frac{5}{82} + \frac{11}{82} = \frac{105}{656} < \frac{15}{92}$$

The second term is $O(t^{15/91})$ if $N \geqslant t^{173/391}$.

For $N < t^{173/391}$, we use the result①

$$\sum_{a\leqslant n\leqslant b} n^{-1/2+it} = O(t^k a^{l-k-1/2})$$

where $a < b < 2a < t/\pi$, and $k = 97/696$, $l = 480/696$. The sum is $O(t^{15/92})$ since

① 222-223.

$$\frac{97}{696}+\left(\frac{480}{696}-\frac{97}{696}-\frac{1}{2}\right)\cdot\frac{173}{391}=\frac{97}{696}+\frac{35\times 173}{696\times 391}<\frac{15}{92}$$

By the approximate functional equation, we have

$$\xi(1/2+\mathrm{i}t)=O(t^{15/92+\varepsilon}),\quad \varepsilon>0$$

where the constant implied by O depends only on ε.

黎曼 ζ 函数的一种推广
——Ⅰ. $Z_{n,k}(s)$ 的全面解析开拓[①]

§1 引　论

黎曼 ζ 函数有种种有趣的推广，本文将提出一个新的推广. 在全文中，永远假定 n 是偶数. 命

$$Z_{n,k}(s) = \sum_{x_1=-\infty}^{\infty} \cdots \sum_{x_k=-\infty}^{\infty}{}' \frac{1}{(x_1^n + \cdots + x_k^n)^s} \tag{1.1}$$

式中"′"表 $x_1, \cdots, x_k$ 不同时为零，而依黎曼 ζ 函数论中的惯例，常设 $s = \sigma + \mathrm{i}t$. 当(1.1)的右端绝对收敛时，显然

$$Z_{n,k}(s) = \sum_{m=1}^{\infty} \frac{B(m)}{m^s} \tag{1.2}$$

式中

$$B(m) = \sum_{x_1=-\infty}^{\infty} \cdots \sum_{\substack{x_k=-\infty \\ x_1^n+\cdots+x_k^n=m}}^{\infty} 1 \tag{1.3}$$

表 $x_1^n + \cdots + x_k^n = m$ 的整数解的个数.

如果把(1.1)再推广一些，不难使它包括 Epstein Z 函数，

① 原载：数学学报，1955，5(3)：285-294。

例如把(1.1)右边的 $x_1^n+\cdots+x_k^n$ 换成 k 个线性函数的 n 次方幂的和就是一个顶简单的推广方法．但为明确计，我们宁愿就上面这个形式上较特殊而实际上最重要的情形来讨论.

本文将分作若干篇发表，本篇 I 将建立函数 $Z_{n,k}(s)$ 的一些基本性质，最主要的是它可以像 $\zeta(s)$ 一样开拓到全平面，其唯一的奇点是一个简单极点.

§2 $Z_{n,k}(s)$ 的几个简单性质

为简便计，今后用 v 表 $\frac{1}{n}$

$$v=\frac{1}{n}. \tag{2.1}$$

定理2.1 级数(1.1)当 $\sigma>kv$ 时绝对收敛，当 $\sigma\leqslant kv$ 时发散．又当 $\sigma>kv$ 时

$$Z_{n,k}(s)\leqslant A\left(1+\frac{1}{\sigma-kv}\right) \tag{2.2}$$

式中 A 代表一个正的绝对常数.

证 (1)因多重级数的收敛就是绝对收敛，所以只须考虑 $s=\sigma$ 的情形：

$$\sum_{x_1=-\infty}^{\infty}\cdots\sum_{x_k=-\infty}^{\infty}{}'\frac{1}{(x_1^n+\cdots+x_k^n)^{\sigma}} \tag{2.3}$$

显然

$$\sum_{\substack{x_1=-N\\ |x_i|\leqslant|x_1|,i=2,\cdots,k}}^{N}{}'\frac{1}{(x_1^n+\cdots+x_k^n)^{\sigma}}\leqslant 2\sum_{x_1=1}^{N}\frac{(2x_1+1)^{k-1}}{x_1^{n\sigma}}\leqslant 2\cdot 3^{k-1}\sum_{x_1=1}^{N}\frac{1}{x_1^{n\sigma-k+1}} \tag{2.4}$$

式中“′”表 $x_1\neq 0$．若 $\sigma>kv$，则当 $N\to+\infty$ 时上式右端有界．显然若用 $x_j(j=2,\cdots,k)$ 代替上式之 x_1 亦得同样结论．由此可见(2.3)绝对收敛.

(2)另一方面

$$\sum_{\substack{x_1=-N\\ |x_i|\leqslant|x_1|,i=2,\cdots,k}}^{N}{}'\frac{1}{(x_1^n+\cdots+x_k^n)^{\sigma}}\geqslant 2\sum_{x_1=1}^{N}\frac{(2x_1+1)^{k-1}}{(kx_1^n)^{\sigma}}\geqslant 2^k\sum_{x_1=1}^{N}k^{\sigma}\frac{1}{x_1^{n\sigma-k+1}}$$

若 $\sigma\leqslant kv$，上式右端显然随 N 趋向 $+\infty$；故当 $\sigma\leqslant kv$ 时，级数(2.3)发散.

(3)由(2.4)

$$\sum_{i=1}^{k}\sum_{\substack{x_i=-N\\ |x_j|\leqslant|x_i|,j\neq i}}^{N}{}'\frac{1}{(x_1^n+\cdots+x_k^n)^{\sigma}}\leqslant 2\cdot 3^{k-1}k\sum_{x=1}^{N}\frac{1}{x^{n\sigma-k+1}}\leqslant$$

$$2\cdot 3^{k-1}k\left\{1+\int_1^N \frac{\mathrm{d}x}{x^{n\sigma-k+1}}\right\}\leqslant A\left(1+\frac{1}{n\sigma-k}\right)$$

于是定理随之成立.

定理2.2 除以 $s=kv$ 为简单极点外, $Z_{n,k}(s)$ 可以解析地开拓到 $\sigma=kv-v$ 之右. 在极点 $s=kv$, $Z_{n,k}(s)$ 的残数是

$$P=2^k kvT_k \text{ 而 } T_k=\frac{\Gamma^k(1+v)}{\Gamma(1+kv)} \tag{2.5}$$

证 (1) 当 $0\leqslant x<1$ 时,命 $S(x)=0$,而于 $x\geqslant 1$ 时

$$S(x)=\sum_{0\leqslant m\leqslant x}B(m)$$

则对于正整数 m 即有

$$B(m)=S(m)-S(m-1)$$

故当 $\sigma>kv$ 时,由(2.5) 得

$$Z_{n,k}(s)=\sum_{m=1}^{\infty}\frac{S(m)-S(m-1)}{m^s}=\sum_{m=1}^{\infty}S(m)\left(\frac{1}{m^s}-\frac{1}{(m+1)^s}\right)=$$

$$\sum_{m=1}^{\infty}S(m)s\int_m^{m+1}\frac{\mathrm{d}x}{x^{s+1}}=s\int_1^{\infty}\frac{S(x)\mathrm{d}x}{x^{s+1}} \tag{2.6}$$

(2) 现在要证明当 $x\to+\infty$ 时,

$$S(x)=S_k(x)=2^kT_kx^{kv}+\omega_k(x)x^{kv-v} \tag{2.7}$$

式中 $|\omega_k(x)|$ 是一个有界函数,其上界只与 n 及 k 有关. 我们只要证明(2.7) 对于正整数 $x=N$ 成立即可. 这因为知道(2.7) 对正整数成立之后,不难看出(2.7) 对所有正数 x 都成立.

显然

$$S_1(N)=2N^v+1-2\theta,\quad 0<\theta<1$$

故(2.7) 对于 $S_1(N)$ 成立. 今设(2.7) 对于 $S_k(N)$ 成立,则

$$S_{k+1}(N)=\sum_{-N^v\leqslant t\leqslant N^v}S_k(N-t^n)=$$

$$2^kT_k\sum_{-N^v\leqslant t\leqslant N^v}(N-t^n)^{kv}+\sum_{-N^v\leqslant t\leqslant N^v}\omega_k(N-t^n)(N-t^n)^{kv-v}=$$

$$2^kT_k\int_{-N^v}^{N^v}(N-t^n)^{kv}\mathrm{d}t+2^{k+1}\theta'T_kN^{kv}+N^{kv}A_k(N)$$

式中 $-1\leqslant\theta'\leqslant 1$, $|A_k(N)|<2\sup|\omega_k(N)|$. 但

$$\int_{-N^v}^{N^v}(N-t^n)^{kv}\mathrm{d}t=2\int_0^{N^v}(N-t^n)^{kv}\mathrm{d}t=2vN^{(k+1)v}\int_0^1(1-x)^{kv}x^{v-1}\mathrm{d}x=$$

$$2vN^{(k+1)v}\frac{\Gamma(kv+1)\Gamma(v)}{\Gamma(kv+v+1)}$$

故

$$S_{k+1}(N)=2^{k+1}T_{k+1}N^{(k+1)v}+\omega_{k+1}(N)N^{kv}$$

其中 $|\omega_{k+1}(N)|$ 的上界只与 n 及 k 有关．这证明(2.7)常成立①.

(3) 把(2.7)代入(2.6),即得:当 $\sigma > kv$ 时

$$Z_{n,k}(s) = \frac{2^k T_k s}{s-kv} + s\int_1^{\infty} \frac{\omega_k(x)\,\mathrm{d}x}{x^{s-kv+1+v}} \tag{2.8}$$

利用把 $\frac{\omega_k(x)}{x^{s-kv+1+v}}$ 展成 s 的幂级数(显然当 $1 \leqslant x \leqslant X$ 时一致收敛)然后分项积分的方法,可以证明当 X 一定时

$$f_X(s) = s\int_1^X \frac{\omega_k(x)\,\mathrm{d}x}{x^{s-kv+1+v}} = s\sum_{m=0}^{\infty}\frac{s^m}{m!}\int_1^X \frac{\omega_k(x)\log^m x}{x^{-kv+1+v}}\mathrm{d}x$$

是 s 的整函数$\left(这因为\left|\int_1^X \frac{\omega_k(x)\log^m x}{x^{-kv+1+v}}\mathrm{d}x\right| \leqslant \log^m X\int_1^X \frac{\omega_k(x)\,\mathrm{d}x}{x^{-kv+1+v}}\right)$. 又当 $X \to +\infty$ 时,在 $\sigma \geqslant kv - v + \varepsilon(\varepsilon > 0)$ 半面内,$f_x(s)$ 一致地趋于极限函数

$$s\int_1^{\infty} \frac{\omega_k(x)\,\mathrm{d}x}{x^{s-kv+1+v}} = f(s)$$

故 $f(s)$ 在 $\sigma > kv - v$ 时是解析的,因此 $Z_{n,k}(s)$ 除以 $s = kv$ 为简单极点(其相当的残数显然是 $P = 2^k kvT_k$)外,在半面 $\sigma > kv - v$ 上是解析的②.

定理 2.3　当 $\sigma > kv - v$ 而 $|t| \to \infty$ 时

$$Z_{n,k}(s) = O(|s|)$$

证　由(2.8)及下式即得本定理

$$\int_1^{\infty} \frac{\omega_k(x)\,\mathrm{d}x}{x^{\sigma-kv+1+v}} = O\left(\int_1^{\infty}\frac{\mathrm{d}x}{x^{1+v}}\right) = O(1)$$

§3　$Z_{n,k}(s)$ 的全面开拓

在上节已经证明 $Z_{n,k}(s)$ 并非以 $\sigma = kv$ 为自然边界而可以解析地开拓到 $\sigma = kv - v$ 之右(但以 $s = kv$ 为奇点). 下面证明 $Z_{n,k}(s)$ 可以解析地开拓到全平面,但以 $s = kv$ 为唯一奇点．我们要用几个引理:

引理 3.1(Poisson 公式)　设 $f(x)$ 是确定在 $0 \leqslant x < +\infty$ 的连续函数,且当 $x \to +\infty$ 时下降至0. 又设 $f(x) \in L(0,\infty)$,$\alpha > 0$, $\alpha\beta = 2\pi$,而

$$g(y) = \sqrt{\frac{2}{\pi}}\int_0^{\infty} f(t)\cos yt\,\mathrm{d}t$$

---

① 参看 Виноградов, Метод тригонометрических сумм в теории чисел, 第一章,引理 3.

② 参看 Ingham, The Distribution of Prime Numbers, 第二章,第 1,2 两节.

则

$$\sqrt{\alpha}\left\{\frac{1}{2}f(0)+\sum_{n=1}^{\infty}f(n\alpha)\right\}=\sqrt{\beta}\left\{\frac{1}{2}g(0)+\sum_{n=1}^{\infty}g(n\beta)\right\} \tag{3.1}$$

引理 3.2 当 $\omega>0$(及 n 是正的偶数)时

$$\frac{1}{2}+\sum_{x=1}^{\infty}\mathrm{e}^{-x^n\omega}=\frac{1}{\omega^v}\left\{\Gamma(1+v)+2\omega^{2hv}\sum_{y=1}^{\infty}\frac{(-1)^h}{(2\pi y)^{2h}}\int_0^{\infty}\left(\frac{\mathrm{d}^{2h}}{\mathrm{d}x^{2h}}\mathrm{e}^{-x^n}\right)\cos\frac{2\pi yx}{\omega^v}\mathrm{d}x\right\} \tag{3.2}$$

式中 h 可以是任何正整数．又如把一函数看成是自己的 0 次导数，则上式当 $h=0$ 时仍然成立.

证 (1) 在引理 3.1 中可令

$$f(x)=\mathrm{e}^{-x^n},\quad \alpha=\omega^v,\quad \beta=\frac{2\pi}{\alpha}=\frac{2\pi}{\omega^v}$$

则

$$g(y)=\sqrt{\frac{2}{\pi}}\int_0^{\infty}\mathrm{e}^{-t^n}\cos yt\mathrm{d}t$$

而

$$\omega^{v/2}\left\{\frac{1}{2}+\sum_{x=1}^{\infty}\mathrm{e}^{-x^n\omega}\right\}=\frac{\sqrt{2\pi}}{\omega^{v/2}}\left\{\frac{1}{2}\sqrt{\frac{2}{\pi}}\int_0^{\infty}\mathrm{e}^{-x^n}\mathrm{d}x+\sum_{y=1}^{\infty}\sqrt{\frac{2}{\pi}}\int_0^{\infty}\mathrm{e}^{-x^n}\cos\frac{2\pi yx}{\omega^v}\mathrm{d}x\right\}$$

因 $\int_0^{\infty}\mathrm{e}^{-x^n}\mathrm{d}x=v\int_0^{\infty}u^{v-1}\mathrm{e}^{-u}\mathrm{d}u=v\Gamma(v)=\Gamma(1+v)$，故

$$\frac{1}{2}+\sum_{x=1}^{\infty}\mathrm{e}^{-x^n\omega}=\frac{1}{\omega^v}\left\{\Gamma(1+v)+2\sum_{y=1}^{\infty}\int_0^{\infty}\mathrm{e}^{-x^n}\cos\frac{2\pi yx}{\omega^v}\mathrm{d}x\right\} \tag{3.3}$$

(2) 今将证当 h 是正整数时

$$\int_0^{\infty}\mathrm{e}^{-x^n}\cos\frac{2\pi xy}{\omega^v}\mathrm{d}x=(-1)^h\left(\frac{w^v}{2\pi y}\right)^{2h}\int_0^{\infty}\left(\frac{\mathrm{d}^{2h}}{\mathrm{d}x^{2h}}\mathrm{e}^{-x^n}\right)\cos\frac{2\pi xy}{\omega^v}\mathrm{d}x \tag{3.4}$$

如果把 e^{-x^n} 看做是自己的0次导数，显然上式对于 $h=0$ 成立．今假定上式成立而证用 $h+1$ 换 h 后仍成立.

用分部积分法两次，由(3.4)得

$$\int_0^{\infty}\mathrm{e}^{-x^n}\cos\frac{2\pi xy}{\omega^v}\mathrm{d}x=(-1)^h\left(\frac{\omega^v}{2\pi y}\right)^{2h+2}\left[\left(\frac{\mathrm{d}^{2h+1}}{\mathrm{d}x^{2h+1}}\mathrm{e}^{-x^n}\right)\cos\frac{2\pi xy}{\omega^v}\right]_0^{\infty}+(-1)^{h+1}\left(\frac{\omega^v}{2\pi y}\right)^{2h+2}\int_0^{\infty}\left(\frac{\mathrm{d}^{2h+2}}{\mathrm{d}x^{2h+2}}\mathrm{e}^{-x^n}\right)\cos\frac{2\pi xy}{\omega^v}\mathrm{d}x$$

上面第一项事实上等于0. 这因为一方面

$$\frac{\mathrm{d}^{2h+1}}{\mathrm{d}x^{2h+1}}\mathrm{e}^{-x^n}=P(x)\mathrm{e}^{-x^n}$$

其中 $P(x)$ 是一个多项式，故当 $x\to\infty$ 时，上式 $\to 0$；另一方面

$$\frac{\mathrm{d}^{2h+1}}{\mathrm{d}x^{2h+1}}\mathrm{e}^{-x^n} = \frac{\mathrm{d}^{2h+1}}{\mathrm{d}x^{2h+1}}\left(1 - x^n + \frac{x^{2n}}{2!} - \frac{x^{3n}}{3!} + \cdots\right)$$

上式右端在分项微分之后，不含常数项（因 n 是偶数），故当 $x = 0$ 时，上式为0. 因此(3.4) 常成立.

(3) 把(3.4) 代入(3.3) 即得(3.2).

定理3.1 $Z_{n,k}(s)$ 除在 $s = kv$ 有一简单极点（其相应的残数为 $P = 2^k kvT_k$）外，可以解析地开拓到全平面.

证 (1) 利用当 $\sigma > 0$ 时 $\Gamma(s)$ 的公式

$$\Gamma(s) = \int_0^\infty x^{s-1}\mathrm{e}^{-x}\mathrm{d}x$$

可以证明，当 $\sigma > kv$ 时

$$Z_{n,k}(s) = \frac{1}{\Gamma(s)}\int_0^\infty \omega^{s-1}\left[\left(\sum_{x=-\infty}^{\infty}\mathrm{e}^{-x^n\omega}\right)^k - 1\right]\mathrm{d}\omega \tag{3.5}$$

现在把证明的详细步骤叙述如下：当 $\omega > 0$ 时

$$\left(\sum_{x=-\infty}^{\infty}\mathrm{e}^{-x^n\omega}\right)^k - 1 = \sum_{m=1}^{\infty}B(m)\mathrm{e}^{-m\omega} \tag{3.6}$$

式中 $B(m)$ 的定义见(1.3). 由(2.7)，$S(x) = O(x^{kv})$. 由 $B(m)$ 与 $S(m)$ 的定义知 $B(m) = O(m^{kv})$. 故(3.6) 右边的级数当 $\omega \geqslant \varepsilon > 0$ 时是一致收敛的. 前已假定 $\sigma > kv$，于是当 $0 < \varepsilon < N$ 时

$$\begin{aligned}
&\frac{1}{\Gamma(s)}\int_\varepsilon^N \omega^{s-1}\left[\left(\sum_{x=-\infty}^{\infty}\mathrm{e}^{-x^n\omega}\right)^k - 1\right]\mathrm{d}\omega = \frac{1}{\Gamma(s)}\int_\varepsilon^N \omega^{s-1}\sum_{m=1}^{\infty}B(m)\mathrm{e}^{-\omega m}\mathrm{d}\omega = \\
&\sum_{m=1}^{\infty}\frac{1}{\Gamma(s)}\frac{B(m)}{m^s}\int_{m\varepsilon}^{mN}\omega^{s-1}\mathrm{e}^{-\omega}\mathrm{d}\omega = \\
&\sum_{m=1}^{\infty}\frac{1}{\Gamma(s)}\frac{B(m)}{m^s}\left\{\int_0^\infty - \int_{mN}^\infty - \int_\infty^{m\varepsilon}\right\}\omega^{s-1}\mathrm{e}^{-\omega}\mathrm{d}\omega = \\
&Z_{n,k}(s) - \frac{1}{\Gamma(s)}\sum_{m=1}^{\infty}\frac{B(m)}{m^s}\int_{mN}^\infty \omega^{s-1}\mathrm{e}^{-\omega}\mathrm{d}\omega - \\
&\frac{1}{\Gamma(s)}\sum_{m=1}^{\infty}\frac{B(m)}{m^s}\int_0^{m\varepsilon}\omega^{s-1}\mathrm{e}^{-\omega}\mathrm{d}\omega = \\
&Z_{n,k}(s) - \frac{1}{\Gamma(s)}\sum\nolimits_1 - \frac{1}{\Gamma(s)}\sum\nolimits_2
\end{aligned}$$

式中

$$\left|\sum\nolimits_1\right| \leqslant \sum_{m=1}^{\infty}\frac{B(m)}{m^\sigma}\int_N^\infty \omega^{\sigma-1}\mathrm{e}^{-\omega}\mathrm{d}\omega \to 0，当 N \to \infty$$

而

$$\left|\sum\nolimits_2\right| \leqslant \sum_{m=1}^{M}\frac{B(m)}{m^\sigma}\int_0^{\varepsilon M}\omega^{\sigma-1}\mathrm{e}^{-\omega}\mathrm{d}\omega + \sum_{m=M+1}^{\infty}\frac{B(m)}{m^\sigma}\int_0^\infty \omega^{\sigma-1}\mathrm{e}^{-\omega}\mathrm{d}\omega$$

可先选M使上式右边第二项小于任意指定正数之半. M选定后,当ε充分小时,第一项也就小于该指定正数之半. 故当$\varepsilon \to 0$时,$\sum_2 \to 0$. 因此当$\sigma > kv$时,(3.5)成立.

(2) 由(3.5)知

$$Z_{n,k}(s) = \frac{1}{\Gamma(s)}\left\{\int_0^1 \omega^{s-1}\left[\left(\sum_{x=-\infty}^{\infty} e^{-x^n\omega}\right)^k - 1\right]d\omega + \int_1^{\infty} \omega^{s-1}\left[\left(\sum_{x=-\infty}^{\infty} e^{-x^n\omega}\right)^k - 1\right]d\omega\right\} \tag{3.7}$$

我们知道$\frac{1}{\Gamma(s)}$是整函数①,所以只须讨论花括弧内两个积分. 今顺次用I_1,I_2代表它们.

先考虑I_2. 当$\omega(0 < \omega < +\infty)$一定时,$\omega^s\left[\left(\sum_{x=-\infty}^{\infty} e^{-x^n\omega}\right)^k - 1\right]$是$s$的解析函数,而当$1 \leqslant \omega < \infty$时,它又是$\omega$与$s$的连续函数. 今将证$I_2$在半面$\sigma \leqslant a$($a$表任意实数)上一致收敛.

由(3.6),

$$\left|\omega^{s-1}\left[\left(\sum_{x=-\infty}^{\infty} e^{-x^n\omega}\right)^k - 1\right]\right| < \omega^{a-1}\sum_{m=1}^{\infty} B(m)e^{-m\omega} < \omega^{a-1}e^{-\omega}\sum_{m=1}^{\infty} B(m)e^{-(m-1)\omega}$$

故I_2在$\sigma \leqslant a$时一致收敛. 因此I_2代表s的一个整函数②.

其次考虑I_1. 由引理3.2,当$\sigma > kv$时

$$I_1 = \int_0^1 2^k\omega^{s-kv-1}\left\{\Gamma(1+v) + 2\omega^{2hv}\sum_{y=1}^{\infty}\frac{(-1)^h}{(2\pi y)^{2h}}\int_0^{\infty}\left(\frac{d^{2h}}{dx^{2h}}e^{-x^n}\right)\cos\frac{2\pi yx}{\omega^v}dx\right\}^k d\omega - \frac{1}{s} =$$
$$\frac{2^k\Gamma^k(1+v)}{s-kv} - \frac{1}{s} + \int_0^1 2^k\omega^{s-kv-1}\left[\left\{\Gamma(1+v) + 2\omega^{2hv}\sum_{y=1}^{\infty}\frac{(-1)^h}{(2\pi y)^{2h}}\int_0^{\infty}\left(\frac{d^{2h}}{dx^{2h}}e^{-x^n}\right)\cos\frac{2\pi yx}{\omega^v}dx\right\}^k - \Gamma^k(1+v)\right]d\omega =$$
$$\frac{2^k\Gamma^k(1+v)}{s-kv} - \frac{1}{s} + I_3$$

式中I_3可以写成下面的形式

$$I_3 = \int_0^1 2^k\omega^{s-1-kv+2hv}\Phi_{2h}(\omega)d\omega$$

式中$\Phi_{2h}(\omega)$当$0 < \omega \leqslant 1$时是连续的有界的函数,其有界性可以证明如下:显然

---

① 参看 Titchmarsh, Theory of functions,第二版,第149页.

② 参看 Titchmarsh, Theory of functions, 第二版,第94-100页.

$$\left|\sum_{y=1}^{\infty}\frac{(-1)^h}{(2\pi y)^{2h}}\int_0^{\infty}\left(\frac{d^{2h}}{dx^{2h}}e^{-x^n}\right)\cos\frac{2\pi yx}{\omega^v}dx\right|\leqslant$$

$$\sum_{y=1}^{\infty}\frac{1}{(2\pi y)^{2h}}\int_0^{\infty}\left|\frac{d^{2h}}{dx^{2h}}e^{-x^n}\right|dx=$$

$$\sum_{y=1}^{\infty}\frac{1}{(2\pi y)^{2h}}\int_0^{\infty}|\phi_{2h}(x)|e^{-x^n}dx<\infty$$

其中 $\phi_{2h}(x)$ 是 x 的一个多项式．由此不难看出 $|\Phi_{2h}(\omega)|$ 有界.

因此,当 h 充分大时即当 $\sigma>kv-2hv=-(2h-k)v$ 时,$\omega^{s-1-kv+2hv}\Phi_{2h}(\omega)$ 是 s 与 $\omega(0\leqslant\omega\leqslant1)$ 的连续函数．因 h 可取任意大的值,故 I_3 代表 s 的一个整函数.

根据以上对于 I_1 及 I_2 的讨论,由(3.7)即得

$$Z_{n,k}^n(s)=\frac{1}{\Gamma(s)}\left\{\frac{2^k\Gamma^k(1+v)}{s-kv}-\frac{1}{s}\right\}+\Phi(s)=$$

$$\frac{2^k\Gamma^k(1+v)}{\Gamma(s)}\cdot\frac{1}{s-kv}-\frac{1}{\Gamma(s+1)}+\Phi(s)$$

式中 $\Phi(s)$ 代表 s 的一个整函数．由此,显见 $Z_{n,k}(s)$ 只有一个奇点 $s=kv$. 这是一个简单极点,其相当残数是

$$\frac{2^k\Gamma^k(1+v)}{\Gamma(kv)}=\frac{2^kkv\Gamma^k(1+v)}{\Gamma(1+kv)}=P$$

这结果与定理2.2相合．定理至此证毕.

总结以上的讨论,我们可以为 $Z_{n,k}(s)$ 得到下面的表示式:

定理 3.2

$$Z_{n,k}(s)=\frac{2^k\Gamma^k(1+v)}{\Gamma(s)}\frac{1}{s-kv}-\frac{1}{\Gamma(s+1)}+$$

$$\frac{1}{\Gamma(s)}\left\{\int_1^{\infty}\omega^{s-1}\left[\left(\sum_{x=-\infty}^{\infty}e^{-x^n\omega}\right)^k-1\right]d\omega+\int_0^1 2^k\omega^{s-kv-1}\left[\left(\Gamma(1+v)+\right.\right.\right.$$

$$\left.\left.\left.2\omega^{2hv}\sum_{y=1}^{\infty}\frac{(-1)^h}{(2\pi y)^{2h}}\int_0^{\infty}\left(\frac{d^{2h}}{dx^{2h}}e^{-x^n}\right)\cos\frac{2\pi yx}{\omega^v}dx\right)^k-\Gamma^k(1+v)\right]d\omega\right\}\tag{3.8}$$

这个表示式可以适用于全平面,式中 h 可取任意正整数值,且若把一函数看做是自己的0次导数,则上式中 h 可以是0. 又在 $h=0$ 时,(3.8)还可以写成下列较好看的形式(* 号表示和数系取柯西主值):

$$Z_{n,k}(s)=\frac{1}{\Gamma(s)}\left\{\frac{2^k\Gamma^k(1+v)}{s-kv}-\frac{1}{s}+\int_1^{\infty}\omega^{s-1}\left[\left(\sum_{x=-\infty}^{\infty}e^{-x^n\omega}\right)^k-1\right]d\omega+\right.$$

$$\left.\int_0^1 2^k\omega^{s-kv-1}\left[\left(\sum_{y=-\infty}^{\infty}{}^{*}\int_0^{\infty}e^{-x^n}\exp\frac{2\pi iyx}{\omega^v}dx\right)^k-\Gamma^k(1+v)\right]d\omega\right\}\tag{3.9}$$

黎曼 ζ 函数的一种推广
——Ⅱ. $Z_{n,k}(s)$ 的阶①

§1 引 论

在 $\sigma \leqslant kv - v$ 的情形下,要想估计当 $t \to \infty$ 时 $Z_{n,k}(s)$ 的阶是比较困难的. 本篇的目的就是要证明:当 $A_1 < \sigma < A_2$ 而 $t \to \infty$ 时,可以找到一个正数 A(与 A_1, A_2 有关)使

$$Z_{n,k}(s) = O(t^A) \tag{1.1}$$

在本文以后各篇中,就会显出这个结果的用处. 像在第 Ⅰ 篇一样,我们永远假定 n 是正的偶数而 $v = \frac{1}{n}$.

§2 两个简单的引理

引理 2.1 设 $\varphi(z)$ 是多项式而 α 与 λ 是满足

$$\alpha\lambda > 0, \ |\alpha| < \frac{\pi}{2n} \tag{2.1}$$

① 原载:数学学报, 1956, 6(1):1-11.

的两个实数，则

$$\int_0^{\infty}\varphi(x)e^{-x^n+\lambda ix}dx = e^{i\alpha}\int_0^{\infty}\varphi(e^{i\alpha}x)\exp\{-e^{in\alpha}x^n+\lambda ie^{i\alpha}x\}dx \qquad (2.2)$$

式中积分路线都是沿着实数轴而取的.

证 设 $z = re^{i\theta}$ 则当 $\lambda\theta > 0$ 且 $|\theta| < \frac{\pi}{2n}$ 时

$$\mathrm{Re}\{z^n - i\lambda z\} = r^n\cos n\theta + \lambda r\sin\theta > 0$$

设用 A 表点 $z = R(R > 0)$，B 表 $z = Re^{i\alpha}$，$\widehat{AB}$ 表圆 $|z| = R$ 上面的一段劣弧，则

$$\left\{\int_{OA}+\int_{\widehat{AB}}+\int_{BO}\right\}\varphi(z)e^{-z^n+\lambda iz}dz = 0$$

在 $\widehat{AB}$ 上，

$$|\varphi(z)e^{-z^n+\lambda iz}| = |\varphi(Re^{i\theta})|e^{-(R^n\cos n\theta+\lambda R\sin\theta)} = O(R^{-1}),\ 当\ R\to+\infty$$

故若用 L 表示延长 OB 所得的半线，则

$$\int_0^{\infty}\varphi(x)e^{-x^n+\lambda ix}dx = \int_L\varphi(z)e^{-x^n+\lambda iz}dz = e^{i\alpha}\int_0^{\infty}\varphi(e^{i\alpha}x)\exp\{-e^{in\alpha}x^n+\lambda ie^{i\alpha}x\}dx$$

引理 2.2 当 $\sigma < 0$ 时

$$Z_{n,k}(s) = \frac{2^k}{\Gamma(s)}\int_0^{\infty}\omega^{s-1-kv}\left[\left\{\Gamma(1+v)+2\sum_{y=1}^{\infty}\int_0^{\infty}e^{-x^n}\cos\frac{2\pi yx}{\omega^v}dx\right\}^k-\Gamma^k(1+v)\right]d\omega \qquad (2.3)$$

即

$$Z_{n,k}(s) = \frac{2^k}{\Gamma(s)}\sum_{k'=1}^{\infty}\binom{k}{k'}\Gamma^{k-k'}(1+v)\int_0^{\infty}\omega^{s-1-kv}\times\left\{2\sum_{y=1}^{\infty}\int_0^{\infty}e^{-x^n}\cos\frac{2\pi yx}{\omega^v}dx\right\}^{k'}d\omega \qquad (2.4)$$

证 当 $\sigma < 0$ 时

$$\int_1^{\infty}\omega^{s-1}d\omega = -\frac{1}{s},\quad \int_1^{\infty}\omega^{s-1-kv}d\omega = -\frac{1}{s-kv}$$

故在(Ⅰ.3.8)① 内取 $h = 0$，即得

$$Z_{n,k}(s) = \frac{1}{\Gamma(s)}\left\{\int_1^{\infty}\omega^{s-1}\left[\left(\sum_{x=-\infty}^{\infty}e^{-x^n\omega}\right)^k-2^k\Gamma^k(1+v)\omega^{-kv}\right]d\omega+\int_0^1 2^k\omega^{s-kv-1}\left[\left(\Gamma(1+v)+2\sum_{y=1}^{\infty}\int_0^1 e^{-x^n}\cos\frac{2\pi yx}{\omega^v}dx\right)^k-\Gamma^k(1+v)\right]d\omega\right\}$$

---

① 我们用(Ⅰ.3.8)表第Ⅰ篇的(3.8). 我们又用引理Ⅰ.3.2表第Ⅰ篇的引理3.2. 其他类推.

用引理 Ⅰ.3.2(取 $h=0$) 变化上面花括弧内第一个积号下的函数,再合并两个积分,即得(2.3). 从此易得(2.4).

§3 主要引理

引理3.1 当 $\sigma=-(2M+1)\frac{v}{2}$ 而 M 是充分大的正整数时可以找到一个正数 A,使当 $t\to\infty$ 时

$$Z_{n,k}(s)=O(t^A) \tag{3.1}$$

证 (1) 由(2.4)可知只要考虑

$$I=\int_0^\infty \omega^{s-1-kv}\left\{2\sum_{y=1}^{\infty}\int_0^\infty \mathrm{e}^{-x^n}\cos\frac{2\pi yx}{\omega^v}\mathrm{d}x\right\}^{k'}\mathrm{d}\omega=$$

$$\int_0^\infty \omega^{s-1-kv}\left\{\lim_{N\to\infty}\sum_{y=-N}^{N}{}'\int_0^\infty \mathrm{e}^{-x^n}\mathrm{e}^{\frac{2\pi\mathrm{i}yx}{\omega^v}}\mathrm{d}x\right\}^{k'}\mathrm{d}\omega,\quad 1\leqslant k'\leqslant k \tag{3.2}$$

式中“′”表 $y\neq 0$.

今将用归纳法证明:当 $h\geqslant 1$ 且为整数时

$$\sum_{y=-N}^{N}{}'\int_0^\infty \mathrm{e}^{-x^n}\mathrm{e}^{\frac{2\pi\mathrm{i}yx}{\omega^v}}\mathrm{d}x\ \sum_{y=-N}^{N}{}'\frac{(-1)^h}{\left(\frac{2\pi\mathrm{i}y}{\omega^v}\right)^h}\int_0^\infty\left(\frac{\mathrm{d}^h}{\mathrm{d}x^h}\mathrm{e}^{-x^n}\right)\mathrm{e}^{\frac{2\pi\mathrm{i}yx}{\omega^v}}\mathrm{d}x \tag{3.3}$$

若将一函数看成是自己的0次导数,则上式当 $h=0$ 时显然成立. 又上式右端可以写成

$$\sum_{y=-N}^{N}{}'\frac{(-1)^h}{\left(\frac{2\pi\mathrm{i}y}{\omega^v}\right)^h}\int_0^\infty\left(\frac{\mathrm{d}^h}{\mathrm{d}x^h}\mathrm{e}^{-x^n}\right)\mathrm{d}\,\frac{\mathrm{e}^{\frac{2\pi\mathrm{i}yx}{\omega^v}}}{\frac{2\pi\mathrm{i}y}{\omega^v}}=$$

$$\sum_{y=-N}^{N}{}'\frac{(-1)^h}{\left(\frac{2\pi\mathrm{i}y}{\omega^v}\right)^{h+1}}\left\{\left[\left(\frac{\mathrm{d}^h}{\mathrm{d}x^h}\mathrm{e}^{-x^n}\right)\mathrm{e}^{\frac{2\pi\mathrm{i}yx}{\omega^v}}\right]_0^\infty-\int_0^\infty\left(\frac{\mathrm{d}^{h+1}}{\mathrm{d}x^{h+1}}\mathrm{e}^{-x^n}\right)\mathrm{e}^{\frac{2\pi\mathrm{i}yx}{\omega^v}}\mathrm{d}x\right\} \tag{3.4}$$

上面右端方括弧内的 $\frac{\mathrm{d}^h}{\mathrm{d}x^h}\mathrm{e}^{-x^n}$ 是 x 的多项式与 e^{-x^n} 之积,故当 $x\to+\infty$ 时 $\frac{\mathrm{d}^h}{\mathrm{d}x^h}\mathrm{e}^{-r^n}\to 0$. 又当 h 是奇数时,因

$$\frac{\mathrm{d}^h}{\mathrm{d}x^h}\mathrm{e}^{-x^n}=\frac{\mathrm{d}^h}{\mathrm{d}x^h}\sum_{\mu=0}^{\infty}\frac{(-x^n)^\mu}{\mu!}=\sum_{\mu=0}^{\infty}\frac{\mathrm{d}^h}{\mathrm{d}x^h}\frac{(-x^n)^\mu}{\mu!}$$

不含常数项,故当 $x=0$ 时其值为0. 若 h 是偶数则因当 $x=0$ 时,$\left(\frac{\mathrm{d}^h}{\mathrm{d}x^h}\mathrm{e}^{-x^n}\right)\mathrm{e}^{\frac{2\pi\mathrm{i}yx}{\omega^v}}$ 的值与 y 无关,设为 c,则因

$$\sum_{y=-N}^{N}{}' \frac{(-1)^h}{\left(\frac{2\pi i y}{\omega^v}\right)^{h+1}} \cdot c = 0$$

故由(3.4)得

$$\sum_{y=-N}^{N}{}' \frac{(-1)^h}{\left(\frac{2\pi i y}{\omega^v}\right)^{h}} \int_0^\infty \left(\frac{d^h}{dx^h} e^{-x^n}\right) e^{\frac{2\pi i y x}{\omega^v}} dx =$$

$$\sum_{y=-N}^{N}{}' \frac{(-1)^{h+1}}{\left(\frac{2\pi i y}{\omega^v}\right)^{h+1}} \int_0^\infty \left(\frac{d^{h+1}}{dx^{h+1}} e^{-x^n}\right) e^{\frac{2\pi i y x}{\omega^v}} dx$$

故(3.3)当 h 换成 $h+1$ 后仍成立. 故(3.3)恒成立.

(2) 由(3.3),可将(3.2)写成

$$I = \int_0^\infty \omega^{s-1-kv} \prod_{j=1}^{k'} \left\{ \sum_{y_j=-\infty}^{\infty}{}' \frac{(-1)^{h_j}}{\left(\frac{2\pi i y_j}{\omega^v}\right)^{h_j}} \int_0^\infty \left(\frac{d^{h_j}}{dx^{h_j}} e^{-x^n}\right) e^{\frac{2\pi i y x}{\omega^v}} dx \right\} d\omega$$

式中 $h_1, h_2, \cdots, h_{k'}$ 可以是任意选定的大于 1 的一串整数(注意花括号内每一积分的绝对值小于与 y 无关的一个常数). 上式也可以写成

$$I = (-1)^R \int_0^\infty \omega^{s-1-kv+Rv} \times$$

$$\prod_{j=1}^{k'} \left\{ \sum_{y_j=-\infty}^{\infty}{}' \frac{1}{(2\pi i y_j)^{h_j}} \int_0^\infty \left(\frac{d^{h_j}}{dx^{h_j}} e^{-x_j^n}\right) e^{\frac{2\pi i y_j x_j}{\omega^v}} dx_j \right\} d\omega \tag{3.5}$$

式中 $R = \sum_{j=1}^{k'} h_j$.

(3) 令 $\frac{d^h}{dx^h} e^{-x^n} = \varphi_k(x) e^{-x^n}$, $\lambda = \frac{2\pi y}{\omega^v}$, $\alpha\lambda > 0$ 且 $|\alpha| < \frac{\pi}{2n}$,则由引理2.1得

$$\int_0^\infty \left(\frac{d^h}{dx^h} e^{-x^n}\right) e^{\frac{2\pi i y x}{\omega^v}} dx = \int_0^\infty \varphi_h(x) e^{-x^n + i\lambda x} dx =$$

$$e^{i\alpha} \int_0^\infty \varphi_h(e^{\alpha i} x) \exp\left\{ -e^{n\alpha i} x^n + \frac{2\pi i y}{\omega^v} e^{\alpha i} x \right\} dx$$

用 $\omega^v x$ 代最后一积分中的 x 即得

$$\int_0^\infty \left(\frac{d^h}{dx^h} e^{-x^n}\right) e^{\frac{2\pi i y x}{\omega^v}} dx = e^{\alpha i} \omega^v \int_0^\infty \varphi_h(e^{\alpha i} \omega^v x) \exp\{ -e^{n\alpha i} \omega x^n + 2\pi i y e^{\alpha i} x \} dx$$

因此由(3.5)得$\left(\text{假定 } \alpha_j y_j > 0, |\alpha_j| < \frac{\pi}{2n}\right)$

$$I = (-1)^R \int_0^\infty \omega^{s-1-kv+Rv+k'v} \times$$

$$\prod_{j=1}^{k'}\left\{\sum_{y_j=-\infty}^{\infty}{}'\frac{e^{\alpha_j i}}{(2\pi i y_j)^{h_j}}\int_0^{\infty}\varphi_{hj}(e^{\alpha_j i}\omega^v x_j)\exp[-e^{n\alpha_j i}\omega x_j^n+2\pi i e^{\alpha_j i}y_j x_j]dx_j\right\}d\omega \tag{3.6}$$

(4) 当 $x_j>0$ 时

$$\text{Re } e^{n\alpha_j i}\omega x_j^n=\omega x_j^n\cos n\alpha_j>0$$
$$\text{Re } 2\pi i\, e^{\alpha_j i}x_j y_j=-2\pi x_j y_j\sin\alpha_j<0$$

故

$$\int_0^{\infty}|\varphi_{hj}(e^{\alpha_j i}\omega^v x_j)\exp[-e^{n\alpha_j i}\omega x_j^n+2\pi i e^{\alpha_j i}y_j x_j]|dx_j\leqslant$$
$$\int_0^{\infty}|\varphi_{hj}(e^{\alpha_j i}\omega^v x_j)|\exp[-\omega x_j^n\cos n\alpha_j-2\pi x_j y_j\sin\alpha_j]dx_j\leqslant$$
$$\int_0^{\infty}|\varphi_{hj}(e^{\alpha_j i}\omega^v x_j)|\exp[-\omega x_j^n\cos n\alpha_j]dx_j<+\infty \tag{3.7}$$

又因 $h_j\geqslant 2$,故(3.6)右边花括弧内各级数都是绝对收敛级数. 因此(3.6)可写成

$$I=(-1)^R\int_0^{\infty}d\omega\sum_{y_1=-\infty}^{\infty}{}'\cdots\sum_{y_{k'}=-\infty}^{\infty}{}'\frac{e^{iT}\omega^{S-1}}{(2\pi i y_1)^{h_1}\cdots(2\pi i y_{k'})^{h_{k'}}}\times$$
$$\int_0^{\infty}\cdots\int_0^{\infty}\varphi h_1(e^{\alpha_1 i}\omega^v x_1)\cdots\varphi h_{k'}(e^{\alpha_{k'}i}\omega^v x_{k'})\times$$
$$\exp\left\{-\omega\sum_{j=1}^{k'}e^{n\alpha_j i}x_j^n+2\pi i\sum_{j=1}^{k'}e^{\alpha_j i}y_j x_j\right\}dx_1\cdots dx_{k'} \tag{3.8}$$

式中(S,T 是新记号,R 是旧记号)

$$S=s-kv+Rv+k'v,\ T=\sum_{j=1}^{k'}\alpha_j,\ R=\sum_{j=1}^{k'}h_j \tag{3.9}$$

(5) 由本引理的假设,我们可选定 $h_j\geqslant 2$ 使

$$\text{Re } S=\frac{v}{2} \tag{3.10}$$

考虑多重级数

$$\sum_{y_1=-\infty}^{\infty}{}'\cdots\sum_{y_{k'}=-\infty}^{\infty}{}'\frac{|\omega^{S-1}|}{(2\pi i y_1)^{h_1}\cdots(2\pi y_{k'})^{h_{k'}}}\times$$
$$\left|\int_0^{\infty}\cdots\int_0^{\infty}\varphi h_1(e^{\alpha_1 i}\omega^v x_1)\cdots\varphi h_{k'}(e^{\alpha_{k'}i}\omega^v x_{k'})\times\right.$$
$$\left.\exp\left\{-\omega\sum_{j=1}^{k'}e^{n\alpha_j i}x_j^u+2\pi i\sum_{j=1}^{k'}e^{\alpha_j i}y_j x_j\right\}dx_1\cdots dx_{k'}\right| \tag{3.11}$$

由(3.7)可知上面的 k' 重积分的绝对值不超过

$$\int_0^{\infty}\cdots\int_0^{\infty}|\varphi h_1(e^{\alpha_1 i}\omega^v x_1)\cdots\varphi h_{k'}(e^{\alpha_{k'}i}\omega^v x_{k'})|\times$$

$$\exp\{-\omega\sum_{j=1}^{k'}x_j^n\cos n\alpha_j-2\pi\sum_{j=1}^{k'}x_jy_j\sin\alpha_j\}\mathrm{d}x_1\cdots\mathrm{d}x_{k'}\tag{3.12}$$

设多项式 $\varphi_{hj}(x_j)=\sum_{\mu=0}^{m_j}c_{j,\mu}x_j^{\mu}$，则当 $\omega\leqslant 1$，$x_j\geqslant 0$ 时

$$|\varphi_{hj}(e^{\alpha_j i}\omega^v x_j)|\leqslant\sum_{\mu=0}^{m_j}|c_{j,\mu}|x_j^{\mu}=\Phi_j(x_j)\text{（新记号）}$$

而(3.12)不超过（因 $|y_i|\geqslant 1$）

$$\int_0^\infty\cdots\int_0^\infty\Phi_1(x_1)\cdots\Phi_{k'}(x_{k'})\exp\{-2\pi\sum_{j=1}^{k'}x_j|\sin\alpha_j|\}\mathrm{d}x_1\cdots\mathrm{d}x_{k'}=$$

$$\prod_{j=1}^{k'}\int_0^\infty\Phi_j(x_j)\exp\left\{-2\pi x_j|\sin\alpha_j|\right\}\mathrm{d}x_j<\infty\tag{3.13}$$

故如将(3.11)自0积分至1（对于 ω）所得为一收敛的积分.

另一方面当 $\omega\geqslant 1$ 时，(3.12)不超过

$$\omega^{-k'v}\int_0^\infty\cdots\int_0^\infty|\varphi_{h_1}(e^{\alpha_1 i}x)\cdots\varphi h_{k'}(e^{\alpha_{k'}i}x)|\exp\{-\sum_{j=1}^{k'}x_j^n\cos n\alpha_j\}\mathrm{d}x_1\cdots\mathrm{d}x_{k'}\leqslant$$

$$\omega^{-k'v}\int_0^\infty\cdots\int_0^\infty\Phi_{h_1}(x_1)\cdots\Phi_{h_{k'}}(x_{k'})\exp\{-\sum_{j=1}^{k'}x_j^n\cos n\alpha_j\}\mathrm{d}x_1\cdots\mathrm{d}x_{k'}=$$

$$\omega^{-k'v}\prod_{j=1}^{k'}\int_0^\infty\Phi_{h_j}(x_j)\exp\left\{-x_j^n\cos n\alpha_j\right\}\mathrm{d}x_j\tag{3.14}$$

故由(3.10)，若把(3.11)自1积分至 $+\infty$ 亦得收敛的积分.

因此若把(3.11)自0积分至 $+\infty$，所得为收敛的积分.

(6) 由(3.13)及(3.14)可以看出：k' 重级数(3.11)在 $0<\omega_0\leqslant\omega\leqslant\omega_1<+\infty$ 时是一致收敛的. 因此，(3.8)由第一个积分号下的 k' 重级数在 $0<\omega_0<\omega<\omega_1<+\infty$ 时也是一致收敛的. 故可用逐项积分法自 ω_0 积至 ω_1. 由一著名的定理[1]，根据(5)的结果，我们可以把那个 k' 重级数由0积至 $+\infty$. 这样，我们就可以把(3.8)内第一个积分号移到所有 $\sum$ 号之后，得到

$$I=(-1)^R\sum_{y_1=-\infty}^{\infty}{}'\cdots\sum_{y_{k'}=-\infty}^{\infty}{}'\frac{e^{iT}}{(2\pi iy_1)^{h_1}\cdots(2\pi iy_{k'})^{h_{k'}}}\int_0^\infty\omega^{s-1}\mathrm{d}\omega\times$$

$$\int_0^\infty\cdots\int_0^\infty\varphi h_1(e^{\alpha_1 i}\omega^v x_1)\cdots\varphi h_{k'}(e^{\alpha_{k'}i}\omega^v x_{k'})\times$$

$$\exp\{-\omega\sum_{j=1}^{k'}e^{n\alpha_j i}x_j^n+2\pi i\sum_{j=1}^{k'}e^{\alpha_j i}y_i x_j\}\mathrm{d}x_1\cdots\mathrm{d}x_{k'}\tag{3.15}$$

不仅如此，由(5)内对于(3.12)这个 k' 重积分的讨论，我们知道上式右边的

$k'+1$ 累次积分是绝对收敛的,同时不难看出下列积分(看成对于 x_μ 的积分,$\mu=1,2,\cdots,k'$)

$$\int_0^\infty \mathrm{d}x_\mu \int_0^\infty \cdots \int_0^\infty \varphi_{h_\mu}(\mathrm{e}^{\alpha_\mu \mathrm{i}}\omega^v x_\mu)\varphi_{h_{\mu+1}}(\mathrm{e}^{\alpha_{\mu+1}\mathrm{i}}\omega^v x_{\mu+1})\cdots\varphi_{h_{k'}}(\mathrm{e}^{\alpha_{k'}\mathrm{i}}\omega^v x_{k'})\times$$
$$\exp\{-\omega\sum_{j=\mu}^{k'}\mathrm{e}^{n\alpha_j\mathrm{i}}x_j^n+2\pi\mathrm{i}\sum_{j=\mu}^{k'}\mathrm{e}^{\alpha_j\mathrm{i}}y_jx_j\}\mathrm{d}x_\mu\cdots\mathrm{d}x_{k'}$$

在 $0<\omega_0\leqslant\omega\leqslant\omega_1<+\infty$ 时是一致收敛的.因此由一个著名的定理①我们可以把(3.15)内的第一个积分号移到所有积分号之后.于是得到

$$I=(-1)^R\sum_{y_1=-\infty}^{\infty}{}'\cdots\sum_{y_{k'}=-\infty}^{\infty}{}'\frac{\mathrm{e}^{\mathrm{i}T}}{(2\pi\mathrm{i}y_1)^{h_1}\cdots(2\pi\mathrm{i}y_{k'})^{h_{k'}}}\times$$
$$\int_0^\infty\cdots\int_0^\infty\exp\{2\pi\mathrm{i}\sum_{j=1}^{k'}\mathrm{e}^{\alpha_j\mathrm{i}}y_jx_j\}\mathrm{d}x_1\cdots\mathrm{d}x_{k'}\times$$
$$\int_0^\infty\omega^{S-1}\{\prod_{j=1}^{k'}\varphi_{h_j}(\mathrm{e}^{\alpha_j\mathrm{i}}\omega^v x_j)\}\exp\{-\omega\sum_{j=1}^{k'}\mathrm{e}^{n\alpha_j\mathrm{i}}j^{\mathrm{i}}x_j^n\}\mathrm{d}\omega \tag{3.16}$$

(7)上式右边最内一积分为

$$J=\int_0^\infty\omega^{S-1}\left\{\prod_{j=1}^{k'}\varphi_{h_j}(\mathrm{e}^{\alpha_j\mathrm{i}}\omega^v x_j)\right\}\mathrm{e}^{-\omega\Lambda}\mathrm{d}\omega \tag{3.17}$$

式中 $\Lambda=\sum_{j=1}^{k'}\mathrm{e}^{n\alpha_j\mathrm{i}}x_j^n$.因当 $x_j\geqslant 0$ 时,由3)内对于 α_j 的假定,有

$$\operatorname{Re}\Lambda=\sum_{j=1}^{k'}x_j^n\cos n\alpha_j\geqslant 0 \tag{3.18}$$

且上式中的"="号只在 $x_1=x_2=\cdots=x_{k'}=0$ 时才成立,故除在 $x_1=x_2=\cdots=x_{k'}=0$ 时以外,都可设

$$-\frac{\pi}{2}<\arg\Lambda=\Omega<\frac{\pi}{2}$$

于是(3.17)内积分号下的函数的圆弧

$$|\omega|=\rho,\quad |\arg\omega|\leqslant|\Omega|,\quad \Omega\arg\omega\leqslant 0$$

上的绝对值的上界当 $\rho\to+\infty$ 时为 $O(\rho^{-1})$.因此像在引理2.1那样,我们可以用 $\frac{\omega}{\Lambda}$ 代(3.17)中的 ω 而得

$$J=\frac{1}{\Lambda^S}\int_0^\infty\omega^{s-1}\left\{\prod_{j=1}^{k'}\varphi_{hj}\left(\mathrm{e}^{\alpha_j\mathrm{i}}\omega^v\frac{x_j}{\Lambda^v}\right)\right\}\mathrm{e}^{-\omega}\mathrm{d}\omega$$

---

① 参看[1],54－55页.我们把所讨论的积分看成 $k'+1$ 重的累次积分,然后逐步移动(3.15)内第一个积分号,以至最后.如用Fubini定理可以更简单些.

前已设 $\varphi_{hj}(x)=\sum_{\mu=0}^{m_j}c_{j,\mu}x_j^{\mu}$,故上式可以写成

$$J=\sum\frac{C_{\lambda_1,\lambda_2,\cdots\lambda_{k'}}x_1^{\lambda_1}\cdots x_k^{\lambda_{k'}}}{\Lambda^{s+v(\lambda_1+\cdots+\lambda_{k'})}}\int_0^{\infty}\omega^{s+v(\lambda_1+\cdots+\lambda_{k'})-1}\mathrm{e}^{-\omega}\mathrm{d}\omega$$

其中 $C_{\lambda_1,\lambda_2,\cdots\lambda_{k'}}=C_{1,\lambda_1}C_{2,\lambda_2}\cdots C_{k',\lambda_{k'}}\mathrm{e}^{(\alpha_1\lambda_1+\cdots+\alpha_k\lambda_k)\mathrm{i}}$,而 λ_j 分别自 0 变到 m_j. 上式即 $\left(注意已选好 \operatorname{Re}S=\frac{v}{2}\right)$

$$J=\sum\Gamma(S+v(\lambda_1+\cdots+\lambda_{k'}))\frac{C_{\lambda_1,\cdots,\lambda_{k'}}x_1^{\lambda_1}\cdots x^{\lambda'_{k'}}}{\Lambda^{S+v(\lambda_1+\cdots+\lambda_{k'})}}$$

故由(3.16)得

$$I=(-1)^R\sum_{y_1=-\infty}^{\infty}{}'\cdots\sum_{y_{k'}=-\infty}^{\infty}{}'\frac{\mathrm{e}^{\mathrm{i}T}}{(2\pi\mathrm{i}y_1)^{h_1}\cdots(2\pi\mathrm{i}y_{k'})^{h_{k'}}}\sum\Gamma(S+v(\lambda_1+\cdots+\lambda_{k'}))\times$$

$$C_{\lambda_1,\cdots,\lambda_{k'}}\int_0^{\infty}\cdots\int_0^{\infty}\exp\{2\pi\mathrm{i}\sum_{j=1}^{k'}\mathrm{e}^{\alpha_j\mathrm{i}}y_jx_j\}\frac{x_1^{\lambda_1}\cdots x_{k'}^{\lambda_{k'}}}{\Lambda^{S+v(\lambda_1+\cdots+\lambda_{k'})}}\mathrm{d}x_1\cdots\mathrm{d}x_{k'}\tag{3.19}$$

(8) 今取

$$|\alpha_1|=|\alpha_2|=\cdots=|\alpha_{k'}|=\frac{1}{|t|}$$

则当 $|t|$ 充分大时,即满足 $|\alpha_j|<\frac{\pi}{2n}$ 的条件. 由

$$\Lambda=\sum_{j=1}^{k'}x_j^n\cos n\alpha_j+\mathrm{i}\sum_{j=1}^{k'}x_j^n\sin n\alpha_j$$

得

$$|\Lambda|\geqslant\cos\frac{n}{|t|}\sum_{j=1}^{k'}x_j^n\left(\geqslant x_j^n\cos\frac{n}{|t|}\right)$$

$$|\arg\Lambda|=\left|\arctan\frac{\sum_{j=1}^{k'}x_j^n\sin n\alpha_j}{\sum_{j=1}^{k'}x_j^n\cos n\alpha_j}\right|\leqslant$$

$$\arctan\left(\tan\frac{n}{|t|}\right)=\frac{n}{|t|}$$

因 $\operatorname{Re}S=\frac{v}{2}$,$\operatorname{Im}S=t$,故

$$|\Lambda^S|=|\Lambda|^{\frac{v}{2}}|\mathrm{e}^{(\mathrm{i}\arg\Lambda)(\frac{v}{2}+\mathrm{i}t)}|=$$

$$|\Lambda|^{\frac{v}{2}}|\mathrm{e}^{-\mathrm{i}t\arg\Lambda}|>C\left(\sum_{j=1}^{k'}x_j^n\right)^{\frac{v}{2}}$$

式中 C 是一个适当的正的常数. 又因 $|y_j|\geqslant1$, $y_j\alpha_j>0$,及当 $|\alpha|\leqslant\frac{\pi}{2}$ 时

$|\sin\alpha| > \frac{2}{\pi}|\alpha|$,故(3.19)右边的 k' 重积分的绝对值不超过

$$O\left[\int_0^\infty\cdots\int_0^\infty \exp\left\{-2\pi\sum_{j=1}^{k'}(y_j\sin\alpha_j)x_j\right\}\frac{\mathrm{d}x_1\cdots\mathrm{d}x_{k'}}{(x_1^n+\cdots+x_{k'}^n)^{v/2}}\right]=$$

$$O\left[\int_0^\infty\cdots\int_0^\infty \exp\left\{-4\sum_{j=1}^{k'}\frac{x_j}{|t|}\right\}\frac{\mathrm{d}x_1\cdots\mathrm{d}x_{k'}}{(x_1^n+\cdots+x_{k'}^n)^{v/2}}\right]=$$

$$O\left[|t|^{k'-\frac{1}{2}}\int_0^\infty\cdots\int_0^\infty \exp\left\{-4\sum_{j=1}^{k'}x_j\right\}\frac{\mathrm{d}x_1\cdots\mathrm{d}x_{k'}}{(x_1^n+\cdots+x_{k'}^n)^{v/2}}\right]=$$

$$O(t^{k'-\frac{1}{2}})$$

(利用 $\frac{x_1^n+\cdots+x_{k'}^n}{k'}\geqslant(x_1^n\cdots x_{k'}^n)^{\frac{1}{k'}}$,可证明上面最后的 k' 重积分收敛,且不超过 $k'^{-\frac{v}{2}}\left(\int_0^\infty e^{-4x}x^{-\frac{1}{2k'}}\mathrm{d}x\right)^{k'}$). 因 $h_j\geqslant 2$,故由(3.19)得

$$I \ll |t|^{k'-\frac{1}{2}}\sum\Gamma(S+v(\lambda_1+\cdots+\lambda_{k'})) \tag{3.20}$$

我们知道当 x 一定而 $y\to\pm\infty$ 时

$$|\Gamma(x+\mathrm{i}y)| \sim e^{-\frac{1}{2}\pi|y|}|y|^{x-\frac{1}{2}}\sqrt{2\pi}\text{①} \tag{3.21}$$

故由(2.4)及(3.20)得

$$Z_{n,k}(S) = O(t^A)$$

§4　结　　论

我们现在可以证明下面的定理,在证明中要屡次用到(Ⅰ.3.8)那个公式,因此把它写在下面

$$Z_{n,k}(S) = \frac{2^k\Gamma^k(1+v)}{\Gamma(s)}\frac{1}{s-kv}-\frac{1}{\Gamma(s+1)}+$$
$$\frac{1}{\Gamma(s)}\left\{\int_1^\infty\omega^{s-1}\left[\left(\sum_{x=-\infty}^{\infty}e^{-x^n\omega}\right)^k-1\right]\mathrm{d}\omega+\int_0^1 2^k\omega^{s-kv-1}\left[\left(\Gamma(1+v)+\right.\right.\right.$$
$$\left.\left.\left.2\omega^{2hv}\sum_{y=1}^{\infty}\frac{(-1)^h}{(2\pi y)^{2h}}\int_0^\infty\left(\frac{\mathrm{d}^{2h}}{\mathrm{d}x^{2h}}e^{-x^n}\right)\cos\frac{2\pi yx}{\omega^v}\mathrm{d}x\right)^k-\Gamma(1+v)\right]\mathrm{d}\omega\right\} \tag{Ⅰ.3.8}$$

这个表示式除去奇点 $S=kv$ 外可以适用于全平面,式中 h 可取任意正整数值,且若把一函数看成是自己的0次导数,则 h 也可以是0.

---

① 参看[1]第151页(4.42节).

定理4.1　设A_1,A_2是任意二常数,满足$A_1 < A_2$,则当$A_1 \leqslant \sigma \leqslant A_2$而$t \to \infty$时,可以找到一个常数$A$(与$A_1,A_2$有关)使

$$Z_{n,k}(s) = O(t^A) \tag{4.1}$$

一致的成立(即O中所隐含的常数只与A_1,A_2有关).

证　当$\sigma \geqslant \sigma_0 > kv$时,$|Z_{n,k}(s)| \leqslant Z_{n,k}(\sigma_0)$. 今考虑$\sigma \leqslant \sigma_0$的情形. 由(Ⅰ.3.8)易知$Z_{n,k}(\bar{s}) = \overline{Z_{n,k}(s)}$.(式中$\bar{z}$表$z$的共轭复数),故只须讨论$t \to +\infty$的情形. 由引理3.1知道当$M$是充分大的整数时,在半线

$$\sigma = -(2M+1)\frac{v}{2},\ t \geqslant 1 \quad 及 \quad \sigma = \sigma_0,\ t \geqslant 1$$

上(4.1)成立(对于适当的A而言). 我们要证明在$A_1 \leqslant \sigma \leqslant A_2$, $t \geqslant 1$时

$$Z_{n,k}(s) = O(e^t) = O(e^{e^{\varepsilon t}}) \tag{4.2}$$

式中ε表任意正数. 这可以根据(Ⅰ.3.8)来证明. 因当$|z| \to \infty$时

$$\log \Gamma(z) = \left(z - \frac{1}{2}\right)\log z - z + \frac{1}{2}\log 2\pi + O(1/|z|)$$

对于$-\pi + \delta \leqslant \arg z \leqslant \pi - \delta$一致的成立①,故当$A_1 \leqslant \sigma \leqslant A_2$而$t \to +\infty$时(Ⅰ.3.8)右边前两项$= O(e^t)$. 又(Ⅰ.3.8)右边花括号外的因子也是$O(e^t)$,而花括号内部的两个积分的绝对值分别小于下面两个积分

$$\int_1^{\infty} \omega^{\sigma-1}\left[\left(\sum_{x=-\infty}^{\infty} e^{-x^n\omega}\right)^k - 1\right]d\omega$$

及

$$\int_0^1 2^k \omega^{\sigma-kv-1}\left[\left\{\Gamma(1+v) + 2\omega^{2hv}\sum_{y=1}^{\infty}\frac{1}{(2\pi y)^{2h}}\int_0^{\infty}\left|\frac{d^{2h}}{dx^{2h}}e^{-x^n}\right|dx\right\}^k - \Gamma^k(1+v)\right]d\omega$$

其中h可取充分大的值. 上面两积分都是收敛的,且与t无关,故等于$O(1)$. 因此(4.2)成立. 根据以上的讨论,可知可以应用一个已知的定理6)得到:当$-(2M+1)\frac{v}{2} \leqslant \sigma \leqslant \sigma_0$时(4.1)成立. 又因$M$可以任意大,所以定理成立.

参考书目

[1] Titchmarsh, Theory of functions, 第二版,44-45页(1.77节).

[2] Littlewood, Lectures on the theory of functions, 108(定理108的推论).

① 参看[1],151页(4.42)节.

黎曼 ζ 函数的一种推广 ——Ⅲ. $Z_{n,k}(s)$ 的均值公式[①]

§1 引 论

关于 $\zeta(s)$,我们有所谓均值公式(或均值定理),如:

$$\lim_{T\to\infty}\frac{1}{T}\int_1^T |\zeta(\sigma+\mathrm{i}t)|^2\mathrm{d}t=\zeta(2\sigma),\quad \sigma>\frac{1}{2} \tag{1.1}$$

$$\int_0^T\left|\zeta\left(\frac{1}{2}+\mathrm{i}t\right)\right|^2\mathrm{d}t\sim T\log T \tag{1.2}$$

本篇的目的就是要为 $Z_{n,k}(s)$ 建立类似的公式.

当 $\sigma>kv$ 时我们很容易为 $Z_{n,k}(s)$ 建立类似(1.1)的公式②,在这种情形下,我们可以把 $Z_{n,k}(s)$ 表成绝对收敛级数的和:

$$Z_{n,k}(s)=\sum_{x_1=-\infty}^{\infty}\cdots\sum_{x_k=-\infty}^{\infty}{}'\frac{1}{(x_1^n+\cdots+x_k^n)^s}=\sum_{m=1}^{\infty}\frac{B(m)}{m^s} \tag{1.3}$$

其中“′”表 $x_1,\cdots,x_k$ 不同时为零,而 $B(m)$ 表

① 原载:数学学报,1956,6(3):347-361.

② 像在第Ⅰ,Ⅱ两篇一样,我们永远假定 n 是正偶数而 $v=\frac{1}{n}$.

$$x_1^n + \cdots + x_k^n = m$$

的整数解的组数. 因此,当 $T \geqslant 1$ 时

$$\frac{1}{T}\int_1^T | Z_{n,k}(\sigma + \mathrm{i}t) |^2 \mathrm{d}t =$$

$$\frac{1}{T}\int_1^T \sum_{m_1=1}^{\infty}\sum_{m_2=1}^{\infty} \frac{B(m_1)}{m_1^{\sigma+\mathrm{i}t}} \frac{B(m_2)}{m_2^{\sigma-\mathrm{i}t}} \mathrm{d}t =$$

$$\sum_{m=1}^{\infty} \frac{B^2(m)}{m^{2\sigma}} + \frac{1}{T} \sum_{\substack{m_1=1 \\ m_1 \neq m_2}}^{\infty} \sum_{m_2=1}^{\infty} \frac{B(m_1)B(m_2)}{(m_1 m_2)^{\sigma}} \frac{\left(\frac{m_1}{m_2}\right)^{\mathrm{i}T} - \left(\frac{m_1}{m_2}\right)^{\mathrm{i}}}{\mathrm{i}\log \frac{m_1}{m_2}}$$

故

$$\lim_{T\to\infty} \frac{1}{T}\int_1^T | Z_{n,k}(\sigma + \mathrm{i}t) |^2 \mathrm{d}t = \sum_{m=1}^{\infty} \frac{B^2(m)}{m^{2\sigma}}, \quad \sigma > kv \tag{1.4}$$

当 $\sigma \leqslant kv$ 时,均值公式的建立就困难得多. 在为 $\zeta(s)$ 建立均值公式时有许多方法,其中方法之一是先证明形如

$$\int_0^{\infty} \left|\zeta\left(\frac{1}{2} + \mathrm{i}t\right)\right|^2 \mathrm{e}^{-\delta t} \mathrm{d}t \sim \frac{1}{\delta}\log\frac{1}{\delta}, \quad \delta \to 0 \tag{1.5}$$

的公式. 我们不妨称(1.5)为梯其玛什(Titchmarsh)型均值公式. 本篇也要先为 $Z_{n,k}(s)$ 建立梯其玛什型均值公式. 为简洁计,我们只讨论 $0 < \sigma < kv - v$ 的情形.

§2　几个引理,一对傅里叶变形

引理 2.1　(梅林(Mellin)反转公式①)设 κ 是实数而

(1) $y^{\kappa-1}f(y) \in L(0,\infty)$;

(2) $f(y)$ 在 $y = x(0 < x < \infty)$ 的一个邻域内囿变;

(3) $F(s) = \int_0^{\infty} f(y) y^{s-1} \mathrm{d}y,\ s = \kappa + \mathrm{i}t$;

则

$$\frac{1}{2}\{f(x+0) + f(x-0)\} = \frac{1}{2\pi \mathrm{i}} \lim_{T\to\infty} \int_{\kappa-\mathrm{i}T}^{\kappa+\mathrm{i}T} F(s) x^{-s} \mathrm{d}s$$

引理 2.2　下列二函数是一对傅里叶变形

---

① Titchmarsh, Introduction to the theory of Fourier integrals(Oxford,1937),第 1.29 节. 以后把这一本书记作 TF1.

$$f(t) = \frac{1}{\sqrt{2\pi}}\Gamma(a+\mathrm{i}t)Z_{n,k}(a+\mathrm{i}t)\mathrm{e}^{-\mathrm{i}(c+\mathrm{i}t)(\pi/2-\delta)}$$

$$F(\xi) = \mathrm{e}^{a\xi}\{(\sum_{x=-\infty}^{\infty}\mathrm{e}^{-x^n\mathrm{i}\mathrm{e}^{\xi-\mathrm{i}\delta}})^k - j - j'R(\omega)\} \tag{2.1}$$

式中 $0<\delta<\pi$，a 不等于 0 及 kv，$\omega = \mathrm{i}\mathrm{e}^{\xi-\mathrm{i}\delta}$，

$$R(\omega) = 2^k\Gamma^k(1+v)\omega^{-kv} \tag{2.2}$$

而

$$j = \begin{cases} 1, & 当\ a>0, \\ 0, & 当\ a<0, \end{cases} \quad j' = \begin{cases} 1, & 当\ a<kv \\ 0, & 当\ a>kv \end{cases}$$

证 (1) 当 $\sigma > kv$ 时，由(Ⅰ.3.5)① 知道

$$Z_{n,k}(s) = \frac{1}{\Gamma(s)}\int_0^{\infty}\omega^{s-1}[(\sum_{x=-\infty}^{\infty}\mathrm{e}^{-x^n\omega})^k - 1]\mathrm{d}\omega \tag{2.3}$$

在 $(0,\infty)$ 内函数 $(\sum_{x=-\infty}^{\infty}\mathrm{e}^{-x^n\omega})^k - 1$ 是单调下降的，故在每一点 ω，$\omega>0$ 的附近，这函数是囿变的．又当 $\omega\to+\infty$ 时

$$(\sum_{x=-\infty}^{\infty}\mathrm{e}^{-x^n\omega})^k - 1 < (\sum_{x=-\infty}^{\infty}\mathrm{e}^{-|x|\omega})^k - 1 = \left(\frac{1+\mathrm{e}^{-\omega}}{1-\mathrm{e}^{-\omega}}\right)^k - 1 = O(\mathrm{e}^{-\omega})$$

故对于任何实数 κ 都有

$$\omega^{\kappa-1}\{(\sum_{x=-\infty}^{\infty}\mathrm{e}^{-x^n\omega})^k - 1\}\in L(0,\infty)$$

又从定理Ⅱ.4.1 及(Ⅱ.3.21)得 $\Gamma(a+\mathrm{i}t)Z_{n,k}(a+\mathrm{i}t) = o(\mathrm{e}^{(-\pi/2+\varepsilon)|t|})$ $(\varepsilon>0)$．因此，可以引用引理 2.1 得到

$$(\sum_{x=-\infty}^{\infty}\mathrm{e}^{-x^n\omega})^k - 1 = \frac{1}{2\pi\mathrm{i}}\int_{c-\mathrm{i}\infty}^{c+\mathrm{i}\infty}\Gamma(s)Z_{n,k}(s)\omega^{-s}\mathrm{d}s \tag{2.4}$$

在上式中假定了 $c>kv$，$\omega>0$．设 $s = c+\mathrm{i}t$，则

$$\omega^{-s} = \mathrm{e}^{-(c+\mathrm{i}t)(\log\omega+\mathrm{i}\arg\omega)} = \mathrm{e}^{-(c\log\omega - t\arg\omega)+\mathrm{i}(t\log\omega+c\arg\omega)}$$

我们容易看出上式两边当 $\mathrm{Re}\,\omega>0$ 时都是 ω 的解析函数$\left(\omega\right.$ 的辐角应取在 $-\frac{\pi}{2}$ 与 $\left.\frac{\pi}{2}\right.$ 之间$\left.\right)$．因此上式当 $\mathrm{Re}\,\omega>0$ 时恒成立．命

$$\omega = \mathrm{i}\mathrm{e}^{\xi-\mathrm{i}\delta} = \mathrm{e}^{\xi+\mathrm{i}(\frac{\pi}{2}-\delta)} = \mathrm{e}^{\xi}(\sin\delta + \mathrm{i}\cos\delta),\quad 0<\delta<\pi$$

则得

$$(\sum_{x=-\infty}^{\infty}\mathrm{e}^{-x^n\omega})^k - 1 = \frac{1}{2\pi}\int_{-\infty}^{\infty}\Gamma(c+\mathrm{i}t)Z_{n,k}(c+\mathrm{i}t)\mathrm{e}^{-(c+\mathrm{i}t)\xi-\mathrm{i}(c+\mathrm{i}t)(\pi/2-\delta)}\mathrm{d}t$$

---

① 我们用(Ⅰ.3.5)表示 Ⅰ 内公式(3.5)，用定理Ⅱ.4.1.表示 Ⅱ 内定理4.1等．又 Ⅰ 登在数学学报第5卷第3期(1955)第244-285页；Ⅱ 登在第6卷第1期(1956)第1-11页．

这证明当 $c > kv$ 时

$$e^{c\xi}\{(\sum_{x=-\infty}^{\infty} e^{-x^n\omega})^k - 1\} = \frac{1}{2\pi}\int_{-\infty}^{\infty} \Gamma(c+\mathrm{i}t)Z_{n,k}(c+\mathrm{i}t)e^{-\mathrm{i}(c+\mathrm{i}t)(\pi/2-\delta)}e^{-\mathrm{i}t\xi}\mathrm{d}t$$

因而得到一对傅里叶变形

$$f(t) = \frac{1}{\sqrt{2\pi}}\Gamma(c+\mathrm{i}t)Z_{n,k}(c+\mathrm{i}t)e^{-\mathrm{i}(c+\mathrm{i}t)(\pi/2-\delta)}$$

$$F(\xi) = e^{c\xi}\{(\sum_{x=-\infty}^{\infty} e^{-x^n\omega})^k - 1\}, \quad \omega = \mathrm{i}e^{\xi-\mathrm{i}\delta}$$

这证明了引理中当 $a = c > kv$ 的情形.

(2) 当 $|s| \to \infty$ 时

$$\log \Gamma(s) = \left(s - \frac{1}{2}\right)\log s - s + \frac{1}{2}\log 2\pi + O\left(\frac{1}{|s|}\right)$$

对于 $-\pi + \delta \leqslant \arg s \leqslant \pi + \delta (0 < \delta < \pi)$ 一致成立①,由此可以推出当 $a \leqslant \sigma \leqslant c$ 而 $|t| \to \infty$ 时

$$|\Gamma(\sigma+\mathrm{i}t)| = (1+o(1))e^{-\pi/2|t|}|t|^{\sigma-\frac{1}{2}}\sqrt{2\pi} \tag{2.5}$$

其中 o 所隐含的常数只与 a 及 c 有关. 因此,由定理 Ⅱ.4.1 知(2.4) 右边积分号下的函数当 $a \leqslant \sigma \leqslant c$, $|t| \to \infty$ 时,一致趋于0. 又当 $0 < a < kv$ 时,该函数在带形域 $a \leqslant \sigma \leqslant c$ 内只有一奇点,即简单极点 $s = kv$. 由定理 Ⅰ.2.2,相当的残数是

$$\Gamma(kv)\frac{2^k\Gamma^k(1+v)}{\Gamma(kv)}\omega^{-kv} = R(\omega)$$

因而可将(2.4) 右边积分路线移到 $\sigma = a$ 而得到

$$\begin{aligned}&(\sum_{x=-\infty}^{\infty} e^{-x^n\omega})^k - j - R(\omega) = \\ &\frac{1}{2\pi\mathrm{i}}\int_{a-\mathrm{i}\infty}^{a+\mathrm{i}\infty}\Gamma(s)Z_{n,k}(s)\omega^{-s}\mathrm{d}s = \\ &\frac{1}{2\pi}\int_{-\infty}^{\infty}\Gamma(a+\mathrm{i}t)Z_{n,k}(a+\mathrm{i}t)\omega^{-a-\mathrm{i}t}\mathrm{d}t\end{aligned} \tag{2.6}$$

式中 $j = 1$ 而 $0 < a < kv$. 当 $a < 0$ 时,由(Ⅰ.3.8) 知道在带形域 $a \leqslant \sigma \leqslant c$ 内,(2.4) 右边的被积函数除以 $s = kv$ 为奇点外,还有一奇点 $s = 0$,其相当的残数为 -1. 这证明当 $a < 0$ 时,(2.6) 中的 j 应为0.

(3) 由定理 Ⅱ.4.1 及(2.5),$\Gamma(a+\mathrm{i}t)Z_{n,k}(a+\mathrm{i}t) = o(e^{-|t|})$. 故(2.6) 最左及最右两端,当 $\mathrm{Re}\ \omega > 0$ 时都是 ω 的解析函数. 因此上式当 $\mathrm{Re}\ \omega >$

① Titchmarsh, Theory of functions(第二版)4.42, Example(i).

$0\left(可取 -\frac{\pi}{2} < \arg\omega < \frac{\pi}{2}\right)$时恒成立．命

$$\omega = \mathrm{i}e^{\xi-\mathrm{i}\delta} = e^{\xi+\mathrm{i}(\pi/2-\delta)} = e^{\xi}(\sin\delta + \mathrm{i}\cos\delta),\ 0 < \delta < \pi$$

即得

$$\left(\sum_{x=-\infty}^{\infty} e^{-x^n\omega}\right)^k - j - R(\omega) =$$

$$\frac{1}{2\pi}\int_{-\infty}^{\infty} \Gamma(a+\mathrm{i}t)Z_{n,k}(a+\mathrm{i}t)e^{-a\xi-\mathrm{i}\xi t-\mathrm{i}(a+\mathrm{i}t)(\pi/2-\delta)}\mathrm{d}t$$

故

$$e^{a\xi}\left\{\left(\sum_{x=-\infty}^{\infty} e^{-x^n\omega}\right)^k - j - R(\omega)\right\} =$$

$$\frac{1}{2\pi}\int_{-\infty}^{\infty} \Gamma(a+\mathrm{i}t)Z_{n,k}(a+\mathrm{i}t)e^{-\mathrm{i}(a+\mathrm{i}t)(\pi/2-\delta)}e^{-\mathrm{i}\xi t}\mathrm{d}t$$

由此得到一对傅里叶变形：

$$f(t) = \frac{1}{\sqrt{2\pi}}\Gamma(a+\mathrm{i}t)Z_{n,k}(a+\mathrm{i}t)e^{-\mathrm{i}(a+\mathrm{i}t)(\pi/2-\delta)}$$

$$F(\xi) = e^{a\xi}\left\{\left(\sum_{x=-\infty}^{\infty} e^{-x^n\omega}\right)^k - j - R(\omega)\right\},\quad \omega = \mathrm{i}e^{\xi-j\delta}$$

式中 $0 \neq a < kv$ 而

$$j = \begin{cases} 1, & 当\ a > 0 \\ 0, & 当\ a < 0 \end{cases}$$

引理 2.3（帕塞瓦（Parseval）等式①） 设 $f(x) \in L(-\infty,\infty)$ 并且它的傅里叶变形是 $F(x) \in L(-\infty,\infty)$，则

$$\int_{-\infty}^{\infty} |f(x)|^2\mathrm{d}x = \int_{-\infty}^{\infty} |F(x)|^2\mathrm{d}x$$

引理 2.4② 设 $f(x) \in L^p(-\infty,\infty)\ (1 < p \leqslant 2)$，则

$$F_b(x) = \frac{1}{\sqrt{2\pi}}\int_{-b}^{b} f(t)e^{\mathrm{i}xt}\mathrm{d}t$$

以指数 $p' = \frac{p}{p-1}$ 平均收敛到极限函数 $F(x)$，并满足

$$\int_{-\infty}^{\infty} |F(x)|^{p'}\mathrm{d}x \leqslant \frac{1}{(2\pi)^{\frac{1}{2}p'-1}}\int_{-\infty}^{\infty} |f(x)|^p\mathrm{d}x$$

又几乎到处有

$$F(x) = \frac{1}{\sqrt{2\pi}}\frac{\mathrm{d}}{\mathrm{d}x}\int_{-\infty}^{\infty} f(t)\frac{e^{\mathrm{i}xt}-1}{\mathrm{i}t}\mathrm{d}t$$

① TFI，2.2 节定理 35 及 2.1 节公式（2.1.3）．

② TFI，4.1 节定理 74．

§3 梯其玛什型均值公式

本节的目的是要为 $Z_{n,k}(s)$ 建立类似于(1.5)的均值公式,即梯其玛什型均值公式. 为清楚起见,我们把证明的若干部分写成一串的引理:

引理3.1 设 $0 < a < kv$,则当 $\delta \to +0$ 时

$$\frac{1}{\sqrt{2\pi}}\int_0^\infty t^{2a-1}(1+o(1))\mid Z_{n,k}(a+\mathrm{i}t)\mid^2 \mathrm{e}^{-2\delta t}\mathrm{d}t = \int_0^\infty u^{2a-1}\left|\Big(\sum_{x=-\infty}^{\infty}\mathrm{e}^{-x^n\omega}\Big)^k - 1 - \frac{2^k\Gamma^k(1+v)}{\omega^{kv}}\right|^2\mathrm{d}u \tag{3.1}$$

式中 $\omega = \mathrm{i}ne^{-\mathrm{i}\delta}$.

证 我们知道当 $t\to\infty$ 时

$$\Gamma(a+\mathrm{i}t) = \exp\left\{-\frac{\pi}{2}\mid t\mid\right\}\mid t\mid^{a-\frac{1}{2}}\sqrt{2\pi}(1+o(1)) \tag{3.2}$$

(见(2.5)),故由定理 Ⅱ.4.1 知道当 δ 充分小而 $t\to\infty$ 时

$$\Gamma(a+\mathrm{i}t)Z_{n,k}(a+\mathrm{i}t)\exp\left\{t\left(\frac{\pi}{2}-\delta\right)\right\} = O(t^{A_1}\mathrm{e}^{-\delta\mid t\mid}) \tag{3.3}$$

式中 A_1 只与 a 有关,又 O 中所隐含的常数也只与 a 有关. 这表明引理2.2中的 $f(t)$ 是属于 $L(-\infty,\infty)$ 的. 又当 $0 < a < kv$ 时引理2.2中的 $F(\xi)$ 是

$$F(\xi) = \mathrm{e}^{a\xi}\left\{\Big(\sum_{x=-\infty}^{\infty}\mathrm{e}^{-x^n\mathrm{e}^{\xi}(\sin\delta+\mathrm{i}\cos\delta)}\Big)^k - 1 - \frac{2^k\Gamma^k(1+v)}{(\mathrm{i}\mathrm{e}^{\xi-\mathrm{i}\delta})^{kv}}\right\}$$

像在引理2.2的证明中一样,当 $\xi\to+\infty$ 时,我们有

$$\mid F(\xi)\mid \leqslant \mathrm{e}^{a\xi}\left\{\Big(\sum_{x=-\infty}^{\infty}\mathrm{e}^{-x^n\mathrm{e}^{\xi}\sin\delta}\Big)^k - 1 + \frac{2^k\Gamma^k(1+v)}{\mathrm{e}^{kv\xi}}\right\} = O(\mathrm{e}^{a\xi-\mathrm{e}^{\xi}\sin\delta}) + O(\mathrm{e}^{(a-kv)\xi})$$

设用 $f_a(t)$ 及 $F_a(\xi)$ 记引理2.2中的 $f(t)$ 及 $F(\xi)$ 则 $f_{a/2}(t)\in L(-\infty,\infty)$ 而

$$F_a(\xi) = \mathrm{e}^{a\xi/2}F_{a/2}(\xi) = \frac{\mathrm{e}^{a\xi/2}}{\sqrt{2\pi}}\int_{-\infty}^{\infty}f_{a/2}(t)\mathrm{e}^{-\mathrm{i}\xi t}\mathrm{d}t = O(\mathrm{e}^{a\xi/2})$$

由以上的讨论知道 $F(\xi)\in L(-\infty,\infty)$. 因此,当 $0 < a < kv$ 时,可以把引理2.3应用到引理2.2中的 $f(t)$ 及 $F(\xi)$ 得到

$$\frac{1}{2\pi}\int_{-\infty}^{\infty}\mid\Gamma(a+\mathrm{i}t)Z_{n,k}(a+\mathrm{i}t)\mathrm{e}^{t(\frac{\pi}{2}-\delta)}\mid^2\mathrm{d}t = \int_{-\infty}^{\infty}\mathrm{e}^{2a\xi}\left|\Big(\sum_{x=-\infty}^{\infty}\mathrm{e}^{-x^n\omega}\Big)^k - 1 - \frac{2^k\Gamma^k(1+v)}{\omega^{kv}}\right|^2\mathrm{d}\xi =$$

$$\int_0^\infty u^{2a-1}\left|\left(\sum_{x=-\infty}^{\infty}\mathrm{e}^{-x^n\omega}\right)^k-1-\frac{2^k\Gamma^k(1+v)}{\omega^{kv}}\right|^2\mathrm{d}u \tag{3.4}$$

由(3.2),当$\delta\to+0$时,(3.4)的最左端可以写成

$$\frac{1}{\sqrt{2\pi}}\int_{-\infty}^{\infty}(1+o(1))\mid t\mid^{2a-1}\mid Z_{n,k}(a+\mathrm{i}t)\mid^2\mathrm{e}^{-\pi(|t|-t)-2\delta t}\mathrm{d}t$$

因此,根据定理Ⅱ.4.1立得(3.1).

引理3.2 设$m\geqslant c$,则任何一个包含x与y的m次多项式一定可以写成下列三个类型的项之和:

A.	$A(x-y)^\lambda y^\mu$	$\mu\geqslant c$,	$\lambda+\mu\leqslant m$
B.	$A(x-y-1)^\lambda y^\mu$	$\mu<c$,	$c\leqslant\lambda+\mu\leqslant m$
C.	$A(x-1)^\lambda y^\mu$	$\mu<c$,	$\lambda+\mu<c$

当$m<c$时,只有C类型的项,引理显然仍成立.

证 设用P表已知多项式.若P不含x,显然可以写成A,C两类型的项之和(此时$\lambda=0$).念设引理对x的m次多项式成立,要证对x的$m+1$次多项式P也成立.任取P内含x^{m+1}的一项,设为$Q=Ax^\lambda y^\mu(\lambda=m+1)$.若$\mu\geqslant c$,则$Q$与A类型的项$A(x-y)^\lambda y^\mu$的差对$x$为$m$次;若$\mu<c$,则应考虑$Q$与B或C类型的项之差(要分$\lambda+\mu\geqslant c$及$\lambda+\mu<c$两种情形),结果也得到$x$的$m$次多项式.对于$P$内每一含$x^{m+1}$的项都可以如此作.这就是说,总可以从$P$减去A,B,C三类型的项,使所余为$x$的$m$次多项式.用归纳法即得本引理.

引理3.3 我们可以把$x^k-y^k-1(k>c)$表成下列形式:

$$x^k-y^k-1=\sum_{\substack{\lambda>0,\mu\geqslant c\\ \lambda+\mu\leqslant k}}c_{\lambda,\mu}(x-y)^\lambda y^\mu+\sum_{\substack{0\leqslant\mu<c\\ c\leqslant\lambda+\mu\leqslant k}}c_{\lambda,\mu}(x-y-1)^\lambda y^\mu+\sum_{\substack{\lambda+\mu<c\\ \lambda>0}}c_{\lambda,\mu}(x-1)^\lambda y^\mu \tag{3.5}$$

式中$c_{\lambda,\mu}$都是常数且$c_{1,k-1}=k$.

证 由引理3.2,可以把x^k-y^k-1表成

$$x^k-y^k-1=\sum_{\substack{\lambda>0,\mu\geqslant c\\ \lambda+\mu\leqslant k}}c_{\lambda,\mu}(x-y)^\lambda y^\mu+\sum_{\substack{0\leqslant\mu<c\\ c\leqslant\lambda+\mu\leqslant k}}c_{\lambda,\mu}(x-y-1)^\lambda y^\mu+\sum_{\substack{\lambda+\mu<c\\ \lambda>0}}c_{\lambda,\mu}(x-1)^\lambda y^\mu+\sum_{0\leqslant\mu\leqslant k}c_\mu y^\mu$$

其中c_μ是常数.命$x=1$即得

$$-y^k=\sum_{\substack{\lambda>0,\mu\geqslant c\\ \lambda+\mu\leqslant k}}c_{\lambda,\mu}(1-y)^\lambda y^\mu+\sum_{\substack{0\leqslant\mu<c\\ c\leqslant\lambda+\mu\leqslant k}}(-1)^\lambda c_{\lambda,\mu}y^{\lambda+\mu}+\sum_{0\leqslant\mu\leqslant k}c_\mu y^\mu$$

由此显见$c_\mu=0,0\leqslant\mu<c$.又命$x=y$即得

$$-1=\sum_{\substack{0\leqslant\mu<c\\ c\leqslant\lambda+\mu\leqslant k}}(-1)^\lambda c_{\lambda,\mu}y^\mu+\sum_{\substack{\lambda+\mu<c\\ \lambda>0}}c_{\lambda,\mu}(y-1)^\lambda y^\mu+\sum_{c\leqslant\mu\leqslant k}c_\mu y^\mu$$

因此又得 $c_\mu = 0, c \leqslant \mu \leqslant k$. 故(3.5)成立. 但还要证 $c_{1,k-1} = k$. 比较(3.5)两边的最高次项得

$$x^k - y^k = \sum_{\substack{\lambda > 0, \mu \geqslant c \\ \lambda + \mu = k}} c_{\lambda,\mu}(x-y)^\lambda y^\mu + \sum_{\substack{0 \leqslant \mu < c \\ c \leqslant \lambda + \mu = k}} c_{\lambda,\mu}(x-y)^\lambda y^\mu$$

因 $\mu < c < k, \lambda + \mu = k$ 隐含 $\lambda \geqslant 1$. 故上式第二项中 $\lambda \geqslant 1$. 用 $x - y$ 除两边,得

$$x^{k-1} + \cdots + y^{k-1} = \sum_{\substack{\lambda > 0, \mu \geqslant c \\ \lambda + \mu = k}} c_{\lambda,\mu}(x-y)^{\lambda-1} y^\mu + \sum_{\substack{0 \leqslant \mu < c \\ \lambda + \mu = k}} c_{\lambda,\mu}(x-y)^{\lambda-1} y^\mu$$

令 $x = y = 1$,即得 $k = c_{1,k-1}$.

定理 3.1 设 an 不是整数而 $0 < a < kv - v$,则当 $\delta \to 0$ 时

$$\int_0^\infty t^{2a-1} | Z_{n,k}(a + \mathrm{i}t) |^2 \mathrm{e}^{-2\delta t} \mathrm{d}t =$$
$$c_1 \delta^{-2(n-1)(kv-v-a)-1}(1 + o(1)) + O(\delta^{-2a}) + O(\delta^{-4-\varepsilon})$$

式中

$$c_1 = k^2 (2\pi)^{1/2} (2\pi v)^{-2(k-na-1)-1} (2\Gamma(1+v))^{2k-2} \times$$
$$\Gamma(2(1-v)(k-na-1)+1)\xi(2(k-na))$$

而 $\varepsilon > 0$.

证 (1) 设 $c = an > [an]$($[x]$ 表 x 的整数部分),则由引理 3.3

$$\int_0^\infty u^{2a-1} \left| \left(\sum_{x=-\infty}^{\infty} \mathrm{e}^{-x^n \omega} \right)^k - 1 - \left(\frac{2\Gamma(1+v)}{\omega^v} \right)^k \right|^2 \mathrm{d}u =$$

$$\int_0^\infty u^{2a-1} \left| \sum_{\substack{\lambda > 0, \mu \geqslant c \\ \lambda + \mu \leqslant k}} c_{\lambda,\mu} (\Phi - \Psi)^\lambda \Psi^\mu + \sum_{\substack{0 \leqslant \mu < c \\ c \leqslant \lambda + \mu \leqslant k}} c_{\lambda,\mu} (\Phi - \Psi - 1)^\lambda \Psi^\mu + \right.$$

$$\left. \sum_{\substack{\lambda + \mu < c \\ \lambda > 0}} c_{\lambda,\mu} (\Phi - 1)^\lambda \Psi^\mu \right|^2 \mathrm{d}u \tag{3.6}$$

式中 $\omega = \mathrm{i}u\mathrm{e}^{-\mathrm{i}\delta}$ 而

$$\Phi = \Phi(u) = \sum_{x=-\infty}^{\infty} \mathrm{e}^{-x^n \omega}, \quad \Psi = \Psi(u) = \frac{2\Gamma(1+v)}{\omega^v}$$

把(3.6)右边积分号下形如 $|W|^2$ 的式子换作 $W\overline{W}$($\overline{W}$ 表 W 的共轭复数),则乘开以后分别积分就得到九个类型的项. 其中三个类型的项,除去一常数因子不算,就可以写成:

$$\mathrm{A} = I_{\lambda,\mu} = \int_0^\infty u^{2a-1} | \Phi - \Psi |^{2\lambda} | \Psi |^{2\mu} \mathrm{d}u, \qquad \lambda > 0, \mu \geqslant c, \lambda + \mu \leqslant k$$

$$\mathrm{B} = I_{\lambda,\mu} = \int_0^\infty u^{2a-1} | \Phi - \Psi - 1 |^{2\lambda} | \Psi |^{2\mu} \mathrm{d}u, \quad 0 \leqslant \mu < c, c \leqslant \lambda + \mu \leqslant k$$

$$\mathrm{C} = I_{\lambda,\mu} = \int_0^\infty u^{2a-1} | \Phi - 1 |^{2\lambda} | \Psi |^{2\mu} \mathrm{d}u, \qquad \lambda > 0, \lambda + \mu < c$$

另外 9 个类型的项的绝对值,则不超过(对于适当的 $\lambda,\mu,\lambda',\mu'$)

$$O(\sqrt{I_{\lambda,\mu}I_{\lambda',\mu'}}),\quad |\lambda-\lambda'|+|\mu-\mu'|\neq 0$$

为说明最后一句话,我们利用斯瓦尔兹(Schwarz)不等式就得到

$$\left|\int_0^\infty u^{2a-1}|\Phi-\Psi|^\lambda\Psi^\mu\cdot\overline{(\Phi-\Psi-1)}^\lambda\bar{\Psi}^\mu\mathrm{d}u\right|\leqslant\sqrt{AB}$$

以后要证明在 A,B,C 三种项中,在适当的条件下,只有 $I_{1,k-1}$ 的阶最大,其余的阶都较低,因此,(3.6) 的主要部分是

$$\int_0^\infty u^{2a-1}|c_{1,k-1}(\Phi-\Psi)|^2|\Psi|^{2k-2}\mathrm{d}u=k^2I_{1,k-1}\tag{3.7}$$

(2) A,B,C 三类型的项都可以写作

$$I_{\lambda,\mu}=(2\Gamma(1+v))^{2\mu}\int_0^\infty u^{2(a-\mu v)}\left|\sum_{x=-\infty}^{\infty}\mathrm{e}^{-x^n\omega}-j-j'\frac{2\Gamma(1+v)}{\omega^v}\right|^{2\lambda}\frac{\mathrm{d}u}{u}$$

其中

$$j=\begin{cases}1, & \text{当}\mu<an,\quad\text{即}\dfrac{a-\mu v}{\lambda}>0\\ 0, & \text{当}\mu>an,\quad\text{即}\dfrac{a-\mu v}{\lambda}<0\end{cases}$$

而

$$j'=\begin{cases}1, & \text{当}\lambda+\mu>an,\quad\text{即}\dfrac{a-\mu v}{\lambda}<v\\ 0, & \text{当}\lambda+\mu<an,\quad\text{即}\dfrac{a-\mu v}{\lambda}>v\end{cases}$$

故由引理 2.2

$$f(t)=\frac{1}{\sqrt{2\pi}}\Gamma\left(\frac{a-\mu v}{\lambda}+\mathrm{i}t\right)Z_{n,1}\left(\frac{a-\mu v}{\lambda}+\mathrm{i}t\right)\mathrm{e}^{-\mathrm{i}\left(\frac{a-\mu v}{\lambda}+\mathrm{i}t\right)\left(\frac{\pi}{2}-\delta\right)}$$

与

$$F(\xi)=\mathrm{e}^{\frac{a-\mu v}{\lambda}\xi}\left\{\sum_{x=-\infty}^{\infty}\mathrm{e}^{-x^n\omega}-j-j'\frac{2\Gamma(1+v)}{\omega^v}\right\}$$

是一对傅里叶变形. 由(3.3) 知道,当 $|t|\to\infty$ 时

$$f(t)=O(|t|^{A_1}\mathrm{e}^{-\delta|t|})\tag{3.8}$$

因此对于任何的 $p(1\leqslant p\leqslant 2)$,均得$\overline{f(t)}\in L^p(-\infty,\infty)$,故引理 2.4 可用,于是得

$$\int_{-\infty}^\infty|F_1(x)^{p'}\mathrm{d}x\leqslant\frac{1}{(2\pi)^{p'/2-1}}\int_{-\infty}^\infty|f(x)|^p\mathrm{d}x\tag{3.9}$$

其中 $p'=\dfrac{p}{p-1}$ 而

$$F_1(x)\doteq\frac{\mathrm{d}}{\mathrm{d}x}\frac{1}{\sqrt{2\pi}}\int_{-\infty}^\infty\overline{f(t)}\frac{\mathrm{e}^{\mathrm{i}xt}-1}{\mathrm{i}t}\mathrm{d}t$$

式中 $\doteq$ 表两边除在一测度是零的集合上以外，恒相等．又由(3.8)，上式右边可以在积分号下取微分．故 $F_1(x)\doteq\overline{F(x)}$．因此，(3.9) 变成

$$\int_{-\infty}^{\infty}|F_1(x)|^{p'}\mathrm{d}x\leqslant\frac{1}{(2\pi)^{p'/2-1}}\int_{-\infty}^{\infty}|f(x)|^{p}\mathrm{d}x$$

由此可见，对于 A,B,C 三类型的项，都有

$$I_{\lambda,\mu}=(2\Gamma(1+v))^{2\mu}\int_0^{\infty}u^{2(a-\mu v)}\left|\sum_{x=-\infty}^{\infty}\mathrm{e}^{-x^n\omega}-j-j'\frac{2\Gamma(1+v)}{\omega^v}\right|^{2\lambda}\frac{\mathrm{d}u}{u}\ll$$

$$\int_{-\infty}^{\infty}\left|\frac{1}{\sqrt{2\pi}}\Gamma\left(\frac{a-\mu v}{\lambda}+\mathrm{i}t\right)Z_{n,1}\left(\frac{a-\mu v}{\lambda}+\mathrm{i}t\right)\exp\left\{-\mathrm{i}\left(\frac{a-\mu v}{\lambda}+\mathrm{i}t\right)\left(\frac{\pi}{2}-\delta\right)\right\}\right|^{h}\mathrm{d}t \tag{3.10}$$

式中 $h=\frac{2\lambda}{2\lambda-1}$.

(3) 今将估计(3.10) 的右边．由(3.2)，当 $t\to\infty$ 时

$$\left|\frac{1}{\sqrt{2\pi}}\Gamma\left(\frac{a-\mu v}{\lambda}+\mathrm{i}t\right)\exp\left\{-\mathrm{i}\left(\frac{a-\mu v}{\lambda}+\mathrm{i}t\right)\left(\frac{\pi}{2}-\delta\right)\right\}\right|\ll$$

$$|t|^{\frac{a-\mu v}{\lambda}-\frac{1}{2}}\mathrm{e}^{-\frac{\pi}{2}(|t|-t)-\delta t}$$

式中所隐含的常数与 δ 及 t 都无关．因此，由(3.10) 及定理 Ⅱ.4.1 当 $\delta\to+0$ 时

$$I_{\lambda,\mu}\ll\int_1^{\infty}t^{\left(\frac{a-\mu v}{\lambda}-\frac{1}{2}\right)h}\mathrm{e}^{-\delta ht}\left|Z_{n,1}\left(\frac{a-\mu v}{\lambda}+\mathrm{i}t\right)\right|^{h}\mathrm{d}t+1\ll$$

$$\int_1^{\infty}t^{\left(\frac{a-\mu v}{\lambda}-\frac{1}{2}\right)h}\mathrm{e}^{-\delta ht}\left|\xi\left(\frac{an-\mu}{\lambda}+n\mathrm{i}t\right)\right|^{h}\mathrm{d}t+1$$

1) 现在考虑 $\frac{an-\mu}{\lambda}>1$ 也就是 $\lambda+\mu<an$ 的情形．在这情形下，因 $\zeta\left(\frac{an-\mu}{\lambda}+n\mathrm{i}t\right)=O(1)$（当 $t\to\infty$），故

$$I_{\lambda,\mu}\ll\int_1^{\infty}t^{\left(\frac{a-\mu v}{\lambda}-\frac{1}{2}\right)h}\mathrm{e}^{-\delta ht}\mathrm{d}t+1=$$

$$\delta^{-\left(\frac{a-\mu v}{\lambda}-\frac{1}{2}\right)h-1}\int_{\delta}^{\infty}|t|^{\left(\frac{a-\mu v}{\lambda}-\frac{1}{2}\right)h}\mathrm{e}^{-ht}\mathrm{d}t+1=$$

$$O\left(\delta^{-\left(\frac{a-\mu v}{\lambda}-\frac{1}{2}\right)h-1}\right)+O(\delta^{-1})$$

因 $\lambda\geqslant1$ 故 $\frac{a-\mu v}{\lambda}\leqslant a$，$1\leqslant h=\frac{2\lambda}{2\lambda-1}\leqslant2$，而

$$I_{\lambda,\mu}=O(\delta^{-2a})+O(\delta^{-1})$$

2) 其次考虑 $0<\frac{an-\mu}{\lambda}<1$ 也就是 $an-\mu>0$ 且 $\lambda+\mu>an$ 的情形．在

这情形下,我们利用$\zeta(s) = O(t^{3/2+\varepsilon})$(当$\sigma \geqslant -\varepsilon, \varepsilon \geqslant 0$)① 可得

$$I_{\lambda,\mu} \ll \int_1^{\infty} t^{(\frac{a-\mu v}{\lambda}-\frac{1}{2})h} e^{-\delta h t} t^{(3/2+\varepsilon)h} dt + 1 =$$

$$\int_1^{\infty} t^{(\frac{a-\mu v}{\lambda}+1+\varepsilon)h} e^{-\delta h t} dt + 1 = O(\delta^{-(\frac{a-\mu v}{\lambda}+1+\varepsilon)h-1}) =$$

$$O(\delta^{-2(v+1+\varepsilon)-1}) = O(\delta^{-4-\varepsilon})$$

(因$h \leqslant 2$, $n \geqslant 2$).

3) 最后考虑$\frac{an-\mu}{\lambda} < 0$也就是$\mu > an$的情形. 在这种情形下,我们利用$\xi(s) = O(t^{1/2} - \sigma)$②($\sigma \leqslant -\varepsilon < 0$)可得

$$I_{\lambda,\mu} \ll \int_1^{\infty} t^{(\frac{a-\mu v}{\lambda}-\frac{1}{2})h} e^{-\delta h t} t^{(\frac{1}{2}-\frac{an-\mu}{\lambda})h} dt + 1 =$$

$$\int_1^{\infty} t^{-(n-1)h\frac{a-\mu v}{\lambda}} e^{-\delta h t} dt + 1 =$$

$$O(\delta^{-(n-1)h\frac{\mu v-a}{\lambda}-1})$$

当a一定时,如果λ越小,μ越大,上式右边的指数就越大. 因为$\lambda \geqslant 1$, $\mu \leqslant k-1$故

$$I_{\lambda,\mu} = \begin{cases} O(\delta^{-(kv-v-a)(n-1)h^{-1}}), & \text{当}\lambda = 1, \mu = k-1 \\ o(\delta^{-(kv-v-a)(n-1)h^{-1}}), & \text{其他情形} \end{cases}$$

(4) 对于$I_{1,k-1}$,我们还要求出它的主要部分. 因为$a < kv - v$,所以

$$I_{1,k-1} = (2\Gamma(1+v))^{2k-2} \int_0^{\infty} u^{2(a-kv+v)} \left| \sum_{x=-\infty}^{\infty} e^{-x^n \omega} - \frac{2\Gamma(1+v)}{\omega^v} \right|^2 \frac{du}{u}$$

这时,我们可以不用不等式(3.9)而用Parseval等式(引理2.3). 现在先验证一对傅里叶变形(参看引理2.2)

$$f(t) = \frac{1}{\sqrt{2\pi}} \Gamma(a-kv+v+it) Z_{n,1}(a-kv+v+it) e^{-i(a-kv+v+it)(\pi/2-\delta)}$$

$$F(\xi) = e^{(a-kv+v)\xi} \left\{ \sum_{x=-\infty}^{\infty} e^{-x^n \omega} - \frac{2\Gamma(1+v)}{\omega^v} \right\}, \quad \omega = e^{\xi + i(\pi/2-\delta)}$$

是否都$\in L(-\infty,\infty)$. 由(3.3),$f(x) \in L(-\infty,\infty)$. 显然当$\xi \to +\infty$时$F(\xi) = O(e^{(a-kv+v)\xi})$. 用$f_{a-kv+v}(t)$及$F_{a-kv+v}(\xi)$表以上一对傅里叶变形,则$f_{-kv+v}(t)$及$F_{-kv+v}(\xi)$也是一对傅里叶变形而$f_{-kv+v}(t) \in L(-\infty,\infty)$. 因此

$$F(\xi) = F_{a-kv+v}(\xi) = e^{a\xi} F_{-kv+v}(\xi) =$$

---

① Titchmarsh, The theory of the Riemann zeta - function (Oxford, 1951)5.1节(有俄文译本). 以后简记作TRZ.

② 同上.

$$e^{a\xi}\frac{1}{\sqrt{2\pi}}\int_{-\infty}^{\infty}f_{-kv+v}(t)e^{-\xi t i}dt = O(e^{a\xi}),\text{当}\xi\to-\infty$$

故 $F(\xi)\in L(-\infty,\infty)$. 由引理 2.2

$$I_{1,k-1} = (2\Gamma(1+v))^{2k-2}\int_{-\infty}^{\infty}\left|\frac{1}{\sqrt{2\pi}}\Gamma(a-kv+v+it)\times Z_{n,1}(a-kv+v+it)e^{-i(a-kv+v+it)(\pi/2-\delta)}\right|^2dt$$

由(3.2),当 $t\to\infty$ 时

$$\left|\frac{1}{\sqrt{2\pi}}\Gamma(a-kv+v)e^{-i(a-kv+v+it)(\pi/2-\delta)}\right| = |t|^{a-kv+v-1/2}e^{-\pi(|t|-t)/2-\delta t}(1+o(1))$$

故当 $\delta\to+0$ 时

$$I_{1,k-1} = (1+o(1))(2\Gamma(1+v))^{2k-2}\int_{v}^{\infty}t^{2(a-kv+v-1/2)}e^{-2\delta t}\cdot|\zeta(na-k+1+nit)|^2dt+O(1)$$

式中积分的下限 v 是为方便而取的. 由此得

$$I_{1,k-1} = (1+o(1))v^{2(a-kv+v)}(2\Gamma(1+v))^{2k-2}\int_{1}^{\infty}t^{2(a-kv+v)-1}e^{-2\delta vt}\times|\zeta(na-k+1+it)|^2dt+O(1)$$

的 $\zeta(s)$ 的函数方程①,当 $t\to+\infty$ 时

$$|\xi(s)| = |\chi(s)\xi(1-s)| \sim \left(\frac{t}{2\pi}\right)^{1/2-\sigma}|\xi(1-s)|$$

故又得

$$I_{1,k-1} = (1+o(1))(2\pi)^{-1}(2\pi v^{v})^{-2(k-na-1)}(2\Gamma(1+v))^{2k-2}\times\int_{1}^{\infty}t^{2(n-1)(kv-v-a)}e^{-2\delta vt}|\zeta(k-na-it)|^2dt+O(1)\tag{3.11}$$

今用 I_0 表上式右边的积分,则因 $k-na>1$

$$\begin{aligned}I_0 &= \int_1^{\infty}t^{2(n-1)(kv-v-a)}e^{-2\delta vt}\sum_{m_1=1}^{\infty}\frac{1}{m_1^{k-na-it}}\sum_{m_2=1}^{\infty}\frac{1}{m_2^{k-na-it}}dt = \\ &\zeta(2(k-na))\int_1^{\infty}t^{2(n-1)(kv-v-a)}e^{-2\delta vt}dt+\\ &2\sum_{m_1=1}^{\infty}\sum_{m_2=1}^{m_1-1}\frac{1}{(m_1m_2)^{k-na}}\int_1^{\infty}t^{2(n-1)(kv-v-a)}e^{-2\delta vt}\left(\frac{m_1}{m_2}\right)^{it}dt = \\ &I_{01}+I_{02}\end{aligned}$$

显然

---

① TRZ, 136, (7.12.6) – (7.12.7).

$$\int_1^{\infty} t^{2(n-1)(kv-v-a)} \mathrm{e}^{-2\delta v t} \mathrm{d}t = (2\delta v)^{-2(n-1)(kv-v-a)-1} \int_0^{\infty} t^{2(n-1)(kv-v-a)} \mathrm{e}^{-t} \mathrm{d}t + O(1) =$$

$$(2\delta v)^{-2(n-1)(kv-v-a)-1} \Gamma(2(n-1)(kv-v-a)+1) + O(1)$$

而

$$\int_1^{\infty} t^{2(n-1)(kv-v-a)} \mathrm{e}^{-2\delta v t} \left(\frac{m_1}{m_2}\right)^{\mathrm{i}t} \mathrm{d}t =$$

$$\left(\log \frac{m_1}{m_2}\right)^{-2(n-1)(kv-v-a)-1} \int_{\log\frac{m_1}{m_2}}^{\infty} t^{2(n-1)(kv-v-a)} \mathrm{e}^{-2\delta v t(\log(m_1/m_2))^{-1}} \mathrm{e}^{\mathrm{i}t} \mathrm{d}t \ll$$

$$\left(\log \frac{m_1}{m_2}\right)^{-2(n-1)(kv-v-a)-1} \max_{\log(m_1/m_2) \leqslant t < \infty} t^{2(n-1)(kv-v-a)} \mathrm{e}^{-2\delta v t(\log(m_1/m_2))^{-1}} \ll$$

$$\left(\log \frac{m_1}{m_2}\right)^{-1} \delta^{-2(n-1)(kv-v-a)} + O(1)$$

故

$$I_{01} = (2\delta v)^{-2(n-1)(kv-v-a)-1} \Gamma(2(n-1)(kv-v-a)+1) \zeta(2(k-na)) + O(1)$$

而

$$I_{02} \ll \sum_{m_1=1}^{\infty} \sum_{m_2=1}^{m_1-1} \frac{\delta^{-2(n-1)(kv-v-a)}}{(m_1 m_2)^{k-na} \log\left(\frac{m_1}{m_2}\right)} = O(\delta^{-2(n-1)(kv-v-a)})$$

合并 I_{01} 及 I_{02} 得

$$I_0 = (2\delta v)^{-2(n-1)(kv-v-a)-1} \Gamma(2(n-1)(kv-v-a)+1) \zeta(2(k-na)) + O(\delta^{-2(n-1)(kv-v-a)}) + O(1)$$

代入(3.11)即得

$$I_{1,k-1} = (1+o(1)) c_0 \delta^{-2(n-1)(kv-v-a)-1} \tag{3.12}$$

其中

$$c_0 = (2\pi)^{-1} (2\pi v^{v})^{-2(k-na-1)} (2v)^{-2(n-1)(kv-v-a)-1} \times (2\Gamma(1+v))^{2k-2} \Gamma(2(n-1)(kv-v-a)+1) \zeta(2(k-na)) = (2\pi v)^{-2(k-na-1)-1} (2\Gamma(1+v))^{2k-2} \times \Gamma(2(1-v)(k-na-1)+1) \zeta(2(k-na)) \tag{3.13}$$

(5) 根据以上各段的讨论,我们得以

$$\int_0^{\infty} u^{2a-1} \left| \left(\sum_{x=-\infty}^{\infty} \mathrm{e}^{-x^n \omega}\right)^k - 1 - \left(\frac{2\Gamma(1+v)}{\omega^{v}}\right)^k \right|^2 \mathrm{d}u =$$

$$(1+o(1)) k^2 c_0 \delta^{-2(n-1)(kv-v-a)-1} + O(\delta^{-2a}) + O(\delta^{-4-\varepsilon})$$

由引理3.1得

$$\frac{1}{\sqrt{2\pi}} \int_0^{\infty} t^{2a-1} \mid Z_{n,k}(a+\mathrm{i}t) \mid^2 \mathrm{e}^{-2\delta t} \mathrm{d}t =$$

$$(1+o(1)) k^2 c_0 \delta^{-2(n-1)(kv-v-a)-1} + O(\delta^{-2a}) + O(\delta^{-4-\varepsilon})$$

定理随之成立.

以上为方便起见假定了 an 不是整数时. 当 an 是整数时,定理应该修改. 这一点,本篇不拟加以讨论.

§4 典型的均值公式

在本节里面,我们要为 $Z_{n,k}(s)$ 建立像(1.1)及(1.2)那样的均值公式,我们不妨称之为典型的均值公式. 为简单计,我们没有除去所有能除去的条件. 现在先提出几个引理:

引理4.1① 若

$$\int_1^{\infty} f(t)\mathrm{e}^{-\delta t}\mathrm{d}t \sim C\delta^{-\alpha}, \quad \alpha > 0$$

则

$$\int_1^{\infty} t^{-\beta} f(t)\mathrm{e}^{-\delta t}\mathrm{d}t \sim C\frac{\Gamma(\alpha-\beta)}{\Gamma(\alpha)}\delta^{\beta-\alpha}, \quad 0 < \beta < \alpha$$

引理4.2 设 an 不是整数而 $2(n-1)(kv-v-a)+1 > \max(2a,4)$,则

$$\int_0^{\infty} | Z_{n,k}(a+\mathrm{i}t) |^2 \mathrm{e}^{-2\delta t}\mathrm{d}t \sim c_2\delta^{-2(n-1)(kv-v-a)+2a-2}$$

其中

$$c_2 = \frac{\Gamma(2(n-1)(kv-v-a)-2a+2)}{\Gamma(2(n-1)(kv-v-a)+1)}c_1$$

而 c_1 的意义见定理3.1.

证 这个引理可以从定理3.1及引理4.1推出.

引理4.3② 设 $\alpha(t)$ 是单调增加函数而积分 $f(x) = \int_0^{\infty} \mathrm{e}^{-st}\mathrm{d}\alpha(t)$ 在 $s > 0$ 时收敛. 又设对于正数 γ 及常数 A,有

$$f(s) \sim \frac{A}{s^r} \quad (s \to 0+)$$

则

$$\alpha(t) \sim \frac{At^r}{\Gamma(\gamma+1)} \quad (t \to \infty)$$

定理4.1 设 $an > 0$ 且不是整数而 $2(n-1)(kv-v-a)+1 > \max(2a,4)$ 则

---

① TRZ, 136, (7.12.6 - 7.12.7).

② Widder, The Laplace transform, Chapter, V. Theorem 4 - 3.

$$\int_0^T |Z_{n,k}(a+\mathrm{i}t)|^2 \mathrm{d}t \sim c_3 T^{2(n-1)(kv-v-a)-2a+2} \quad (T \to +\infty)$$

其中

$$c_3 = 2^{-2(kv-v)+1/2}[2(n-1)(kv-v-a)-2a+2]^{-1}\pi^{-2(k-na)+3/2} \times k^2 v^{2na}\Gamma^2(v)\zeta(2(k-na))$$

证 在引理4.3中,令$\alpha(T) = \int_0^T |Z_{n,k}(a+\mathrm{i}t)|^2 \mathrm{d}t$,则由引理4.2可以得到本定理.

我十分感谢越民义先生耐心审查这篇论文并改正其中演算的错误.

论黎曼 ζ 函数的非明显零点[①]

§1 引 论

1. 引论

黎曼 ζ 函数 $\zeta(s)(s=\sigma+\mathrm{i}t)$ 以 $s=-2,-4,\cdots$ 为零点. 这些零点就是所谓明显零点(trivial zeros),其他的零点就是所谓非明显零点(non-trivial zeros)都含于带形区域 $0<\sigma<1$. 内设用 $N(T)$ 表示满足 $0\leqslant\beta\leqslant1, 0\leqslant\gamma\leqslant T$ 的 $\zeta(s)$ 的零点 $\beta+\mathrm{i}\gamma$ 的个数,并用 $N_0(T)$ 表示满足 $\beta=1/2, 0\leqslant\gamma\leqslant T$ 的 $\zeta(s)$ 的零点个数. 则因 $\zeta(s)$ 在共轭复数上取共轭值,所谓黎曼假说就和下式等价:

$$N_0(T)=N(T),\quad T\geqslant0$$

我们知道当 $T\to\infty$ 时,$N(T)\sim(2\pi)^{-1}T\log T$,所以根据黎曼假设知道 $N_0(T)\sim(2\pi)^{-1}T\times\log T$. A. Selberg[1] 曾证明有一个常数 A 存在使得

$$N_0(T)>AT\log T \tag{1.1}$$

本文将证明

定理 1 当 T 充分大时,$N_0(T)>\frac{1}{60\ 000}N(T)$.

---

① 原载:北京大学学报,1956,2(2):2:165-189.

2. 我们要以下面的引理为依据：

引理 2.1 设 $F(t)$ 是一个定义在 (T_1,T_2) 的实连续函数而 $0 < H < T_2 - T_1$，又设 n 是 $F(t)$ 在 (T_1,T_2) 内变更符号的次数，则

$$\left\{\int_{T_1}^{T_2-H}\left(\int_t^{t+H}|F(v)|\,\mathrm{d}v - \left|\int_t^{t+H}F(v)\,\mathrm{d}v\right|\right)\mathrm{d}t\right\}^2 \leqslant$$

$$nH\int_{T_1}^{T_2-H}\left\{\int_t^{t+H}|F(v)|\,\mathrm{d}v - \left|\int_t^{t+H}F(v)\,\mathrm{d}v\right|\right\}^2\mathrm{d}t \tag{2.1}$$

引理 2.2 设 $F(t)$ 对于所有 t 的值是连续的，并且下面出现的积分都存在. 设 $0 < 2H < T_2 - T_1$ 而 $u = T_2 - T_1 - 2H$. 最后设

$$\int_{-\infty}^{\infty}|F(v)|^2\mathrm{d}v \leqslant \delta_1 H^{-2},\ \int_{-\infty}^{\infty}\left|\int_t^{t+H}F(v)\,\mathrm{d}v\right|^2\mathrm{d}t = \delta'_2 \leqslant \delta_2 \tag{2.2}$$

与

$$\int_{T_1+H}^{T_2-H}|F(v)|\,\mathrm{d}v \geqslant \delta_3 H^{-1}u^{\frac{1}{2}},\ \delta_3 > \delta_2^{\frac{1}{2}}$$

则 $F(t)$ 在 (T_1,T_2) 内变号的次数是

$$n \geqslant \frac{(\delta_3 - {\delta'_2}^{\frac{1}{2}})^2}{\delta_1 - \delta'_2}\frac{u}{H} \geqslant \frac{(\delta_3 - \delta_2^{\frac{1}{2}})^2}{\delta_1}\frac{u}{H} \tag{2.3}$$

引理 2.3 若在引理 2.2 里面再假定 $F(t)$ 以 $f(y)$ 为傅氏变换，则条件 (2.2) 可以用下列条件代替

$$2\int_0^{\infty}|f(y)|^2\mathrm{d}y \leqslant \delta_1 H^{-2},\ 8\int_0^{\infty}|f(y)|^2\frac{\sin^2\frac{1}{2}Hy}{y^2}\mathrm{d}y = \delta'_2 \leqslant \delta_2 \tag{2.2'}$$

这些引理已在[2] 内证明．由于[2] 内对于引理 2 及引理 3 的叙述有些缺点．因而需要改成现在的形式，至于[2] 内的证明只要把 δ_2 改成 δ'_2 就可以了．这些改动并不影响[2] 的其他部分，因为在[2] 内只用到 $n \geqslant \frac{(\delta_3 - \delta_2^{\frac{1}{2}})^2}{\delta_1}\frac{u}{H}$.

上面最后一个引理就是我们估计 $N_0(T)$ 的主要工具，事实上，我们以后取

$$F(t) = -\frac{1}{\sqrt{8\pi}}\pi^{-\frac{1}{4}-\frac{\mathrm{i}}{2}t}\Gamma\left(\frac{1}{4}+\frac{\mathrm{i}}{2}t\right)\zeta\left(\frac{1}{2}+\mathrm{i}t\right)\left|\phi\left(\frac{1}{2}+\mathrm{i}t\right)\right|^2\mathrm{e}^{(\frac{\pi}{4}-\frac{d}{2})t}$$

其中

$$\phi(s) = \sum_{v<\xi}\beta_v v^{-s},\quad |\beta_v| \leqslant 1$$

常数 $\xi = \xi(T) = o(T^{\frac{1}{4}})$ 与 $d = d(T) = O\left(\frac{1}{T}\right)$ 要在以后决定，而常数 $\beta_v = \beta_v(T)$ 则规定如下（参考[1]）：

我们用下式定义 α_v 与 α'_v.

$$\{\zeta(s)\}^{-\frac{1}{2}}=\sum_{v=1}^{\infty}\frac{\alpha_v}{v^s},\ \{\zeta(s)\}^{\frac{1}{2}}=\sum_{v=1}^{\infty}\frac{\alpha'_v}{v^s},\ (\sigma>1),\alpha_1=\alpha'_1=1$$

并令

$$\beta_v=\alpha_v\left(1-\frac{\log v}{\log\xi}\right)^{\alpha},\quad 1\leqslant v\leqslant\xi,\quad \alpha>\frac{1}{2}$$

由 $\zeta(s)$ 的欧拉乘积可以看出当$(\mu,v)=1$时,$\alpha_\mu\alpha_v=\alpha_{\mu v}$,而$|\alpha_v|\leqslant\alpha'_v<1$. 由此,$|\beta_v|\leqslant1$ 而

$$|\phi(s)|=O(\xi^{1-\sigma})$$

我们知道[3]$F(t)$ 的傅氏变换是

$$f(y)=\frac{1}{2}z^{\frac{1}{2}}\phi(0)\phi(1)-z^{-\frac{1}{2}}\sum_{n=1}^{\infty}\sum_{\mu=1}^{\xi}\sum_{v=1}^{\xi}\frac{\beta_\mu\beta_v}{v}\exp\left(-\frac{\pi n^2\mu^2}{z^2v^2}\right)\quad(y\geqslant0)$$

其中 $z=\mathrm{e}^{-\mathrm{i}(\frac{\pi}{4}-\frac{d}{2})-y}$. 为简便设计

$$I=\int_H^{T-H}|F(v)|\,\mathrm{d}v,\ I_1=\int_0^{\infty}|f(x)|^2\mathrm{d}x$$

$$I_2=\int_0^{\infty}|f(x)|^2\frac{\sin^2\frac{1}{2}Hx}{x^2}\mathrm{d}x$$

其中 $H=H(T)=o(T)$. 由(2.3)可知,我们把估计 $N_0(T)$ 的问题化为求 I 的一个适当的下界与 I_1 及 I_2 的适当上界的问题.

3. 积分 I 的一个下界.

引理 3.1

$$I>(1-o(1))\frac{1}{2}\left(\frac{2}{\pi}\right)^{\frac{1}{4}}d^{-\frac{3}{4}}\int_{dH}^{d(T-H)}t^{-\frac{1}{4}}\mathrm{e}^{-\frac{1}{2}t}\mathrm{d}t>$$

$$(1-o(1))\frac{2}{3}\left(\frac{2}{\pi}\right)^{\frac{1}{4}}T^{\frac{3}{4}}\mathrm{e}^{-\frac{dT}{2}}$$

证 当 x 是常数,而 $y\to\pm\infty$ 时,我们有 $\Gamma(x+\mathrm{i}y)\sim\mathrm{e}^{-\frac{1}{2}\pi|y|}|y|^{x-\frac{1}{2}}\sqrt{2\pi}$. 因此,当 $t\to\infty$ 时

$$|F(t)|\sim\frac{1}{2}\left(\frac{2}{\pi}\right)^{\frac{1}{4}}t^{-\frac{1}{4}}\mathrm{e}^{-\frac{d}{2}t}\left|\zeta\left(\frac{1}{2}+\mathrm{i}t\right)\right|\cdot\left|\phi\left(\frac{1}{2}+\mathrm{i}t\right)\right|^2$$

由此可知当 $n>T^{\frac{1}{2}}$ 时,

$$I=\sum_{m=0}^{n}\int_{H+\frac{m}{n}(T-2H)}^{H+\frac{m+1}{n}(T-2H)}|F(v)|\,\mathrm{d}v>$$

$$(1-o(1))\frac{1}{2}\left(\frac{2}{\pi}\right)^{\frac{1}{4}}d^{\frac{1}{4}}\sum_{m=0}^{n}\left\{dH+\frac{m}{n}d(T-2H)\right\}^{-\frac{1}{4}}\mathrm{e}^{-\frac{1}{2}d\{H+\frac{m}{n}(T-2H)\}}\times$$

$$\int_{H+\frac{m}{n}(T-2H)}^{H+\frac{m+1}{n}(T-2H)}\left|\zeta\left(\frac{1}{2}+\mathrm{i}t\right)\right|\cdot\left|\phi\left(\frac{1}{2}+\mathrm{i}t\right)\right|^2\mathrm{d}t>$$

$$(1-o(1))\frac{1}{2}\left(\frac{2}{\pi}\right)^{\frac{1}{4}}d^{-\frac{3}{4}}\int_{dH}^{d(T-H)}e^{-\frac{t}{2}}t^{-\frac{1}{4}}dt>(1-o(1))\frac{2}{3}\left(\frac{2}{\pi}\right)^{\frac{1}{4}}T^{\frac{3}{4}}e^{-\frac{dT}{2}}$$

因为当 $u>T^{\frac{1}{2}}$ 时([2] 引理4),

$$\int_T^{T+u}\zeta\left(\frac{1}{2}+it\right)\varphi^2\left(\frac{1}{2}+it\right)dt=u+o(u)$$

4. 让我们来考虑

$$I_2=\int_0^\infty|f(y)|^2\frac{\sin^2\frac{1}{2}Hy}{y^2}dy$$

其中

$$f(y)=\frac{1}{2}z^{\frac{1}{2}}\varphi(0)\varphi(1)-z^{-\frac{1}{2}}\sum_{n=1}^{\infty}\sum_{\mu=1}^{\zeta}\sum_{v=1}^{\xi}\frac{\beta_\mu\beta_v}{v}\exp\left(-\frac{\pi n^2\mu^2}{z^2v^2}\right)$$

而 $z=\exp\left\{-i\left(\frac{1}{4}\pi-\frac{1}{2}d\right)-y\right\}$. 我们有

$$I_2\leqslant\frac{H^2}{4}\int_0^{\frac{2}{H}}|f(y)|^2dy+\int_{\frac{2}{H}}^{\infty}|f(y)|^2\frac{dy}{y^2}=\frac{H^2}{4}I_{21}+I_{22}(\text{新引进的符号})\tag{4.1}$$

令 $y=\log x$ 与 $G=e^{\frac{2}{H}}$,则

$$I_{21}=\int_1^G\left|\frac{1}{2}x^{-1}\varphi(0)\varphi(1)\exp\left\{-i\left(\frac{\pi}{4}-\frac{d}{2}\right)\right\}-g(x)\right|^2dx$$

其中

$$g(x)=\sum_{n=1}^{\infty}\sum_{\mu=1}^{\xi}\sum_{v=1}^{\xi}\frac{\beta_\mu\beta_v}{v}\exp\left(-\frac{\pi\mu^2n^2}{v^2}e^{i(\pi/2-d)}x^2\right)$$

由于 $\varphi(0)\varphi(1)=O(\xi\log\xi)$ 和 $\alpha_v=o(1)$ 我们有

$$\begin{aligned}I_{21}&\leqslant\int_1^G|g(x)|^2dx+2\int_1^G\frac{\xi\log\xi|g(x)|}{2x}dx+\int_1^G\frac{\xi^2\log^2\xi}{4x^2}dx\leqslant\\&\int_1^G|g(x)|^2dx+O\left\{\xi\log\xi\left(\int_1^G|g(x)|^2dx\right)^{1/2}\right\}+O(\xi^2\log^2\xi)\end{aligned}\tag{4.2}$$

仿此,因 $\int_G^\infty\frac{|\varphi(0)\varphi(1)|^2}{4x^2\log^2x}dx=O\left(\frac{\xi^2\log^2\xi}{G\log^2G}\right)$,我们得到

$$I_{22}\leqslant\int_G^\infty\frac{|g(x)|^2}{\log^2x}dx+O\left\{\left(\frac{\xi^2\log^2\xi}{G\log^2G}\int_G^\infty\frac{|g(x)|^2}{\log^2x}dx\right)^{1/2}\right\}+O\left(\frac{\xi^2\log^2\xi}{G\log^2G}\right)\tag{4.3}$$

今转而讨论 I_1,我们容易得到

$$I_1\leqslant\int_1^\infty|g(x)|^2dx+O\left\{\xi\log\xi\left(\int_1^\infty|g(x)|^2dx\right)^{1/2}\right\}+O(\varepsilon^2\log^2\xi)\tag{4.4}$$

因此,剩下的问题只有去估计

$$I_1^* = \int_1^G |g(x)|^2 dx,\ I_2^* = \int_G^\infty \frac{|g(x)|^2}{\log^2 x} dx,\ I_3^* = \int_1^\infty |g(x)|^2 dx$$

设

$$J(x,\theta) = \int_x^\infty |g(x)|^2 \frac{dx}{x^\theta},\quad 0 < \theta < 1$$

不难看出

$$I_1^* = -\int_1^G x^\theta \frac{\partial J}{\partial x} dx = -[x^\theta J]_1^G + \theta \int_1^G x^{\theta-1} J dx \tag{4.5}$$

而对于充分大的 G 则有

$$\int_0^{1/2} \theta J(G,\theta) d\theta = \int_G^\infty |g(x)|^2 dx \int_0^{1/2} \theta x^{-\theta} d\theta =$$
$$\int_G^\infty |g(x)|^2 \left(\frac{1}{\log^2 x} - \frac{1}{2x^{1/2}\log x} - \frac{1}{x^{1/2}\log^2 x}\right) dx \geqslant$$
$$\int_G^\infty \frac{|g(x)|^2}{\log^2 x} dx - \int_G^\infty \frac{|g(x)|^2}{x^{1/2}} dx$$

即

$$I_2^* \leqslant \int_0^{1/2} \theta J(G,\theta) d\theta + J\left(G\frac{1}{2}\right) \tag{4.6}$$

5. 显然,我们有

$$J(X,\theta) = \sum_{m=1}^\infty \sum_{n=1}^\infty \sum_\kappa \sum_\lambda \sum_\mu \sum_v \frac{\beta_\kappa \beta_\lambda \beta_\mu \beta_v}{\lambda v} \int_X^\infty \exp\left\{-\pi\left(\frac{m^2\kappa^2}{\lambda^2} + \frac{n^2\mu^2}{v^2}\right)x^2 \sin d + \right.$$
$$\left. i\pi\left(\frac{m^2\kappa^2}{\lambda^2} - \frac{n^2\mu^2}{v^2}\right)x^2 \cos d\right\} \frac{dx}{x^\theta}$$

用 $\sum_1$ 表示各项满足 $\frac{m\kappa}{\lambda} = \frac{n\mu}{v}$ 的和而 $\sum_2$ 则表示其余各项之和. 令 $(\kappa v, \lambda\mu) = q$ 则 $\kappa v = aq$, $\lambda\mu = bq$ 而 $(a,b) = 1$,故在 $\sum_1$ 中 $ma = nb$ 因而 $n = ra$, $m = rb(r = 1,2,\cdots)$,故

$$\sum_1 = \sum_\kappa \sum_\lambda \sum_\mu \sum_v \frac{\beta_\kappa \beta_\lambda \beta_\mu \beta_v}{\lambda v} \sum_{r=1}^\infty \int_X^\infty \exp\left(-2\pi \frac{r^2\kappa^2\mu^2}{q^2} x^2 \sin d\right) \frac{dx}{x^\theta}$$

我们先考虑

$$\sum_{r=1}^\infty \int_X^\infty e^{-r^2x^2\eta} \frac{dx}{x^\theta} = \eta^{(1/2)\theta-(1/2)} \sum_{r=1}^\infty \frac{1}{r^{1-\theta}} \int_{Xr\sqrt{\eta}}^\infty e^{-y^2} \frac{dy}{y^\theta} =$$
$$\eta^{(1/2)\theta-(1/2)} \int_{X\sqrt{\eta}}^\infty \frac{e^{-y^2}}{y^\theta} \left(\sum_{r \leqslant y(X\sqrt{\eta})} \frac{1}{r^{1-\theta}}\right) dy$$

因 $\xi(s) = \sum_{n=1}^N \frac{1}{n^s} - \frac{1}{(1-s)N^{s-1}} + O\left(\frac{1}{N^\sigma}\right)$,故关于 r 的和可写成

$$\frac{1}{\theta}\left(\frac{y}{X\sqrt{\eta}}\right)^{\theta}+\xi(1-\theta)+O\left\{\left(\frac{y}{X\sqrt{\eta}}\right)^{\theta-1}\right\}$$

由此可得

$$\sum_{r=1}^{\infty}\int_{X}^{\infty}\mathrm{e}^{-r^2x^2\eta}\frac{\mathrm{d}x}{x^{\theta}}=\frac{1}{\theta X^{\theta}\sqrt{\eta}}\left\{\int_0^{\infty}\mathrm{e}^{-y^2}\mathrm{d}y+O(X\sqrt{\eta})\right\}+$$

$$\zeta(1-\theta)\eta^{(1/2)\theta-(1/2)}\left[\int_0^{\infty}y^{-\theta}\mathrm{e}^{-y^2}\mathrm{d}y+O\left\{\left(\frac{X\sqrt{\eta}}{1-\theta}\right)^{1-\theta}\right\}\right]+O\{X^{1-\theta}\log(X\sqrt{\eta})\}=$$

$$\frac{\sqrt{\pi}}{2\theta X^{\theta}\eta^{1/2}}+\frac{1}{2}\xi(1-\theta)\Gamma\left(\frac{1-\theta}{2}\right)\eta^{(1/2)\theta-(1/2)}+O\left\{\frac{X^{1-\theta}}{\theta(1-\theta)}\log(X\sqrt{\eta})\right\}$$

令 $\eta=2\pi\kappa^2\mu^2q^{-2}\sin d$,我们有

$$\sum\nolimits_1=\frac{S(0)}{2(2\sin d)^{1/2}\theta X^{\theta}}+\frac{1}{2}\zeta(1-\theta)\Gamma\left(\frac{1-\theta}{2}\right)(2\pi\sin d)^{(\theta-1)/2}S(\theta)+$$

$$O\left(\frac{X^{1-\theta}\log(X\xi/d)}{\theta(1-\theta)}\xi^2\log^2\xi\right)\tag{5.1}$$

其中

$$S(\theta)=\sum_{\kappa}\sum_{\lambda}\sum_{\mu}\sum_{v}\left(\frac{q}{\kappa\mu}\right)^{1-\theta}\frac{\beta_{\kappa}\beta_{\lambda}\beta_{\mu}\beta_{v}}{\lambda v}$$

我们已知(见[3]内(7.1))

$$\sum\nolimits_2=O\left(X^{-\theta}\xi^4\log^2\frac{1}{d}\right)\tag{5.2}$$

故由(5.1)与(5.2)得出

$$J(X,\theta)=\frac{S(0)}{2(2\sin d)^{1/2}\theta X^{\theta}}+\frac{1}{2}\xi(1-\theta)\Gamma\left(\frac{1-\theta}{2}\right)(2\pi\sin d)^{(\theta-1)/2}S(\theta)+$$

$$O\left(\frac{X^{1-\theta}\xi^2}{\theta(1-\theta)}\log(X\xi/d)\log^2\xi\right)+O\left(X^{-\theta}\xi^4\log^2\frac{1}{d}\right)\tag{5.3}$$

我们取 $G=\mathrm{e}^{2/H}$ 并选择 d,ξ 与 H 使得

$$d=\frac{A_1}{T},\quad \xi=A_2T^{(1/8)-\varepsilon_1},\ H=\frac{A_3}{\log\xi}>\frac{2}{\log\xi}\tag{5.4}$$

其中 A_1,A_2 和以后的 $A_3,\cdots$ 都是正的常数又 ε_1 和以后的 $\varepsilon_2,\varepsilon_3,\cdots$ 都表任意小的正数. 于是从(5.3)得出

$$J(X,\theta)=\frac{S(0)}{2(2\sin d)^{1/2}\theta X^{\theta}}+\frac{1}{2}\zeta(1-\theta)\Gamma\left(\frac{1-\theta}{2}\right)(2\pi\sin d)^{(\theta-1)/2}S(\theta)+$$

$$O\left\{\left(\frac{X^{1-\theta}}{\theta(1-\theta)}+T^{1/4}X^{-\theta}\right)T^{(1/4)-\varepsilon_2}\right\}\tag{5.5}$$

取 $\theta=\frac{1}{2}$ 并代入(4.5)我们得到

$$I_1^* = \frac{S(0)}{(2\sin d)^{1/2}H} + O(T^{(1/2)-\varepsilon_3}) \tag{5.6}$$

将来要证明 $S(\theta) \geqslant 0$(见(9.2)). 因而上面第二项与 $\zeta(1-\theta)$ 是同号的. 但 $\zeta(1-\theta)$ 当 $0 \leqslant \theta \leqslant 1$ 时是负的,故由(5.5) 得

$$J(X,\theta) \leqslant \frac{S(0)}{2(2\sin d)^{1/2}\theta X^\theta} + O\left\{\left(\frac{X^{1-\theta}}{\theta(1-\theta)} + T^{1/4}X^{-\theta}\right)T^{(1/4)-\varepsilon_2}\right\} \tag{5.7}$$

代入(4.6) 我们得出

$$I_2^* \leqslant \frac{HS(0)}{4(2\sin d)^{1/2}} + O(T^{(1/2)-\varepsilon_4}) \tag{5.8}$$

将来要证明 $S(\theta) = O(1/\log \xi)$(见(9.14)). 把(5.6) 及(5.8) 代入(4.2) 和(4.3) 即得

$$I_{21} \leqslant \frac{S(0)}{(2\sin d)^{1/2}H} + O(T^{(1/2)-\varepsilon_5})$$

$$I_{22} \leqslant \frac{HS(0)}{4(2\sin d)^{1/2}} + O(T^{(1/2)-\varepsilon_6})$$

故由(4.1)

$$I_2 \leqslant \frac{HS(0)}{2(2\sin d)^{1/2}} + O(T^{(1/2)-\varepsilon_7}) \tag{5.9}$$

6. 现在考虑 $I_3^* = J(1,0)$. 如 §5,我们可以写成

$$I_3^* = \sum_{m=1}^{\infty}\sum_{n=1}^{\infty}\sum_{\kappa}\sum_{\lambda}\sum_{\mu}\sum_{v}\frac{\beta_\kappa\beta_\lambda\beta_\mu\beta_v}{\lambda v}\int_1^\infty \exp\left\{-\pi\left(\frac{m^2\kappa^2}{\lambda^2}+\frac{n^2\mu^2}{v^2}\right)x^2\sin d + \right.$$
$$\left. \mathrm{i}\pi\left(\frac{m^2\kappa^2}{\lambda^2}-\frac{n^2\mu^2}{v^2}\right)x^2\cos d\right\}\mathrm{d}x = \sum\nolimits_1^* + \sum\nolimits_2^*$$

其中 $\sum_1^* + \sum_2^*$ 是对应于 $\sum_1$ 及 $\sum_2$ 的项. 因为 $\theta = 0$ 时 $\sum_2$ 变成 $\sum_2^*$. 故由(5.2) 我们得到

$$\sum\nolimits_2^* = O\left(\xi^4\log^2\frac{1}{\alpha}\right) = O(T^{(1/2)-\varepsilon_8}) \tag{6.1}$$

另一方面,

$$\sum\nolimits_1^* = \sum_{\kappa}\sum_{\lambda}\sum_{\mu}\sum_{v}\frac{\beta_\kappa\beta_\lambda\beta_\mu\beta_v}{\lambda v}\sum_{r=1}^{\infty}\int_1^\infty \exp\left(-2\pi\frac{r^2\kappa^2\mu^2}{q}x^2\sin d\right)\mathrm{d}x$$

现在,

$$\sum_{r=1}^{\infty}\int_1^\infty \mathrm{e}^{-r^2x^2\eta}\mathrm{d}x = \eta^{-1/2}\int_{\sqrt{\eta}}^\infty \mathrm{e}^{-y^2}\sum_{r\leqslant y/\sqrt{\eta}} + \frac{1}{r}\mathrm{d}y =$$
$$\eta^{-1/2}\int_{\sqrt{\eta}}^\infty \mathrm{e}^{-y^2}\left[\log\frac{y}{\sqrt{\eta}} + C + O\left(\frac{\sqrt{\eta}}{y}\right)\right]\mathrm{d}y$$

其中 C 是一常数. 最后的式子等于

$$\eta^{-1/2}\left\{\int_0^\infty e^{-y^2}\log\frac{y}{\sqrt{\eta}}dy + O(\eta^{1/2}\log\eta) + A_4\right\} =$$

$$-\frac{\sqrt{\pi}}{4}\eta^{-1/2}\log\eta + A_5\eta^{-1/2} + O(\log\eta)$$

令 $\eta = 2\pi\kappa^2\mu^2 q^{-2}\sin d$,我们由(5.4)得到

$$\sum_1^{*} = -\frac{S^*}{4(2\sin d)^{1/2}} + \frac{A_6 S(0)}{(2\sin d)^{1/2}} + O\left(\log d^{-1}\sum_\kappa\sum_\lambda\sum_\mu\sum_v\frac{1}{\lambda v}\right)$$

其中

$$S^* = \sum_\kappa\sum_\lambda\sum_\mu\sum_v\frac{\beta_\kappa\beta_\lambda\beta_\mu\beta_v}{\lambda v}\frac{q}{\kappa\mu}\log\left(2\pi\frac{\kappa^2\mu^2}{q^2}\sin d\right)$$

因 $S(0) = O\left(\frac{1}{\log\xi}\right)$[证明见 §9,参看(9.14)]及

$$\log d^{-1}\sum\sum\sum\sum\frac{1}{\lambda v} = O(\xi^2\log^2\xi\log d^{-1}) = O(T^{1/4}\log^3 T)$$

我们有

$$\sum_1^{*} = -\frac{S^*}{4(2\sin d)^{1/2}} + O\left(\frac{T^{1/2}}{\log T}\right) \tag{6.2}$$

把(6.1)及(6.2)加起来,我们得到

$$I_3^* = -\frac{S^*}{4(2\sin d)^{1/2}} + O\left(\frac{T^{1/2}}{\log T}\right) \tag{6.3}$$

这就给出(4.4)的第一项的一个估计. 将来要证明 $S^* = O(1)$[看(9.17)],故由(4.4)

$$I_1 \leqslant -\frac{S^*}{4(2\sin d)^{1/2}} + O\left(\frac{T^{1/2}}{\log T}\right) \tag{6.4}$$

7. 假定我们能证明(见(9.14))

$$S(0) \leqslant \frac{A_0}{\log\xi}, \quad -S^* \leqslant A^* \tag{7.1}$$

则由(6.4),(5.9)及引理3.1,

$$I_1 \leqslant (1+o(1))\frac{A^*}{4(2\sin d)^{1/2}}, \quad I_2 \leqslant (1+o(1))\frac{HA_0\log^{-1}\xi}{2(2\sin d)^{1/2}}$$

$$I \geqslant \tilde{A}T^{3/4}$$

其中$\left(\text{取 } d = \frac{1}{2T}\right)$

$$\tilde{A} = \frac{2}{3}\left(\frac{2}{\pi}\right)^{1/4}e^{-dT/2} = \frac{2}{3}\left(\frac{2}{\pi}\right)^{1/4}e^{-1/4} \tag{7.2}$$

由引理2.3($T_1 = 0$, $T_2 = T$)

$$N_0(T) \geqslant (1-o(1))\frac{2(2\sin d)^{1/2}}{A^* H^2}\left\{\widetilde{A}HT^{1/4} - \frac{2A_0^{1/2}H^{1/2}}{(2\sin d)^{1/4}}\log^{-1/4}\xi\right\}^2 \frac{T}{H} =$$

$$8(1-o(1))\left\{\frac{1}{2}\widetilde{A}H^{1/2}T^{1/4}(2\sin d)^{1/4} - A_0^{1/2}\log^{-1/2}\xi\right\}^2 \frac{T}{A^* H^2}$$

取 H 使得

$$\frac{1}{2}\widetilde{A}H^{1/2}T^{1/4}(2\sin d)^{1/4} = 2A_0^{1/2}\log^{-1/2}\xi$$

即使得

$$H^2 = \frac{128A_0^2}{\widetilde{A}^4 T\sin d}\frac{1}{\log^2\xi}$$

我们有

$$N_0(T) \geqslant 8(1-o(1))\frac{A_0 T\log^{-1}\xi}{A^* H^2} =$$

$$(1-o(1))\frac{\widetilde{A}^4 T\sin d}{16A_0A^*}T\log\xi =$$

$$(1-o(1))\frac{T\log T}{648\pi e A_0 A^*} \tag{7.3}$$

8. 在估计 $S(0)$ 及 S^* 之前我们要先证明几个引理.

引理 8.1 当 $\operatorname{Re} a = a_1 > 1/2$ 及 k 充分大时

$$\frac{1}{\Gamma(a+1)}\sum_{\substack{\kappa\leqslant k\\(\kappa,\rho)=1}}\frac{\alpha_\kappa}{\kappa}\log^a\frac{k}{\kappa} = \frac{1}{\Gamma\left(a+\frac{1}{2}\right)}\sum_{\kappa\leqslant k}{}^{*}\frac{\alpha'_\kappa}{\kappa}\log^{a-(1/2)}\frac{k}{\kappa} + \tag{8.1}$$

$$O\left[(\log^{a_1-(3/2)}k + \log^{(a_1/2)-(1/4)}k)\prod_{p|\rho}\left(1-\frac{1}{p}\right)^{-1/2}\right]$$

其中 * 号表示 κ 的一切素因数都除尽 ρ 并且 $\alpha_\kappa,\alpha'_\kappa$ 分别是 $\{\zeta(s)\}^{-1/2}$ 及 $\{\zeta(s)\}^{1/2}$ 的狄氏级数的系数(参看 §3). 我们取平方根的符号使得 $\alpha_1 = \alpha'_1 = 1$.

证 当 $c>0$ 及 $\operatorname{Re} z>0$ 时,我们有

$$\frac{1}{\Gamma(z)} = \frac{1}{2\pi}\int_{-\infty}^{\infty}e^{\alpha+iu}(c+iu)^{-z}du = \frac{1}{2\pi i}\int_{c-i\infty}^{c+i\infty}\frac{e^s}{s^z}ds$$

这公式是 Laplace 证明的(参看 Whittaker-Watson, Modern analysis 第 4 版, 245-246 页例 1),故当 $\operatorname{Re} b>0$ 时

$$\frac{1}{2\pi i}\int_{1-i\infty}^{1+i\infty}\frac{x^s}{s^{b+1}}ds = \begin{cases}0, & 0\leqslant x\leqslant 1\\ \dfrac{1}{\Gamma(b+1)}\log^b x, & 1<x\end{cases} \tag{8.2}$$

当 $\sigma>0$ 时,我们有

$$\sum_{\substack{\kappa=1\\(\kappa,\rho)=1}}^{\infty}\frac{\alpha_\kappa}{\kappa^{1+s}}=\prod_{p|\rho}\left(1-\frac{1}{p^{1+s}}\right)^{-1/2}\frac{1}{\sqrt{\zeta(1+s)}}$$

因此,由(8.2)得

$$\frac{1}{\Gamma(a+1)}\sum_{\substack{\kappa\leqslant k\\(\kappa,\rho)=1}}\frac{\alpha_\kappa}{\kappa}\log^a\frac{k}{\kappa}=\frac{1}{2\pi i}\int_{1-i\infty}^{1+i\infty}\frac{k^s}{s^{a+1}}\prod_{p|\rho}\left(1-\frac{1}{p^{1+s}}\right)^{-1/2}\frac{ds}{\sqrt{\zeta(1+s)}}$$

我们把积分路线推到 $\sigma=0$ 去,为了避免通过原点,可以绕着一个以原点为中心,以 r 为半径并且整个在虚轴右边的半圆,这样我们就得到

$$\frac{1}{\Gamma(a+1)}\sum_{\substack{\kappa\leqslant k\\(\kappa,\rho)=1}}\frac{\alpha_\kappa}{\kappa}\log^a\frac{k}{\kappa}=\frac{1}{2\pi i}\left\{\int_C+\int_{-i\infty}^{-ir_1}+\int_{ir_1}^{i\infty}\right\}\frac{k^s}{s^{a+1}}\prod_{p|\rho}\left(1-\frac{1}{p^{1+s}}\right)^{-1/2}\frac{ds}{\sqrt{\zeta(1+s)}}\tag{8.3}$$

其中 $r_1>r$ 并且 C 包含一个半圆和两个线段. 上述步骤是合理的,这因为当 $\sigma\geqslant1$ 时我们有:当 $t\to\infty$ 时 $1/\xi(s)=O\{\log t^{A_7}\}$(参看 Ingham, The Distribution of prime numbers, Theorem 10).

我们知道 $|\zeta(1+it)|^{-1}<A_8|t|$ 是对于一切的 t 值(不论大或小)一致成立的,故(8.3)右边最后两个积分的绝对值小于(取 $r_1=\log^{-1/2}k$)

$$A_9\int_{r_1}^{\infty}\frac{dt}{t^{a_1+(1/2)}}\prod_{p|\rho}\left(1-\frac{1}{p}\right)^{-1/2}\leqslant A_{10}r_1^{(1/2)-a_1}\prod_{p|\rho}\left(1-\frac{1}{p}\right)^{-1/2}\leqslant A_{10}\log^{(1/2)a_1-(1/4)}k\prod_{p|\rho}\left(1-\frac{1}{p}\right)^{-1/2}\tag{8.4}$$

当 $|s|\leqslant r_1$ 时,我们有 $\zeta^{-1/2}(1+s)=s^{1/2}+A_1s^{3/2}+\cdots$,取 $r_1=\frac{1}{\log k}$,我们得到:沿 C 的积分是

$$\int_C\frac{k^s}{s^{a+1}}\prod_{p|\rho}\left(1-\frac{1}{p^{1+s}}\right)^{-1/2}s^{1/2}ds+O\left[\log^{a_1-3/2}k\prod_{p|\rho}\left(1-\frac{1}{p}\right)^{-1/2}\right]=$$
$$\left\{\int_C+\int_{-i\infty}^{-ir_1}+\int_{ir_1}^{i\infty}\right\}\frac{k^s}{s^{a+(1/2)}}\prod_{p|\rho}\left(1-\frac{1}{p^{1+s}}\right)^{-1/2}ds+$$
$$O\left[\log^{a_1-(3/2)}k\prod_{p|\rho}\left(1-\frac{1}{p}\right)^{-1/2}\right]+O\left[\log^{(a_1/2)-(1/4)}k\prod_{p|\rho}\left(1-\frac{1}{p}\right)^{-1/2}\right]\tag{8.5}$$

在(8.5)右边的积分等于(根据(8.2))

$$\frac{1}{2\pi i}\int_{1-i\infty}^{1+i\infty}\frac{k^s}{s^{a+(1/2)}}\prod_{p|\rho}\left(1-\frac{1}{p^{1+s}}\right)^{-1/2}ds=\frac{1}{\Gamma\left(a+\frac{1}{2}\right)}\sum_{\kappa\leqslant k}{}^{*}\frac{\alpha'_\kappa}{\kappa}\log^{a-(1/2)}\frac{k}{\kappa}\tag{8.6}$$

由(8.4),(8.5)及(8.6)我们看到(8.3)的右边等于

$$\frac{1}{\Gamma\left(a+\frac{1}{2}\right)}\sum_{\kappa\leqslant k}{}^{*}\frac{\alpha'_{\kappa}}{\kappa}\log^{a-(1/2)}\frac{k}{\kappa}+O\left\{(\log^{(a_1/2)-(1/4)}k+\log^{a_1-(3/2)}k)\prod_{p|\rho}\left(1-\frac{1}{p}\right)^{-1/2}\right\}$$

这正是我们所要证明的.

引理 8.2 设 λ_1 与 λ_2 是正的, ξ_1 与 ξ_2 是大于 1 的, n 是一个正的整数而 p 是一个素数,则

$$\left|\sum_{l+m=n}{}'\alpha_p^l\alpha_p^m\log^{\lambda_1}\frac{\xi_1}{p^l}\log^{\lambda_2}\frac{\xi_2}{p^m}\right|<Cn^{-3/2}\log^{\lambda_1+\lambda_2}\xi \tag{8.7}$$

其中 $\xi=\max(\xi_1,\xi_2)$, $C=4e^{5/3}\pi^{-1/2}$ 而"′"表示 m 与 n 通过满足 $p^l\leqslant\xi_1$ 与 $p^m\leqslant\xi_2$ 的非负整数.

证 (8.7) 的左边不超过

$$\log^{\lambda_1+\lambda_2}\xi\sum_{l+m=n}|\alpha_{p^l}\alpha_{p^m}| \tag{8.8}$$

因为 $\alpha_{p^l}=(-)^l\frac{\frac{1}{2}\left(\frac{1}{2}-1\right)\cdots\left(\frac{1}{2}-l+1\right)}{l!}$ 是负的或等于 1,要看 $l>0$ 或 $l=0$ 而定. 所以我们知道当 $n>1$ 时, (8.8) 等于

$$\log^{\lambda_1+\lambda_2}\xi\left(\sum_{l+m=n}\alpha_{p^l}\alpha_{p^m}-4\alpha_p{}^n\right)=-4\log^{\lambda_1+\lambda_2}\xi\cdot\alpha_p{}^n$$

(这因为 $\sum_{l+m=n}\alpha_{p^l}\alpha_{p^m}$ 是在

$$[\{\zeta(s)\}^{-1/2}]^2=\zeta^{-1}(s)=\prod_p\left(1-\frac{1}{p^s}\right)=\sum_{n=1}^{\infty}\frac{\mu(n)}{n^s}$$

中 $\frac{1}{p^{ns}}$ 的系数,因而当 $n>1$ 时它等于 0). 由 Stirling 公式

$$|\alpha_p{}^n|=\frac{\frac{1}{2}\cdot\frac{1}{2}\cdot\frac{3}{2}\cdot\cdots\cdot\frac{2n-3}{2}}{1\cdot2\cdot3\cdot\cdots\cdot n}=\frac{1}{\sqrt{\pi}}\frac{\Gamma\left(\frac{2n-1}{2}\right)}{\Gamma(n+1)}=$$

$$\frac{1}{\sqrt{\pi}}\frac{\left(n-\frac{1}{2}\right)^{n-1}e^{-n+(1/2)}e^{\theta_1/(6(2n-1))}}{(n+1)^{n+(1/2)}e^{-n-1}e^{\theta_2/(12(n+1))}}\quad(0<\theta_1<1,0<\theta_2<1)<$$

$$\frac{1}{\sqrt{\pi}}\cdot\frac{1}{n^{3/2}}\cdot e^{3/2}\cdot e^{1/6}=\frac{e^{5/3}}{\sqrt{\pi}}n^{-3/2}$$

从此立刻得到引理.

引理 8.3 设 ρ 是不超过 ξ^2 的一个整数而 λ_1 与 λ_2 都是正数,则当 ε 是任意正数而 ξ 充分大时,我们有

$$\sum_{\rho|D}{}^{*}\frac{1}{D}\sum_{\substack{d_1d_2=D\\d_1\leqslant\xi/\kappa,d_2\leqslant\xi/v}}\alpha_{d_1}\alpha_{d_2}\log^{\lambda_1}\frac{\xi}{d_1\kappa}\log^{\lambda_2}\frac{\xi}{d_2v}=$$

$$\frac{1}{\rho}\sum_{\substack{d_1d_2=\rho\\ d_1\leqslant\xi/\kappa,d_2\leqslant\xi/v}}\alpha_{d_1}\alpha_{d_2}\log^{\lambda_1}\frac{\xi}{d_1\kappa}\log^{\lambda_2}\frac{\xi}{d_2v}+R \tag{8.9}$$

其中 $|R|<\varepsilon\log^{\lambda_1+\lambda_2}\xi\frac{1}{\rho}\prod_{p|\rho}\left(1-\frac{1}{p}\right)^{-1}$. 而星号表示 D 通过一切那种类型的正整数,就是它只以 ρ 的素因数为素因数,又除去当 ρ 不是下列形式的数时,(8.9) 右边第一项应该删去:

$$\rho^*=p_1\cdots p_jp_{j+1}^{l_1}\cdots p_{j+g}^{l_g} \tag{8.10}$$

其中 $g<C_\varepsilon$ 而 $p_{j+i}>C_{\xi,\varepsilon}$,又 $p_1,\cdots p_{j+h}$ 是不同的素数,C_ε 是一个常数(与 λ_1,λ_2 及 ε 有关),而 $C_{\xi,\varepsilon}$ 是另一个常数(与 $\lambda_1,\lambda_2,\varepsilon$ 及 § 有关) 并且 $C_{\xi,\varepsilon}$ 随 $\xi\to\infty$ 而趋于无穷.

证 为便利计我们用 $p^j\ /\!/\ N$ 来表示 p^j 除尽 N 但 p^{j+1} 则否. 设

$$n\geqslant2,\ p^n\ /\!/\ D,\ p^l\ /\!/\ d_1 \text{ 与 } p^m\ /\!/\ d_2$$

设 $d_1=ap^l$ 而 $d_2=bp^m$. 则因当 $(\mu,v)=1$ 时 $\alpha_\mu\alpha_v=\alpha_{\mu v}$,(8.9) 左边的内部和等于

$$\sum_a\sum_{b\,p^n=D}\alpha_a\alpha_b\sum\sum{}'\alpha_{p^l}\alpha_{p^m}\log^{\lambda_1}\frac{\xi}{a\kappa p^l}\log^{\lambda_2}\frac{\xi}{bvp^m} \tag{8.11}$$

其中"′"表示 l 与 m 满足条件:$p^l\leqslant\xi/a\kappa$, $p^m\leqslant\xi/bv$ 与 $l+m=n$.

令

$$\sum_p=\sum\sum{}'\alpha_{p^l}\alpha_{p^m}\log^{\lambda_1}\frac{\xi}{a\kappa p^l}\log^{\lambda_2}\frac{\xi}{bvp^m} \tag{8.12}$$

若 $\xi/a\kappa$ 与 ξ/bv 之中有一个小于 $\xi^{\varepsilon'}(0<\varepsilon'<1)$ 而 $\lambda=\min(\lambda_1,\lambda_2)$,则

$$\left|\sum_p\right|\leqslant\varepsilon'^{\lambda}\log^{\lambda_1,\lambda_2}\xi\sum\sum{}^*|\alpha_{p^l}\alpha_{p^m}|\leqslant$$

$$\varepsilon'^{\lambda}\log^{\lambda_1+\lambda_2}\xi\sum_{l+m=n}\sum\alpha'_{p^l}\alpha'_{p^m}=\varepsilon'^{\lambda}\log^{\lambda_1+\lambda_2}\xi \tag{8.13}$$

现在假定 $\xi/a\kappa$ 与 ξ/bv 都大于 $\xi^{\varepsilon'}$,那么我们或者得到 $p^n\leqslant\xi^{\varepsilon'2}$ 或是得到 $p^n>\xi^{\varepsilon'2}$.

在第一种情形下

$$\log^{\lambda_1}\frac{\xi}{a\kappa p^l}\log^{\lambda_2}\frac{\xi}{bvp^m}=\log^{\lambda_1}\frac{\xi}{a\kappa}\log^{\lambda_2}\frac{\xi}{bv}\left(1-\frac{\log p^l}{\log\frac{\xi}{a\kappa}}\right)^{\lambda_1}\left(1-\frac{\log p^m}{\log\frac{\xi}{bv}}\right)^{\lambda_2}=$$

$$\log^{\lambda_1}\frac{\xi}{a\kappa}\log^{\lambda_2}\frac{\xi}{bv}(1+\theta(l))$$

其中 $|\theta(l)|<A'\varepsilon'$ 且 A' 是一常数(只与 λ_1 及 λ_2 有关). 故(因 $|a_v|<\alpha'_v$)

$$\sum_p=\log^{\lambda_1}\frac{\xi}{a\kappa}\log^{\lambda_2}\frac{\xi}{bv}\sum_{l+m=n}\sum\alpha_{p^l}\alpha_{p^m}-$$

$$-\varepsilon''\log^{\lambda_1}\frac{\xi}{a\kappa}\log^{\lambda_2}\frac{\xi}{bv}\sum_{l+m=n}\sum\alpha'_{p^l}\alpha'_{d^m},$$

其中 $|\varepsilon''|<A'\varepsilon'$. 我们曾证明当 $n>1$ 时, $\sum\limits_{l+m=n}\alpha_{p^l}\alpha_{p^m}=0$, 我们同样可以证明 $\sum\limits_{l+m=n}\alpha'_{p^l}\alpha'_{p^m}=1$, 故

$$\left|\sum\nolimits_p\right|\leqslant A'\varepsilon'\log^{\lambda_1+\lambda_2}\xi \tag{8.14}$$

在第二种情形中,我们从引理 8.2 可以推出

$$\left|\sum\nolimits_p\right|<\frac{C}{n^{3/2}}\log\xi=\varepsilon'''\log^{\lambda_1+\lambda_2}\xi,\text{ 当 } n>\left(\frac{C}{\varepsilon'''}\right)^{2/3} \tag{8.15}$$

由(8.13), (8.14) 与(8.15),我们可以下结论说

$$\left|\sum\nolimits_p\right|\leqslant\varepsilon^{(4)}\log^{\lambda_1+\lambda_2}\xi,\ \varepsilon^{(4)}=\max(\varepsilon'^{\lambda},A'\varepsilon',\varepsilon''')$$

除了当 $n=1$ 或

$$p^n>\xi^{\varepsilon'^2}\text{ 与 }1<n<\left(\frac{C}{\varepsilon'''}\right)^{2/3},$$

即

$$p>\xi^{\varepsilon'^2/n}>\xi^{\varepsilon'^2(\varepsilon'''/C)^{2/3}}$$

以外都是成立的. 因此利用 $\sum\limits_{a}\sum\limits_{b\,p^n=D}\alpha'_a\alpha'_b=1$ 这个等式一般可以得到

$$\left|\sum_{\substack{d_1d_2=D\\ d_1\leqslant\xi/\kappa,d_2\leqslant\xi/v}}\sum\alpha_{d_1}\alpha_{d_2}\log^{\lambda_1}\frac{\xi}{d_1\kappa}\log^{\lambda_2}\frac{\xi}{d_2v}\right|\leqslant\varepsilon^{(4)}\log^{\lambda_1+\lambda_2\xi}\sum_{a}\sum_{b\,p^n=D}\alpha'_a\alpha'_b=$$

$$\varepsilon^{(4)}\log^{\lambda_1+\lambda_2}\xi \tag{8.16}$$

上式不成立的情形只有:D 或者无平方因数(也就是说等于 ρ) 或者可以写成

$$D^*=p_1\cdots p_rp_{r+1}^{n_1}\cdots p_{r+h}^{n_h} \tag{8.17}$$

其中 $p_1,\cdots,p_{r+h}$ 是不同的素数,而

$$p_{r+i}^{n_i}>\xi^{\varepsilon'^2},\quad 1<n_i<\left(\frac{C}{\varepsilon'''}\right)^{2/3}$$

即

$$p_{r+i}>\xi^{\varepsilon'^2/n_i}>\xi^{\varepsilon^2(\varepsilon'''/C)^{2/3}}=\xi^{\kappa},\quad \kappa\text{ 是新记号} \tag{8.18}$$

因为 $\rho\leqslant\xi^2$, 所以大于 $\xi^{\varepsilon'^2\left(\frac{\varepsilon'''}{C}\right)^{2/3}}$ 的素因数个数一定小于或等于

$$\frac{\log\xi^2}{\log[\xi^{\varepsilon'^2(\varepsilon'''/C)^{2/3}}]}=\frac{2}{\varepsilon'^2\left(\frac{\varepsilon'''}{C}\right)^{2/3}}=C\varepsilon',(\text{新符号}) \tag{8.19}$$

现在

$$\sum_{\rho|D}{}^*\frac{1}{D}\sum_{\substack{d_1d_2=D\\ d_1\leqslant\xi/\kappa,d_2\leqslant\xi/v}}\alpha_{d_1}\alpha_{d_2}\log^{\lambda_1}\frac{\xi}{d_1\kappa}\log^{\lambda_2}\frac{\xi}{d_2v}=\sum{}'+\sum{}'' \tag{8.20}$$

其中$\sum''$表示其中D或者无平方因数,或者可以写成(8.17)的各项之和,而$\sum'$表示其他各项之和. 于是由(8.16)

$$\left|\sum{}'\right| \leqslant \sum_{\rho \mid D}{}' \frac{1}{D} \cdot \varepsilon^{(4)} \log^{\lambda_1+\lambda_2}\xi \leqslant \varepsilon^{(4)} \log^{\lambda_1+\lambda_2}\xi \cdot \frac{1}{\rho} \prod_{p \mid \rho} \left(1 - \frac{1}{p}\right)^{-1} \tag{8.21}$$

另一方面

$$\sum{}'' = \frac{1}{\rho} \sum_{\substack{d_1 d_2 = \rho \\ d_1 \leqslant \xi/\kappa,\, d_2 \leqslant \xi/v}} \alpha_{d_1} \alpha_{d_2} \log^{\lambda_1} \frac{\xi}{d_1 \kappa} \log^{\lambda_2} \frac{\xi}{d_2 v} +$$

$$\sum_{\substack{\rho \mid D^* \\ \rho \neq D^*}} \frac{1}{D^*} \sum_{\substack{d_1 d_2 = D^* \\ d_1 \leqslant \xi/\kappa,\, d_2 \leqslant \xi/v}} \alpha_{d_1} \alpha_{d_2} \log^{\lambda_1} \frac{\xi}{d_1 \kappa} \log^{\lambda_2} \frac{\xi}{d_2 v}$$

其中右边第一项除了当ρ可以表成(8.17)的形式D^*时以外,都应该删去. 至于上式右边第二项的绝对值则不超过

$$\log^{\lambda_1+\lambda_1}\xi \sum_{\substack{\rho \mid D^* \\ \rho \neq D^*}} \frac{1}{D^*} \sum_{d_1 d_2 = D^*} \alpha'_{d_1} \alpha'_{d_2} \leqslant \log^{\lambda_1+\lambda_1}\xi \sum_{\substack{\rho \mid D^* \\ D^* \neq \rho}} \frac{1}{D^*}$$

由(8.18)及(8.19),知道上式不超过

$$\log^{\lambda_1+\lambda_1}\xi \cdot \frac{1}{\rho} \prod_{p \mid \rho,\, p > \xi^k} \left(1 - \frac{1}{p}\right)^{-1} <$$

$$\log^{\lambda_1+\lambda_1}\xi \cdot \frac{1}{\rho} \left\{ \left(1 - \frac{1}{\xi^\kappa}\right)^{-C'\xi} - 1 \right\} < \varepsilon^{(5)} \frac{\log^{\lambda_1+\lambda_1}\xi}{\rho}$$

其中$\varepsilon^{(5)} \to 0$当$\xi \to \infty$. 故结合(8.21)我们看出(8.20)右边的式子等于

$$\frac{1}{\rho} \sum_{\substack{d_1 d_2 = \rho \\ d_1 \leqslant \xi/\kappa,\, d_2 \leqslant \xi/v}} \alpha_{d_1} \alpha_{d_2} \log^{\lambda_1} \frac{\xi}{d_1 \kappa} \log^{\lambda_2} \frac{\xi}{d_2 v} + R$$

其中$|R| < \varepsilon \log^{\lambda_1+\lambda_2 \xi} \cdot \frac{1}{\rho}\left(1 - \frac{1}{\rho}\right)^{-1}$而$\varepsilon$可以选得任意小(我们可以先选得$\varepsilon$充分小再取$\xi$充分大). 这就完成了引理的证明.

引理 8.4 设ρ是不超过ξ^2的一个整数而$\lambda_1 > 1/2, \lambda_2 > 1/2$及$|\lambda_1 - \lambda_2| \leqslant 1$,则任给$\varepsilon_0 > 0$当$\xi$充分大时我们就有

$$\left| \sum_{\substack{\kappa \leqslant \xi \\ \rho \mid \kappa v}} \sum_{v \leqslant \xi} \frac{\alpha_\kappa \alpha_v}{\kappa v} \left(1 - \frac{\log \kappa}{\log \xi}\right)^{\lambda_1} \left(1 - \frac{\log v}{\log \xi}\right)^{\lambda_2} \right| \leqslant$$

$$\frac{\Gamma(\lambda_1 + 1)\Gamma(\lambda_2 + 1)}{\Gamma\left(\lambda_1 + \frac{1}{2}\right)\Gamma\left(\lambda_2 + \frac{1}{2}\right)} \frac{1}{\log^{\lambda_1+\lambda_2}\xi} \frac{1}{\rho} \log^{\lambda_1+\lambda_2-1} \frac{\xi}{\sqrt{\rho}} \prod_{p \mid \rho} \left(1 - \frac{1}{p}\right)^{-1} +$$

$$\frac{\varepsilon_0}{\log \xi} \frac{1}{\rho} \prod_{p \mid \rho} \left(1 - \frac{1}{p}\right)^{-2} \tag{8.22}$$

证 由于当$(v_1,v_2)=1$时$\alpha_{v_1}\alpha_{v_2}=\alpha_{v_1v_2}$,不难推出

$$\sum_{\substack{\kappa\leqslant\xi\\ \rho\mid\kappa v}}\sum_{v\leqslant\xi}\frac{\alpha_\kappa\alpha_v}{\kappa v}\left(1-\frac{\log\kappa}{\log\xi}\right)^{\lambda_1}\left(1-\frac{\log v}{\log\xi}\right)^{\lambda_2}=$$

$$\frac{1}{\log^{\lambda_1+\lambda_2}\xi}\sum_{\rho\mid d_1d_2}^{*}\sum^{*}\frac{\alpha_{d_1}\alpha_{d_2}}{d_1d_2}\sum_{\substack{\kappa'\leqslant\xi/d_1\\(\kappa',\rho)=1}}\frac{\alpha_{\kappa'}}{\kappa'}\log^{\lambda_1}\frac{\xi}{\kappa'd_1}\times\sum_{\substack{v'\leqslant\xi/d_2\\(v',\rho)=1}}\frac{\alpha'_v}{v'}\log^{\lambda_2}\frac{\xi}{v'd_2}\tag{8.23}$$

其中星号用来表示d_1与d_2只通过以ρ的素因数为素因数的那些数,由引理8.1知道(8.23)的绝对值不超过下式的绝对值

$$\frac{\Gamma(\lambda_1+1)\Gamma(\lambda_2+1)}{\Gamma\left(\lambda_1+\frac{1}{2}\right)\Gamma\left(\lambda_2+\frac{1}{2}\right)}\frac{1}{\log^{\lambda_1+\lambda_2}\xi}\sum_{\rho\mid d_1d_2}^{*}\sum^{*}\frac{\alpha_{d_1}\alpha_{d_2}}{d_1d_2}\times$$

$$\left[\sum_{\kappa'\leqslant\xi/d_1}^{*}\frac{\alpha'_{\kappa'}}{\kappa'}\log^{\lambda_1-1/2}\frac{\xi}{\kappa'd_1}+O\left\{\left(\log^{\lambda_1-3/2}\frac{\xi}{d_1}+\log^{(\lambda_1/2)-(1/4)}k\right)\prod_{p\mid\rho}\left(1-\frac{1}{p}\right)^{-1/2}\right\}\right]\times$$

$$\left[\sum_{v'\leqslant\xi/d_2}^{*}\frac{\alpha'_{v'}}{v'}\log^{\lambda_2-1/2}\frac{\xi}{v'd_2}+O\left\{\left(\log^{\lambda_2-3/2}\frac{\xi}{d_1}+\log^{(\lambda_2/2)-(1/4)}k\right)\prod_{p\mid\rho}\left(1-\frac{1}{p}\right)^{-1/2}\right\}\right]\tag{8.24}$$

容易看出

$$\sum_{\rho\mid d_1d_2}^{*}\sum^{*}\frac{|\alpha_{d_1}\alpha_{d_2}|}{d_1d_2}\leqslant\sum_{\rho\mid d_1d_2}^{*}\frac{\alpha'_{d_1}\alpha'_{d_2}}{d_1d_2}=\sum_{\rho\mid D}^{*}\frac{1}{D}\sum_{d_1d_2=D}\alpha'_{d_1}\alpha'_{d_2}=\frac{1}{\rho}\prod_{p\mid\rho}\left(1-\frac{1}{p}\right)^{-1}$$

其中星号表示所有D的素因数都是ρ的素因数. 又

$$\sum_{\kappa'\leqslant\xi/d}^{*}\frac{\alpha'_\kappa}{\kappa'}\leqslant\prod_{p\mid\rho}\left(1-\frac{1}{p}\right)^{-1/2}$$

故(8.24)等于

$$\frac{\Gamma(\lambda_1+1)\Gamma(\lambda_2+1)}{\Gamma\left(\lambda_1+\frac{1}{2}\right)\Gamma\left(\lambda_2+\frac{1}{2}\right)}\frac{1}{\log^{\lambda_1+\lambda_2}\xi}\sum_{\rho\mid d_1d_2}^{*}\sum^{*}\frac{\alpha_{d_1}\alpha_{d_2}}{d_1d_2}\times$$

$$\sum_{\substack{\kappa'\leqslant\xi/d_1\\ v'\leqslant\xi/d_2}}^{*}\sum^{*}\frac{\alpha_{\kappa'}\alpha_{v'}}{\kappa'v'}\log^{\lambda_1-1/2}\frac{\xi}{\kappa'd_1}\log^{\lambda_2-1/2}\frac{\xi}{v'd_2}+O\left[\frac{1}{\log^{1+\delta}\xi}\frac{1}{\rho}\prod_{p\mid\rho}\left(1-\frac{1}{p}\right)^{-2}\right]\tag{8.25}$$

其中

$$2\delta=\min\left(\lambda_1-\frac{1}{2},\ \lambda_2-\frac{1}{2}\right)$$

让我们用$\sum'$表示上面的四重和,则由引理8.3及$|\alpha_v|\leqslant\alpha'$,这个不等式,我们便有

$$\sum{}' = \sum_{\substack{\kappa'<\xi \\ \kappa'v'\leqslant\xi^2/\rho}}{}^{*}\sum_{v'<\xi}{}^{*}\frac{\alpha'_{\kappa'}\alpha'_{v'}}{\kappa'v'}\times\sum_{\substack{\rho\mid d_1d_2 \\ d_1\leqslant\xi/\kappa' \\ d_2\leqslant\xi/v'}}{}^{*}\sum{}^{*}\frac{\alpha_{d_1}\alpha_{d_2}}{d_1d_2}\log^{\lambda_1-1/2}\frac{\xi}{\kappa'd_1}\log^{\lambda_2-1/2}\frac{\xi}{v'd_2}\leqslant$$

$$\sum_{\substack{\kappa'\leqslant\xi \\ \kappa'v'\leqslant\xi^2/\rho}}{}^{*}\sum_{v'\leqslant\xi}{}^{*}\frac{\alpha'_{\kappa'}\alpha'_{v'}}{\kappa'v'}\times\Big\{\frac{1}{\rho}\sum_{d_1d_2=\rho}\alpha'_{d_1}\alpha'_{d_2}\log^{\lambda_1-1/2}\frac{\xi}{d_1\kappa'}\log^{\lambda_2-1/2}\frac{\xi}{d_2v'}+$$

$$\frac{\varepsilon}{\rho}\log^{\lambda_1+\lambda_2-1}\xi\times\prod_{p\mid\rho}\left(1-\frac{1}{p}\right)^{-1}\Big\}$$

其中除了当ρ具有引理8.3中所述的形式外,都可以省去花括弧中的第一项.因为

$$\sum_{\kappa'=1}^{\infty}{}^{*}\sum_{v'=1}^{\infty}{}^{*}\frac{\alpha'_{\kappa'}\alpha'_{v'}}{\kappa'v'}=\Big[\prod_{p\mid\rho}\left(1-\frac{1}{p}\right)^{-1/2}\Big]^2=\prod^{p\mid\rho}\left(1-\frac{1}{p}\right)^{-1}$$

所以

$$\sum{}'\leqslant\sum_{\substack{\kappa'\leqslant\xi \\ \kappa'v'\leqslant\xi^2/\rho}}{}^{*}\sum_{v'\leqslant\xi}{}^{*}\frac{\alpha'_{\kappa'}\alpha'_{v'}}{\kappa'v'}\frac{1}{\rho}\sum_{d_1d_2=\rho}\sum\frac{\alpha'_{d_1}\alpha'_{d_2}}{2}\Big(\log^{\lambda_1-1/2}\frac{\xi}{d_1\kappa'}\log^{\lambda_2-1/2}\frac{\xi}{d_2v'}+$$

$$\log^{\lambda_1-1/2}\frac{\xi}{d_2v'}\log^{\lambda_2-1/2}\frac{\xi}{d_1\kappa'}\Big)+\frac{\varepsilon}{\rho}\prod_{p\mid\rho}\left(1-\frac{1}{p}\right)^{-2}\log^{\lambda_1+\lambda_2-1}\xi \qquad (8.26)$$

容易验证当$0\leqslant X\leqslant 1$时$X^a(1-X)^b+X^b(1-X)^a$的最大值是$1/2^{a+b-1}$式中a与b是正数其差不超过1.取$X=x/(x+y)$可以推出当x,y与a,b是正数而$|a-b|\leqslant 1$时我们有

$$\frac{x^ay^b+x^by^a}{2}\leqslant\left(\frac{x+y}{2}\right)^{a+b}$$

因此,(8.26)右边第一项不超过

$$\sum_{\substack{\kappa'\leqslant\xi \\ \kappa'v'\leqslant\xi^2/\rho}}{}^{*}\sum_{v'\leqslant\xi}{}^{*}\frac{\alpha'_{\kappa'}\alpha'_{v'}}{\kappa'v'}\frac{1}{\rho}\sum_{d_1d_2=\rho}\sum\alpha'_{d_1}\alpha'_{d_2}\log^{\lambda_1+\lambda_2-1}\frac{\xi}{\sqrt{\rho\kappa'v'}}=$$

$$\sum_{\substack{\kappa'\leqslant\xi \\ \kappa'v'\leqslant\xi^2/\rho}}{}^{*}\sum_{v'\leqslant\xi}{}^{*}\frac{\alpha'_{\kappa'}\alpha'_{v'}}{\kappa'v'}\frac{1}{\rho}\log^{\lambda_1+\lambda_2-1}\frac{\xi}{\sqrt{\rho\kappa'v'}}\leqslant\frac{1}{\rho}\log^{\lambda_1+\lambda_2-1}\frac{\xi}{\sqrt{\rho}}\prod_{p\mid\rho}\left(1-\frac{1}{p}\right)^{-1}$$

引理随之成立.

9. 现在我们可以估计$S(0)$及S^*.

设

$$\phi_{-\theta}(\rho)=\rho^{1-\theta}\sum_{m\mid\rho}\frac{\mu(m)}{m^{1-\theta}}=\rho^{1-\theta}\prod_{p\mid\rho}\left(1-\frac{1}{\rho^{1-\theta}}\right)$$

$$\phi_0(\rho)=\phi_0(\rho)$$

其中$\mu(m)$是Möbius函数,则

$$q^{1-\theta}=\sum_{\rho\mid q}\phi_{-\theta}(\rho)=\sum_{\rho\mid(\kappa v,\lambda\mu)}\phi_{-\theta}(\rho)=\sum_{\rho\mid\kappa v,\rho\mid\lambda\mu}\phi_{-\theta}(\rho) \qquad (9.1)$$

故当 $0 \leqslant \theta \leqslant 1$ 时

$$S(\theta) = \sum_{\rho \leqslant \xi^2} \phi_{-\theta}(\rho) \sum_{\rho | \kappa v} \sum \sum_{\rho | \lambda\mu} \sum \frac{\beta_\kappa \beta_\lambda \beta_\mu \beta_v}{\kappa^{1-\theta} \lambda \mu^{1-\theta} v} =$$

$$\sum_{\rho \leqslant \xi^2} \phi_{-\theta}(\rho) \left(\sum_{\rho | \kappa v} \frac{\beta_\kappa \beta_v}{\kappa^{1-\theta} v} \right)^2 \geqslant 0 \tag{9.2}$$

特别有

$$S(0) = \sum_{\rho \leqslant \xi^2} \phi(\rho) \left(\sum_{\rho | \kappa v} \frac{\beta_\kappa \beta_v}{\kappa v} \right)^2 \tag{9.3}$$

另一方面

$$S^* = \sum_\kappa \sum_\lambda \sum_\mu \sum_v \frac{\beta_\kappa \beta_\lambda \beta_\mu \beta_v}{\lambda v} \frac{q}{\kappa\mu} \log\left(2\pi \frac{\kappa^2 \mu^2}{q^2} \sin d \right) =$$

$$2 \sum_\kappa \sum_\lambda \sum_\mu \sum_v \frac{\beta_\kappa \beta_\lambda \beta_\mu \beta_v}{\lambda v} \frac{q}{\kappa\mu} (\log \kappa\mu - \log q) +$$

$$\sum_\kappa \sum_\lambda \sum_\mu \sum_v \frac{\beta_\kappa \beta_\lambda \beta_\mu \beta_v}{\lambda v} \frac{q}{\kappa\mu} \log (2\pi \sin d) =$$

$$-2 \sum_\kappa \sum_\lambda \sum_\mu \sum_v \frac{\beta_\kappa \beta_\lambda \beta_\mu \beta_v}{\lambda v} \frac{q \log q}{\kappa\mu} +$$

$$4 \sum_\kappa \sum_\lambda \sum_\mu \sum_v \frac{\beta_\kappa \beta_\lambda \beta_\mu \beta_v}{\lambda v} \frac{q}{\kappa\mu} \log \mu -$$

$$\log(2\pi \sin d)^{-1} \sum_\kappa \sum_\lambda \sum_\mu \sum_v \frac{\beta_\kappa \beta_\lambda \beta_\mu \beta_v}{\lambda v} \frac{q}{\kappa\mu} =$$

$$-2S_1 + 4S_2 - S_3 \text{（新引用符号）} \tag{9.4}$$

对于 θ 微分(9.1) 即得

$$-q^{1-\theta} \log q = \sum_{\rho | \kappa v, \rho | \lambda\mu} \frac{\partial}{\partial\theta} \phi_{-\theta}(\rho) = -\sum_{\rho | \kappa v, \rho | \lambda\mu} \phi^*_{-\theta}(\rho)$$

其中

$$\phi^*_{-\theta}(\rho) = \rho^{1-\theta} \log \rho \prod_{p | \rho} \left(1 - \frac{1}{\rho^{1-\theta}} \right) + \rho^{1-\theta} \prod_{p | \rho} \left(1 - \frac{1}{\rho^{1-\theta}} \right) \sum_{p | \rho} \frac{\log \rho}{\rho^{1-\theta} - 1}$$

特别是

$$\phi^*(\rho) = \phi^*_0(\rho) = \phi(\rho) \left(\log \rho + \sum_{p | \rho} \frac{\log p}{p - 1} \right) \tag{9.5}$$

由此可知

$$S_1 = \sum_{p \leqslant \xi^2} \phi(\rho) \left(\log \rho + \sum_{p | \rho} \frac{\log \rho}{p - 1} \right) \sum_{\rho | \kappa v} \sum \sum_{\rho | \lambda\mu} \sum \frac{\beta_\kappa \beta_\lambda \beta_\mu \beta_v}{\kappa \lambda \mu v} =$$

$$\sum_{p \leqslant \xi^2} \phi(\rho) \left(\log \rho + \sum_{p | \rho} \frac{\log \rho}{p - 1} \right) \left(\sum_{\rho | \kappa v} \frac{\beta_\kappa \beta_v}{\kappa v} \right)^2 \tag{9.6}$$

对于是 S_1 相当的表示式是

$$S_2 = \sum_{\rho\leq\xi^2}\phi(\rho)\Big(\sum_{\rho|\kappa v}\frac{\beta_\kappa\beta_v}{\kappa v}\Big)\Big(\sum_{\rho|\lambda\mu}\frac{\beta_\lambda\beta_\mu}{\lambda\mu}\log\mu\Big) =$$
$$\sum_{\rho\leq\xi^2}\phi(\rho)\log\xi\Big(\sum_{\rho|\kappa v}\frac{\beta_\kappa\beta_v}{\kappa v}\Big)^2 -$$
$$\sum_{\rho\leq\xi^2}\phi(\rho)\Big(\sum_{\rho|\kappa v}\frac{\beta_\kappa\beta_v}{\kappa v}\Big)\Big(\sum_{\rho|\lambda\mu}\frac{\beta_\lambda\beta_\mu}{\lambda\mu}\log\frac{\xi}{\mu}\Big) \tag{9.7}$$

最后我们有

$$S_3 = \log(2\pi\sin d)^{-1}S(0) \tag{9.8}$$

把(9.6),(9.7) 与(9.8) 代入(9.4) 便有

$$S^* = -2\sum_{\rho\leq\xi^2}\phi(\rho)\Big(\log\rho + \sum_{p|\rho}\frac{\log p}{p-1}\Big)\Big(\sum_{\rho|\kappa v}\frac{\beta_\kappa\beta_v}{\kappa v}\Big)^2 +$$
$$4\sum_{\rho\leq\xi^2}\phi(\rho)\log\xi\Big(\sum_{p|\kappa v}\frac{\beta_\kappa\beta_v}{\kappa v}\Big)^2 -$$
$$4\sum_{\rho\leq\xi^2}\phi(\rho)\Big(\sum_{\rho|\kappa v}\frac{\beta_\kappa\beta_v}{\kappa v}\Big)\Big(\sum_{\rho|\lambda\mu}\frac{\beta_\lambda\beta_\mu}{\lambda\mu}\log\frac{\xi}{\mu}\Big) - \log(2\pi\sin d)^{-1}S(0)$$

故

$$-S^* \leq 4\sum_{\rho\leq\xi^2}\phi(\rho)\Big(\sum_{\rho|\kappa v}\frac{\beta_\kappa\beta_v}{\kappa v}\Big)\Big(\sum_{\rho|\lambda\mu}\frac{\beta_\lambda\beta_\mu}{\lambda\mu}\log\frac{\xi}{\mu}\Big) +$$
$$2\sum_{\rho\leq\xi^2}\phi(\rho)\sum_{p|\rho}\frac{\log p}{p-1}\Big(\sum\sum_{\rho|\kappa v}\frac{\beta_\kappa\beta_v}{\kappa v}\Big)^2 + \log(2\pi\sin d)^{-1}S(0) =$$
$$4S_1^* + 2S_2^* + \log(2\pi\sin d)^{-1}S(0) \tag{9.9}$$

因 $\beta_v = \alpha_v\Big(1 - \frac{\log v}{\log\xi}\Big)^\alpha$, $\alpha > \frac{1}{2}$,由引理 8.4 我们得到

$$S(0) \leq \sum_{\rho\leq\xi^2}\phi(\rho)\left\{\frac{\Gamma^2(\alpha+1)}{\Gamma^2\Big(\alpha+\frac{1}{2}\Big)}\frac{1}{\log^{2\alpha}\xi}\frac{1}{\rho}\log^{2\alpha-1}\frac{\xi}{\sqrt{\rho}}\prod_{p|\rho}\Big(1-\frac{1}{\rho}\Big)^{-1} +\right.$$
$$\left.\frac{\varepsilon_0}{\log\xi}\frac{1}{\rho}\prod_{p|\rho}\Big(1-\frac{1}{p}\Big)^{-2}\right\}^2 \leq$$
$$\frac{\Gamma^4(\alpha+1)}{\Gamma^4\Big(\alpha+\frac{1}{2}\Big)}\frac{1}{\log^{4\alpha}\xi}\sum_{\rho\leq\xi^2}\frac{\log^{4\alpha-2}\frac{\xi}{\sqrt{\rho}}}{\rho}\prod_{p|\rho}\Big(1-\frac{1}{p}\Big)^{-1} +$$
$$\frac{\varepsilon_0^2}{\log^2\xi}\sum_{\rho\leq\xi^2}\frac{1}{\rho}\prod_{p|\rho}\Big(1-\frac{1}{p}\Big)^{-3} +$$

$$\frac{\Gamma^2(\alpha+1)}{\Gamma^2\left(\alpha+\frac{1}{2}\right)}\frac{2\varepsilon_0}{\log^{2\alpha+1}\xi}\sum_{\rho\leqslant\xi^2}\frac{\log^{2\alpha-1}\frac{\xi}{\sqrt{\rho}}}{\rho}\prod_{p\mid\rho}\left(1-\frac{1}{p}\right)^{-2}=$$

$$\frac{\Gamma^4(\alpha+1)}{\Gamma^4\left(\alpha+\frac{1}{2}\right)}\frac{1}{\log^{4\alpha}\xi}S'+\frac{\varepsilon_0^2}{\log^2\xi}S''+\frac{\Gamma^2(\alpha+1)}{\Gamma^4\left(\alpha+\frac{1}{2}\right)}\frac{2\varepsilon_0}{\log^{2\alpha+1}\xi}S'''\text{(新符号)}$$

(9.10)

我们有

$$S'=\sum_{\rho\leqslant\xi^2}\frac{\log^{4\alpha-2}\frac{\xi}{\sqrt{\rho}}}{\rho}\sum{}^*\frac{1}{n}$$

其中 $*$ 号表示所有 n 的素因数都除尽 ρ. 故

$$S'=\sum{}'\frac{1}{n}\sum_{\rho\leqslant\xi^2}\frac{\log^{4\alpha-2}\frac{\xi}{\sqrt{\rho}}}{\rho}$$

其中 $'$ 表示 ρ 可以被 n 的一切素因数除尽.

设 $P=P(n)$ 为 n 的一切素因数的乘积,则关于 ρ 的和不超过

$$\sum_{\rho_1\leqslant\xi^2/P}\frac{\log^{4\alpha-2}\frac{\xi}{\sqrt{\rho_1 P}}}{P\rho_1}\leqslant\frac{1}{P}\left(\log^{4\alpha-2}\frac{\xi}{\sqrt{P}}+\int_1^{\xi^2/P}\frac{\log^{4\alpha-2}\frac{\xi}{\sqrt{\rho_1 P}}}{\rho_1}\mathrm{d}\rho_1\right)=$$

$$\frac{1}{P}\left(\frac{2}{4\alpha-1}\log^{4\alpha-1}\frac{\xi}{\sqrt{P}}+\log^{4\alpha-2}\frac{\xi}{\sqrt{P}}\right)$$

故

$$S'\leqslant\left(\frac{2}{4\alpha-1}\log^{4\alpha-1}\xi+\log^{4\alpha-2}\xi\right)\sum_{n=1}^{\infty}\frac{1}{nP}$$

上面关于 n 的和小于或等于

$$\prod_p\left(1+\frac{1}{p^2}+\frac{1}{p^2}+\cdots\right)=\prod_p\left(1+\frac{1}{p(p-1)}\right)=$$

$$\prod_p\frac{1-p^{-6}}{(1-p^{-3})(1-p^{-2})}=\frac{\zeta(2)\zeta(3)}{\zeta(6)}=\frac{\pi^2}{6}\frac{\zeta(3)}{\zeta(6)}$$

故

$$S'\leqslant\frac{\pi^2}{6}\frac{\zeta(3)}{\zeta(6)}\left(\frac{2}{4\alpha-1}\log^{4\alpha-1}\xi+\log^{4\alpha-2}\xi\right)\tag{9.11}$$

另一方面,因为$(1-x)^{-4}<1+2^4x$(当$0<x\leqslant 1/2$),所以

$$S'''\leqslant\log^{2\alpha-1}\xi\sum_{\rho\leqslant\xi^2}\frac{1}{\rho}\prod_{p\mid\rho}\left(1-\frac{1}{p}\right)^{-2}\leqslant\log^{2\alpha-1}\xi\sum_{\rho\leqslant\xi^2}\frac{1}{\rho}\prod_{p\mid\rho}\left(1+\frac{2^4}{p}\right)$$

故

$$S''' \leqslant A\log^{2\alpha-1}\xi \sum_{\rho\leqslant\xi^2}\frac{1}{\rho}\prod_{p|\rho}\left(1+\frac{1}{p^{1/2}}\right)$$

其中 $A=\prod_{p\leqslant 2^8}\left(1+\frac{1}{p}\right)$. 上面关于 ρ 的和不超过

$$\sum_{\rho\leqslant\xi^2}\frac{1}{\rho}\sum_{n|\rho}=\sum_{n\leqslant\xi^2}\sum_{\rho_1\leqslant\xi^2/n}\frac{1}{(n\rho_1)n^{1/2}}=\sum_{n=1}^{\infty}\frac{1}{n^{3/2}}\sum_{\rho_1\leqslant\xi^2/n}\frac{1}{\rho}=O(\log\xi)$$

故

$$S'''=O(\log^{2\alpha}\xi) \tag{9.12}$$

仿此

$$S''=O(\log\xi) \tag{9.13}$$

由(9.10) ~ (9.13),我们可以得到

$$S(0)\leqslant(1+\varepsilon^*)\frac{\pi^2}{3(4\alpha-1)}\frac{\Gamma^4(\alpha+1)}{\Gamma^4\left(\alpha+\frac{1}{2}\right)}\frac{\zeta(3)}{\zeta(6)}\frac{1}{\log\xi}=(1+\varepsilon^*)\frac{A_0}{\log\xi}(\text{新符号}) \tag{9.14}$$

其中当 ξ 充分大时 ε 可以任意小.

其次,我们考虑

$$S_1^*=\sum_{\rho\leqslant\xi^2}\phi(\rho)\left(\sum_{\rho|\kappa v}\frac{\beta_\kappa\beta_v}{\kappa v}\right)\left(\sum_{\rho|\lambda\mu}\frac{\beta_\lambda\beta_\mu}{\lambda\mu}\log\frac{\xi}{\mu}\right)$$

由引理 8.4,知道上式不超过

$$\sum_{\rho\leqslant\xi^2}\phi(\rho)\left\{\frac{\Gamma^2(\alpha+1)}{\Gamma^2\left(\alpha+\frac{1}{2}\right)}\frac{1}{\log^{2\alpha}\xi}\frac{1}{\rho}\log^{2\alpha-1}\frac{\xi}{\sqrt{\rho}}\prod_{p|\rho}\left(1-\frac{1}{p}\right)^{-1}+\frac{\varepsilon_0}{\log\xi}\frac{1}{\rho}\prod_{p|\rho}\left(1-\frac{1}{p}\right)^{-2}\right\}\times$$

$$\left\{\frac{\Gamma(\alpha+1)\Gamma(\alpha+2)}{\Gamma^2\left(\alpha+\frac{1}{2}\right)\left(\alpha+\frac{3}{2}\right)}\frac{1}{\log^{2\alpha}\xi}\frac{1}{\rho}\log^{2\alpha}\frac{\xi}{\sqrt{\rho}}\prod_{p|\rho}\left(1-\frac{1}{p}\right)^{-1}+\varepsilon_0\frac{1}{\rho}\prod_{p|\rho}\left(1-\frac{1}{p}\right)^{-2}\right\}\leqslant$$

$$\frac{\Gamma^3(\alpha+1)}{\Gamma^3\left(\alpha+\frac{1}{2}\right)}\frac{\Gamma(\alpha+2)}{\Gamma\left(\alpha+\frac{3}{2}\right)}\frac{1}{\log^{4\alpha}\xi}\sum_{\rho\leqslant\xi^2}\frac{\log^{4\alpha-1}\left(\frac{\xi}{\sqrt{\rho}}\right)}{\rho}\prod_{p|\rho}\left(1-\frac{1}{p}\right)^{-1}+$$

$$\frac{\varepsilon_0^2}{\log\xi}\sum_{\rho\leqslant\xi^2}\frac{1}{\rho}\prod_{p|\rho}\left(1-\frac{1}{p}\right)^{-3}+$$

$$\frac{\Gamma(\alpha+1)}{\Gamma\left(\alpha+\frac{1}{2}\right)}\frac{\Gamma(\alpha+2)}{\Gamma\left(\alpha+\frac{1}{2}\right)}\frac{\varepsilon_0}{\log^{2\alpha+1}\xi}\sum_{\rho\leqslant\xi^2}\frac{\log^{2\alpha}\left(\frac{\xi}{\sqrt{\rho}}\right)}{\rho}\prod_{p|\rho}\left(1-\frac{1}{p}\right)^{-2}+$$

$$\frac{\Gamma^2(\alpha+1)}{\Gamma^2\left(\alpha+\frac{1}{2}\right)}\frac{\varepsilon_0}{\log^{2\alpha}\xi}\sum_{\rho\leqslant\xi^2}\frac{\log^{2\alpha-1}\left(\frac{\xi}{\sqrt{\rho}}\right)}{\rho}\prod_{p\mid\rho}\left(1-\frac{1}{p}\right)^{-2}$$

我们把上式和 $S(0)$ 的相当的表达式比较一下就可以看出

$$S_1^*\leqslant(1+\varepsilon_1^*)\frac{\pi^2}{3\left[4\left(\alpha+\frac{1}{4}\right)-1\right]}\frac{\Gamma^3(\alpha+1)}{\Gamma^3\left(\alpha+\frac{1}{2}\right)}\frac{\Gamma(\alpha+2)}{\Gamma\left(\alpha+\frac{3}{2}\right)}=$$

$$(1+\varepsilon_1^*)\frac{\pi^2}{12\alpha}\frac{\Gamma^3(\alpha+1)}{\Gamma^3\left(\alpha+\frac{1}{2}\right)}\frac{\Gamma(\alpha+2)}{\Gamma\left(\alpha+\frac{3}{2}\right)}\frac{\zeta(3)}{\zeta(6)} \tag{9.15}$$

其中把 ξ 取得充分大时 ε^* 就可以任意小.

在这儿很容易看出 S_2^* 是可以忽略的. 事实上,

$$\sum_{p\mid\rho}\frac{\log p}{p-1}\leqslant\log(\log\rho+1)\sum_{p\leqslant\log\rho+1}\frac{1}{p-1}+\frac{1}{\log\rho}\sum_{\substack{p\mid\rho\\ p\geqslant\log\rho+1}}\log p=$$

$$O\{\log\log\rho)^2\}$$

故

$$S_2^*=O\{\log\log\xi\}^2S(0)\}=O\left[\frac{(\log\log\xi)^2}{\log\xi}\right]=o(1) \tag{9.16}$$

结合(9.15),(9.16)与(9.14)的结果,我们由(9.9)与 $d=A_1/T,\xi=A_2T^{(1/8)-\varepsilon_1}$ 这些式子可以得到

$$-S^*\leqslant(1+\varepsilon_1^*)\frac{\pi^2}{3\alpha}\frac{\Gamma^3(\alpha+1)}{\Gamma^3\left(\alpha+\frac{1}{2}\right)}\frac{\Gamma(\alpha+2)}{\Gamma\left(\alpha+\frac{3}{2}\right)}\frac{\zeta(3)}{\zeta(6)}+$$

$$(1+\varepsilon_2^*)\frac{8\pi^2}{3(4\alpha-1)}\frac{\Gamma^4(\alpha+1)}{\Gamma^4\left(\alpha+\frac{1}{2}\right)}\frac{\zeta(3)}{\zeta(6)}+o(1)=(1+\varepsilon_3^*)A^*\text{(新符号)} \tag{9.17}$$

其中(今后要沿用)我们用 ε_i^* 表示一个当 ξ 充分大时即任意小的数.

我们可以选 α 使得

$$A_0A^*=\frac{\pi^2}{3(4\alpha-1)}\frac{\Gamma^4(\alpha+1)}{\Gamma^4\left(\alpha+\frac{1}{2}\right)}\frac{\zeta^2(3)}{\zeta^2(6)}\left\{\frac{\pi^2}{3\alpha}\frac{\Gamma^3(\alpha+1)}{\Gamma^3\left(\alpha+\frac{1}{2}\right)}\frac{\Gamma(\alpha+2)}{\Gamma\left(\alpha+\frac{3}{2}\right)}+\right.$$

$$\left.\frac{8\pi^2}{3(4\alpha-1)}\frac{\Gamma^4(\alpha+1)}{\Gamma^4\left(\alpha+\frac{1}{2}\right)}\right\}=$$

$$\frac{\pi^4}{9(4\alpha-1)}\frac{\Gamma^8(\alpha+1)}{\Gamma^8\left(\alpha+\frac{1}{2}\right)}\frac{\zeta^2(3)}{\zeta^2(6)}\left\{\frac{1}{\alpha}\frac{\alpha+1}{\alpha+\frac{1}{2}}+\frac{8}{4\alpha-1}\right\}$$

尽可能的小,但为简单计我们取$\alpha=(1/2)+\varepsilon_4$,其中$\varepsilon_4$是一个很小的正数. 这种取法比 A. Selberg 在他文中[1] 的选法(取$\alpha=1$) 为佳.

在(9.14) 与(9.15) 中取$\alpha=\frac{1}{2}+\varepsilon_4$即得

$$S(0)\leqslant(1+\varepsilon_5^*)\frac{\pi^2}{3}\frac{\Gamma^4\left(\frac{3}{2}\right)}{\Gamma^4(1)}\frac{\zeta(3)}{\zeta(6)}\frac{1}{\log\xi}=(1+\varepsilon_5^*)\frac{\pi^4}{48}\frac{\zeta(3)}{\zeta(6)}\frac{1}{\log\xi}$$

与

$$-S^*\leqslant(1+\varepsilon_1^*)\frac{2\pi^2}{3}\frac{\Gamma^3\left(\frac{3}{2}\right)}{\Gamma^3(1)}\frac{\Gamma\left(\frac{5}{2}\right)}{\Gamma(2)}\frac{\zeta(3)}{\zeta(6)}+(1+\varepsilon_6^*)\frac{\pi^4}{6}\frac{\zeta(3)}{\zeta(6)}\leqslant$$

$$(1+\varepsilon_7^*)\left(\frac{\pi^4}{16}\frac{\zeta(3)}{\zeta(6)}+\frac{\pi^4}{6}\frac{\zeta(3)}{\zeta(6)}\right)=(1+\varepsilon_7^*)\frac{11\pi^4}{48}\frac{\zeta(3)}{\zeta(6)}$$

因此我们可以取

$$A_0=\frac{\pi^4}{48}\frac{\zeta(3)}{\zeta(6)},\quad A^*=\frac{11\pi^4}{48}\frac{\zeta(3)}{\zeta(6)}$$

代入(7.3) 当T充分大时我们就有

$$N_0(T)\geqslant(1-o(1))\frac{T\log T}{9\pi e}\cdot\frac{32}{11\pi^8}\frac{\zeta(6)}{\zeta(3)}=(1-o(1))\frac{32T\log T}{99\pi^9 e}\frac{\zeta(6)}{\zeta(3)}=$$

$$\frac{(1-o(1))}{2\pi}T\log T\frac{64}{99\pi^8 e}\frac{\zeta^2(6)}{\zeta^2(3)}>\frac{N(T)}{60\,000}$$

我因为$\zeta(3)=1.202$与$\zeta(6)=1.017$. 这样我们就证明了引论中所提出的定理.

这个定理的结论是可以略微改进的. 但像比较大的改进,例如接近最后的结果,则比较困难. 还需要进一步的研究,探索才行.

参考书目

[1] Selberg, A., Nerke. Videnskaps. Akad. Oslo, Mat. - Naturv. Klaese, (1942), No. 10,1-59.

[2] 闵嗣鹤,清华大学科学报告,第五卷第四期,1950 年 12 月.

[3] Titchmarsh, E. C., Q. J. O. 18(1947).

谈 $\pi(x)$ 与 $\zeta(s)$①

自从 1896 年 Hadamard 与 de la Vallée Poussin 证明了素数定理

$$\pi(x) \sim \frac{x}{\log x} \quad (x \to \infty)$$

(式中 $\pi(x)$ 表示不超过 x 的素数个数) 以后,已经有不少的数学家对于 $\pi(x)$ 作过更进一步的研究. 他们的结果大致都可以纳入下列形式:

$$\pi(x) = \mathrm{li}\, x + O(x\mathrm{e}^{-A(\log x)^{\mu}}) \tag{1}$$

其中 $\mathrm{li}\, x = \lim\limits_{\varepsilon \to 0^+}\left(\int_0^{1-\varepsilon} \frac{\mathrm{d}t}{\log t} + \int_{1+\varepsilon}^{x} \frac{\mathrm{d}t}{\log t}\right)$,$A$ 是一个充分小的正数, $\mu = \mu' - \varepsilon$,ε 是任意小的正数而 μ' 是其中最重要的常数,其值已由 $\frac{1}{2}$(de la Vallée Poussin) 经过 $\frac{5}{9}$(Чулаков,Titchmarsh) 增加到 $\frac{4}{7}$(可用 И. М. Виноградов 估计三角和新的方法得出,隐含于 Titchmarsh 的书[1] 中,又在华罗庚著《堆垒素数论》的俄文版附录中也曾提及此结果).

证明(1) 的方法是利用它和黎曼 ζ 函数零点的某种分布的等价性. 明白的说有下面的定理:

定理 1 可以找到正数 A 使得(1) 成立这件事的必要而且

---

① 原载:北京大学学报, 1956,2(3):297-302.

充分的条件是:存在着正数 A_1 使得 $\zeta(s)$ 在

$$D: \qquad 1-\frac{a_1}{\log^{\lambda} t^*} \leqslant \sigma$$

内无零点,式中 $t^*=\max(|t|,2)$ 而 $\lambda=\frac{1-\mu}{\mu}$.

条件的充分性是 Ingham 在他的书[2] 中所证明的一个定理(Theorem 22)的特殊情形,而必要性则是 Turán 在他的一篇文章中所证明的(可参考他的书[3]). 当然充分性是老早就为人所知,而等价性则是最近才由 Turán 发现的.

不过把(1)的证明化成了 $\zeta(s)$ 在 D 内的零点分布问题之后,并不能就顺利地得出很好的结果,因为零点的分布并不是很容易搞清的问题. 依照 Чуаков, Titchmarsh 所提供的方法,我们可以进一步利用当 $t\to\infty$ 时 $\zeta(s)$ 在一个形式如 D 的区域内的阶的估计来推出 $\zeta(s)$ 在 D 内没有零点.

这对于我们所谈问题的"最后一步转移"是有重要意义的,因为接着就可以利用 И. М. Виноградов 估计三角和的方法来估计 $\zeta(s)$ 在 $\sigma=1$ 附近(也就是在 D 内)的阶. 现在最好的结果就是这样得出来的.

这里就发生了一个问题,上面最后一步转移是否还有所损失?换句话说,这最后一步转移是否也具有"等价性". 这就是我们要讨论的主要问题. 一旦考虑到这个问题之后,便很自然地联想的李特伍德(Littlewood)的一个结果,他曾证明在黎曼假设之下有

$$\log\zeta(s)=O\{(\log t)^{2-2\sigma+\varepsilon}\},\ \frac{1}{2}<\sigma_0\leqslant\sigma\leqslant 1,\quad \varepsilon>0$$

证明见 Titchmarsh 的书[1] 中的 14.2 节,现在即是采用他的方法来解决我们的问题. 在正式提出我们的定理之前,需要先证明一个引理.

引理 当 $\eta\to 0^+$ 时,$\log\zeta(1+\eta+\mathrm{i}t)=O(\log\eta^{-1})$.

证 当 $\eta>0$ 时

$$\log\zeta(1+\eta+\mathrm{i}t)=\sum_{n=2}^{\infty}\frac{\Lambda_1(n)}{n^{1+\eta+\mathrm{i}t}}$$

式中 $\Lambda_1(n)=\frac{\Lambda_1(n)}{\log n}=1$ 或 0,视 n 是一个素数的幂或不是而定. 显然

$$|\log\zeta(1+\eta+\mathrm{i}t)|\leqslant\sum_{n=2}^{\infty}\frac{\Lambda_1(n)}{n^{1+\eta}}$$

在[1]内 3.14 节我们可以找到公式(3.14.4):

$$\sum_{n<x}\frac{\Lambda_1(n)}{n}=\log\log x+\gamma+o(1) \tag{2}$$

令

$$S(x)=\sum_{n\leqslant x}\frac{\Lambda_1(n)}{n}$$

则当 $a \geqslant 3$ 时

$$\sum_{n=\alpha}^{\infty}\frac{\Lambda_1(n)}{n^{1+\eta}}=\sum_{n=\alpha}^{\infty}\frac{S(n)-S(n-1)}{n^{\eta}}=\sum_{n=\alpha}^{\infty}S(n)\left(\frac{1}{n^{\eta}}-\frac{1}{(n+1)^{\eta}}\right)+\frac{S(a)}{(a+1)^{\eta}}=$$

$$\eta\sum_{n=a}^{\infty}S(n)\int_{n}^{n+1}\frac{\mathrm{d}x}{x^{\eta+1}}=\eta\int_{a}^{\infty}\left(\frac{S([x])}{x^{\eta+1}}+\frac{S(a)}{(a+1)^{\eta}}\right)\mathrm{d}x=$$

$$O\left(\eta\int_{a}^{\infty}\frac{\log\log x}{x^{\eta+1}}\mathrm{d}x\right)+O\left(\frac{\log\log a}{(a+1)^{\eta}}\right)$$

用分部积分可以得出

$$\eta\int_{a}^{\infty}\frac{\log\log x}{x^{\eta+1}}\mathrm{d}x=\frac{\log\log a}{a^{\eta}}+\frac{1}{\eta}\frac{1}{a^{\eta}\log a}-\frac{1}{\eta}\int_{a}^{\infty}\frac{\mathrm{d}x}{x^{1+\eta}\log^2 x}=$$

$$O\left(\frac{1}{\eta a^{\eta}}\right)+O\left(\frac{\log\log a}{a^{\eta}}\right)$$

故

$$\sum_{n=\alpha}^{\infty}\frac{\Lambda_1(n)}{n^{1+\eta}}=O\left(\frac{1}{\eta a^{\eta}}\right)+O\left(\frac{\log\log a}{a^{\eta}}\right)$$

又由(2)

$$\sum_{n=2}^{\infty}\frac{\Lambda_1(u)}{n^{1+\eta}}=O(\log\log a)+O\left(\frac{1}{\eta a^{\eta}}\right)$$

取 $\log a=\eta^{-1}\log\eta^{-1}$ 即得出所需要的结果.

设对于适当的正数 A_1,$\zeta(s)$ 在

$$D_1:\qquad 1-\frac{A_1}{\log^{\lambda}t^*}<\sigma\quad(\lambda>0,\ t^*=\max(|t|,2))$$

内无零点,我们用 λ_1 表示这种实数 λ 的下确界. 又设对于适当的正数 A_2 与 A_3 及满足 $\alpha+\beta=\lambda$ 的适当正数 α 与 β,在

$$D_2\qquad 1-\frac{A_2}{\log^{\alpha}t^*}<\sigma\leqslant 2$$

内

$$\zeta(s)=O(\exp\{A_3\log^{\beta}|t|\})\tag{3}$$

我们用 λ_2 代表这种实数 λ 的下确界. 我们要证明:

定理 2 $\lambda_1=\lambda_2$.

证 (1) 由 Titchmarsh 书[1] 中定理 3.10 可以推出 $\lambda_1\leqslant\lambda_2$,以下要证明 $\lambda_2\leqslant\lambda_1$,不妨只考虑 $t>0$ 的情形.

假定 $\zeta(s)$ 在 D_1 内没有零点,以 $2+\mathrm{i}t$ 为中心,以

$$1+\theta(t^*+1)-\frac{\delta}{2}$$

$$1+\theta(t^*+1)-\delta,\quad 0<\delta<\theta(t^*+1)$$

为半径作二圆(其中 $\theta(t^*)=\dfrac{A_1}{\log^{\lambda+2}t^*}$,见图 1),则两圆都在 D_1 内. 在大圆上(当 t 充分大时)

$$R\{\log\zeta(s)\}=\log|\zeta(s)|<A\log t$$

其中 A 是正的常数. 故由 Borel - Caratheodory 定理,在小圆上有

$$|\log\zeta(s)|\leqslant\frac{2(1+\theta(t^*+1)-\delta)}{\frac{1}{2}\delta}A\log t+\frac{2+2\theta(t^*+1)-\frac{3}{2}\delta}{\frac{1}{2}\delta}.$$

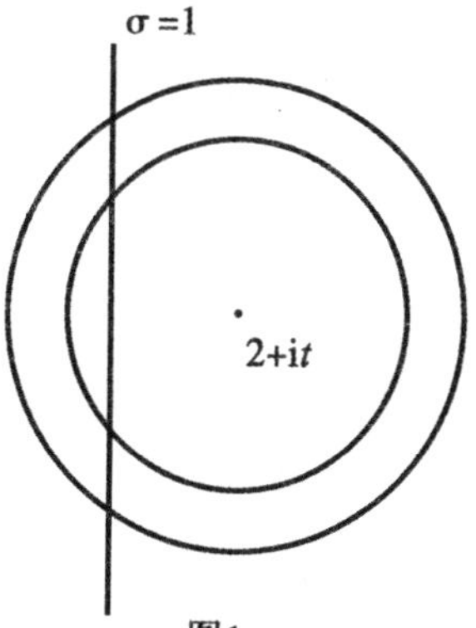

图1

$$\log\zeta(2+it)|<A'\delta^{-1}\log t$$

以上证明了当 t 充分大而

$$\sigma\geqslant1-\frac{A_1}{\log^{\lambda+\varepsilon}t^*}+\delta$$

时,我们有

$$|\log\zeta(s)|<A'\delta^{-1}\log t \tag{4}$$

(2) 其次我们要运用 Hadamard 三圆定理到下列三圆上,他们都以 $\sigma_1+it(1<\sigma_1\leqslant t)$ 为中心,分别通过

$$1+\eta+it,\quad \sigma+it,\quad 1-\theta(t_1)+\delta+it$$

即半径分别为

$$r_1=\sigma_1-1-\eta,\quad r_2=\sigma_1-\sigma,\quad r_3=\sigma_1-(1-\theta(t_1)+\delta)$$

其中我们可以取 $\sigma_1=\log\log t^*$, $t_1=t^*+\log\log t^*$

若 $|\log\zeta(s)|$ 在以上三圆上的极大值分别为 M_1,M_2,M_3,则由 Hadamard 三圆定理

$$M_2\leqslant M_1^{1-a}M_3^a \tag{5}$$

其中(我们取 δ 及 η 使他们随 t^{-1} 变小)

$$a=\log\frac{r_2}{r_1}/\log\frac{r_3}{r_1}=\log\left(1+\frac{1+\eta-\sigma}{\sigma_2-\eta-1}\right)/\log\left(1+\frac{\theta(t_1)+\eta-\sigma}{\sigma_1+\eta-1}\right)=$$

$$\frac{\frac{1+\eta-\sigma}{\sigma_1-\eta-1}-\cdots}{\frac{\theta(t_1)+\eta-\delta}{\sigma_1-\eta-1}-\cdots}=\frac{1+\eta-\sigma}{\theta(t_1)+\eta-\delta}+O\left(\frac{1}{\sigma_1}\right)$$

由(4),$M_3<A\delta^{-1}\log t$. 又容易看出

$$M_1\leqslant A''\log\eta^{-1}\quad(A''>0,\text{常数})$$

故代入(5),即得

$$|\log\zeta(\sigma+\mathrm{i}t)|<(A''\log\eta^{-1})^{1-a}\left(\frac{A\log t}{\delta}\right)^{a}$$

取

$$\eta=\delta=\frac{\theta(t_1)}{\log\log t}$$

则任给 $\varepsilon>0$,当 $\varepsilon'>0$,充分小而

$$\sigma\geqslant 1-\frac{A_1\varepsilon'}{\log^{\lambda}t}$$

时即得

$$\log\zeta(\sigma+\mathrm{i}t)=O\{\log\varepsilon t\}$$

故

$$\lambda_2\geqslant\lambda_1$$

[证完]

设用 μ^* 表示对于适当的正数 A,能使(1)成立的 μ 的上确界,则结合定理2与定理1即得

定理3 $$\mu^*=\frac{1}{1+\lambda_2}$$

由于当 $\sigma\geqslant\sigma_0>0$ 及 $t>0$ 时

$$\zeta(s)=\sum_{n\leqslant t}\frac{1}{n^s}+o(1),\quad s=\sigma+\mathrm{i}t$$

所以我们还可以用

$$\sum_{n\leqslant t}\frac{1}{n^s}=\sum_{n\leqslant t}n^{-\sigma}\mathrm{e}^{-\mathrm{i}t\log n}\tag{6}$$

代替(3)式的 $\zeta(s)$. 这样就把素数定理中误差项的估计,化成看起来很简单的和数(6)的估计了.

参 考 书 目

[1] TITCHMARSH. The Theory of the Riemann Zeta-Function[M]. Oxford: Oxford University Press,1951.

[2] INGHAM. The Distribution of Prime Numbers[M]. Cambridge Tract, 1932.

[3] TURÁN. Eine Neue methode in der Analysis und deren Anwandungen[M]. Akadémiai Kiads Budaperat,1953.

关于 $Z_{n,k}(s)$ 的均值公式①

1. 引论

作者之一曾建立 $Z_{n,k}(s)$ 的均值公式[1]，但由于引用了一个错误的定理（文[1] 中引理 2.4，亦即[2] 内定理 74），因此所得均值公式（文[1] 中定理3.1 与4.1）是需要修改的. 本文的主要目的是改正[1] 内的错误，给出正确的 $Z_{n,k}(s)$ 的均值公式，其次是叙述并讨论关于 $Z_{n,k}(s)$ 的几个猜测. 在全文中用 n 表正偶数，用 v 表 $\frac{1}{n}$.

当然，在[1] 内不牵涉其中引理 2.4 的部分依然是正确的. 为简便计，本文要加以引用，不再证明.

2. $Z_{n,k}(s)$ 的均值公式

在建立这个公式以前，我们需要一系列的引理：

引理 1 设 $0 < a < kv$，则当 $\delta \to +0$ 时

$$I = \frac{1}{\sqrt{2\pi}}\int_0^\infty t^{2a+1}(1+o(1))\,|\,Z_{n,k}(a+\mathrm{i}t)\,|^2 \mathrm{e}^{-2\delta t}\mathrm{d}t =$$

$$\int_0^\infty u^{2a-1}\,|\,\Psi^k - 1 - (A_\delta u^{-v})^k\,|^2 \mathrm{d}u =$$

$$\int_0^1 + \int_1^\infty = I_1 + I_2$$

式中

① 原载：北京大学学报，4(1958)，1：41-50. 合作者：尹文霖.

$$\Psi = \sum_{x=-\infty}^{\infty} e^{-iux^n e^{-i\delta}}, \quad A_\delta = \frac{2\Gamma(1+v)}{(ie^{-i\delta})^v}$$

这就是[1] 内引理 3.1.

引理 2 当 $a < kv$ 时

$$I_2 \ll \delta^{-2kv}, \quad \delta \to +0$$

证 由 $(x+1)^n \geqslant x^n + 1 (x \geqslant 0)$ 及

$$\psi \ll \int_1^{\infty} e^{-x^n u \sin \delta} dx + 1 \ll (u\delta)^{-v} + 1$$

可以得到

$$\left|\left(\sum_{x=-\infty}^{\infty} e^{-x^n iue^{-i\delta}}\right)^k - 1\right| = |\Psi - 1| \sum_{v=0}^{k-1} |\Psi|^v \leqslant$$

$$e^{-u\sin\delta} |\Psi| \sum_{v=0}^{k-1} |\Psi|^v \ll e^{-u\sin\delta}\{(u\delta)^{-kv} + 1\}$$

从此容易推出本引理.

显然,当 $a > 0$ 时

$$I_1 = \int_0^1 u^{2a-1} |\Psi^k - (A_\delta u^{-v})^k|^2 du - 2R\left[\int_0^1 u^{2a-1}\{\Psi^k - (A_\delta u^{-v})^k\} du\right] + \int_0^1 u^{2a-1} du =$$

$$I_2 + O(I_3^{\frac{1}{2}}) + O(1)$$

其中 $R[X]$ 表 X 的实部,而

$$I_3 = \int_0^1 u^{2a-1}\left[\sum_{m=0}^{K-1} (A_\delta u^{-v})^m \Psi^{k-1-m}\right]^2 \cdot |\Psi - A_\delta u^{-v}|^2 du$$

引理 3 当 $a < kv - v$ 时

$$I_{1,k-1} = (2\Gamma(1+v))^{2k-2} \int_0^{\infty} u^{-2(kv-v-a)-1} |\Psi - A_\delta u^{-v}|^2 du =$$

$$(1 + o(1)) c_0 \delta^{-2(n-1)(kv-v-a)-1} \quad (\delta \to +0)$$

证明见[1] 内定理 3.1 证明中之 4),而 c_0 的值见[1] 内公式(3.13).

引理 4 设 $\varepsilon > 0$,则

$$I(\alpha) = \int_0^1 u^{-2\alpha-1} |\Psi - A_\delta u^{-v}|^2 du \ll$$

$$\begin{cases} \delta^{-2(n-1)\alpha-1}, & \alpha > 0 \\ \delta^{-1-\varepsilon}, & \alpha \leqslant 0 \end{cases} \quad (\delta \to +0)$$

实际上,当 $\alpha > 0$ 时

$$I(\alpha) = (1 + o(1)) c_0 (2\Gamma(1+v))^{2-2k} \delta^{-2(n-1)\alpha-1}$$

证 当 $\alpha > 0$ 时

$$\int_1^{\infty} u^{-2\alpha-1} |\Psi - A_\delta u^{-v}|^2 du \ll \int_1^{\infty} u^{-2\alpha-1}(u\delta)^{-2v} du + \int_1^{\infty} u^{-2\alpha-1} du \ll \delta^{-2v}$$

故由引理 3,

$$I(\alpha)=\int_0^\infty u^{-2\alpha-1}\mid \Psi-A_\delta u^{-v}\mid^2\mathrm{d}u+O(\delta^{-2v})=$$
$$(1+o(1))c_0(2\Gamma(1+v))^{2-2k}\delta^{-2(n-1)\alpha-1}$$

又当 $\alpha\leqslant 0$ 时,显然 $I(\alpha)\leqslant I\left(\frac{\varepsilon}{2(n-1)}\right)\ll\delta^{-1-\varepsilon}$. 引理证毕.

将来我们会看到:证明本文主要定理的关键,在于估计下列形式的积分:

$$\int_0^1 u^{2\sigma-1}\Psi^{2h}\mid \Psi-A_\delta u^{-v}\mid^2\mathrm{d}u$$

我们首先要估计

$$\Psi=\sum_{x=-\infty}^{\infty}\mathrm{e}^{-\mathrm{i}x^n u e^{\mathrm{i}\delta}}=$$
$$2\sum_{0\leqslant x\leqslant A_1u^{-\frac{1}{n-1}}}+2\sum_{x>A_1u^{-\frac{1}{n-1}}}-1=$$
$$2\Psi_1+2\Psi_2-1$$

其中 A_1 是适当小的正数.

引理 5 设 $f(x)$ 为在 (a,b) 上具有连续的单调下降的一级导数的实函数, $f'(b)=\alpha, f'(a)=\beta$. 又设 $g(x)>0$ 及单调下降, $g'(x)$ 连续, 且 $\mid g'(x)\mid$ 单调下降,则

$$\sum_{a<n\leqslant b}g(n)\mathrm{e}^{2\pi\mathrm{i}f(n)}=\sum_{a-\eta<v<\beta+\eta}\int_a^b g(x)\mathrm{e}^{2\pi\mathrm{i}\{f(x)-vx\}}\mathrm{d}x+$$
$$O\{g(a)\log(\beta-\alpha+2)\}+O\{\mid g'(a)\mid\}$$

式中 η 为小于 1 的任意正常数. 这个引理见于[3] 内第 4. 10 节.

引理 6 设 $F(x)$ 为在 (a,b) 上二次可微的实函数, $F''(x)\geqslant r>0$, $g(x)/F'(x)$ 单调及 $\mid g(x)\mid\leqslant M$,则

$$\left|\int_a^b g(x)\mathrm{e}^{\mathrm{i}F(x)}\mathrm{d}x\right|\leqslant\frac{8M}{\sqrt{r}}$$

这个引理见于[3] 内第 4. 5 节.

引理 7 当 A_1 适当小时

$$\Psi_1=\frac{\Gamma(1+v)}{(\mathrm{i}u\mathrm{e}^{-\mathrm{i}\delta})^v}+O(u^{\frac{1}{2(n-1)}}),\quad\delta\to+0$$

证 取

$$g(x)=\mathrm{e}^{-x^n u\sin\delta}$$
$$f(x)=-\frac{1}{2\pi}x^n u\cos\delta=\frac{F}{2\pi}$$
$$f'(x)=-\frac{n}{2\pi}x^{n-1}u\cos\delta$$
$$f''(x)=-\frac{n(n-1)}{2\pi}x^{n-2}u\cos\delta$$

取 A_1 适当小使当 $0 \leqslant x \leqslant A_1 u^{-\frac{1}{n-1}}$ 时，$|f'(x)| < \frac{1}{2}$. 显然 $|g(x)| \leqslant 1$，而

$$g'(x) = -nx^{n-1}u\sin\delta e^{-x^n u}\sin\delta$$

$$g''(x) = e^{-x^n u\sin\delta}(n^2x^{2n-2}u^2\sin^2\delta - n(n-1)x^{n-2}u\sin\delta) = e^{-x^n n\sin\delta}nx^{n-2}u\sin\delta(nx^n u\sin\delta - n + 1)$$

故 $g'(x)$ 至多有 n 个极值. 又当 $|f'(x)| < \frac{1}{2}$ 时

$$|g'(x)| = O(\delta)$$

在引理5中取 $\eta = \frac{1}{2}$，即得

$$\Psi_1 = \int_0^{A_1 u^{-\frac{1}{n-1}}} e^{-x^n u(\sin\delta + i\cos\delta)}dx + O(1)$$

又当 $u^{-\frac{1}{n-1}} = O(x)$ 时

$$F''(x) \geqslant Au^{\frac{1}{n-1}} > 0, \quad A > 0 \text{ 为一常数}$$

甲故引理6，

$$\int_{A_1 u^{-\frac{1}{n-1}}}^{\infty} e^{-iux^n e^{-i\delta}}dx = O(u^{-\frac{1}{2(n-1)}})$$

因此，

$$\Psi_1 = \int_0^{\infty} e^{-iux^n e^{-i\delta}}dx + O(u^{-\frac{1}{2(n-1)}}) = \frac{\Gamma(1+v)}{(iue^{-\delta})^{iv}} + O(u^{-\frac{1}{2(n-1)}})$$

引理8　设 $h \geqslant 1$，$r - q \geqslant 1$，$f(x)$ 是在 (q,r) 上二次可微分的实函数，且满足

$$\lambda \leqslant -f''(x) \leqslant h\lambda$$

又设 $g(x)$ 在 (q,r) 上单调下降及 $0 < g(x) \leqslant M$，则

$$\sum_{q<x\leqslant r} g(x)e^{2\pi i f(x)} = O\{hM(r-q)\lambda^{\frac{1}{2}}\} + O(M\lambda^{-\frac{1}{2}})$$

证　若 $g(x) \equiv 1$ 则引理即[3]内定理5.9的一部分. 由阿贝尔引理一般情形.

引理9

$$\Psi_2 = O(\delta^{-\frac{1}{2}})$$

$$\Psi = A_\delta u^{-v} + O(u^{-\frac{1}{2(n-1)}}) + O(\delta^{-\frac{1}{2}})$$

证　设 $g(x) = e^{-x^n u\sin\delta}$，$f(x) = -\frac{1}{2\pi}x^n u\sin\delta$，我们要估计

$$\sum_a = \sum_{a<x\leqslant 2a} g(x)e^{2\pi i f(x)}$$

在引理8中取

$$\lambda = \frac{n(n-1)}{2\pi}a^{n-2}u\cos\delta,\ h = 2^{n-2},\ M = \mathrm{e}^{-a^n u}\sin\delta$$

则

$$\lambda \leqslant -f''(x) \leqslant h\lambda,\ 0 \leqslant g(x) \leqslant M$$

因此,当 $a \geqslant \frac{1}{2}A_1 u^{-\frac{1}{n-1}}$ 时

$$\sum_a = O(\mathrm{e}^{-a^n u\sin\delta}a^{\frac{n}{2}}u^{\frac{1}{2}}) + O(\mathrm{e}^{-a^n u\sin\delta}a^{-\frac{n-2}{2}}u^{-\frac{1}{2}}) =$$

$$O(\mathrm{e}^{-a^n u\sin\delta}a^{\frac{n}{2}}u^{\frac{1}{2}}) = O(\mathrm{e}^{-\frac{2}{\pi}a^n u\delta}\sqrt{a^n u\delta}\delta^{-\frac{1}{2}})$$

设 $a_0 = (u\delta)^{-v}$,则 $\sum_{a_0} = O(\delta^{-\frac{1}{2}})$,而

$$\Psi_2 < \sum_{m=-\infty}^{\infty}{}^{*}\sum_{2^m a_0}$$

其中 * 表示 m 满足 $2^m a_0 \geqslant \frac{1}{2}A_1 u^{-\frac{1}{n-1}}$. 故

$$\Psi_2 \ll \sum_{m=-\infty}^{\infty}\mathrm{e}^{-\frac{2}{\pi}2^{mn}}2^{\frac{mn}{2}}\delta^{-\frac{1}{2}} \ll \delta^{-\frac{1}{2}}$$

引理前半已证明,结合引理7,后半即证明.

引理10 当 $a < kv - v$ 及 $\varepsilon > 0$ 时

$$I_3\begin{cases} \ll \delta^{-2(n-1)(kv-va)^{-1}} + \delta^{-k+na-2a-\varepsilon} & ,n \geqslant 2 \\ = \{k^2 c_0\delta^{-2(n-1)(kv-va)^{-1}} + O(\delta^{-k+na-2a-\varepsilon})\}\{1+o(1)\} & ,n > 2 \end{cases}$$

证

$$I_3 = \int_0^1 u^{2a-1}\left|\sum_{m=0}^{k-1}(A_\delta u^{-v})^m\Psi^{k-1-m}\right|^2 |\Psi - A_\delta u^{-v}|^2\mathrm{d}u =$$

$$\sum_{m_1=0}^{k-1}\sum_{m_2=0}^{k-1}J(m_1,m_2) \tag{1}$$

其中

$$J(m_1,m_2) = \int_0^1 u^{2a-1-(m_1+m_2)v}A_0^{m_1}\overline{A}_0^{m_1}\Psi^{k-1-m_1}\overline{\Psi}^{k-1-m_2}|\psi - A_\delta u^{-v}|^2\mathrm{d}u$$

显然

$$J(k-1,k-1) = \{2\Gamma(1+v)\}^{2k-2}I(kv-v-a) \tag{2}$$

从引理2的证明可以知道,当 $u\delta < 1$ 时,$\Psi \ll (u\delta)^{-v}$. 因此,当 $a < kv - v$ 时,由引理4,

$$\int_{\delta^{n/2-1}}^1 u^{2a-1-(m_1+m_2)v}|\overline{\psi}^{2k-2-m_1-m_2}|\cdot|\Psi - A_\delta u^{-v}|^2\mathrm{d}u \ll$$

$$\delta^{-2(k-1)v}\int_{\delta^{n/2-1}}^1 u^{-2(kv-v-a)-1}|\Psi - A_\delta u^{-v}|^2\mathrm{d}u \ll \tag{3}$$

$$\delta^{-2(k-1)v-(\frac{n}{2}-1)\cdot 2(kv-v-a)}I(0) \ll \delta^{-k+na-2a-\varepsilon}$$

根据引理9内对于 Ψ 的估计并(最后)用到Hölder不等式,即得

$$\int_0^{\delta(n/2)-1} u^{2a-1-(m_1+m_2)v} A_0^{m_1} \bar{A}_0^{m_2} \Psi^{k-1-m_1} \bar{\Psi}^{k-1-m_2} |\Psi - A_\delta u^{-v}|^2 dv =$$

$$\{2\Gamma(1+v)\}^{2k-2} \int_0^{\delta(n/2)-1} u^{2a-1-2(k-1)r} (1 + O(u^{v-\frac{1}{2(n-1)}}) + O(u^v \delta^{-\frac{1}{2}}))^{k-1-m_1} \times$$

$$(1 + O(u^{v-\frac{1}{2(n-1)}})) + O(u^v \delta^{-\frac{1}{2}})^{k-1-m_2} |\Psi - A_\delta u^{-v}|^2 du =$$

$$\{2\Gamma(1+v)\}^{2k-2} \int_0^{\delta^{\frac{n}{2}-1}} u^{2a-1-2(k-1)v} |\Psi - A_\delta u^{-v}|^2 du +$$

$$O\Big\{\int_0^{\delta^{\frac{n}{2}-1}} u^{2a-1-2(k-1)v} (u^{v-\frac{1}{2(n-1)}} + u^v \delta^{-\frac{1}{2}} +$$

$$u^{(2k-2-m_1-m_2)(v-\frac{1}{2(n-1)})} + (u^v \delta^{-\frac{1}{2}})^{2k-2-m_1-m_2}) \times |\Psi - A_\delta u^{-v}|^2 du\} =$$

$$\{2\Gamma(1+v)\}^{2k-2} \int_0^{\delta^{\frac{n}{2}-1}} u^{2a-1-2(k-1)v} |\Psi - A_\delta u^{-v}|^2 du +$$

$$O(J_1) + O(J_2) + O(J_1^{\frac{1}{2k-2}} J^{\frac{2k-3}{2k-2}}) + O(J_2^{\frac{1}{2k-2}} J^{\frac{2k-3}{2k-2}}) \tag{4}$$

式中 $J = J(k-1, k-1)$ 而

$$J_1 = \int_0^{\delta^{n/2-1}} u^{2a-1-(m_1+m_2)v-\frac{1}{2(n-1)}(2k-2-m_1-m_2)} |\Psi - A_\delta u^{-v}|^2 du$$

$$J_2 = \int_0^{\delta^{n/2-1}} u^{2a-1-(m_1+m_2)v} \delta^{-k+1+\frac{1}{2}(m_1+m_2)} |\Psi - A_\delta u^{-v}|^2 du$$

由引理4,

$$J_2 \ll \delta^{-k+1+\frac{1}{2}(m_1+m_2)+\Delta(m_1+m_2)-1}$$

其中

$$\Delta(m_1+m_2) = \begin{cases} \left(\frac{n}{2}-1\right)[2a-(m_1+m_2)v] - \varepsilon, & 2a-(m_1+m_2)v \geqslant 0 \\ (n-1)[2a-(m_1+m_2)v], & 2a-(m_1+m_2)v < 0 \end{cases}$$

若 $2\alpha - (m_1+m_2)v \geqslant 0$,则

$$J_2 \ll \delta^{-k+\frac{m_1+m_2}{2}+(\frac{n}{2}-1)[2\alpha-(m_1+m_2)v]-\varepsilon} = \delta^{-k+na-2a+(m_1+m_2)v-\varepsilon} \ll$$

$$\delta^{-k+na-2a-\varepsilon} \tag{5}$$

若 $2a - (m_1+m_2)v < 0$,则

$$J_2 \ll \delta^{-k+\frac{1}{2}(m_1+m_2)+(n-1)[2a-(m_1+m_2)v]} =$$

$$\delta^{-k-\frac{1}{2}(m_1+m_2)+(m_1+m_2)v+2(n-1)a}.$$

由此,当 $m_1 + m_2 \leqslant 2k-3$ 时

$$J_2 \ll \delta^{-2k+\frac{3}{2}+2kv-3v+2(n-1)a} = \delta^{-2(n-1)(kv-v)+2(n-1)a-\frac{1}{2}-v} =$$

$$\begin{cases} O\{I(kv-v-a)\}, & n=2 \\ o\{I(kv-v-a)\}, & n>2 \end{cases} \tag{6}$$

另一方面,当 $m_1+m_2\leqslant 2k-3$ 时

$$(m_1+m_2)v+\frac{1}{2(n-1)}(2k-2-m_1-m_2)\begin{cases}=2(kv-v), & n=2\\ <2(kv-v), & n>2\end{cases}$$

故

$$J_1=\begin{cases}O\{I(kv-v-a)\}, & n=2\\ o\{I(kv-v-a)\}, & n>2\end{cases} \tag{7}$$

由(2)至(7)知道当 $a<kv-v$ 时

$$J_1(m_1,m_2)=\begin{cases}\ll J(k-1,k-1)+O(\delta^{-k+na-2a-\varepsilon}) & n=2\\ =\{J(k-1,k-1)+O(\delta^{-k+na-2a-\varepsilon})\}\{1+o(1)\} & n>2\end{cases}$$

代入(1)后,由(2)及引理4可得本引理中的结论.

定理1 设 $0<a<kv-v$ 则当 $\delta\to0^+$ 时

$$I=\frac{1}{\sqrt{2\pi}}\int_0^\infty t^{2a-1}\mid Z_{n,k}(a+\mathrm{i}t)\mid^2\mathrm{e}^{-2\delta t}\mathrm{d}t\ll$$
$$\delta^{-2(n-1)(kv-v-a)-1}+\delta^{-n(kv-a)-2a-s}$$

又当 $n>2$ 及 $a<kv-2kv^2-v+2v^2$ 时

$$I=(2\pi)^{-\frac{1}{2}}c_1\delta^{-2(n-1)(kv-v-a)-1}(1+o(1))$$

式中 $c_1=(2\pi)^{\frac{1}{2}}k^2c_0$.

证 由引理1,引理2及引理10可知当 $0<a<kv-v$ 时

$$I\ll\delta^{-2(n-1)(kv-v-a)-1}+\delta^{-n(kv-a)-2a-s}+\delta^{-2kv}$$

上面右边第三项比第二项小,可以略去. 又当 $n>2$ 时,我们根据同样的三个引理可以得到比较精密的结果

$$I=\{k^2c_0\delta^{-2(n-1)(kv-v-a)-1}+O(\delta^{-k+na-2a-s})\}\{1+o(1)\}$$

式中 ε 可以任意小. 定理随之成立.

定理2 设 $0<a<kv$,则

$$\int_0^T\mid Z_{n,k}(a+\mathrm{i}t)\mid^2\mathrm{d}t\ll T^{2(n-1)(kv-v-a)-2a+2}+T^{n(kv-a)+1+s},\quad \varepsilon<0$$

又当 $n>2$ 及 $a<kv-2kv^2-v+2v^2$ 时

$$\int_0^T\mid Z_{n,k}(a+\mathrm{i}t)\mid^2\mathrm{d}t\sim c_3T^{2(n-1)(kv-v-a)-2a+2}$$

式中 c_3 是与 k,n 及 a 有关的常数,其明确的表达式见[1]内定理4.1.

这定理的证明与[1]内定理4.1的证明相似.

3. 几个猜想

设用 $\mu(\sigma)=\mu_z(\sigma)$ 表示能使

$$Z_{n,k}(\sigma+\mathrm{i}t)=O(\mid t\mid^\xi)$$

成立的 ξ 的下确界. 又用 $v(\sigma)=v_z(\sigma)$ 表示能使

$$\frac{1}{T}\int |Z_{n,k}(\sigma+\mathrm{i}t)|^2\mathrm{d}t = O(T^{\xi})$$

成立的ξ的下确界. 由已知的定理,$\mu(\sigma)$ 与$v(\sigma)$ 都是向下凸的,连续的,非负的及单调下降的(参考[8] 内9.41 节及[4] 引理2).

当$\sigma \geqslant kv$时,我们知道$\mu(\sigma) = v(\sigma) = 0$. 又当$\sigma \leqslant kv - 2kv^2 - 2v + 2v^2$及$n > 2$时由上节定理2 知道$v(\sigma) = 2(k-1)(1-v) - 2na + 1$. 这说明当$n > 2$时$v(\sigma)$ 的图象至少包含两个半线.

仿照Lindelöff对于$\zeta(s)$ 的猜想,我们可以作以下的猜测,即$\mu(\sigma)$ 与$v(\sigma)$ 的图象都是由两个半线组成的. 更确切地说,就是

$$\mu(\sigma) = \frac{1}{2}v(\sigma) = \begin{cases} 0, & \sigma \geqslant kv - kv^2 - \dfrac{v}{2} + v^2 \\ (n-1)(kv - v - \sigma) - \sigma + \dfrac{1}{2}, & \text{其他} \end{cases}$$

为方便计,我们称以上的猜想为(对于$Z_{n,k(s)}$ 的) 狭义Lindelöff猜想. 但是根据Richert 的一个结果([4] 内Satz8),

$$v(\sigma) \geqslant 2(kv - \sigma) - 1$$

取$\sigma = kv - kv^2 - \dfrac{v}{2} + v^2$,则在狭义Lindelöff 猜想下,由上面不等式得

$$k \leqslant \frac{n^2}{2} - \frac{n}{2} + 1$$

这是狭义Lindelöff 猜想成立的一个必要条件.

当$n = 2$及k是偶数时,汪成义在他的毕业论文[5] 中曾证明

$$v(\sigma) = \begin{cases} 0, & \sigma > \dfrac{k-1}{2} \\ k - 2\sigma - 1, & \dfrac{1}{2} \leqslant \sigma \leqslant \dfrac{k-1}{2} \\ k - 4\sigma, & \sigma < \dfrac{1}{2} \end{cases}$$

为了避免狭义Lindelöff 猜想的局限性,参考了上面的特殊结果,我们还可以作以下的猜想,即

$$\mu(\sigma) = \frac{1}{2}v(\sigma) = \max\left\{0, kv - \sigma - \frac{1}{2}, (n-1)(kv - v - \sigma) - \sigma + \frac{1}{2}\right\}$$

还可以称为广义Lindelöff 猜想.

关于$Z_{n,k}(s)$ 的零点分布,我们所知甚少. 当σ充分大时,显然$Z_{n,k}(s) \neq 0$. 是否当$\sigma > kv$时$Z_{n,k}(s) \neq 0$ 还是未解决的问题. 从$Z_{n,k}(s)$ 的积分表达式

[看[6]内公式(3.8)]容易看出 $Z_{n,k}(s)$ 有简单零点 $s=-1,-2,\cdots$. 是否当 $\sigma<0$ 时只有这些零点,也是问题. 这样说来,我们对于零点分布如果作任何推测,似乎都是为时过早的. 但由本节以上的讨论,是相当于 $\zeta(s)$ 的临界线 $\sigma=\frac{1}{2}$ 的,看来不是 $\sigma=\frac{kv}{2}$ 而是 $\sigma=kv-kv^2-\frac{v}{2}+v^2$. Kober[7] 曾证明当 $k=n=2$ 时,$Z_{n,k}(s)$ 在 $\sigma=\frac{1}{2}$ 上有无穷多的零点. 是否在一般情形下,$Z_{n,k}(s)$ 在 $\sigma=kv-kv^2-\frac{v}{2}+v^2$ 上都有无穷多零点. 这是一个很有趣的问题.

参考书目

[1] 闵嗣鹤,数学学报,6:3,1956.

[2] TITCHMARSH E C. Introduction to the Theory of Fourier Integrals[M]. Oxford: University press, 1937.

[3] TITCHMARSH E C. The Theory of the Riemann Zeta-Function[M]. Oxford: University Press, 1951.

[4] RICHERT H E. Beiträge Zur Summierbarkeit Dirichletschen Reihen mit Anwendungen auf die Zahlentheorie[M]. Nachrichten Jahrgang, Nr. 5, 1956.

[5] 汪成义. Epstein ζ 函数的中值公式(未发表),1957.

[6] 闵嗣鹤,数学学报,5:3,1955.

[7] Kober H. Proc. Lon. Soc. Math. 42, 1936 - 7.

[8] Titchmarsh E C. The Theory of Functions[M]. Oxford: University Press, 1944.

关于多重积分的近似计算①

1. 设函数$f(x_1,\cdots,x_s)$对于每一个变数x_v而言都以1为周期. 又设这函数在单位s维立方体$0\leqslant x_v\leqslant 1, v=1,\cdots,s$上面,可以展成绝对收敛的傅里叶级数:

$$f(x_1,\cdots,x_s)=\sum_{m_1,\cdots,m_s=-\infty}^{\infty}C(m_1,\cdots,m_s)\exp[2\pi i(m_1x_1+\cdots+m_sx_s)] \tag{1}$$

用σ表各傅里叶系数绝对值之和,即

$$\sigma=\sum_{m_1,\cdots,m_s=-\infty}^{\infty}|C(m_1,\cdots,m_s)|$$

Н. М. Коробов 曾证明[1]下列重要的定理:

定理1 设$p\geqslant s$且为素数,$\xi_v(k)=\left\{\frac{k^v}{p^2}\right\}(v=1,\cdots,s)$(这里$\{A\}$表$A$的小数部分). 如果在单位$s$维立方体上面,微商$\frac{\partial^{2s}f(x_1,\cdots,x_s)}{\partial x_1^2\cdots\partial x_s^2}$是连续的,并且对于任意整数组

$$j_1\leqslant j_2\leqslant\cdots\leqslant j_r,\quad 1\leqslant r\leqslant s,\ 1\leqslant j_1,\ j_r\leqslant s$$

而言,微商$\frac{\partial^{2r}f(x_1,\cdots,x_s)}{\partial x_{j_1}^2\cdots\partial x_{j_r}^2}$的绝对值有一公共的上界$C$,则当$N=p^2$时下列不等式成立:

① 原载:北京大学学报,5(1959),2:127-130.

$$\left|\int_0^1\cdots\int_0^1 f(x_1,\cdots,x_s)\,dx_1\cdots dx_s-\frac{1}{N}\sum_{k=1}^{N}f[\xi_1(k),\cdots,\xi_s(k)]\right|\leqslant\frac{(s-1)\sigma}{\sqrt{N}}+\frac{sC}{10N}\tag{2}$$

他的证明很简短，唯一用到比较特别的工具是下列关于三角和的估计：

$$\left|\sum_{k=1}^{p^2}\exp\left[2\pi i\,\frac{m_1k+\cdots+m_sk^s}{p^2}\right]\right|\leqslant(s-1)p$$

这不等式成立的条件是 $m_1,\cdots m_s$ 之中至少有一个被 p 除不尽.

在利用 (2) 计算多重积分时，我们会感到误差项还不够好，Б. В. Гнеденко[2] 即曾提出把误差项改进为 $O(N^{-1})$ 的问题.

另一方面在文[4] 中指出用 Колмогоров[3] 的方法可证明，无论如何取 $\xi_{N,v}(k)$ 及 $C_N(k)(v=1,\cdots,s;k=1,\cdots,N)$ 至少有一函数 $f(x_1,\cdots,x_s)$ 存在，满足下列条件

(1) $\dfrac{\partial^r}{\partial x_{j_1}^{r_1}\cdots\partial x_{j_t}^{r_t}}f(x_1,\cdots,x_s)(1\leqslant j_1<j_2<\cdots<j_t\leqslant s;1\leqslant t\leqslant s;r_1+\cdots+r_t=r\leqslant m)$ 存在并且其绝对值以 C 为公共上界.

(2) $\left|\int_0^1\cdots\int_0^1 f(x_1,\cdots,x_s)\,dx_1\cdots dx_s-\frac{1}{N}\sum_{k=1}^{N}C_N(k)f[\xi_{N,1}(k),\cdots,\xi_{N,s}(k)]\right|\geqslant ACN^{-\frac{m}{s}}$，其中 A 与 N 无关.

这说明：当 $\dfrac{m}{s}$ 不大时，误差即不能太小．本文的主要目的是证明下面的定理：

定理 2 设 n 为正整数而 $N=n^s$. 又设在单位 s 维立方体上面 $\dfrac{\partial^m f}{\partial x_v^m}$, $v=1,\cdots,s_r$ 是连续的，并且其绝对值以 M 为公共上界，则当 $m>s$ 时

$$\left|\int_0^1\cdots\int_0^1 f(x_1,\cdots,x_s)\,dx_1\cdots dx_s-\frac{1}{N}\sum_{x_1,\cdots,x_s=1}^{n}f\left(\frac{x_1}{n},\cdots,\frac{x_s}{n}\right)\right|\leqslant$$

$$\frac{3^s-1}{(2\pi)^m}\xi^s\left(\frac{m}{s}\right)MN^{-\frac{m}{s}}\text{①}\tag{3}$$

这里的误差比 Коробов 所得更小，而且如果不考虑与 N 无关的常数，那么根据 Колмоголов 的结果，就可以看出：这定理是“最佳可能”的．又在以下的证明中并未用到 Коробов 所用的三角和，因此，证明也更为简单.

---

① 此处 $\zeta(\alpha)$ 表黎曼 ζ 函数，当 $\alpha>1$ 时，$\zeta(\alpha)=\sum\limits_{k=1}^{\infty}\frac{1}{k^{\alpha}}$.

证 由(1)得①

$$\frac{1}{n^s}\sum_{x,\cdots,x_s=1}^{n} f\left(\frac{x_1}{n},\cdots,\frac{x_s}{n}\right)=C(0,\cdots,0)+$$

$$\frac{1}{n^s}\sum_{m_1,\cdots,m_s=-\infty}^{\infty} C(m_1,\cdots,m_s)\sum_{x_1,\cdots,x_s=1}^{n}\exp[2\pi\mathrm{i}(m_1x_1+\cdots+m_sx_s)/n]=$$

$$\int_0^1\cdots\int_0^1 f(x_1,\cdots,x_s)\mathrm{d}x_1\cdots\mathrm{d}x_s+R$$

其中“′”表 $m_1,\cdots,m_s$ 不同时为0,而

$$R=\frac{1}{n^s}\sum_{m_1,\cdots,m_s=-\infty}^{\infty}{}' C(m_1,\cdots,m_s)\prod_{v=1}^{s}\sum_{x_v=1}^{n}\exp[2\pi\mathrm{i}m_vx_v/n]$$

当 a 是整数时,我们知道

$$\sum_{x=1}^{n}\exp(2\pi\mathrm{i}ax/n)=\begin{cases}n, & a\equiv 0(\bmod n)\\ 0, & a\not\equiv 0(\bmod n)\end{cases}$$

因此

$$R=\sum_{m_1,\cdots,m_s=-\infty}^{\infty}{}' C(m_1,\cdots,m_s) \tag{4}$$

$$m_v\equiv 0(\bmod n),\quad v=1,\cdots,s$$

但

$$C(m_1,\cdots,m_s)=\int_0^1\cdots\int_0^1 f(t_1,\cdots,t_s)\exp[2\pi\mathrm{i}(m_1t_1+\cdots+m_st_s)]\mathrm{d}t_1\cdots\mathrm{d}t_s$$

故若 $m_v\neq 0$,就可以用分部积分法 m 次得到

$$\int_0^1 f(t_1,\cdots,t_s)\mathrm{e}^{2\pi\mathrm{i}m_vt_v}\mathrm{d}t_v=\frac{(-1)^m}{(2\pi\mathrm{i}m_v)^m}\int_0^1\frac{\partial}{\partial t_v^m}f(t_1,\cdots,t_s)\mathrm{e}^{2\pi\mathrm{i}m_vt_v}\mathrm{d}t_v$$

[这里用到了$f(t_1,\cdots,t_s)$对于 t_v 的周期性及由此推出的 m 级以下的各微商的周期性]. 因此

$$|C(m_1,\cdots,m_s)|\leqslant\frac{M}{(2\pi m_v)^m}$$

这不等式对于每一个不为0的 m_v 都成立. 设恰好有 h 个不为0,即 $m_{i_1},\cdots,m_{i_h}$,则把所能得到的 h 个不等式连乘起来再开 h 次方,即得

$$|C(m_1,\cdots,m_s)|\leqslant\frac{M}{(2\pi)^m|m_{i_1},\cdots,m_{i_h}|^{m/h}} \tag{5}$$

因此,代入(4)即得

---

① 这里当然已假定了本篇开首对$f(x_1,\cdots,x_s)$所作的一切假设. 其实(1)的绝对收敛性是可以从后面的(5)推出来的,因此(1)的右边可以证明是收敛于$f(x_1,\cdots,x_s)$的(证法仿一个变数的情形).

$$|R| \leqslant \frac{M}{(2\pi)^m}\sum_{h=1}^{s}\binom{s}{h}\sum_{\substack{m_1,\cdots,m_h=-\infty\\ 0\neq m_v\equiv 0(\bmod n)\\ v=1,\cdots,h}}^{\infty}\frac{1}{|m_1\cdots m_h|^{m/h}} =$$

$$\frac{M}{(2\pi)^m}\sum_{h=1}^{s}\binom{s}{h}\frac{1}{n^m}\sum_{\substack{m'_1,\cdots,m'_h=-\infty\\ m'_v\neq 0,v=1,\cdots,h}}^{\infty}\frac{1}{|m'_1\cdots m'_h|^{m/h}} \leqslant$$

$$\frac{M}{(2\pi)^m}\frac{1}{n^m}\zeta^s\left(\frac{m}{s}\right)\sum_{h=1}^{s}\left(\frac{s}{h}\right)2^h =$$

$$\frac{3^s-1}{(2\pi)^m}\zeta^s\left(\frac{m}{s}\right)MN^{-\frac{m}{s}}$$

定理证毕.

参 考 书 目

[1] Корбов, Н. М., ДАН, 115:6, 1062 - 5, 1957.

[2] Б. В. 格涅坚科,数学进展,4:4, 1958.

[3] Колмогоров, А. Н., ДАН. 108:3, 385 - 8, 1956.

[4] Гелвфанд, И. М., А. С. Фролов, Н. Н. Ченцов. *изв · высших.* учебных заведений, Mar, 1958. 5.

关于定积分及重积分的近似计算①

1. 在 H. M. Коробов 的短文[1] 及我的短文[2] 中都曾论及多理积分的近似计算法. 但这些计算方法有一种不方便之处,即积分函数必须具有一种很难满足的周期性. 本文的目的是就定积分及重积分的情形加以讨论,说明在积分函数不具有那种周期性的情形之下,怎样增加一些其他的条件(可微性条件)并改变一下计算的方法使得误差仍然很小.

2. 定积分的近似计算.

本节先讨论定积分的情形.

引理 1 存在着一个 $m-1$ 级多项式 $P(x)$ 满足下列条件:

(1) $P(0)=P'(0)=\cdots=P^{(m-1)}(0)=0$;

(2) $P(1)=b_0,\ P'(1)=b_1,\cdots,P^{(m-1)}(1)=b_{m-1}$.

更具体地说,设

$$\Delta=\begin{vmatrix} 1 & 0 & 0 & \cdots & 0 \\ m & 1 & 0 & \cdots & 0 \\ m(m-1) & 2m & 1 & \cdots & 0 \\ \vdots & \vdots & \vdots & & \vdots \\ \dfrac{m!}{1} & \dbinom{m-1}{2}\dfrac{m!}{2!} & \dbinom{m-1}{2}\dfrac{m!}{3!} & \cdots & 1 \end{vmatrix}$$

其中第 r 行(横行)为

$$\frac{m!}{(m-r+1)!},\binom{r-1}{1}\frac{m!}{(m-r+1)!},\cdots,$$

① 原载:北京大学学报,5(1959),3:203-208.

$$\binom{r-1}{j}\frac{m!}{(m-r+j)!},\cdots,1,0,\cdots,0$$

又设 λ_j 为用 $b_0,b_1,\cdots,b_{m-1}$ 代替 Δ 内第 j 列所得的行列式之值,则

$$P(x) = x^m \sum_{j=0}^{m-1}\frac{\lambda_j}{j!}(x-1)^j$$

证 设 $P(x) = x^m Q(x)$,则 $P^{(v)}(0) = 0,\ v = 1,\cdots,m-1$,而

$$P(1) = Q(1),\ P^{(\mu)}(1) = \sum_{j=0}^{\mu}\binom{\mu}{j}\frac{m!}{(m-\mu+j)!}Q^{(j)}(1)$$

令 $P^{(v)}(1) = b_v(v = 1,\cdots,m-1)$,再用 Cramer 法则求 $Q^{(j)}(1)$ 即得 $Q^{(j)}(1) = \lambda_j$. 引理随之成立.

引理 2 设 $f(x)$ 在 $(0,1)$ 上有 m 级连续微商(在端点的微商系左或右微商),又设

$$f(1) = f(0),\ f^{(\mu)}(1) = f^{(\mu)}(0),\quad \mu = 1,\cdots,m-1$$
$$|f^{(m)}(x)| \leqslant M,\quad 0 \leqslant x \leqslant 1$$

则当 n 为正整数及 $m > 1$ 时

$$\left|\int_0^1 f(x)\mathrm{d}x - \frac{1}{n}\sum_{x=1}^{n} f\left(\frac{x}{n}\right)\right| \leqslant AMn^{-m}$$

其中

$$A = \frac{\zeta(m)}{2^{m-1}\pi^m}$$

证 设

$$F(x) = \begin{cases} f(x), & 0 \leqslant x < 1 \\ f(x-k), & k \leqslant x < k+1,\quad k = \pm 1,\ \pm 2,\ \cdots \end{cases}$$

则 $F(x)$ 是以 1 为周期的函数且有 $m-1$ 级连续微商. 又当 $x \neq 0,\ \pm 1,\ \pm 2,\ \cdots$, 时,$m$ 级微商 $F^{(m)}(x)$ 也存在并连续,且 $F^{(m)}(k \pm 0)$ 都存在而且恒得

$$|F^{(m)}(x)| \leqslant M$$

根据文[2] 中的一个定理(注意其证明中并未用到像 $F^{(m)}(k+0) = F^{(m)}(k-0)$ 这种条件),立得本引理所需要的结果.

定理 1 (1) 设 $f(x)$ 在 $[0,1]$ 上有 m 级连续微商(在端点的微商系左或右微商).

(2) 设

$$f(1) - f(0) = b_0$$
$$f^{(\mu)}(1) - f^{(\mu)}(0) = b_\mu,\quad \mu = 1,\cdots,m-1$$

而 λ_μ 的定义见引理 1. 又设 $P(x)$ 为由引理定出的多项式而

$$|f^{(m)}(x) - P^{(m)}(x)| \leqslant M$$

在以上条件下

$$\left|\int_0^1 f(x)\,\mathrm{d}x - \frac{1}{n}\sum_{x=1}^{n} f\left(\frac{x}{n}\right) - \sum_{j=0}^{m-1}(-1)^j \frac{m!}{(m+j-1)!}\lambda_j\right| \leqslant AMn^{-m}$$

其中

$$A = \frac{\zeta(m)}{2^{m-1}\pi^m}$$

证　利用引理1,可以找到多项式 $P(x)$. 令

$$f_1(x) = f(x) - P(x)$$

则

$$f_1(1) = f(1) - [f(1) - f(0)] = f_1(0)$$

$$f_1^{(\mu)}(1) = f^{(\mu)}(1) - [f^{(\mu)}(1) - f^{(\mu)}(0)] = f_1^{(\mu)}(0)$$

$$\mu = 1,2,\cdots,m-1$$

而

$$|f_1^{(m)}(x)| \leqslant M$$

因此,由引理2,得本定理所需要的结果.

为方便计,我们把 λ_j 写成

$$\lambda_j = \sum_{v=0}^{m-1} c_{j,v}(m) b_v = \sum_{v=0}^{m-1} c_{j,v}(m)[f^{(v)}(1) - f^{(v)}(0)] \tag{2.1}$$

3. 重积分的近似计算.

有了上节的结果,我们很自然地想到多重积分的情形. 在这里只以二重积分为例加以讨论.

关键性的问题是怎样推广引理1到二元的情形.

首先设(A)　$f(x,y)$ 在正方域 $0 \leqslant x \leqslant 1, 0 \leqslant y \leqslant 1$ 上连续,并有连续的偏微商

$$f_{x^\lambda}(x,y),\quad \lambda = 1,2,\cdots,m$$

根据引理1,我们可以找到一个函数 $P(x,y)$ 满足

$$P_{x^\mu}(0,y) = 0,\quad \mu = 0,1,\cdots,m-1$$

$$P_{x^\mu}(1,y) = f_{x^\mu}(1,y) - f_{x^\mu}(0,y),\quad \mu = 0,1,\cdots,m-1$$

其中 $P_{x^0}(1,y)$ 表 $P(1,y)$,其他类似的表达式有类似的意义. 这函数的表达式如下:

$$P(x,y) = x^m \sum_{j=0}^{m-1} \frac{\lambda_j(y)}{j!}(x-1)^j$$

而由(2.1)

$$\lambda_j(y) = \sum_{v=0}^{m-1} c_{j,v}(m)[f_{x^v}(1,y) - f_{x^v}(0,y)]$$

令

$$F(x,y)=f(x,y)-P(x,y)$$

则

$$F_{x^\mu}(1,y)-F_{x^\mu}(0,y),\quad \mu=0,\cdots,m-1 \tag{3.1}$$

其次又设(B)$f_{x^\mu y^v}(1,y)$,$f_{x^\mu x^v}(0,y)$ 在 $0\leqslant y\leqslant 1$ 上连续($0\leqslant\mu,v\leqslant m$),其中 $f_{x^0y^v}$ 表 f_{y^v},$f_{x^vy^0}$ 表 f_{x^v}.

再用引理1,就可以得到 $Q(x,y)$ 满足

$$\left.\begin{aligned}&Q_{y^\mu}(x,0)=0\\&Q_{y^\mu}(x,1)=F_{y^\mu}(x,1)-F_{y^\mu}(x,0)\end{aligned}\right.,\quad \mu=0,\cdots,m-1$$

函数 $Q(x,y)$ 有下面的表达式

$$Q(x,y)=y^m\sum_{j=0}^{m-1}\frac{\Lambda_j(x)}{j!}(y-1)^j \tag{3.2}$$

而

$$\Lambda_j(x)=\sum_{v=0}^{m-1}c_{j,v}(m)[F_{y^v}(x,1)-F_{y^v}(x,0)] \tag{3.3}$$

令

$$\Phi(x,y)=F(x,y)-Q(x,y)$$

则

$$\Phi_{y^\mu}(x,1)=\Phi_{y^\mu}(x,0),\quad \mu=0,1,\cdots,m-1 \tag{3.4}$$

现在要问:是否还可以得到

$$\Phi_{x^\mu}(1,y)=\Phi_{x^\mu}(0,y),\quad \mu=0,1,\cdots,m-1 \tag{3.5}$$

即

$$F_{x^\mu}(1,y)-Q_{x^\mu}(1,y)=F_{x^\mu}(0,y)-Q_{x^\mu}(0,y)$$

由(3.1)知上式即

$$Q_{x^\mu}(1,y)=Q_{x^\mu}(0,y),\quad \mu=0,1,\cdots,m-1$$

由(3.2)知道,我们只需要

$$\Lambda_j^{(\mu)}(1)=\Lambda_j^{(\mu)}(0),\quad (\mu=0,1,\cdots,m-1)$$

由(3.3)及(3.1)(注意(3.1)系 y 的恒等式,因此,两边可以对 y 屡次微分),知道上式成立.

最后,我们还可以把 $\Phi(x,y)$ 写成:

$$\begin{aligned}\Phi(x,y)=\;&f(x,y)-P(x,y)-Q(x,y)=\\&f(x,y)-x^m\sum_{j=0}^{m-1}\frac{(x-1)^j}{j!}\sum_{v=0}^{m-1}c_{j,v}(m)[f_{x^v}(1,y)-f_{x^v}(0,y)]-\\&y^m\sum_{j=0}^{m-1}\frac{(y-1)^j}{j!}\sum_{v=0}^{m-1}c_{j,v}(m)[f_{y^v}(x,1)-f_{y^v}(x,0)]+\\&x^my^m\sum_{i,j=0}^{m-1}\frac{(x-1)^i(y-1)^j}{i!j!}\times\end{aligned}$$

$$\sum_{\mu,v=0}^{m-1} c_{i,v}(m)c_{j,v}(m)[f_{x^v y^\mu}(1,1)-f_{x^v y^\mu}(1,0)-$$
$$f_{x^v y^\mu}(0,1)+f_{x^v y^\mu}(0,0)]$$

容易看出,利用(3.4),(3.5) 我们可以扩充 $\Phi(x,y)$ 的定义,使得它成为对 x 及 y 都以1为周期的连续函数,并且 $\Phi_{x^{m-1}}$,$\Phi_{y^{m-1}}$ 都存在及连续. 又除了 x 或 y 为整数的情形以外,Φ_{x^m},Φ_{y^m} 也连续并在区域 $0\leqslant x,y\leqslant 1$ 上有界.

利用以上的结果,我们根据[2] 内的一个定理即得

$$\left|\int_0^1\int_0^1\Phi(x,y)\,\mathrm{d}x\mathrm{d}y-\frac{1}{n^2}\sum_{x=1}^{n}\sum_{y=1}^{n}\Phi\left(\frac{x}{n},\frac{y}{n}\right)\right|\leqslant\frac{3^s-1}{(2\pi)^m}\zeta^{(s)}\left(\frac{m}{s}\right)MN^{-\frac{m}{s}}$$

其中 M 为 $\Phi_{x^m}(x,y)$, $\Phi_{y^m}(x,y)$ 在 $0\leqslant x,y\leqslant 1$ 上的一个公共上界.

但

$$\int_0^1\int_0^1 f(x,y)\,\mathrm{d}x\mathrm{d}y=\int_0^1\int_0^1\Phi(x,y)\,\mathrm{d}x\mathrm{d}y+\int_0^1\int_0^1 P(x,y)\,\mathrm{d}x\mathrm{d}y+\int_0^1\int_0^1 Q(x,y)\,\mathrm{d}x\mathrm{d}y$$

而 $P(x,y)$ 及 $Q(x,y)$ 对两变数之一是多项式,因此,上式右边第二三两个积分可以结合普通的积分法及上节所述定积分的近似计算法去求出其近似值. 这样,我们已经给出一个求上式左边重积分的近似计算法.

不难看出,重积分的近似计算也可以用类似的方式去进行.

参 考 书 目

[1] Коробов, Н. М., ДАН, 115, 6, 1062-5, 1957.
[2] 闵嗣鹤,北京大学学报(自然科学)5:2, 127-130. 1959.

ON THE NUMERICAL INTEGRATION OF DOUBLE AND MULTIPLE INTEGRALS①

1. We express the non-negative integer v in the scale of two as follows:

$$v = a''_s a'_s \cdots a''_1 a'_1 \qquad (1)$$

where a'_i, $a''_i = 0$ or 1 and a''_s and a''_s never vanish simultaneously except for $v = 0$, and in the latter case $s = 1$. Set

$$x_v = a'_1 a'_2 \cdots a'_s$$
$$y_v = a''_1 a''_2 \cdots a''_s$$

and

$$S(M,N) = \sum_{v=M}^{M+N-1} f(x_v, y_v)$$

where M and N are non-negative integers and $f(x,y)$ is any function defined on the unit square $U: 0 \leqslant x, y \leqslant 1$; then for

$$M = 4^r l, N = 4^r$$

l and r being non-negative integers, we have

$$x_{M+v} = x_M + x_v,\ y_{M+v} = y_M + y_v$$

and so

$$S(M,N) = \sum_{v=0}^{N-1} f(x_M + x_v, y_M + y_v)$$

① 原载:*Science Record*,3(1959),11:531-533.

It is easy to see that for $0 \leqslant v \leqslant N$,

$$x_v = \frac{h}{2^r}, y_v = \frac{k}{2^r}$$

where h and k are integers satisfying $0 \leqslant h, k \leqslant 2^r - 1$ and that

$$S(M,N) = \sum_{h=0}^{z^r-1} \sum_{k=0}^{z^r-1} f(x_M + \frac{h}{2^r}, y_M + \frac{k}{2^r}) \tag{2}$$

2. Now let $f(x,y)$ be continuous and with continuous partial derivatives. $\frac{\partial^i f}{\partial x^i}, \frac{\partial^i f}{\partial y^i}, i = 1, \cdots, \kappa$, where $\kappa \geqslant 2$ and let M be an upper bound to each of the functions $\left|\frac{\partial^\kappa f}{\partial x^k}\right|, \left|\frac{\partial^\kappa f}{\partial y^k}\right|$ and finally let $f(x,y)$ be periodic with respect to each of the variables.

Using the Fourier expansion for $f(x,y)$, y being considered as a constant, we can prove that

$$\frac{1}{2^r} \sum_{h=0}^{2v-1} f\left(\frac{h}{2^r}, y\right) = \int_0^1 f(x,y)\,\mathrm{d}x + R_1$$

where

$$| R_1 | \leqslant \frac{\zeta(\kappa) M}{(2\pi \cdot 2^r)^\kappa}.$$

From this we can derive similarly that

$$\frac{1}{4^r} \sum_{h=0}^{2^r-1} \sum_{k=0}^{2^r-1} f\left(\frac{h}{2^r}, \frac{k}{2^r}\right) = \int_0^1 \int f(x,y)\,\mathrm{d}x\mathrm{d}y + R_2 \tag{3}$$

where

$$| R_2 | \leqslant \frac{2\zeta(\kappa) M}{(2\pi \cdot 2^r)^\kappa}$$

3. Let

$$N = c_0 \cdot 4^r + c_1 \cdot 4^{r-1} + \cdots + c_r$$

$$M_s = c_0 \cdot 4^r + \cdots + c_{r-s-1} \cdot 4^{s+1}, N_s = c_{r-s} \cdot 4^s$$

where $c_i = 0, 1$ or 3; then

$$\left| \int_0^1 \int f(x,y)\,\mathrm{d}x\mathrm{d}y - \frac{1}{N} \sum_{v=0}^{N-1} f(x_v, y_v) \right| \leqslant \frac{1}{N} \sum_{s=0}^{r} N_s D_s \tag{4}$$

and

$$D_s = \max_{0 \leqslant j \leqslant c_{r-s}-1} \left| \int_0^1 \int f(x,y)\,\mathrm{d}x\mathrm{d}y - \frac{1}{4^s} \sum_{v=M_s+i\cdot 4^s}^{M_s+j\cdot 4^s+4^s-1} f(x_v, y_v) \right| =$$

$$\max_{0 \leqslant j \leqslant c_{r-s}-1} \left| \int_0^1 \int f(\alpha_j + x, \beta_j + y)\,\mathrm{d}x\mathrm{d}y - \frac{1}{4^s} \sum_{v=0}^{4^s-1} f(\alpha_j + x_v, \beta_j + y_v) \right|$$

where $a_j = x_{M_s+j\cdot 4^s}$, $\beta_j = y_{M_s+j\cdot 4^s}$. From (3) and (2) we have

$$D_s \leqslant \frac{2\zeta(\kappa)M}{(2\pi\cdot 2^s)^\kappa},$$

and hence we have, by (4)

$$\left|\int_0^1\int f(x,y)\,dxdy - \frac{1}{N}\sum_{v=0}^{N-1} f(x_v,y_v)\right| \leqslant \frac{6A_r\zeta(\kappa)}{(2\pi)^\kappa}MN^{-1} \qquad (5)$$

Where $A_r = \{1-2^{-(\kappa-2)}\}^{-1}$ for $\kappa > 2$ and $A_r = r+1$ for $\kappa = 2$. In case N is a multiple of $4^s (s \geqslant 1)$, the error may be estimated in a better way. In particular for $N = 4^r$, the error does not exceed

$$\frac{2\zeta(\kappa)M}{(2\pi)^\kappa}N^{-\kappa/2} \qquad (6)$$

In the general case, the error can not be less than $O(N^{-1})$ and this is seen through the example $f(x,y) = e^{2\pi i(\lambda x+\mu y)}$ $(\lambda\mu \neq 0)$.

4. If $f(x,y)$ is not periodic with respect to each of the variables we have to replace the sum

$$\frac{1}{N}\sum_{v=0}^{N-1} f(x_v,y_v)$$

by a more complex one while x_v and y_v remain the same. Further, we have to assume that

(A) $$f(x,y),\ \frac{\partial^i f}{\partial x^i},\ \frac{\partial^i f}{\partial y^i},\quad i = 1,\cdots,\kappa$$

and

$$\Delta_x \frac{\partial^{i+j} f}{\partial_{x^i}\partial_{y^j}},\quad \Delta y\frac{\partial^{i+j} f}{\partial_{x^i}\partial_{y^j}},\quad 1 \leqslant i+j \leqslant \kappa$$

are all continuous on $U: 0 \leqslant x,y \leqslant 1$;

(B) $$\left|\frac{\partial^\kappa f}{\partial x^\kappa}\right|,\ \left|\frac{\partial^\kappa f}{\partial y^\kappa}\right|,\ \left|\Delta_x\frac{\partial^\kappa f}{\partial_{x^i}\partial_{y^{\kappa-i}}}\right|,\ \left|\Delta_y\frac{\partial^\kappa f}{\partial_{x^i}\partial_{y^{\kappa-i}}}\right|,$$

$i = 0,\cdots,\kappa$, have the same upper bound M. Here Δ_x and Δ_y are defined by the relations:

$$\Delta_x g(x,y) = g(1,y) - g(0,y)$$
$$\Delta_y g(x,y) = g(x,1) - g(x,0)$$

ON CONCRETE EXAMPLES AND THE ABSTRACT THEORY OF THE GENERALIZED ANALYTIC FUNCTIONS①

Ⅰ. Introduction

Unlike the theory of analytic functions, the theory of generalized analytic functions or pseudo-analytic functions as developed by И. Н. Bekya[1] and L. Bers[2] independently, consists of a great number of existence theorems without concrete examples. An objective of this paper is to treat some typical special cases with the aim of obtaining very concrete results. On the other hand we shall make the first attempt of building up an abstract theory of certain operators on some Banach spaces, which will include the theory of generalized analytic functions as a special case.

---

① 原载：*Scientia Sinica*, 12(1963), 9: 1270-1283.

Ⅱ. Concrete Results for Special Equations

1. *The Solutions of the Equation* $\partial_{\bar{z}}\omega = \lambda\bar{\omega}$

It is well-known that an analytic function $f(z)$ can be represented by a power series in z near every regular point. Analogous to this is the fact that a generalized analytic function can be represented by a formal power series[3]. The existence of the so-called formal powers was proved, but the"formal powers"themselves, so far as I am aware, have never been concretely constructed even for the very simple equation $\partial_{\bar{z}}\omega = \bar{\omega}$. In this sections we shall study the solutions of the equation $\partial_{\bar{z}}\omega = \lambda\bar{\omega}$, where λ is a polynomial in z and $\bar{z}$. As is well-known, the general equation $\partial_{\bar{z}}\omega + A\omega + B\bar{\omega} = 0$ can be reduced to an equation of the form $\partial_{\bar{z}}\omega_1 + B_1\bar{\omega}_1 = 0$, and in case $A = 0$, $B \in L_p(\bar{G})$, $p > 2$ the coefficient B can be approximated by a polynomial in z and $\bar{z}$. Our consideration reveals the significance of the equation to be considered.

Now consider the equation

$$\partial_{\bar{z}}\omega = \lambda\bar{\omega} \tag{1.1}$$

where

$$\lambda = \sum_{j=0}^{m} \lambda_j(z)\bar{z}^j, \lambda_j(z) = \sum_{i=0}^{m-1} c_{ij}z^i \tag{1.2}$$

and c_{ij} are constants.

For any function $f(z)$ which can be represented near $z = 0$ by a power series in $\bar{z}$ of the form

$$f(z) = \sum_{j=0}^{\infty} a_j(z)\bar{z}^j$$

where $a_j(z)$ are functions analytic near $z = 0$, we introduce the operator $\int \mathrm{d}\bar{z}$ defined by

$$\int f(z)\,\mathrm{d}\bar{z} = \sum_{j=0}^{\infty} a_j(z)\frac{\bar{z}^{j+1}}{j+1} \tag{1.3}$$

We introduce also the operator Ω defined by

$$\Omega f = \int \lambda\bar{f}\,\mathrm{d}\bar{z} \tag{1.4}$$

which is not meaningless if $\bar{f}$ can be represented by a power series in $\bar{z}$ of the mentioned form.

For a function $\Phi(z)$ analytic near $z = 0$, the equation(1.1)has the following"formal solution":

$$\omega(z) = \Phi + \Omega\Phi + \Omega^2\Phi + \cdots \tag{1.5}$$

In fact, inserting this formally into the left-hand side of (1.1), we have

$$\partial_{\bar{z}}\omega = \partial_{\bar{z}}\Omega\Phi + \partial_{\bar{z}}\Omega\Omega\Phi + \cdots = \partial_{\bar{z}}\Omega\omega = \lambda\bar{\omega} \tag{1.6}$$

To justify this, we have to consider the convergence of the series in (1.5) and (1.6). Our next object is not only to justify (1.6) but also to get a more comprehensive form for the solution $\omega(z)$.

Since the operator Ω is linear(with respect to real coefficients), it is benificial to consider the cases $\Phi(z) = z^k$, iz^k. Now, let us first consider the case $\Phi(z) = z^k$. It is easy to verify that

$$\Omega^{2n}z^k = \sum \bar{c}_{ij}c_{i_1j_1}\bar{c}_{i_2j_2}\cdots c_{i_{2n-1}j_{2n-1}} \times \frac{z^{j+i_1+j_2+\cdots+i_{2n-1}+k+n}\bar{z}^{i+j_1+i_2+\cdots+j_{2n-1}+n}}{[j,i_1,j_2,\cdots,j_{2n-2};k][i,j_1,j_2,\cdots,j_{2n-1};0]} \tag{1.7}$$

$$\Omega^{2n+1}z^k = \sum c_{ij}\bar{c}_{i_1j_1}c_{i_2j_2}\cdots c_{i_{2n}j_{2n}} \times \frac{z^{i+j_1+i_2+\cdots+i_{2n}+n}\bar{z}^{j+i_1+j_2+\cdots+j_{2n}+k+n+1}}{[i,j_1,i_2,\cdots,j_{2n-1;0}][j,i_1,j_2,\cdots,j_{2n};k]} \tag{1.8}$$

Where $\sum$ denotes that $i,j,i_1,j_1,\cdots$run respectively through $0,1,\cdots,m$ but, $i_v + j_v \leqslant m$ and

$$[i,j_1,i_2,\cdots,j_{2n-1};0] =$$
$$(i,j_1+1)(i+j_1+i_2+j_3+2)\cdots(i+j_1+i_2+\cdots+j_{2n-1}+n)$$
$$[j,i_2,j_2,\cdots,j_{2n};k] =$$
$$(j+k+1)(j+i_1+j_2+k+2)\cdots(j+i_1+j_2+\cdots+j_{2n}+k+n+1)$$

Therefore, for $\Phi(z) = z^k$, (1.5)can be written as

$$\omega(z) = z^kE_k(z) + \bar{z}^{k+1}\tilde{E}_{k+1}(z) \tag{1.9}$$

where

$$E_k(z) = 1 + \sum_{n=0}^{\infty}\sum \bar{c}_{ij}c_{i_1j_1}\cdots c_{i2n-1j2n-1} \times \frac{z^{j+i_1+j_2+\cdots+i_{2n-1}+n}\bar{z}^{i+j_1+i_2+\cdots+j_{2n-1}+n}}{[j,i_1,\cdots,j_{2n-2};k][i,j_1,i_2,\cdots,j_{2n-1};0]}$$

and

$$\tilde{E}_{k+1}(z) = \sum_{n=0}^{\infty}\sum c_{ij}\bar{c}_{i_1j_1}c_{i_2j_2}\cdots c_{i_{2n}j_{2n}} \times \frac{z^{i+j_1+i_2+\cdots+i_{2n}+n}\bar{z}^{j+i_1+j_2+\cdots+j_{2n}+n}}{[i,j_1,\cdots,j_{2n-1};0][j,i_1,j_2,\cdots,j_{2n};k]}$$

Analogously, we have for $\Phi(z) = iz^k$,

$$\omega(z) = iz^k E_k(z) - i\bar{z}^{k+1}\tilde{E}_{k+1}(z) \tag{1.10}$$

and generally we have for

$$\Phi(z) = \sum_{k=0}^{\infty} c_k z^k$$

$$\omega(z) = \sum_{k=0}^{\infty} [c_k z^k E_k(z) + \bar{c}_k \bar{z}^{k+1} \tilde{E}_{k+1}(z)] \tag{1.11}$$

In order to verity the convergence of the series(1.11)and(1.5), we put

$$\max_{i,j} | c_{ij} | = C, \max(1, | z |) = \rho \tag{1.12}$$

then on account of(1.7)and(1.8)we have

$$| z^{-k}\Omega^{2n} z^k | \leqslant C^{2n} \sum \frac{1}{n!n!} | z |^{i+j+i_1+j_1+\cdots+i_{2n-1}+j_{2n-1}+2n} \tag{1.13}$$

$$| \bar{z}^{-k-1}\Omega^{2n+1} z^k | \leqslant C^{2n+2} \sum \frac{1}{n!(n+1)!} | z |^{i+j+i_1+j_1+\cdots+i_{2n}+j_{2n}+2n}$$

and hence

$$| z^{-k}\Omega^{2n} z^k | \leqslant C^{2n}(m+1)^{2n}\rho^{2(m+1)n}/n!n!$$

$$| \bar{z}^{-k-1}\Omega^{2n+1} z^k | \leqslant C^{2n+2}(m+1)^{2n+2}\rho^{2(m+1)n+m}/n!(n+1)! \tag{1.14}$$

It follows that $F_k(z)$ and $\tilde{E}_{k+1}(z)$ have a bound independent of k and z provided that z lies in a fixed circle, and hence that(1.11)converges whenever $\Phi(z) = \sum_{k=0}^{\infty} ckz^k$ is convergent.

Analogous to(1.13)are the inequalities:

$$\begin{aligned} | z^{-k}\Omega^{2n} iz^k | &\leqslant C^{2n} \sum \frac{1}{n!n!} | z |^{i+j+i_1+j_1+\cdots+i_{2n-1}+j_{2n-1}+2n} \\ | \bar{z}^{-k-1}\Omega^{2n+1} iz^k | &\leqslant C^{2n+2} \sum \frac{1}{n!(n+1)!} | z |^{i+j+i_1+j_1+\cdots+i_{2n}+j_{2n}+2n} \end{aligned} \tag{1.15}$$

In view of(1.13)and(1.15)we have

$$\begin{aligned} | \Omega^{2n}\Phi | &\leqslant 2C^{2n} \sum \frac{\rho^{i+j+\cdots+i_{2n-1}+j_{2n-1}+2n}}{n!n!} \sum_{k=0}^{\infty} | c_k || z |^k \\ | \Omega^{2n+1}\Phi | &\leqslant 2C^{2n+2} \sum \frac{\rho^{i+j+i_1+j_1+\cdots+i_{2n}+j_{2n}+2n}}{n!(n+1)!} \sum_{k=0}^{\infty} | c_k || z |^{k+1} \end{aligned} \tag{1.16}$$

Thus the convergence of(1.5)follows from that of $\Phi(z) = \sum_{k=0}^{\infty} c_k z^k$.

To justify(1.6)ew have also to study the convergence of the series obtained by"differentiating"(1.5)with respect to $\bar{z}$. Here we omit the details.

Furthermore, it is evident that a solution for(1.1)which is valid near $z = z_0$ instead of $z = 0$ can be obtained in just the same way.

2. *The Generdlity of the Solution*

In this section we discuss the generality of the solution obtained in the previous section. We shall prove that every generalized solution of the equation(1.1) can be represented by a series of the form

$$\omega(z) = \sum_{k=0}^{\infty}[a_k(a - z_0)^k E_k(z - z_0) + \bar{a}_k(\overline{z - z_0})^{k+1}\tilde{E}_k + 1(z - z_0)] \quad (2.1)$$

near each of its regular point $z = z_0$. For simplicity we take $z_0 = 0$.

As is well-known the solution $\omega(z)$ has the generalized partial derivatives $\partial_{\bar{z}}\omega$ and $\partial_z\omega$ near its regular points. Hence, under the assumption that λ is a polynomial in z and $\bar{z}$ (or more generally an analytic function of the two variables z and $\bar{z}$), the solution $\omega(z)$ has derivatives of all orders and consequently according to a well-known theorem these derivatives are ordinary formal derivatives[1]. The solution $\omega(z)$ must, therefore, be a classical solution.

Let us, first, take for granted that the solution $\omega(z)$ can be expanded into a power series in z and $\bar{z}$ near $z = 0$ as follows

$$\omega(z) = \sum_{m=0}^{\infty}\sum_{n=0}^{\infty} c_{mn} z^m \bar{z}^n \quad (2.2)$$

where

$$c_{mn} = \frac{1}{m!n!}[\partial_{z^m\bar{z}^n}\omega(z)]_{z=0} \quad (2.3)$$

Let

$$\Phi(z) = \sum_{m=0}^{\infty} c_{mn} z^m \quad (2.4)$$

then we may construct the solution

$$\omega_0(z) = \Phi + \Omega\Phi + \Omega^2\Phi + \cdots \quad (2.5)$$

as before. It follows immediately that

$$\partial_{z^m}[\omega(z) - \omega_0(z)] = 0, \quad z = 0; m = 0,1,\cdots \quad (2.6)$$

Noting that $\omega(z) - \omega_0(z)$ is a solution of (1.1), we prove without difficulty that

$$\partial_{z^m\bar{z}^n}[\omega(z) - \omega_0(z)] = 0, \quad z = 0; m,n = 0,1,\cdots \quad (2.7)$$

This shows that $\omega(z) = \omega_0(z)$.

It remains to show that $\omega(z)$ can be actually represented by a series of the form (2.2) This, in fact, can be proved by either making use of the generalized Cauchy integral formula or consulting the known theory of partial differential equations (see section 4 below and[4]).

3. *The Special Case* $\partial_{\bar z}\omega = \lambda_0 z^p \bar z^q$ *Where* λ_0 *Is a Consiant and* p, q *Are Nonnegative Integers*

Let $r = p + q + 1$ and $s = \frac{k+q+1}{r}$. The solution corresponding to $\Phi(z) = z^k$ is

$$\omega(z) = z^k E_k(z) + \bar z^{k+1}\tilde{E}_{k+1}(z) \tag{3.1}$$

where

$$E_k(z) = 1 + \sum_{n=1}^{\infty}\frac{(|\lambda_0|r^{-1})^{2n}|z|^{2nr}}{n!s(s+1)\cdots(s+n-1)} = \Gamma(s)\left(i\frac{|\lambda_0 z^r|}{r}\right)^{1-s}J_{s-1}\left(2i\frac{|\lambda_0 z^r|}{r}\right) \tag{3.1$_1$}$$

and

$$\widetilde{E}_{k+1}(z) = \sum_{n=1}^{\infty}\frac{\lambda_0 s^{-1}r^{-1}z^p\bar z^p(|\lambda_0|r^{-1})^{2n}|z|^{2nr}}{n!(s+1)(s+2)\cdots(s+n)} = \frac{\lambda_0 z^p\bar z^q}{k+q+1}E_{k+r}(z) = \Gamma(s)\lambda_0 r^{-1}z^p\bar z^q\left(i\frac{|\lambda_0 z^r|}{r}\right)^{-s}J_s\left(2i\frac{|\lambda_0 z^r|}{r}\right) \tag{3.1$_2$}$$

Analogous to this is the solution corresponding to $\Phi = iz^k$:

$$\omega(z) = iz^k E_k(z) - i\bar z^{k+1}\widetilde{E}_{k+1}(z) \tag{3.2}$$

Generally speaking, corresponding to the function $\Phi(z) = \sum_{k=0}^{\infty}\alpha_k z^k$ is the solution

$$\omega(z) = \sum_{k=0}^{\infty}[a_k z^k E_k(z) + \bar a_k \bar z^{k+1}\widetilde{E}_k(z)] = \tag{3.3}$$

$$\sum_{k=0}^{\infty}\Gamma(s)\left[a_k z^k\left(i\frac{|\lambda_0 z^r|}{r}\right)^{1-s}J_{s-1}\left(2i\frac{|\lambda_0 z^r|}{r}\right) + \bar a_k\lambda_0 r^{-1}\bar z^{k+1}z^p\bar z^q\left(i\frac{|\lambda_0 z^r|}{r}\right)^{-s}J_s\left(2i\frac{|\lambda_0 z^r|}{r}\right)\right] \tag{3.3$_1$}$$

In particular, for $p = q = 0$, we have

$$\omega(z) = \sum_{k=0}^{\infty}k!\left[a_k\left(\frac{z}{i|\lambda_0 z|}\right)^k J_k(2i|\lambda_0 z) + \bar a_k\lambda_0\left(\frac{\bar z}{i|\lambda_0 z|}\right)^{k+1}J_{k+1}(2i|\lambda_0 z|)\right] \tag{3.3$_2$}$$

From (3.3) we have

$$a_k = \frac{1}{k!}[\partial_z^k\omega(z)]_{z=0} \tag{3.4}$$

In the case $p = q = 0$, Lee-chung obtained a maximum modulus principle stronger than that of the analytic function. A proof is given below:

Near $z = z_0$, $\omega(z)$ can be represented by the series

$$\omega(z) = \sum_{k=0}^{\infty} [a_k(z - z_0)^k E_k(z - z_0) + \bar{a}_k(\overline{z - z_0})^{k+1} \tilde{E}_{k+1}(z - z_0)] \quad (3.5)$$

For sufficiently small $\rho > 0$, we have

$$\frac{1}{2\pi i}\int_{|z-z_0|=\rho} \frac{\omega(z)\,dz}{z - z_0} = \sum_{k=0}^{\infty} \frac{1}{2\pi i}\int_{|z-z_0|=\rho} [a_k(z - z_0)^{k-1} E_k(\rho) +$$

$$\bar{a}_k \rho^{2(k+1)} (z - z_0)^{-k-2} \tilde{E}_{k+1}(\rho)]\,dz =$$

$$a_0 E_0(\rho) = \alpha_0 \sum_{n=0}^{\infty} \frac{(|\lambda_0|\rho)^{2n}}{n!n!} = a_0 I_0(|\lambda_0|\rho)$$

Therefore

$$|\omega(z_0)| = |a_0| \leqslant \frac{1}{2\pi i_0(|\lambda_0|\rho)} \left| \int_{|z-z_0|=\rho} \frac{\omega(z)}{z - z_0} dz \right| \leqslant$$

$$\frac{1}{I_0(|\lambda_0|\rho)} \max_{|z-z_0|=\rho} |\omega(z)| \leqslant \max_{|z-z_0|=\rho} |\omega(z)|$$

From this we first obtain the ordinary maximum modulus principle and then the stronger maximum modulus principle:

$$|\omega(z)| \leqslant \frac{M}{I_0(\lambda_0 R)}$$

where M is the maximum of the modulus of $\omega(z)$ on the boundary of a region at each point $z = z_0$ near which $\omega(z)$ can be represented by a series of the form (3.5) and R is the distance of z from the boundary of the region.

4. *A Method for Finding the Fundamental Kernels*

Consider the equation

$$\partial_{\bar{z}}\omega = \lambda\bar{\omega} \quad (4.1)$$

where $\lambda = \lambda_0(z) + \bar{z}\lambda^*(z,\bar{z})$, $\lambda_0(z)$ being an integral function of z and $\lambda^*(z,\bar{z})$, and an integral function of z and $\bar{z}$. We may find a solution of (4.1) of the following form:

$$\omega(z) = \frac{1}{z} + G\log z\bar{z} + H \equiv -2X_1(z) \quad (4.2)$$

where G and H are integral functions of z and $\bar{z}$. In fact, inserting (4.2) into (4.1) we have

$$0 = \partial_{\bar{z}}\omega - \lambda\bar{\omega} = \frac{G - \bar{\lambda}}{\bar{z}} + (G_{\bar{z}} - \lambda\bar{G})\ln z\bar{z} + H_{\bar{z}} - \lambda\bar{H} \quad (4.3)$$

We choose G such that

$$G_{\bar{z}} - \lambda\bar{G} = 0$$

We may take, for example,

$$G = \sum_{n=0}^{\infty} \Omega^n \lambda_0(z) = \lambda_0(z) + \bar{z}G^*(z,\bar{z}) \tag{4.4}$$

Then, substituting(4.4)into(4.3), we have

$$H_{\bar{z}} - \lambda\bar{H} = \frac{\lambda - G}{\bar{z}} = \lambda^*(z,\bar{z}) - G^*(z,\bar{z})$$

and therefore, we may take

$$H = \sum_{n=0}^{\infty} \Omega^n \int (\lambda^*(z,\bar{z}) - G^*(z,\bar{z}))\,d\bar{z} \tag{4.5}$$

It is worthwhile to note that the functions G and H thus obtained are integral functions of z and $\bar{z}$. In the same way we obtain another solution

$$\omega(z) = \frac{1}{z^i} + G_1 \ln z\bar{z} + H_1 \equiv -2X_2(z) \tag{4.6}$$

where

$$G_1 = \sum_{n=0}^{\infty} \Omega^n i\lambda_0(z)$$

$$H_1 = \sum_{n=0}^{\infty} \Omega^n \int \left(-\frac{G_1 - i\lambda}{\bar{z}} \right) d\bar{z} \tag{4.7}$$

The solutions $X_i(z)$, $i = 1,2$, have a singular point at $z = 0$, To obtain analogous solutions with $z = t$ as a singular point, we may make the change of variable $z = z' + t$, obtain the solutions with $z' = 0$ as a singular point and put $z = z' + t$ in the results obtained. Thus we obtain the fundamental solutions with $z = t$ as a singular point:

$$X_i(z,t), \quad i = 1,2 \tag{4.8}$$

Corresponding to the fundamental solutions the fundamental kernels are given by the well-known formulae:

$$\Omega_1(z,t) = X_1(z,t) + iX_2(z,t)$$

$$\Omega_2(z,t) = X_1(z,t) - iX_2(z,t) \tag{4.9}$$

In the particular case $\lambda \equiv 1$, wc put

$$E = \sum_{n=0}^{\infty} \frac{z^n \bar{z}^n}{n!n!}, G = \sum_{n=0}^{\infty} \left(1 + \frac{1}{2} + \cdots + \frac{1}{n}\right) \frac{z^n \bar{z}^n}{n!n!} \tag{4.10}$$

Then adapting the above method we obtain the fundamental solutions

$$X_1(z,t) = \frac{E(z-t)}{2(t-z)} - [E(z-t) + E_{\bar{z}}(z-t)]\ln|z-t| + G(z-t) - G_{\bar{z}}(z-t) \tag{4.11$_1$}$$

$$X_2(z,t) = \frac{E(z-t)}{2i(t-z)} - \mathrm{i}[E(z-t) - E_{\bar z}(z-t)]\ln|z-t| +$$

$$\mathrm{i}G(z-t) - iG_{\bar z}(z-t) \tag{4.11$_2$}$$

We may, however, verify directly that these are fundamental solutions. Hence we obtain the fundamental kernels:

$$\Omega_1(z,t) = \frac{E(z-t)}{t-z} - 2E_z(z-t)\ln|z-t| + 2G_z(z-t) \tag{4.12$_1$}$$

$$\Omega_2(z,t) = -2E(z-t)\ln|z-t| + 2G(z-t) \tag{4.12$_2$}$$

5. *The Beltrami Equation*

In the theory of the generalized analytic functions, an important role is played by the complete homeomorphisms for the Beltrami equation

$$\partial_{\bar z}\omega = q\partial_z\omega \tag{5.1}$$

where $|q| \leqslant q_0 < 1$ and q is a measurable function. Various methods have been devised for proving the existence of a complete homeomorphism. According to Bekya[1], we first establish the existence of a local homeomorphism for (5.1) under the condition that q is Höldercontinuous, and then the existence of a complete homeomorphism under the same condition. The existence of the complete homeomorphism for (5.1) in general is proved by a method of approximation. But the measurable function q can be, in fact, approximated by a polynomial in z and $\bar z$, so that we may restrict ourselves to the case that $q = \lambda(z, \bar z)$ is a polynomial in z and $\bar z$, Here we give a very short existence proof of a local homeomorphism for this special but important case.

We introduce the operator:

$$\Omega = \int d\bar z \lambda \partial_z \tag{5.2}$$

which means differentiating formally with respect to z, multiplying by λ and integrating with respect to $\bar z$ formally(see § 1). This operator is applicable to any integral function of z and $\bar z$. Now let

$$\lambda = \sum_{j=0}^{m} \lambda_j \bar z^j, \quad \lambda_j = \sum_{v=0}^{m-j} c_{vj} z^v \tag{5.3}$$

Then it is easy to verify that

$$\Omega^n z = \sum_{j=0}^{m}\sum_{j_1=0}^{m}\cdots\sum_{j_{n-1}=0}^{m} \frac{A_{j,j_1,\cdots,j_{n-1}} \bar z^{j+j_1+\cdots+j_{n-1}+n}}{(j+1)(j+j_1+2)\cdots(j+\cdots+j_{m-1}+n)} \tag{5.4}$$

where

$$A_{j,j_1,\cdots,j_{n-1}} = \sum \lambda_j^{(k_j)} \lambda_{j_1}^{(k_{j1})} \cdots \lambda_{j_{n-1}}^{(k_{j_{n-1}})} \tag{5.5}$$

and $k_j, k_{j_1}, \cdots, k_{j_{n-1}}$ run respectively through all integers satisfying the conditions

$$0 \leqslant k_j \leqslant \min(m, n-v-1), k_j + \cdots + k_{j_{n-1}} = n-1 \qquad (5.6)$$

Let

$$\sum_{j,v} |c_{jv}| = A \qquad (5.7)$$

then, for $|z| \leqslant 1$,

$$|\lambda_j^{(k)}| \leqslant Am^m \qquad (5.8)$$

$$|A_{j,\cdots,j_{n-1}}| \leqslant A^n m^{mn} m^n \qquad (5.9)$$

One deduces from these inequalities that the series

$$\omega(z) = z + \Omega z + \cdots + \Omega^n z + \cdots \qquad (5.10)$$

converges absolutely and uniformly in a neighbourhood of $z = 0$ and that $\omega(z)$ satisfies (5.1) (with $q = \lambda$).

That (5.10) gives a local homeomorphism follows from the fact that

$$J = \left|\frac{\partial\omega}{\partial z}\right|^2 - \left|\frac{\partial\omega}{\partial\bar{z}}\right|^2 = (1 - |\lambda|^2)\left|\frac{\partial\omega}{\partial z}\right|^2 \neq 0$$

the last inequality being justified by

$$\frac{\partial\omega}{\partial z} = 1 + \partial_z \sum_{n=0}^{\infty} \Omega_z^m \omega = 1 + O(|z|) \to 1, (z \to 0)$$

Obviously a local homeomorphism near any point $z = z_0$ in the region considered can be obtained in exactly the same way.

Ⅲ. A Generalization of the Theory of the Generalized Analytic Functions

1. Let A be a commutative algebra over the complex field. Let H, B and B_1 be subsets of A which are themselves Banach spaces. The norm of an element f is denoted by $|f|$, $\|f\|$ or $\|f\|_1$, according as $f \in H$, B or B_1. The space H is supposed to be a commutative Banach algebra (= a normed ring with a unit) such that① $HB \subset B$ and that

$$h_1 h_2 \leqslant K |h_1| \cdot |h_2|, \quad h_1, h_2 \in H \qquad (1.1)$$

where K is an absolute constant.

Let ∂ be a linear operator defined over $D \subset A$ subject to the following conditions

① We denote the set of all elements hb ($h \in H$, $b \in B$) by HB.

(1) If $f \in D$, $g \in D \cap H$, $\partial g \in B$, then $fg \in D$ and

$$\partial fg = f\partial g + g\partial f \tag{1.2}$$

(2) If $\varphi(z)$ is holomorphic in $|z| < R$, $f \in D \cap H$ and $K|f| < R$, then $\varphi(f) \in D$ and

$$\partial\varphi(f) = \varphi'(f)\partial f \tag{1.3}$$

(This means that a power series in f can be differentiated term by term.)

Let σ be a bounded linear (with respect to real coefficients) completely continuous operator satisfying $\sigma B \subset H \cap D$ and

$$\partial\sigma f = f \tag{1.4}$$

Finally, let A_0 be the set of all elements of D satisfying $\partial f = 0$. We assume that $A_0 H \subset B_1$ (hence $A_0 \subset B_1$) and that every $\varphi \in A_0$ gives a continuous mapping of H into B_1 so that $\varphi H \subset B_1$.

Now let $F(\omega)$ ($\omega \in B_1$) be any operator (usually non-linear) which maps B_1 into B. We consider the equation

$$\partial\omega = \omega F(\omega) \tag{1.5}$$

Suppose $\omega \in D \cap B_1$ be any solution of (1.5) then in view of (1.4) - (1.5) we have

$$\partial\omega e^{-\sigma F(w)} = w\partial e^{-\sigma F(w)} + e^{-\sigma F(w)}\partial w = e^{-\sigma F(w)}(\partial\omega - \omega F(\omega)) = 0$$

hence

$$we^{-\sigma F(w)} = \varphi \in A_0$$

and

$$\omega = \varphi e^{\sigma F(w)} \tag{1.6}$$

Conversely, given $\varphi \in A_0$ and $w = \varphi e^{\sigma F(w)} \in D \cap B_1$, we have as before

$$0 = \partial we^{-\sigma F(w)} = e^{-\sigma F(w)}(\partial w - wF(w))$$

So w satisfies (1.5).

From now on we introduce the additional conditions on F that F is a continuous mapping of $A.H$ into B and that there exists a constant A independent of w such that

$$\| F(\omega) \| \leqslant A \tag{1.7}$$

for all $\omega \in D \cap B_1$. We claim: for any $\varphi \in A_0$ there exists $\omega \in D \cap B_1$ for which (1.6) holds. In fact, inserting $\omega = \varphi e^{\omega}$ into (1.6), one finds

$$\varphi e^{\omega} = \varphi e^{\sigma F(\varphi_e \omega)} \tag{1.8}$$

Therefore we have to prove the existence of an $\omega \in H$ satisfying

$$\omega = \sigma F(\varphi e^{\omega}) \tag{1.9}$$

We shall make use of Schauder's fixed – point theorem. Consider the set M:

$$\omega = \sigma g,\ g \in B,\ \|g\| \leqslant M,\ M \geqslant A$$

where M is a constant. The set M is obviously convex but not necessarily closed. So we replace M by its closure $\overline{M}$ which is both convex and closed. When ω runs through $\overline{M}$, the left-hand side of (1.9) runs through a compact set; this follows from (1.7) and the complete continuity of the operator σ. Therefore the operator defined by the left-hand side of (1.9) maps a closed convex set $\overline{M} \subset H$ into a compact subset (since $M \geqslant A$).

It remains to verify the continuity of this operator. Since σ is a bounded operator there exists a constant C such that the inequality

$$|\sigma F(\varphi e^{\omega_1}) - \sigma F(\varphi e^{\omega_0})| \leqslant C \| F(\varphi e^{w_1}) - F(\varphi e^{\omega_0}) \|$$

is valid for all ω_0, $\omega_1 \in \overline{M}$. Since F is continuous the right-hand side of the above inequality tends to zero with $\varphi e^{\omega_1} - \varphi e^{\omega_0}$ and the latter tends to zero with $|e^{\omega_1} - e^{\omega_0}|$ according to our assumption on $A_0\,H$, since $\varphi \in A_0$ and $e^{\omega} \in H$ as $\omega \in H$. Further we have by (1.1)

$$|e^{\omega_1} - e^{\omega_0}| = \left| \sum_{n=0}^{\infty} \frac{1}{n!}(\omega_1^n - \omega_0^n) \right| \leqslant \sum_{n=0}^{\infty} \frac{1}{n!} |\omega_1^n - \omega_0^n| =$$

$$\sum_{n=0}^{\infty} \frac{1}{n!} \left| \sum_{r=0}^{m-1} \binom{n}{r} \omega_0^r (\omega_1 - \omega_0)^{n-r} \right| \leqslant$$

$$\sum_{n=0}^{\infty} \frac{K^{n-1}}{n!} \sum_{r=0}^{n-1} \binom{n}{r} |\omega_0|^r |\omega_1 - \omega_0|^{n-r}$$

$$\rightarrow 0 (\text{as } \omega_1 \rightarrow \omega_0)$$

This proves that the operator on the right-hand side of (1.9) is continuous. By Schauder's fixed-point theorem, there exists $\omega \in \overline{M}$ for which (1.9) holds.

Our considerations prove the "principle of similarity":

Theorem 1 *If $F(\omega)$ is a continuous mapping of $A_0 H$ into B and if for every $\omega \in D \cap B_1$, we have always*

$$\| F(\omega) \| \leqslant A \tag{1.10}$$

where A is a constant independent of ω, then every solution $\omega \in B_1$ of the equation

$$\partial \omega = \omega F(\omega) \tag{1.11}$$

can be written as

$$\omega = \varphi e^{\sigma F(\omega)} \tag{1.12}$$

where $\varphi \in A_0$. Conversely, given $\varphi \in A_0$ we can always find a solution $\omega \in B_1$ of (1.11) *for which* (1.12) *holds.*

2. Now consider the equation

$$\partial_{\bar{z}} w = wf(z,w) \equiv F(z,w) \tag{2.1}$$

where $z \in G$, G being a bounded region on the z plane, $w \in L^1(\bar{G})$, $\partial_{\bar{z}}\omega$ is the generalized derivative of ω with respect to $\bar{z}$, and f and F are functions of z and ω.

We assume that

$$L^p(f,\bar{G}) \leqslant A, \quad p > 2 \tag{2.2}$$

for all $\omega \in L^1(\bar{G})$, where A is a constant independent of ω and that $f(z,\omega)$ is a continuous mapping of $[\mathscr{U}_0(G) \cap L^1(\bar{G})] G_a(\bar{G})$ into $L^p(\bar{G})$.

In §1 we take A to be the set of all measurable functions defined on $\bar{G}$, $B_1 = L^1(\bar{G})$, $B = L^p(\bar{G})$, $p > 2$, $H = C_a(\bar{G})$, $a = \frac{p-2}{p}$ [or simply $H = C\bar{G}$]. Evidently $HB \subset B$ and (1.1) holds①. We take

$$A_0 = \mathscr{U}_0(G) \cap L^1(\bar{G})$$

We take $\partial = \partial_{\bar{z}}$, $D = D_{\bar{z}}(G)$ and $\sigma = T_G$. We are going to verify (1.2), i. e.,

$$\partial_{\bar{z}} fg = f\partial_{\bar{z}} g + g\partial_{\bar{z}} f \tag{2.3}$$

provided that f and $\partial_{\bar{z}} f \in L^1(\bar{G})$, $g \in C_a(\bar{G})$ and $\partial_{\bar{z}} g \in L^p(\bar{G})$.

We have

$$f = F(z) + T_G f_1, \quad g = G(z) + T_G g_1$$

where

$$F(z) \in L^1(\bar{G}) \cap \mathscr{U}_0(G),\ f_1 \in L^1(\bar{G}),\ T_G f_1 \in L^r(\bar{G}), \quad 1 \leqslant r < 2$$
$$G(z) \in C_a(\bar{G}) \cap \mathscr{U}_0(G),\ g_1 \in L^p(\bar{G}),\ T_G g_1 \in L^a(\bar{G})$$

Since

$$fg = FG + GT_G f_1 + FT_G g_1 + T_G f_1 T_G g_1 \tag{2.4}$$

and each of the first three terms on the right-hand side of (2.4) contains at least a factor $\in \cap\, \mathscr{U}_0(G) \cap L^1(\bar{G})$, we need only to prove (2.3) for $f = T_G f_1$ and $g = T_G g_1$, that is, for all $\varphi \in D^0_\infty(G)$ we have, writing T for T_G,

$$\iint_G [(Tf_1 Tg_1)\partial_{\bar{z}}\varphi + (f_1 Tg_1 + g_1 Tf_1)\varphi]\, dxdy = 0 \tag{2.5}$$

Taking a sequence of functions $g_n \in D^0_\infty(G)$ which converges to g_1 according to the norm of $L^p(\bar{G})$, we have

---

① We have $C_a(fg, \bar{G}) \leqslant C_a(f, \bar{G})C(g,\bar{G}) + C(f,\bar{G})C_a(g,\bar{G}) \leqslant 2C_a(f,\bar{G})C_a(g,\bar{G})$.

$$\iint_G [(Tf_1 Tg_n)\partial_{\bar z}\varphi + (f_1 g_n + g_n Tf_1)\varphi]\,dxdy = 0 \tag{2.6}$$

We know that Tg_n tends uniformly to Tg_1 as $n \to \infty$. Also $\varphi Tf_1 \in L^q(\bar G)\left(q = \frac{p}{p-1}\right)$.

Making $n \to \infty$, We obtain(2.5)from(2.6). This proves(1.2).

Evidently (1.3) and (1.4) are true. Also it is evident that $A_0 H \subset B_1$ and that $f = \varphi h$ gives a continuous mapping of H into B_1 if φ is a given function belonging to $A_0 \cap B_1 = \mathscr{U}_0(G) \cap L^1(\bar G)$.

In view of our assumptions on $f(z, w)$ we can apply Theorem 1 to obtain the principle of similarity of the solutions of (2.1). This result contains L. Bers's result[2] on pseudo-analytic functions as a special case.

Now we introduce the new condition that

$$L^p\left(\frac{F(z, w_1) - F(z, w_2)}{w_1 - w_2}, G\right) < \infty, \ p > 2 \tag{2.7}$$

for all $\omega_1, \omega_2 \in L^1(\bar G)$ where $\frac{F(z, w_1) - F(z, w_2)}{w_1 - w_2}$ should be replaced by 0 when $\omega_1 = \omega_2$.

From(2.1)we have

$$w(z) = \Phi(z) + T_G[w(z)f(z, w)] \tag{2.8}$$

where $\Phi \in \mathscr{U}_0(G) \cap L^1(\bar G)$. We are going to prove that for any given function $\Phi(z) \in C(\bar G)$, (2.9) has at most one solution $\in C(\bar G)$.

Without loss of generality we may put $f(z,w) = 0$ if z is outside G. Suppose, on the contrary, that (2.9) has two solutions $w_1, w_2 \in C(\bar G)$, then

$$w_0(z) \equiv w_1(z) - w_2(z) = T_G(F(z, w_1) - F(z, w_2)) \tag{2.9}$$

can be continued continuously by means of (2.10) to the exterior of G_1. On the whole plane, we have

$$\partial_{\bar z} w_0 = F(z, w_1) - F(z, w_2) = w_0 \frac{F(z, w_1) - F(z, w_2)}{w_1 - w_2} \tag{2.10}$$

In view of (2.8) we can prove as in the previous section that for any bounded region $G^* \supset G$, a function $\varphi(z) \in \mathscr{U}_0(G^*)$ can be found such that

$$w_0 = \varphi e^{T_{G^*}F^*} \tag{2.11}$$

where

$$F^* = \frac{F(z, w_1) - F(z, w_2)}{w_1 - w_2}$$

for $w_1 \neq w_2$ and $F^* = 0$ for $w_1 = w_2$. Since $F^* = 0$ if z is outside G, w_0 and

$T_{G*}F^*$ are both analytic outside G. Thus φ can be continued analytically to the whole plane. Since w_1 and w_2 are solutions of (2.9), $w = w_1 - w_2 = 0$ at $z = \infty$. Hence $\varphi(z) = 0$ at $z = \infty$. So it is a constant. This proves that $w_0 = w_1 - w_2 = 0$, *i. e.*, (29) has at most one solution.

It follows that (2.9) defines an operator:

$$w(z) = \Omega\Phi \tag{2.12}$$

This operator, whenever it has any meaning, gives a unique result. In particular, to any solution $w(z)$ which belongs to $C(\bar{G})$ we have from (2.8), assuming that the boundary T of G is a simple smooth curve.

$$\Phi(z) = \frac{2}{2\pi i}\int_c \frac{\omega(\zeta)}{\zeta - z}d\zeta \tag{2.13}$$

In this case (2.12) has a unique solution. Therefore we have the generalized Cauchy formula

$$w(z) = \Omega\frac{1}{2\pi i}\int_c \frac{w(\zeta)}{\zeta - z}d\zeta \tag{2.14}$$

Added in proof. I am informed that Yan Chang-ling has investigated the solutions of eq. (1.1) with constant coefficient λ.

References

[1] Bekya И. Н. 1959 Обобμенные АнаΛитцеские Функццц, Физматтиз.

[2] Bers, L. 1953 Theory *of* Pseudo-analytic Functions, New York.

[3] Bers, L. 1956 *Comm. Pure App. Math.* ,9 ,693-711.

[4] Morrey, C. B. Jr. ,& Nirenberg, L. 1957 Comm, Pure Appl. Math. ,10.

独立自主发展石油地震数字处理①

地震勘探数字处理中的某些数学模型

1. 动校正量的快速计算法

地震反射波时距曲线是一支双曲线

$$t = \sqrt{t_0^2 + \frac{x^2}{v^2}} \tag{1.1}$$

其中 v 是地震波传播速度，x 是炮点与检波点之间的距离，t_0 是回声时间，t 是接收时间.

所谓动校正，就是要把双曲线(1.1) 校成直线 $t = t_0$. 因此，把下面的 Δt 称为动校正量，即

$$\Delta t = t - t_0 = \sqrt{t_0^2 + \frac{x^2}{v^2}} - t_0 \tag{1.2}$$

动校正是石油地震勘探资料处理中最基本最大量的一种处理，因此要大量反复地计算式(1.2). 由于(1.2) 中包含开方运算，这就使得计算时间过长. 为此，我们采用了动校正量的快速计算法，它的原理如下：

把(1.2) 改写为

① 原载：数学学报，18(1975)，4：231-246.

$$\Delta t = t_0\left(\sqrt{1+\frac{x^2}{v^2t_0^2}}-1\right)$$

令

$$\lambda = \frac{x}{vt_0},\ F(\lambda) = \sqrt{1+\lambda^2}-1$$

于是(1.2) 变为

$$\Delta t = t_0 F(\lambda) \tag{1.3}$$

作 $F(\lambda)$ 的数值表,λ 的抽样间隔为 $\Delta\lambda$,它是根据计算精度而确定的,λ 的下限为 0,λ 的上限取为 λ_{max}.

$$\lambda_{max} = \frac{x_{max}}{t_{0min}\cdot v_{min}}$$

把 $F(\lambda)$ 表存入内存,于是动校正量 Δt 的计算只需有两次乘法、一次除法和一次查表即可得到,这样就大大节省了计算时间.

若计算精度要求误差不超过 1 ms,根据地震资料的特点,采取 λ 的抽样间隔 $\Delta\lambda = 2^{-10}$. 可以证明,快速计算法所产生的误差是允许的. 事实上,对一给定的 x,v,t,有 $\lambda = \frac{x}{vt_0}$,动校正量为 $\Delta t = t_0F(\lambda)$,在快速计算法中,λ 由于查表的需要而变为 λ_1,按四舍五入的取法,有 $|\lambda-\lambda_1| \leqslant \frac{1}{2}\Delta\lambda = 2^{-11}$,由快速算法得到的动校正量为 $\widetilde{\Delta t} = t_0F(\lambda_1)$. 现在要估计 Δ 与 $\widetilde{\Delta t}$ 之间的误差. 由微商中值定理可得

$$\Delta t - \widetilde{\Delta t} = t_0[F(\lambda)-F(\lambda_1)] = t_0\frac{\lambda_\mu}{\sqrt{1+\lambda_\mu^2}}(\lambda-\lambda_1)$$

其中 λ_μ 在 λ 与 λ_1 之间. 因此

$$|\lambda_\mu| = |\lambda+\lambda_\mu-\lambda| \leqslant \lambda + |\lambda-\lambda_1|$$

于是

$$\begin{aligned}|\Delta t - \widetilde{\Delta t}| &\leqslant t_0|\lambda_\mu||\lambda-\lambda_1| \leqslant \\ & t_0\lambda|\lambda-\lambda_1| + t_0|\lambda-\lambda_1|^2 \leqslant \\ & \frac{x}{2v}\cdot 2^{-10} + \frac{t_0}{2^{10}}\cdot\frac{1}{4}\cdot 2^{-10}\end{aligned}$$

在一般资料中,x 最大为3 000 m,v 最小为1.5 m/ms,t_0 最大为5 000 ms,因此

$$\frac{x}{2v} \leqslant 1\,000,\ \frac{t_0}{2^{10}} < 5$$

所以

$$|\Delta t - \widetilde{\Delta} t| < \left(1\,000 + \frac{5}{4}\right)2^{-10} < 1$$

这说明,快速算法的精度是完全合乎要求的.

2. 自适应加权叠加

(1) 自适应加权叠加.

设有 n 道记录 $x_1(t), x_2(t), \cdots, x_n(t)$,它们为

$$x_i(t) = s(t) + n_i(t), i = 1, 2, \cdots, n \tag{2.1}$$

其中 $s(t)$ 为信号,$n_i(t)$ 为噪声.

为了去掉噪声、获得信号,通常采用算术平均方法(称为普通水平叠加)即求 $\bar{x}(t)$,

$$\bar{x}(t) = \frac{1}{n}\sum_{i=1}^{n} x_i(t)$$

这种方法对压制噪声,一般来说还是好的. 但是,缺点是没有考虑到信号、噪声之间的强弱关系,因而可采用加权叠加的办法.

记

$$\bar{x}_i(t) = \frac{1}{n = 1}\sum_{\substack{j=1 \\ j \neq i}}^{n} x_j(t)$$

设对第 i 道的权系数为 w_i,取它使下式

$$I = \sum_{t'=t-T/2}^{t+T/2} [w_i x_i(t') - \bar{x}_i(t')]^2 \tag{2.2}$$

达最小.

我们注意,

$$\bar{x}_i(t) = \frac{1}{n-1}\left[\sum_{j=1}^{n} x_j(t) - x_i(t)\right] = \frac{n}{n-1}\bar{x}(t) - \frac{1}{n-1}x_i(t)$$

因此(2.2)可写为

$$\begin{aligned} I &= \sum_{|t'-t| \leqslant T/2}\left[w_i x_i(t') + \frac{1}{n-1}x_i(t') - \frac{n}{n-1}\bar{x}(t')\right]^2 = \\ &\frac{n^2}{(n-1)^2}\sum_{|t'-t| \leqslant T/2}\left[\frac{n-1}{n}\left(w_i + \frac{1}{n-1}\right)x_i(t') - \bar{x}(t')\right]^2 = \\ &\frac{n^2}{(n-1)^2}\sum_{|t'-t| \leqslant T/2}[\beta_i x_i(t') - \bar{x}(t')]^2 \end{aligned} \tag{2.3}$$

其中

$$\beta_i = \frac{n-1}{n}\left(w_i + \frac{1}{n-1}\right) \tag{2.4}$$

由(2.4)可得

$$w_i = \frac{n\beta_i - 1}{n - 1} \tag{2.5}$$

为了使(2.3)达最小,由$\frac{\partial I}{\partial \beta_i} = 0$可得

$$\beta_i = \frac{\gamma_{x_i\bar{x}_j}(T,t)}{\gamma_{ii}(T,t)}, \quad i = 1,2,\cdots,n \tag{2.6}$$

同样由$\frac{\partial I}{\partial w_i} = 0$可得

$$w_i = \frac{\gamma_{x_i\bar{x}_j}(T,t)}{\gamma_{ii}(T,t)}, \quad i = 1,2,\cdots,n \tag{2.7}$$

其中

$$\gamma_{ii}(T,t) = \sum_{|t'-t| \leqslant T/2} x_i(t')x_i(t')$$

$$\gamma_{x_i\bar{x}}(T,t) = \sum_{|t'-t| \leqslant T/2} x_i(t')\bar{x}_i(t')$$

$$\gamma_{x_i\bar{x}j}(T,t) = \sum_{|t'-t| \leqslant T/2} x_i(t')\bar{x}_i(t')$$

用(2.7)求w_i,首先要计算n个$\bar{x}_i(t')$,而用(2.6)求β_i,只要计算1个$\bar{x}(t')$就行了.由此,由(2.6)和(2.5)计算加权系数w_i,要比直接由(2.7)计算w_i方便得多,速度要快得多.

从(2.6)和(2.7)可以看出,当T固定以后,β_i、w_i实际上是t的函数,因此,我们以后把β_i、w_i都写成$\beta_i(t)$和$w_i(t)$.所谓加权叠加就是求

$$\bar{x}(t) = \sum_{i=1}^{n} w_i(t)x_i(t) \tag{2.8}$$

由于权系数$w_i(t)$是随着时间t而变化的,我们就称这种叠加为自适应加权叠加.

(2)对自适应加权叠加的分析

在模型(2.1)中,我们再假定

$$\begin{cases} n_i(t)\text{与}s(t)\text{不相关,即}\gamma_{sn_i}(T,t) = 0 \\ n_i(t)\text{彼此间的相关函数为} \\ \gamma_{n_in_j}(T,t) = \delta(i-j)\gamma_{nn}(T,t)\text{①} \end{cases} \tag{2.9}$$

其中

$$\delta(i) = \begin{cases} 1, i = 0 \\ 0, i \neq 0 \end{cases}$$

在(2.9)的条件下,由(2.6)和(2.7)可得

① 这说明不同道的噪声的相关函数是相同的.

$$\beta_i(t) = \frac{\gamma_{ss}(T,t) + \frac{1}{n}\gamma_{nn}(T,t)}{\gamma_{ss}(T,t) + \gamma_{nn}(T,t)} \tag{2.10}$$

$$w_i(t) = \frac{\gamma_{ss}(T,t)}{\gamma_{ss}(T,t) + \gamma_{nn}(T,t)} \tag{2.11}$$

由(2.11)和(2.8)可得

$$\bar{x}(t) = \frac{\gamma_{ss}(T,t)}{\gamma_{ss}(T,t) + \gamma_{nn}(T,t)} \sum_{i=1}^{n} x_i(t) = n\frac{\gamma_{ss}(T,t)}{\gamma_{ss}(T,t) + \gamma_{nn}(T,t)}\bar{x}(t) \tag{2.12}$$

上式说明了普通水平叠加 $\bar{x}(t)$ 与自适应加权叠加 $\bar{x}(t)$ 在(2.9)条件下的关系.当信号比噪声强时,加权系数(2.11)比较大,可接近于1;当信号比噪声弱时,加权系数(2.11)比较小,可接近于0.这样,自适应加权叠加就起到了增强信号压制噪声干扰的作用.

设信噪比 $q(t) = \gamma_{ss}(T,t)/\gamma_{nn}(T,t)$,当 $q(t_1) > q(t_2)$ 时,则有 $\{w_i(t_1)/w_i(t_2)\} > \{\beta_i(t_1)/\beta_i(t_2)\}$,这说明权系数 $w_i(t)$ 随着信噪比强弱的相对变化比 $\beta_i(t)$ 灵敏,因此通常采用的是 $w_i(t)$.

在应用中,权系数 $w_i(t)$ 可用递推方法求得,当曲线 $w_i(t)$ 不够平滑、变化剧烈时,我们可用平均平滑方法对 $w_i(t)$ 作一加工处理,平均平滑公式为

$$\tilde{w}_i(t) = \frac{1}{T_1 + 1}\sum_{|t-s| \leq T_1} w_i(s)$$

3. 随机时移的消去

设有 N 道地震记录 $x_n(t)$:

$$x_n(t) = S(t + \tau_n), n = 1,2,\cdots,N \tag{3.1}$$

其中 τ_n 为随机时移量,或称他们为剩余校正量.

对 τ_n,可以假定它们是相互独立、相同分布的随机变量,均值为0,概率密度为对称函数,例如在[$-\lambda,\lambda$]上均匀分布,或服从正态分布 $N(0,\sigma)$(见[1]).

按照通常有水平叠加法得到

$$\tilde{x}(t) = \frac{1}{N}\sum_{n=1}^{N} x_n(t) \tag{3.2}$$

我们希望 $\tilde{x}(t)$ 能近似 $s(t)$.但实际情况如何呢?我们从频率域来看.

设 $s(t)$ 的频谱为

$$S(\omega) = | S(\omega) | e^{i\Phi(\omega)} \tag{3.3}$$

(3.2)的频率形式为

$$\tilde{X}(\omega) = | S(\omega) | e^{i\Phi(\omega)} \frac{1}{N}\sum_{n=1}^{N} e^{i\tau_n\omega} \tag{3.4}$$

假定 τ_n 在 $[-\lambda,\lambda]$ 上均匀分布，由概率统计理论知道

$$\frac{1}{N}\sum_{n=1}^{N} e^{i\tau_n\omega} = Ee^{i\tau_n\omega} = \frac{1}{2\lambda}\int_{-\lambda}^{\lambda} e^{i\tau\omega} d\tau = \frac{\sin\lambda\omega}{\lambda\omega} \tag{3.5}$$

从(3.4)知，$\tilde{X}(\omega)$ 与 $S(\omega)$ 相差一个因子 $\frac{1}{N}\sum_{n=1}^{N} e^{i\tau_n\omega}$，这个因子相当于 $\frac{\sin\lambda\omega}{\lambda\omega}$，只有在 $\omega=0$ 时它才为 1. 如何去掉这个因子呢？我们知道：

$$\frac{\frac{1}{N}\sum_{n=1}^{N} e^{i\tau_n\omega}}{\left|\frac{1}{N}\sum_{n=1}^{N} e^{i\tau_n\omega}\right|} = \frac{\frac{\sin\lambda\omega}{\lambda\omega}}{\left|\frac{\sin\lambda\omega}{\lambda\omega}\right|} = \begin{cases} 1, 2m\pi \leqslant |\lambda\omega| \leqslant (2m+1)\pi, m=0,1,\cdots \\ -1, \quad \text{其他} \end{cases}$$

令

$$G(\omega) = \begin{cases} 1, \quad 2m\pi \leqslant |\lambda\omega| \leqslant (2m+1)\pi, \quad m=0,1,\cdots \\ -1, \quad \text{其他} \end{cases}$$

于是有

$$G(\omega)\cdot\frac{\frac{1}{N}\sum_{n=1}^{N} e^{i\tau_n\omega}}{\left|\frac{1}{N}\sum_{n=1}^{N} e^{i\tau_n\omega}\right|} = 1$$

但是，决定 $G(\omega)$ 的参数 λ 很难知道，因此 $G(\omega)$ 并不好求.

现在我们假定 τ_n 服从正态分布 $N(0,\sigma)$，则

$$Ee^{i\tau_n\omega} = \frac{1}{\sqrt{2\pi}\sigma}\int_{-}^{\infty} \infty\, e^{i\tau\omega} e^{-\tau^2/(2\sigma^2)} d\tau = e^{-(\sigma^2/2)\omega} \tag{3.6}$$

这时有

$$\frac{\frac{1}{N}\sum_{n=1}^{N} e^{i\tau_n\omega}}{\left|\frac{1}{N}\sum_{n=1}^{N} e^{i\tau_n\omega}\right|} = \frac{e^{-(\sigma^2/2)\omega}}{e^{-(\sigma^2/2)}\omega} = 1 \tag{3.7}$$

因此，在 τ_n 服从正态分布的假定下，根据式(3.7)，可以去掉因子 $\frac{1}{N}\sum_{n=1}^{N} e^{i\tau_n\omega}$，其步骤如下：

(1) 求 $x_n(t)$ 的振幅谱 $|X_n(\omega)|$ 与 $e^{i\Phi_n(\omega)}$，其中 $\Phi_n(\omega)$ 为 $x_n(t)$ 的相位谱.

由(3.1)知 $x_n(t)$ 的相位谱 $\Phi_n(\omega)=\tau_n\omega+\Phi(\omega)$. 我们之所以求 $e^{i\Phi_n(\omega)}$ 而不先求相位谱 $\Phi_n(\omega)$，原因是在计算上求 $e^{i\Phi_n(\omega)}$ 较容易，而求 $\Phi_n(\omega)$ 要用反三角函数，工作量大，精度还难保证.

(2) 把 $e^{i\Phi_n(\omega)}$ 叠加得

$$F(\omega) = \sum_{n=1}^{N} e^{i\Phi_n(\omega)} = e^{i\Phi(\omega)} \sum_{n=1}^{n} e^{i\tau_n\omega}$$

(3) 取 $F(\omega)$ 的模 $|F(\omega)|$:

$$|F(\omega)| = \left|\sum_{n=1}^{N} e^{i\tau_n\omega}\right|$$

(4) 对 $F(\omega)$ 规一化,即

$$\frac{F(\omega)}{|F(\omega)|} = e^{i\Phi(\omega)} \frac{\sum_{n=1}^{N} e^{i\tau_n\omega}}{\left|\sum_{n=1}^{N} e^{i\tau_n\omega}\right|} = e^{i\Phi(\omega)}$$

这样就得到 $e^{i\Phi(\omega)}$,而消除了随机时移 τ_n 的影响.

当然,每一道 $x_n(t)$ 的振幅谱 $|X_n(\omega)|$ 与信号振幅谱 $|S(\omega)|$ 并不完全一致,为了得到 $|S(\omega)|$,我们采用几何平均法:

$$|\tilde{S}(\omega)| = \sqrt[n]{|X_1(\omega)||X_2(\omega)|\cdots|X_N(\omega)|}$$

用 $|\tilde{S}(\omega)|$ 代替 $|S(\omega)|$,这样,由 $|\tilde{S}(\omega)|\dfrac{F(\omega)}{|F(\omega)|}$ 再经富氏反变换,就可得到我们所需的输出记录.

4. 零相位递归滤波

递归滤波可以提高计算速度,在数字滤波中已得广泛应用.

如果已知滤液器的滤波因子 h_t 或频率响应 $H(\omega) = \sum_t h_t e^{-it\omega}$,如何找一个递归滤波与 h_t 或 $H(\omega)$ 很接近,这就是递归滤波的设计问题. 当 $h_t = (h_0, h_1, h_2, \cdots)$ 时,递归滤波的设计问题已有讨论(见[2]).

现在我们按照最小能量标准进行零相位递归滤波的设计. 由于能量既可以用频谱表示也可以用时间函数表示,因此这种设计在时间域和在频率域中是一致的.

(1) 零相位递归滤波的设计问题.

已知滤波器的频谱 $H(\omega)$ 是零相位的,即 $H(\omega) \geqslant 0$,相应 $H(\omega)$ 的时间函数 h_t 则具有对称性:$h_t = h_{-t}$.

要设计 $a_0, a_1, \cdots, a_n$ 和 $b_1, b_2, \cdots, b_m$ 使

$$\frac{\left|\sum_{l=0}^{n} a_l e^{-ilw}\right|^2}{\left|1 + \sum_{l=1}^{m} b_l e^{-il\omega}\right|^2} = \frac{\sum_{l=-n}^{n} a_l e^{-ilw}}{\sum_{l=-m}^{m} \beta_l e^{-il\omega}} \tag{4.1}$$

与 $H(\omega) = \sum_{l=-\infty}^{\infty} h_l e^{-il\omega}$ 很接近,其中 α_l、β_l 分别为 a_l、b_l 的相关函数. 为了使

递归滤波具有稳定性,还要求多项式 $1+\sum_{l=1}^{m} b_l z^l$ 在单位圆内和圆上都无根.

(2) 最小能量标准.

在(4.1) 的分母中,我们不妨设 $\beta_0=1$,这因为:$\beta_0=1+\sum_{l=1}^{m} b_l^2>0$,把(4.1) 的分子、分母同除 β_0,则新的分母系数为 $\beta'_l=\dfrac{\beta_1}{\beta_0}$,这时总有 $\beta'_0=1$.

按照设计问题,我们要求

$$\frac{\sum_{l=-n}^{n} a_l e^{-il\omega}}{\sum_{t=-m}^{m} \beta_l e^{-il\omega}} \approx \sum_{l=-\infty}^{\infty} h_l e^{-il\omega} \tag{4.2}$$

由此可导出近似式

$$\sum_{l=-n}^{n} \alpha_l e^{-il\omega} \approx \sum_{l=-m}^{m} \beta_l e^{-il\omega} \sum_{l=-\infty}^{\infty} h_l e^{-il\omega} = \sum_{l=-\infty}^{\infty} f_l e^{-il\omega} \tag{4.3}$$

其中

$$f_l=\sum_{j=-m}^{m} \beta_j h_{l-j}=h_l+\sum_{j=1}^{m} \beta_j (h_{l-j}+h_{l+j}) \tag{4.4}$$

由于 $h_l=h_{-l}$,$\beta_l=\beta_{-l}$,可知 $f_l=f_{-l}$.

(4.3) 是近似式,我们用能量标准衡量其近似程度,能量 Q 为

$$Q=\frac{1}{2\pi}\int_{-x}^{x}\left|\sum_{l=-n}^{m} \alpha_l e^{-il\omega}-\sum_{l=-\infty}^{\infty} f_l e^{-il\omega}\right|^2 d\omega=\sum_{l=-n}^{n}(\alpha_l-f_l)^2+2\sum_{l=n+1}^{\infty} f_l^2=$$

$$\left[(\alpha_0-f_0)^2+2\sum_{l=1}^{n}(\alpha_l-f_l)^2\right]+2\sum_{l=n+1}^{\infty} f_l^2 \tag{4.5}$$

所谓最小能量标准,就是求 $\alpha_0,\alpha_1,\cdots,\alpha_n$ 和 $\beta_1,\beta_2,\cdots,\beta_m$ 使 Q 达最小.

在(4.5) 中,我们总可以取 $\alpha_l=f_l$,其中 $0\leqslant l\leqslant n$,这时,式(4.5) 的第一部分为0,使 Q 达最小的问题就变为求 $\beta_1,\beta_2,\cdots,\beta_m$ 使

$$Q_1=\sum_{l=n+1}^{\infty} f_l^2 \tag{4.6}$$

达最小.

(3) 求 $\beta_1,\beta_2,\cdots,\beta_m$.

根据(4.4) 和(4.6),由 $\dfrac{\partial Q_1}{\partial \beta_j}=0$,$j=1,2,\cdots,m$,得

$$\sum_{k=1}^{m} \beta_k\left[\sum_{l=n+1}^{\infty}(h_{l-k}+h_{l+k})(h_{l-j}+h_{l+j})\right]=$$

$$-\sum_{l=n+1}^{\infty} h_l(h_{l-j}+h_{l+j}),\quad j=1,2,\cdots,m \tag{4.7}$$

解(4.7) 即可得 $\beta_1, \beta_2, \cdots, \beta_m$.

(4) 求 $b_1, b_2, \cdots, b_m$.

从相关函数 $1, \beta_1, \cdots, \beta_m$ 出发,用多项式求根的方法就可以找出 $b_1, b_2, \cdots, b_m$,其步骤如下:

求多项式

$$z^m \sum_{k=-m}^{m} \beta_k z^h = \beta_{-m} + \beta_{-m+1} z + \cdots + z + \beta_1 z + \cdots + \beta_m z^{2m}$$

的根,把绝对值大于1的根取出来,记为 $z_1, z_2, \cdots, z_m$,造多项式

$$B(z) = \frac{1}{(-1)^m z_1 z_2 \cdots z_m}(z - z_1)(z - z_2)\cdots(z - z_m)$$

这个多项式 $z, z^2, \cdots, z^m$ 前的系数就是我们要求的 $b_1, b_2, \cdots, b_m$.

由于多项式 $B(z)$ 的根在单位圆外,递归滤波的稳定性是得到保证的.

(5) 求 $\alpha_0, \alpha_1, \cdots, \alpha_n$.

在求得 $b_1, b_2, \cdots, b_m$ 之后,我们要求 $\alpha_0, \alpha_1, \cdots, \alpha_n$. 因为我们需要的近似式是(4.2) 而不是(4.3)(式(4.3) 的作用仅在于求 $\beta_1, \beta_2, \cdots, \beta_m$,进而求 $b_1, b_2, \cdots, b_m$),所以我们必须回过头来再从(4.2) 出发求 $\alpha_0, \alpha_1, \cdots, \alpha_n$. 式(4.2) 就是

$$\frac{\sum_{l=-n}^{n} \alpha_l e^{-il\omega}}{\left|1 + \sum_{l=1}^{m} b_l e^{-il\omega}\right|^2} \approx \sum_{l=-\infty}^{\infty} h_l e^{-il\omega}$$

求 $\alpha_0, \alpha_1, \cdots, \alpha_n$ 的步骤如下:

(i) 求 c_l 使 $\dfrac{1}{1 + b_1 e^{-i\omega} + \cdots + b_m e^{-im\omega}} = \sum_{l=0}^{\infty} c_l e^{-il\omega}$.

可用递推公式求 c_l:

$$c_0 = 1$$

$$c_l = \begin{cases} -\sum_{j=0}^{l-1} c_j b_{l-j}, & 1 \leqslant l \leqslant m \\ -\sum_{j=l-m}^{l-1} c_j b_{l-j}, & l > m \end{cases}$$

(ii) 求 g_l 使 $\dfrac{1}{|1 + b_1 e^{-i\omega} + \cdots + b_m e^{-im\omega}|^2} = \sum_{l=-\infty}^{\infty} g_l e^{-il\omega}$.

g_l 实际上就是 c_l 的自相关函数,因此

$$g_l = \sum_{\tau=0}^{\infty} c_\tau + l c_\tau$$

由于自相关函数的对称性($g_l = g_{-l}$),只要计算 $g_0, g_1, g_2, \cdots$ 就行了.

(iii) 求 $\alpha_0,\alpha_1,\cdots,\alpha_n$.

由于

$$\frac{\sum_{l=-n}^{n}\alpha_l e^{-il\omega}}{\left|1+\sum_{l=1}^{m}b_l e^{-il\omega}\right|} = \sum_{l=-n}^{n}\alpha_l e^{-il\omega}\sum_{l=-\infty}^{\infty}g_l e^{-il\omega} = \sum_{l=-\infty}^{\infty}p_l e^{-il\omega}$$

其中

$$p_l = \sum_{k=-n}^{n}\alpha_k g_{l-k} = \alpha_0 g_l + \sum_{k=1}^{n}\alpha_k(g_{l-k}+g_{l+k}) \tag{4.8}$$

因此,衡量(4.2) 近似程度的能量标准是

$$Q_2 = \frac{1}{2\pi}\int_{-\pi}^{\pi}\left|\sum_{l=-\infty}^{\infty}p_l e^{-il\omega} - \sum_{l=-\infty}^{\infty}h_l e^{-il\omega}\right|^2 d\omega = \sum_{l=-\infty}^{\infty}(p_l-h_l)^2 \tag{4.9}$$

根据(4.8)、(4.9),由 $\frac{\partial Q_2}{\partial\alpha_j}=0, j=0,1,\cdots,n$,可得

$$\begin{aligned}&\gamma_{gg}(j)\alpha_0 + \sum_{k=1}^{n}\alpha_k[\gamma_{gg}(k-j)+\gamma_{gg}(k+j)] = \\ &\frac{1}{2}[\gamma_{hg}(j)+\gamma_{hg}(-j)], j=0,1,\cdots,n\end{aligned} \tag{4.10}$$

其中

$$\gamma_{gg}(\tau) = \sum_{l=-\infty}^{\infty}g_{\tau+l}g_l$$

$$\gamma_{hg}(\tau) = \sum_{l=-\infty}^{\infty}h_{\tau+l}g_l$$

解(4.10) 即可得 $\alpha_0,\alpha_1,\cdots,\alpha_n$. 由于在滤波过程中,用 $a_0,a_1,\cdots,a_n$ 比用 $\alpha_0,\alpha_1,\cdots,\alpha_n$ 更节省时间,所以我们不再从 $\alpha_0,\alpha_1,\cdots,\alpha_n$ 出发求 $a_0,a_1,\cdots,a_n$.

(6) 零相位递归滤波公式.

现在我们用递归滤波

$$\frac{\sum_{l=-n}^{n}\alpha_l e^{-il\omega}}{\left|1+\sum_{l=1}^{m}b_l e^{-il\omega}\right|^2}$$

代替 $H_{(\omega)} = \sum_{l=-\infty}^{\infty}h_l e^{-il\omega}$. 设输入记录为 x_t,输出记录为 y_t,递归滤波方式为:

先做正向递归滤波得 u_t

$$u_t = \alpha_0 x_t + \sum_{l=1}^{n}\alpha_l(x_{t-l}+x_{t+l}) - \sum_{l=1}^{m}b_l u_{t-l}$$

其中 $t=0,1,2,\cdots,T$;

再做反向递归滤波得 y_t

$$y_t = u_t - \sum_{l=1}^{m} b_l y_{t+l}$$

其中 $t = T, T-1, T-2, \cdots, 1, 0$.

关于递归滤波方式的原理参看[2].

综上所述,零相位递归滤波的设计,步骤比较多,但是可以由程序自动完成,同时由于 n, m 一般不大,如取 2,3,4,5,因此计算的速度可以是很快的.

最后我们指出,[4] 也讨论了零相位递归滤波的设计问题,但是它的出发点是不妥当的. 它把一个对称函数的频谱 $\sum_{l=-L}^{L} f_l e^{-il\omega} = f_0 + 2\sum_{l=1}^{L} f_l \cos l\omega$ 转换成 $\cos\omega$ 的多项式 $\sum_{l=0}^{L} p_l \cos^l \omega$(因为 $\cos l\omega$ 可表为 $\cos\omega$ 的 l 次多项式),要使两个对称函数的频谱近似,就让其 $\cos^l\omega$ 前的系数近似,在此基础上再应用最小二乘求所要的未知数. 这种做法的问题是:要进行十分繁琐的转换工作,且当 L 为 $+\infty$ 时这种转换实际上是不可能的(因为 $\cos^l\omega$ 前的系数 p_l 依赖于所有的 f_l,是 f_l 的加权求和级数,而收敛性是不保证的),当 L 很大时,由计算带来的误差十分大,同时引起系数 p_l 强烈摆动,最为重要的是,这种做法失去了函数逼近的确切含义,既不是一致逼近,也不是最小平方逼近或者其他一定意义上的逼近,仅仅是一种形式做法. 因此,[4] 的方法是不可取的.

5. 反滤波

反滤波是具有地震勘探数字处理特色的一种滤波,它的主要目的是压缩波形,以起到提高地下反射层的分辨率和压制某些规则干扰(如海水多次反射波)的作用. 现在我们讨论一般反滤波、波形切除反滤波和解反滤波方程的白噪化三个问题.

(1) 一般反滤波.

一般反滤波的数学问题是:已知波 b_t 是物理可实现、能量有限的序列(物理可实现是指:当 $t < 0$ 时,$b_t = 0$;能量有限是指:$\sum_{t=-\infty}^{\infty} b_t^2 = \sum_{t=0}^{\infty} b_t^2 < +\infty$),要求反波 a_t 使

$$b_t * a_t = \delta_t$$

其中 * 表示褶积,即

$$b_t * a_t = \sum_{s=0}^{\infty} b_s a_{t-s}, \delta_t = \begin{cases} 1, & t = 0 \\ 0, & t \neq 0 \end{cases}$$

上式转换成频率域则有

$$B(\omega)A(\omega) = 1 \text{ 或 } A(\omega) = \frac{1}{B(\omega)}$$

其中$B(\omega)$,$A(\omega)$分别是b_t,a_t的频谱($B(\omega)=\sum_t b_t e^{-it\omega}$,$A(\omega)=\sum_t a_t e^{-it\omega}$).

反波α_t的性质完全由波b_t的性质确定:当b_t是最小延迟时(直观上表现为能量集中在波的前面),对于$t<0$有$a_t=0$;当b_t是最大延迟时(能量集中在波的后面),对于$t>0$有$a_t=0$;当b_t是混合延尺时(能量集中在波的中间),则当t从$-\infty$变到$+\infty$时a_t都有值(参见[2]).

但是在实际处理中,我们只能取a_t的有限项. 至于取哪些项,对滤波效果是十分重要的. 根据上面分析,a_t有限项的取法如下:当b_t是最小延迟时,取$a_t=(a_0,a_1,\cdots,a_n)$①;当b_t是混合延迟时,取$a_t=(a_{-m},a_{-m+1},\cdots,a_0,\cdots,a_n)$;当$b_t$是最大延迟时,取$a_t=(a_{-n},a_{-n+1},\cdots,a_0)$,其中$m,n$皆为大于0的整数.

当取$a_t=(a_{-m},\cdots,a_0,\cdots,a_n)$时,我们希望这些$a_j$使

$$Q=\sum_j\left(\sum_{s=-m}^{n}a_s b_{t-s}-\delta_t\right)^2$$

达最小. 由$\frac{\partial Q}{\partial a_j}=0$, $-m\leqslant j\leqslant n$,可得方程

$$\begin{pmatrix}\gamma_{bb}(0) & \gamma_{bb}(1) & \cdots & \gamma_{bb}(n+m)\\ \gamma_{bb}(1) & \gamma_{bb}(0) & \cdots & \gamma_{bb}(n+m-1)\\ \vdots & \vdots & & \vdots\\ \gamma_{bb}(n+m) & \gamma_{bb}(n+m-1) & \cdots & \gamma_{bb}(0)\end{pmatrix}\begin{pmatrix}a_{-m}\\ a_{-m+1}\\ \vdots\\ a_n\end{pmatrix}=\begin{pmatrix}b_m\\ b_{m-1}\\ \vdots\\ b_{-n}\end{pmatrix}\tag{5.1}$$

其中$\gamma_{bb}(j)=\sum_{i=0}^{\infty}b_{i+j}b_t$,它是波$b_t$的自相关函数.

当波b_t是混合延迟时,通过解(5.1),可得到有限长度反波$a_t=(a_{-m},\cdots,a_0,\cdots,a_n)$, 当波$b_t$是最小延迟时, 取$m=0$, 方程(5.1)右端为$(b_0,b_{-1},\cdots,b_{-n})=(b_0,0,\cdots,0)$,这时解方程(5.1)可得到有限长度反波$a_t=(a_0,a_1,\cdots,a_n)$.

对于混合延迟的波b_t,还可用另外的方法求其反波. 这时b_t可表为$b_t=g_t*\tilde{b}_t$,其中g_t为纯相位序列,$\tilde{b}_t$为最小延迟的,且$\gamma_{bb}(j)=\gamma_{\tilde{b}\tilde{b}}(j)$(见[3]). 对纯相位序列$g_t$,有$g_{-t}*g_t=\delta_t$(见[2]). 因此,若$\tilde{b}_t$的反波为$\tilde{a}_t$,则$b_t$的反波$a_t=g_{-t}*\tilde{a}_t$. 然而$b_t*\tilde{a}_t=g_t*\tilde{b}_t*\tilde{a}_t=g_t$,所以$a_t=b_{-t}*\tilde{a}_{-t}*\tilde{a}_t$. 有限长度反波$\tilde{a}_t=(\tilde{a}_0,\cdots,\tilde{a}_n)$可以通过解方程(5.1)(此时$m=0$)得到,于是可得$b_t$的近似反波$a_t$.

应用以上方法,我们解决了蒸汽轮反褶积问题. 由于蒸汽在海水中膨胀和

---

① 意即$a_t=\begin{cases}a_t, & 0\leqslant t\leqslant n,\\ 0, & 其他.\end{cases}$

冷缩,使得蒸汽轮子波 b_t 是混合延迟的波. 为了取好求反波 a_t 中的参数 m 和 n,我们首先将 m 和 n 都取得比较大,解(5.1)得 $\hat{a}_t = (\hat{a}_{-m}, \hat{a}_{-m+1}, \cdots, \hat{a}_{n-1}, \hat{a}_n)$. 由于 m,n 过大,作反褶积的计算量就大,在实际上也无必要,因此根据 $\hat{a}_t$ 的波形,把两端振幅值小的部分截掉,余下 $(-m_0, -m_0+1, \cdots, n_0-1, n_0)$ 位置上的值,其中 $0 < m_0 < m$, $0 < n_0 < n$. 根据这两个参数 m_0、n_0,再解(5.1),得 $a_t = (a_{-m_0}, \cdots, a_0, \cdots, a_{-n_0})$,这就是要求的实用的反波. 关于求反波中的参数 m 和 n,在实践中都可以根据这种方法确定.

(2) 波形切除反滤波.

波形切除反滤波的数学问题是:

已知 $u_t = (u_0, u_1, \cdots, u_\tau, u_{\tau+1}, \cdots)$ 为能量有限的最小延迟序列,令

$$z_t = \begin{cases} u_t, & 0 \leqslant t \leqslant \tau \\ 0, & \text{其他} \end{cases}$$

求 f_t 使

$$f_t * u_t = z_t \tag{5.2}$$

把(5.2)转换为频谱关系则有

$$F(\omega)U(\omega) = Z(\omega) \text{ 或 } F(\omega) = Z(\omega)/U(\omega)$$

由于

$$Z(\omega) = \sum_{t=0}^{\tau} u_t e^{-it\omega} = \sum_{t=0}^{\infty} u_t e^{-it\omega} - \sum_{t=\tau+1}^{\infty} u_t e^{-it\omega}$$

所以

$$F(\omega) = 1 - \sum_{t=\tau+1}^{\infty} u_t e^{-it\omega} \cdot \frac{1}{U(\omega)}$$

因为 u_t 是最小延迟的,所以它的反波 q_t 是物理可实现的,即当 $t<0$ 时 $q_t = 0$(见[2]).

因此有

$$\frac{1}{U(\omega)} = \sum_{t=0}^{\infty} q_t e^{-it\omega}$$

进而有

$$\sum_{t=\tau+1}^{\infty} u_t e^{-it\omega} \cdot \frac{1}{U(\omega)} = \sum_{t=\tau+1}^{\infty} p_t e^{-it\omega}$$

所以

$$F(\omega) = 1 - \sum_{t=\tau+1}^{\infty} p_t e^{-it\omega}$$

上式说明,满足(5.2)的 f_t 其形式为

$$f_t = (f_0, f_1, \cdots, f_\tau, f_{\tau+1}, f_{\tau+2}, \cdots) = (1, 0, \cdots, 0, -p_{\tau+1}, -p_{\tau+2}, \cdots)$$

在实际应用中，只能取 f_t 的有限项

$$\tilde{f}_t = (1,0,\cdots,0,-p_{\tau+1},-p_{\tau+2},\cdots,-p_{\tau+n}) \tag{5.3}$$

选取的 $\tilde{f}_t$ 要使

$$Q = \sum_t [\tilde{f}_t * u_t - z_t]^2$$

达最小. 由 $\frac{\partial Q}{\partial p_{\tau+j}} = 0, j = 1,2,\cdots,n$, 得

$$\begin{pmatrix} \gamma_{uu}(0) & \cdots & \gamma_{uu}(n-1) \\ \gamma_{uu}(1) & \cdots & \gamma_{uu}(n-2) \\ \vdots & & \vdots \\ \gamma_{uu}(n-1) & \cdots & \gamma_{uu}(0) \end{pmatrix} \begin{pmatrix} p_{\tau+1} \\ p_{\tau+2} \\ \vdots \\ p_{\tau+n} \end{pmatrix} = \begin{pmatrix} \gamma_{uu}(\tau+1) \\ \gamma_{uu}(\tau+2) \\ \vdots \\ \gamma_{uu}(\tau+n) \end{pmatrix} \tag{5.4}$$

我们称(5.4) 为波形切除反滤波方程.

当 u_t 为最小延迟时，由满足(5.4) 的 $p_{\tau+1}$ 组成的 $\tilde{f}_t$，使 $\tilde{f}_t * u_t = z_t$.

当 u_t 不是最小延迟时，$u_t = g_t * \hat{u}_t$，其中 g_t 为纯相位序列，$\hat{u}_t$ 为最小延迟序列，且 $\gamma_{uu}(j) = \gamma_{\hat{u}\hat{u}}(j)$，因此，由满足(5.4) 的 $p_{\tau+j}$ 组成的 $\tilde{f}_t$(见(5.3)) 使

$$\tilde{f}_t * u_t = g_t * \hat{z}_t \tag{5.5}$$

其中 $\hat{z}_t = \begin{cases} \hat{u}_t, & 0 \leqslant t \leqslant \tau \\ 0, & \text{其他} \end{cases}$

波形切除反滤波在地震勘探中主要用于消除某些规则干扰(多次波). 这时的地震记录 x_t 的模型为

$$x_t = b_t * c_t * \xi_t \tag{5.6}$$

其中 b_t 为地震子波；ξ_t 为白噪声($E\xi_t = 0, E\xi_t\xi_s = \delta(t-s)$)；$c_t$ 为多次波，具有最小延迟性质，且形式为

$$c_t = \begin{cases} 1, & t = 0 \\ c_{m\alpha}, & t = m\alpha, \quad m = 1,2,\cdots \\ 0, & \text{其他} \end{cases}$$

其中 α 为一正整数.

令 $u_t = b_t * c_t$，于是有

$$u_t = \sum_{s=0}^{\infty} c_s b_{t-s} = \sum_{m=0}^{\infty} c_{m\alpha} b_{t-m\alpha} = \begin{cases} b_t, & 0 \leqslant t \leqslant \alpha - 1 \\ b_t + c_\alpha b_{t-\alpha} + \cdots, & \alpha \leqslant t \end{cases}$$

由此可看出，当 $0 \leqslant t \leqslant \alpha - 1$ 时，u_t 与子波 b_t 是一致的，当 $t \geqslant \alpha$ 时，u_t 的值受到多次波的影响. 为了消除这种影响，一种方法是通过滤波保留 u_t 在 $0 \leqslant t \leqslant$

$\alpha-1$ 的部分,而使 $t \geqslant \alpha$ 的部分为0,这就是前面讨论的波形切除反滤波,其中参数 τ 一般取为 $\alpha-1$. 若地震子波 b_t 为有限长度序列,即 $b_t=(b_0,b_1,\cdots,b_l)$,且 $l<\alpha$,则参数 τ 的选取可使之满足 $l \leqslant \tau \leqslant \alpha-1$,因为这时对每一个 τ 所作的 z_t 都是相同的.

因为 $b_t=g_t * \hat{b}_t$,其中 g_t 为纯相位序列,$\hat{b}_t$ 为最小延迟序列,于是 $u_t=b_t * c_t=g_t * \hat{u}_t$,其中 $\hat{u}_t=\hat{b}_t * c_t$ 为最小延迟序列,对于满足 $\tau \leqslant a-1$ 的 τ,有

$$\hat{z}_t=\begin{cases}\hat{u}_t, & 0 \leqslant t \leqslant \tau \\ 0, & \text{其他}\end{cases}=\begin{cases}\hat{b}_t & 0 \leqslant t \leqslant \tau \\ 0, & \text{其他}\end{cases}$$

因此,按照(5.5)有

$$\tilde{f}_t * u_t=g_t * \hat{z}_t=\sum_{s=0}^{\tau} \hat{b}_s g_{t-s} \tag{5.7}$$

这就是对地震记录中的 $u_t=b_t * c_t$ 进行波形切除反滤波后的结果. 从(5.7)可以看出,当 b_t 为有限长度且 $l<a$ 时,由于 $\tau \geqslant 1$,滤波结果为 $\tilde{f}_t * u_t=b_t$,这表示完全消除了多次波 c_t 的影响;当 b_t 为最小延迟时,$g_t=\delta_t$,$\hat{b}_t=b_t$,滤波结果为

$$\tilde{f}_t * u_t \doteq \hat{z}_t=\begin{cases}b_t, & 0 \leqslant t \leqslant \tau \\ 0, & \text{其他}\end{cases}$$

这相当于对子波 b_t 作了切除;当 b_t 不是最小延迟时,滤波结果为

$$\tilde{f}_t * u_t=\sum_{s=0}^{\tau} \hat{b}_s g_{t-s}=\begin{cases}b_t, & 0 \leqslant t \leqslant \tau \\ b_t-\sum\limits_{s=r+1}^{\tau} \hat{b}_s g_{t-s}, & t>\tau\end{cases}$$

这表明保留了子波 b_t 在 $0 \leqslant t \leqslant \tau$ 的部分,而对以后的部分作了修改,但一般说来,这个修改量是不大的. 综上所述,波形切除反褶积对于消除某些多次波是行之有效的,实践也证明了这一点.

现在说明,在应用中,(5.3)中参数 n 的选取原则. 因为 $u_t=b_t * c_t$,所以 n 的选取既与 b_t 有关,又与 c_t 有关. 但是,$\tilde{f}_t$ 的主要目的是消除 c_t 的影响,而完全消除 c_t 影响的是 c_t 的反波 d_t(由于

$$D(\omega)=\frac{1}{C(\omega)}=\frac{1}{\sum\limits_{m=0}^{\infty} c_{m\alpha} \mathrm{e}^{-\mathrm{i}m\alpha\omega}}=\sum_{m=0}^{\infty} d_{m\alpha} \mathrm{e}^{-\mathrm{i}m\alpha\omega}$$

所以 d_t 的形式为

$$d_t=\begin{cases}1, & t=0, \\ d_{m\alpha}, & t=m\alpha, \quad m=1,2,\cdots \\ 0, & \text{其他}\end{cases}$$

即 d_t 是以 α 为间隔取值的)，因此，n 的选取要使得在 $t>\tau+n$ 时 d_t 的值极其微小. 以海上二次鸣震为例，这时 $C(\omega)=\frac{1}{(1+\lambda e^{-i\alpha\omega})^2}$，因此 $D(\omega)=(1+\lambda e^{-l\alpha\omega})^2=1+2\lambda e^{-i\alpha\omega}+\lambda^2 e^{-i2\alpha\omega}$，$d_t$ 为

$$d_t=\begin{cases}1, & t=0\\ 2\lambda, & t=\alpha\\ \lambda^2, & t=2\alpha\\ 0, & \text{其他}\end{cases}$$

所以选 $\tau+n\geqslant 2\alpha$ 就行了，因为 $t>\tau+n$ 时 $d_t=0$. 在这种情况下，当 b_t 为有限长度且 $l<\alpha$，取 τ 在 $l\leqslant\tau\leqslant\alpha-1$ 之间. 这时有 $d_t*u_t=b_t=\sum_{s=0}^{\tau}\hat{b}_s g_{t-s}$，与(5.7) 比较，并注意到 $\tilde{f}_t$ 是由最小平方原则求出，因此 $\tilde{f}_t=d_t$，同时(5.7) 为等式而不是近似式.

在应用中，$u_t=b_t*c_t$ 往往并不知道，但在(5.6) 的模型下，有 $\gamma_{xx}(t)=\gamma_{uu}(t)$，其中 $\gamma_{xx}(t)=Ex(t+s)x(s)$，$\gamma_{uu}(t)=\sum_s u(t+s)u(s)$，这样，就可由(5.4) 求由 $\tilde{f}_t$，以进行波形切除反褶积.

我们指出，这里讨论的波形切除反褶积和通常所谓的预测反褶积是一致的. 但后者仅局限在正则平稳序列预测分解定理的基础之上，而现在的分析，撇开了平稳过程的理论，完全从波形本身出发讨论，这样就更直观，而且分析更为深入细致，如对非最小延迟时的分析，对参数 τ 与 n 的分析.

(3) 解反滤波方程的白噪化.

在以上讨论中，都要遇到解类似于(5.1) 的方程. 但是直接解(5.1)，效果往往不好，甚至非常糟，这是指解出的 $a_t=(a_{-m},\cdots,a_0,\cdots,a_n)$ 自始至终振幅值摆动剧烈，同时滤波结果 b_t*a_t 与 δ_t 相差太远. 在理论上说，只要 $b_t\neq 0$，方程(5.1) 左端的系数矩阵总是正定的. 发生以上情况的原因何在呢?我们以(5.1) 来分析，当 $n,m\to+\infty$ 时，(5.1) 就变为

$$\gamma_{bb}(t)*a_t=b_{-t}$$

化为频率域则有

$$R_{bb}(\omega)A(\omega)=\overline{B(\omega)}$$

即

$$A(\omega)=\frac{\overline{B(\omega)}}{R_{bb}(\omega)} \tag{5.8}$$

其中 $R_{bb}(\omega)=|B(\omega)|^2$.

当 $|B(\omega)|$ 有 0 点或接近于 0 的点时，$A(\omega)$ 就不存在或异常，因此 a_t 就不存在或不稳定(即衰减很慢). 这就是发生以上情况的内因.

补救的办法就是:把(5.1)左边的 $\gamma_{bb}(t)$ 变为 $\tilde{\gamma}_{bb}(t)$:

$$\tilde{\gamma}_{bb}(t) = \gamma_{bb}(t) + \gamma_{nn}(t)$$

其中

$$\gamma_{nn}(t) = \begin{cases} \alpha, & t = 0 \\ 0, & t \neq 0 \end{cases}$$

通常取 a 在 0 到 $0.2\gamma_{bb}(0)$ 之间.

由于 $\gamma_{nn}(t)$ 是白噪的相关函数,因此上述做法就称为白噪化.

$\tilde{\gamma}_{bb}(t)$ 可写为

$$\tilde{\gamma}_{bb}(t) = \begin{cases} \gamma_{bb}(0) + \alpha, & t = 0 \\ \gamma_{bb}(t), & t \neq 0 \end{cases}$$

$\tilde{\gamma}_{bb}(t)$ 相应的频谱为 $R_{bb}(\omega) + \alpha$. 按照(5.8),白噪化以后所得到的反波 α'_t 的频谱就为

$$A'(\omega) = \frac{\overline{B(\omega)}}{R_{bb}(\omega) + \alpha} = \frac{\overline{B(\omega)}}{|B(\omega)|^2 + \alpha}.$$

由于上式的分母总 $\geqslant \alpha > 0$,因此 a'_t 就稳定,即 a'_t 的值衰减较快.

用这样的 a'_t 作反褶积,效果如何呢?是相当好的,因为

$$Q = \sum_t (b_t * a'_t - \delta_t)^2 = \frac{1}{2\pi}\int_{-\pi}^{\pi} |B(\omega)A'(\omega) - 1|^2 \mathrm{d}\omega =$$

$$\frac{1}{2\pi}\int_{-\pi}^{\pi}\left[\frac{\alpha}{|B(\omega)|^2 + \alpha}\right]^2 \mathrm{d}\omega$$

而

$$\frac{\alpha}{|B(\omega)|^2 + \alpha} = 1 - \frac{|B(\omega)|^2}{|B(\omega)|^2 + \alpha}$$

当 $|B(\omega)| \neq 0$ 时,随着 α 单调下降逐向 0,$\dfrac{\alpha}{|B(\omega)|^2 + \alpha}$ 也单调下降逐向 0,而当 $b_t \neq 0$ 且为能量有限的物理可实现序列时,$|B(\omega)| \neq 0$ 是几乎处处成立的,因此当 $\alpha \to 0$ 时 $Q \to 0$. 这就是说,我们可以选取一个适当的 α,既使得 α'_t 稳定,又使得 Q 值较小. 由 a'_t 稳定,就可以取有限长度的 $\tilde{a}'_t = (a'_{-m}, \cdots, a'_0, \cdots, a'_n)$ 很好近似 a'_t,因此,经过白噪化(即把 $\gamma_{aa}(t)$ 换成 $\tilde{\gamma}_{bb}(t)$)后,再解(5.1),就可以得到较好的反波 $\tilde{a}'_t$ 和较好的滤波效果. 大量实际的例子也证实了这一点.

(待续)

参考书目

[1] 燃料化学工业部石油地球物理勘探局计算中心站,北京大学数学力学系等编. 地震勘探数字技术,第一册[M]. 北京:科学出版社,1973 年.

[2] 燃料化学工业部石油地球物理勘探局计算中心站,北京大学数学力学系等编. 地震勘探数字技术,第二册[M]. 北京:科学出版社,1974 年.
[3] 舒立华. 纯相位序列的能量传递性质[M]. 数学学报,1974,(1):20-27.
[4] RAYMANDO AGUILERA,ETC. Design of recursive filters[J]. Geophysics, 35:2,247-253.

独立自主发展石油地震数字处理(续完)[①]

地震数字处理中的某些数学模型

6. 镶边滤波

地震记录 $x(t)$ 是 t 的连续函数,当我们以时间 Δ 为采样间隔时就得一个时间序列 $x(n\Delta)$. $x(n\Delta)$ 的频谱是以 $1/\Delta$ 为周期的对称函数. 为了对 $x(n\Delta)$ 进行滤波,经常采用的滤波器频谱为图 6.1 所示的带通滤波. 这种带通滤波的频谱由于不连续,所以相应的时间序列衰减很慢,这使滤波效果受到影响. 改进的办法就是把带通滤波变成镶边带通滤波,如图 6.2 所示.

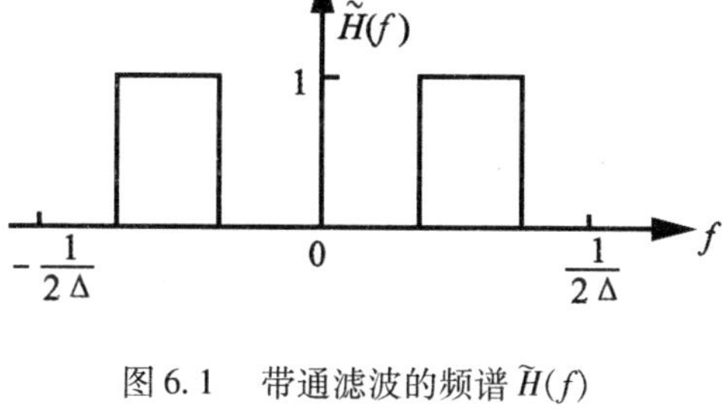

图 6.1　带通滤波的频谱 $\tilde{H}(f)$

① 原载:数学学报,1976,19(1):63-72.

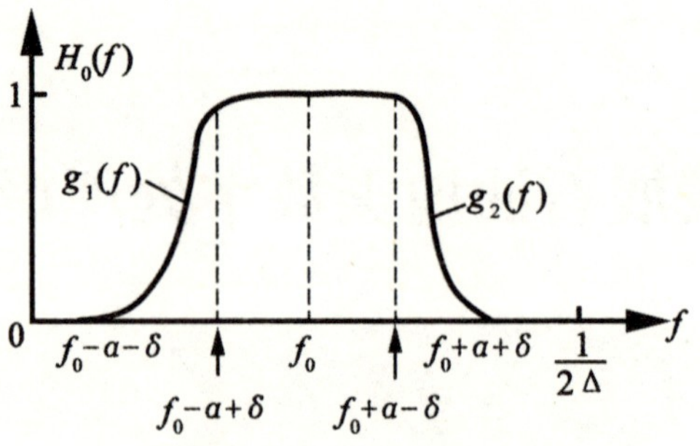

图 6.2　镶边带通滤波的频谱 $H_0(f)$

现在我们主要对镶边滤波的截尾误差作一理论分析（参看[1]第二章）.

(1) 镶边滤波截尾误差讨论之一.

设形如图 6.2 所示的函数 $H_0(f)$ 满足：

$$H_0(f+\frac{1}{\Delta}) = H_0(f)$$

$$H_0(-f) = H_0(f)$$

$$a+\delta < f_0 < \frac{1}{2\Delta} - a - \delta$$

当 $0 \leqslant f \leqslant \frac{1}{2\Delta}$ 时，

$$H_0(f) = \begin{cases} 1, & \text{当} \mid f-f_0 \mid \leqslant \alpha-\delta \\ g_1(f), & \text{当} \mid f-f_0+\alpha \mid \leqslant \delta \\ g_2(f), & \text{当} \mid f-f_0-\alpha \mid \leqslant \delta \\ 0, & \text{其他} \end{cases}$$

$H_0(f)$ 有 r 阶微商 $H_0^{(r)}(f)$，并且

$$\mid g_1^{(r)}(f) \mid \leqslant M_1, \quad \text{当} \mid f-f_0+\alpha \mid \leqslant \delta$$

$$\mid g_2^{(r)}(f) \mid \leqslant M_2, \quad \text{当} \mid f-f_0-\alpha \mid \leqslant \delta$$

我们现在说明什么是截尾误差.

把 $H_0(f)$ 展成富氏级数

$$H_0(f) = \sum_{v=-\infty}^{\infty} C_v e^{-2\pi i f v \Delta} = \sum_{v=-\infty}^{\infty} C_v \cos 2\pi f v \Delta\text{①}$$

其中

$$C_v = \Delta\int_{-1/2\Delta}^{1/2\Delta} H_0(f) e^{2\pi i f v \Delta} df$$

① 利用 $H_v(-f) = H_0(f)$，可得到 $C_{-v} = C_v$.

C_v 就是相应于 $H_0(f)$ 的时间序列或滤波因子. 在时间域进行滤波时,只能取有限的一部分滤波因子 C_v,其中 $v=0,\pm1,\cdots,\pm N$,相应这个一部分滤波因子的频谱为

$$H(f)=\sum_{v=-N}^{N}C_v\cos 2\pi fv\Delta$$

$H_0(f)$ 与 $H(f)$ 有一个误差

$$R_N(f)=H_0(f)-H(f)=2\sum_{v=N+1}^{\infty}C_v\cos 2\pi fv\Delta$$

我们称 $R_N(f)$ 为截尾误差. 现在我们的目的就是要对最大误差

$$\varepsilon=\max|R_N(f)|$$

作一估计.

反复利用分部积分法可得到

$$C_v=\Delta\left(-\frac{1}{2\pi iv\Delta}\right)^r\int_{-1/2\Delta}^{1/2\Delta}H_0^{(r)}(f)\mathrm{e}^{2\pi ifv\Delta}\mathrm{d}f$$

注意 $H(-f)=H(f)$,易得 $H^{(r)}(-f)=(-1)^rH^{(r)}(f)$,因此

$$C_v=\Delta\left(-\frac{1}{2\pi iv\Delta}\right)^r\int_{0}^{1/2\Delta}H_0^{(r)}(f)[\mathrm{e}^{2\pi ifv\Delta}+(-1)^r\mathrm{e}^{-2\pi ifv\Delta}]\mathrm{d}f$$

由此可得到

$$R_N(f)=2\Delta\int_0^{1/2\Delta}H_0^{(r)}(\varphi)K(\varphi)\mathrm{d}\varphi=$$
$$2\Delta\left\{\int_{f_0-a-\delta}^{f_0-a+\delta}g_1^{(r)}(\varphi)K(\varphi)\mathrm{d}\varphi+\int_{f_0+a-\delta}^{f_0+a+\delta}g_2^{(r)}(\varphi)K(\varphi)\mathrm{d}\varphi\right\}$$

其中

$$K(\varphi)=\sum_{v=N+1}^{\infty}\left(-\frac{1}{2\pi iv\Delta}\right)^r[\mathrm{e}^{2\pi i\varphi v\Delta}+(-1)^t\mathrm{e}^{-2\pi i\varphi v\Delta}]\cos 2\pi fv\Delta$$

对 $K(\varphi)$ 作一估计,

$$|K(\varphi)|\leqslant\sum_{v=N+1}^{\infty}\frac{2}{(2\pi v\Delta)^r}\leqslant\frac{2}{(2\pi\Delta)^r}\int_N^{\infty}\frac{\mathrm{d}u}{u^r}=\frac{2}{(r-1)(2\pi\Delta)^rN^{r-1}}$$

因此可得到

$$|R_N(f)\|\leqslant 2\Delta\frac{2}{(r-1)(2\pi\Delta)^rN^{r-1}}(2\delta M_1+2\delta M_2)=$$
$$\frac{4\delta(M_1+M_2)}{\pi(r-1)(2\pi\Delta N)^{r-1}}$$

这样就得到最大误差的估计

$$\varepsilon\leqslant\frac{4\delta(M_1+M_2)}{\pi(r-1)(2\pi\Delta N)^{r-1}}$$

(2) 镶边滤波截尾误差讨论之二.

现在我们对镶边滤波截尾误差作另一估计，并在一定条件下给出最优的镶边函数 $g_1(f)$ 和 $g_2(f)$.

为了叙述简便，我们把镶边滤波的频谱取成图 6.3 的 $H(f)$，$H(f)$ 满足：$H(f+2\pi)=H(f)$，$H(f)=H(-f)$，$H^{(r)}(f)\in C[0,\pi]$（意即 $H(f)$ 的 r 次微商 $H^{(r)}(f)$ 在 $[0,\pi]$ 上连续）. 这时有

$$H(f)=\frac{a_0}{2}+\sum_{n=1}^{\infty}a_n\cos nf,a_n=\frac{2}{\pi}\int_0^{\pi}H(x)\cos nx\mathrm{d}x=\frac{2}{\pi}\mathrm{Re}\int_0^{\pi}H(x)\mathrm{e}^{\mathrm{i}nx}\mathrm{d}x$$

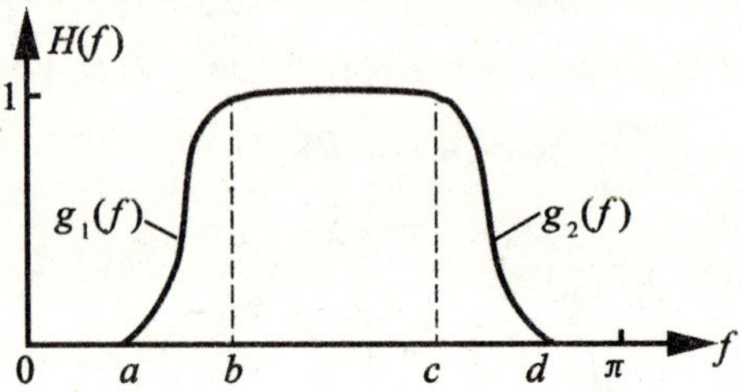

图 6.3　镶边带通滤波的频谱 $H(f)$

反复利用分部积分法可得

$$a_n=\frac{2}{\pi}\mathrm{Re}\int_0^{\pi}H^{(r)}(x)\frac{\mathrm{e}^{\mathrm{i}nx}}{(-\mathrm{i}n)^r}\mathrm{d}x$$

截尾误差为

$$R_N(f)=\sum_{n=N+1}^{\infty}a_n\cos nf=\frac{2}{\pi}\int_0^{\pi}H^{(r)}(x)\mathrm{Re}\sum_{n=N+1}^{\infty}\frac{\cos nf\cdot\mathrm{e}^{\mathrm{i}nx}}{(-\mathrm{i}n)^r}\mathrm{d}x$$

根据 Schwartz 不等式有

$$R_N^2(f)\leqslant\frac{4}{\pi^2}\int_0^{\pi}[H^{(r)}(f)]^2\mathrm{d}x\int_0^{\pi}\left[\mathrm{Re}\sum_{n=N+1}^{\infty}\frac{\cos nf\mathrm{e}^{\mathrm{i}nx}}{(-\mathrm{i}n)^r}\right]^2\mathrm{d}x$$

上式右端第二个积分，当 $r=2m$ 时，则有

$$\int_0^{\pi}\left[\mathrm{Re}\sum_{n=N+1}^{\infty}\frac{\cos nf\mathrm{e}^{\mathrm{i}nx}}{(-\mathrm{i}n)^r}\right]^2\mathrm{d}x=\int_0^{\pi}\left[\sum_{n=N+1}^{\infty}\frac{\cos nf\cos nx}{n^r}\right]^2\mathrm{d}x=$$

$$\sum_{n_1=N+1}^{\infty}\sum_{n_2=N+1}^{\infty}\frac{\cos n_1f}{n_1^r}\frac{\cos n_2f}{n_2^r}\int_0^{\pi}\cos n_1x\cos n_2x\mathrm{d}x=\frac{\pi}{2}\sum_{n=N+1}^{\infty}\frac{\cos^2nf}{n^{2r}}\leqslant$$

$$\frac{\pi}{2}\sum_{n=N+1}^{\infty}\frac{1}{n^{2r}}\leqslant\frac{\pi}{2}\int_N^{\infty}\frac{\mathrm{d}u}{u^{2r}}=\frac{\pi}{2}\frac{1}{(2r-1)N^{2r-1}}$$

因此

$$R_N^2(f)\leqslant\frac{2}{\pi}\frac{1}{(2r-1)N^{2r-1}}\int_0^{\pi}[H^{(r)}(x)]^2\mathrm{d}x=$$

$$\frac{2}{\pi}\frac{1}{(2r-1)N^{2r-1}}\left[\int_a^b[g_1^{(r)}(x)]^2dx+\int_0^d[g_2^{(r)}(x)]^2dx\right] \qquad (6.1)$$

这就是对截尾误差的估计. 当 r 为奇数时,结论是相同的.

(6.1) 式中的 $g_1(f), g_2(f)$ 可任意选择, 但为了使 $H^{(r)}(f) \in [0,1]$, $g_1(f)g_2(f)$ 必须满足

$$\left.\begin{aligned}&g_1(b)=g_2(c)=1, g_1(a)=g_2(d)=0\\&g_1^{(v)}(a)=g_1^{(v)}(b)=g_2^{(v)}(c)=g_2^{(v)}(d)=0(v=1,2,\cdots,r)\\&g_1^{(v)}(f)\in C[a,b], g_2^{(\gamma)}(f)\in C[c,d]\end{aligned}\right\} \qquad (6.2)$$

在(6.2)条件下,使(6.1)达到最小的 $g_1(x), g_2(x)$ 是

$$g_1(x)=C_1\int_a^x(x-a)^{r-1}(b-x)^{r-1}dx \qquad (6.3)$$

$$g_2(x)=C_2\int_x^d(x-c)^{r-1}(d-x)^{r-1}dx \qquad (6.4)$$

其中

$$C_1^{-1}\int_a^b(x-a)^{r-1}(b-x)^{r-1}dx$$

$$C_2^{-1}\int_c^d(x-c)^{r-1}(d-x)^{r-1}dx$$

现在来证明. 在(6.1)中的两个积分可分开来考虑,以第一项为例:设

$$g(x)=g_1(x)+\psi(x)$$

其中 $g_1(x)$ 由(6.3)给出, $\psi(x)$ 满足 $\psi(a)=\psi(b)=\psi^{(v)}(a)=\psi^{(v)}(b)=0(v=1,2,\cdots,r)$ 和 $\psi^{(r)}(x)\in[a,b]$, 则

$$\int_a^b[g^{(r)}(x)]^2dx=\int_a^b[g_1^{(r)}(x)]^2dx+2\int_a^b g_1^{(r)}(x)\psi^{(r)}(x)dx+\int_a^b[\psi^{(r)}(x)]^2dx$$

其中

$$\int_a^b g_1^{(r)}(x)\psi^{(r)}(x)dx=\int_a^b g_1^{(r)}(x)d\psi^{(r-1)}(x)=-\int_a^b g_1^{(r+1)}(x)\psi^{(r-1)}(x)dx=$$

$$(-1)^r\int_a^b g_1^{(2r)}(x)\psi(x)dx=0$$

(因为 $g_1(x)$ 是 $2r-1$ 次多项式),因此

$$\int_a^b[g^{(r)}(x)]^2dx=\int_a^b[g_1^{(r)}(x)]^2dx+\int_a^b[\psi^{(r)}(x)]^2dx\geqslant\int_a^b[g_1^{(r)}(x)^?]dx$$

证明完毕. 对于 $g_2(x)$ 可同样讨论.

当 $g_1(x), g_2(x)$ 为(6.3),(6.4)时,有

$$\int_a^b[g_1^{(r)}(x)]^2dx=\frac{1}{(b-a)^{2r-1}}\cdot\frac{(2r-1)!(2r-2)!}{[(r-1)!]^2} \qquad (6.5)$$

$$\int_c^d[g_2^{(r)}(x)]^2dx=\frac{1}{(d-c)^{2r-1}}\cdot\frac{(2r-1)!(2r-2)!}{[(r-1)!]^2} \qquad (6.6)$$

因此按(6.1)有

$$R_N^2(f) \leqslant \frac{2}{\pi N^{2r-1}} \cdot \frac{[(2r-2)!]^2}{[(r-1)!]^2}\left[\frac{1}{(b-a)^{2r-1}} + \frac{1}{(d-c)^{2r-1}}\right]$$

关于(6.5),(6.6)的推导以及在(6.3),(6.4)情况下 a_n 的计算,可参看[1]P118.

7. 二维滤波

我们主要讨论一种二维滤液——钟形带通滤波,并着重分析其误差(参看[1]第二章).

(1) 连续的钟形带通滤波.

地震记录实际上是时间 t 与距离 x 的二元函数 $g(t,x)$,当 t 与 x 为连续变化时,$g(t,x)$ 的二维富氏变换为 $G(f,k)$,其中 f 为频率,k 为波数. $g(t,x)$ 与 $G(f,k)$ 的关系为

$$G(f,k) = \int_{-\infty}^{\infty}\int_{-\infty}^{\infty} g(t,x)\mathrm{e}^{-2\pi\mathrm{i}(ft+kx)}\mathrm{d}t\mathrm{d}x$$

$$g(t,x) = \int_{-\infty}^{\infty}\int_{-\infty}^{\infty} G(f,k)\mathrm{e}^{2\pi\mathrm{i}(ft+kx)}\mathrm{d}f\mathrm{d}k$$

常用的一种连续二维滤波是连续带通滤波,其谱如图7.1所示,

$$\widetilde{H}(\varphi,K) = \begin{cases}1,(\varphi,K) \in D \text{ 或 } D' \\ 0,\text{其他}\end{cases} \qquad (7.1)$$

相应的时间距离函数为

$$\tilde{h}(t,x) = \iint_{D\cup D} \mathrm{e}^{2\pi\mathrm{i}(\varphi t+Kx)}\mathrm{d}\varphi\mathrm{d}K = 2\iint_D \cos 2\pi\varphi t\cos 2\pi Kx\mathrm{d}\varphi\mathrm{d}K$$

所谓连续的钟形带通滤波,是指其时间距离函数为

$$h(t,x) = 2\mathrm{e}^{-\lambda t^2-\mu x^2}\iint_D \cos 2\pi\varphi t\cos 2\pi Kx\,\mathrm{d}\varphi\mathrm{d}K \qquad (7.2)$$

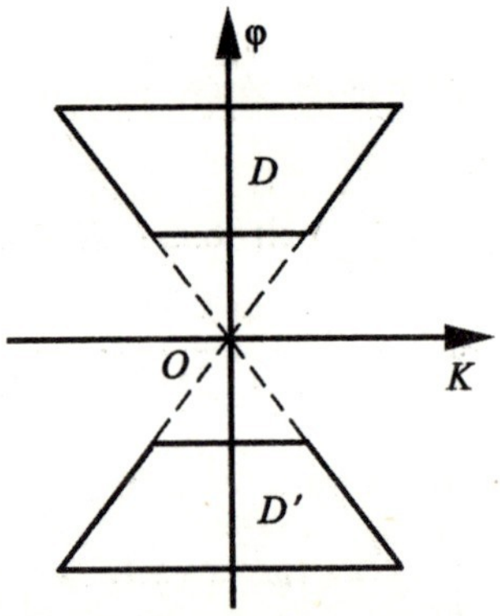

图7.1 连续带通滤波的谱 $\widetilde{H}(\varphi,K)$

相应的谱(或称频波响应)是

$$H_0(f,k) = \int_{-\infty}^{\infty}\int_{-\infty}^{\infty} h(t,x)\mathrm{e}^{-2\pi\mathrm{i}(ft+kx)}\mathrm{d}t\mathrm{d}x \qquad (7.3)$$

把(7.2)代入(7.3),并用 D^* 表示由 D 和 D' 组成的区域,则有

$$H_0(f,k) = \frac{\pi}{\sqrt{\lambda\mu}}\iint_{D^*} \mathrm{e}^{-\pi^2(\varphi-f)^2/\lambda-\pi^2(K-k)^2/\mu}\mathrm{d}\varphi\mathrm{d}K \qquad (7.4)$$

(2) 离散的钟形带通滤波.

设时间 t 和空间 x 的抽样间隔 Δ 和 ∇ 都为1,则相应(7.2)的离散的钟形

带通滤波权函数为

$$h(v_1,v_2) = 2e^{-\lambda v_1^2-\mu v_2^2}\iint\limits_D \cos 2\pi\varphi v_1 \times \cos 2\pi K v_2 \mathrm{d}\varphi \mathrm{d}K$$
$$(v_j = 0, \pm 1, \pm 2,\cdots, j = 1,2) \tag{7.5}$$

相应(7.5)的频波响应为

$$H_1(f,k) = \sum_{v_1=-\infty}^{\infty}\sum_{v_2=-\infty}^{\infty} h(v_1,v_2)e^{-2\pi i(fv_1+kv_2)} \tag{7.6}$$

现在我们要对$H_1(f,k)$的取值情况作一估计. 首先对图7.2作一说明. 由于区域对K轴是对称的,我们在图7.2只画了上半平面中$0 \leqslant \varphi \leqslant \frac{1}{2}$, $-\frac{1}{2} \leqslant K \leqslant \frac{1}{2}$的情况. 图中实线梯形为区域$D$,两个虚线梯形的上、下底与$D$的上、下底距离为$\delta_1(>0)$,两个斜边与$D$的斜边的距离为$d = \sqrt{\delta_1^2+\delta_2^2}(\delta_2>0)$. 小虚线梯形围成的区域记为$D_{内}$,大虚线梯形以外的区域记为$D_{外}$.

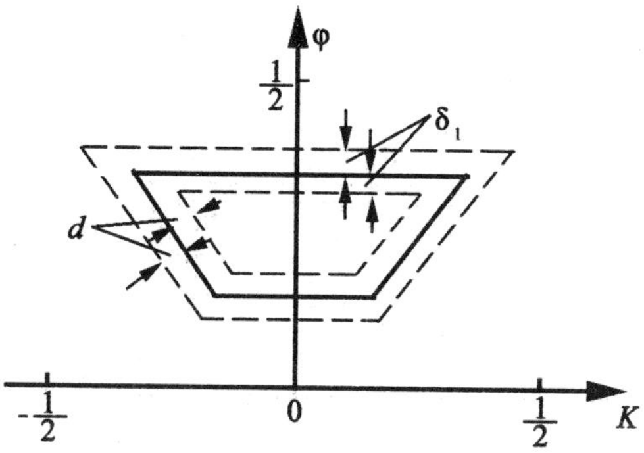

图7.2

根据二维泊松式,可以证明①

$$H_1(f,k) = \sum_{v_1=-\infty}^{\infty}\sum_{v_2=-\infty}^{\infty} H_0(f+v_1,k+v_2) =$$
$$\frac{\pi}{\sqrt{\lambda\mu}}\sum_{v_1=-\infty}^{\infty}\sum_{v_2=-\infty}^{\infty}\iint\limits_{D^*} e^{-\pi^2(\varphi-f-v_1)^2/\lambda-\pi^2(K-k-v_2)^2/\mu}\mathrm{d}\varphi\mathrm{d}K =$$
$$\frac{\pi}{\sqrt{\lambda\mu}}\sum_{v_1=-\infty}^{\infty}\sum_{v_2=-\infty}^{\infty}\iint\limits_{D^*_{v_1v_2}} e^{-\pi^2(\varphi-f)^2/\lambda-\pi^2(K-k)^2/\mu}\mathrm{d}\varphi\mathrm{d}K \tag{7.7}$$

其中域$D^*_{v_1v_2}$表示将D^*沿φ轴移动v_1单位长,再沿K轴移动v_2单位长所得到的

① 参看[1]149.

区域. 由于 $D_{00}^* = D^*$ 在单位正方形($|\varphi| < \frac{1}{2}, |K| < \frac{1}{2}$) 之内,因此 $D_{v_1 v_2}^*(v_i = 0, \pm 1, \pm 2, \cdots, j = 1,2)$ 不相重叠.

由(7.7) 可以得到:

当$(f,k) \in D_{内}$ 时

$$\frac{\pi}{\sqrt{\lambda\mu}} \iint\limits_{\substack{|\varphi - f| \leqslant \delta_1 \\ |K-k| \leqslant \delta_2}} e^{-\pi^2(\varphi-f)^2/\lambda - \pi^2(K-k)^2/\mu} d\varphi dK \leqslant H_1(f,k) \leqslant$$

$$\frac{\pi}{\sqrt{\lambda\mu}} \int_{-\infty}^{\infty}\int_{-\infty}^{\infty} e^{-\pi^2(\varphi-f)^2/\lambda - \pi^2(K-k)^2/\mu} d\varphi dK \tag{7.8}$$

当$(f,k) \in D_{外}$ 时

$$0 \leqslant H_1(f,k) \leqslant \frac{\pi}{\sqrt{\lambda\mu}} \int_{-\infty}^{\infty}\int_{-\infty}^{\infty}\limits_{\substack{|\varphi - f| \geqslant \delta_1 \\ 或 |K-k| \geqslant \delta_2}} e^{-\pi^2(\varphi-f)^2/\lambda - \pi^2(K-k)^2/\mu} d\varphi dK \tag{7.9}$$

由于

$$\frac{\pi}{\sqrt{\lambda\mu}} \int_{-\infty}^{\infty}\int_{-\infty}^{\infty} e^{-\pi^2(\varphi-f)^2/\lambda - \pi^2(K-k)^2/\mu} d\varphi dK = 1 \tag{7.10}$$

$$\frac{\pi}{\sqrt{\lambda\mu}} \iint\limits_{\substack{|\varphi - f| \geqslant \delta_1 \\ 或 |K-k| \geqslant \delta_2}} e^{-\pi^2(\varphi-f)^2/\lambda - \pi^2(K-k)^2/\mu} d\varphi dK \leqslant$$

$$\frac{2}{\sqrt{\pi}}\left[\frac{e^{-\pi^2\delta_1^2/\lambda}}{\sqrt{\pi^2\delta_1^2/\lambda}} + \frac{e^{-\pi^2\delta_2^2/\mu}}{\sqrt{\pi^2\delta_2^2/\mu}}\right]① \tag{7.11}$$

根据(7.8),(7.9) 可得

$$H_1(f,k) = \begin{cases} 1 + R, & 当(f,k) \in D_{内} \\ R', & 当(f,k) \in D_{外} \end{cases} \tag{7.12}$$

其中 $|R|$ 和 $|R'|$ 都不超过

$$R_0 = \frac{2}{\sqrt{\pi}}\left[\frac{e^{-\pi^2\delta_1^2/\lambda}}{\sqrt{\pi^2\delta_1^2/\lambda}} + \frac{e^{-\pi^2\delta_2^2/\mu}}{\sqrt{\pi^2\delta_2^2/\mu}}\right] \tag{7.13}$$

(3) 有限项钟形带通滤波及其截尾误差.

在进行二维数字滤波时,只能取(7.5) 的有限项

$$h(v_1,v_2) = 2e^{-\lambda v_1^2 - \mu v_2^2}\iint\limits_D \cos 2\pi\varphi v_1 \cos 2\pi K v_2 \, d\varphi dK \tag{7.14}$$

$$(v_j = 0, \pm 1, \pm 2, \cdots, \pm N_j, j = 1,2)$$

相应(7.14) 的二维数字滤波的频波响应为

---

① 详细推导可参看[1],151.

$$H(f,k)=\sum_{v_1=-N_1}^{N_1}\sum_{v_2=-N_2}^{N_2}h(v_1,v_2)\mathrm{e}^{-2\pi\mathrm{i}(fv_1+kv_2)}=\sum_{v_1=-\infty}^{\infty}\sum_{v_2=-\infty}^{\infty}h(v_1,v_2)\mathrm{e}^{-2\pi\mathrm{i}(fv_1+hv_2)}-\sum_{\substack{|v_1|\geqslant N_1+1\\ \text{或}|v_2|\geqslant N_2+1}}\sum h(v_1,v_2)\mathrm{e}^{-2\pi\mathrm{i}(fv_1+kv_2)}=H_1(f,k)-R_1(f,k)\qquad(7.15)$$

其中 $R_1(f,k)$ 为截尾误差.

现在对截尾误差作一估计,易知

$$|R_1(f,k)|\leqslant\sum_{\substack{|v_1|\geqslant N_1+1\\ \text{或}|v_2|\geqslant N_2+1}}\sum|h(v_1,v_2)|\leqslant\sum_{\substack{|v_1|\geqslant N_1+1\\ |v_2|\geqslant N_2+1}}\sum 2\mathrm{e}^{-\lambda v_1^2-\mu v_2^2}|D|\leqslant$$

$$4|D|\left[\sum_{v_1=-\infty}^{\infty}\mathrm{e}^{-\lambda v_1^2}\sum_{v_2=N_2+1}^{\infty}\mathrm{e}^{-\mu v_2^2}+\sum_{v_2=-\infty}^{\infty}\mathrm{e}^{-\mu v_2^2}\sum_{v_1=N_1+1}^{\infty}\mathrm{e}^{-\lambda v_1^2}\right]\qquad(7.16)$$

其中 $|D|$ 为区域 D 的面积.

由于

$$\sum_{v_1=-\infty}^{\infty}\mathrm{e}^{-\lambda v_1^2}=1+2\sum_{v_1=1}^{\infty}\mathrm{e}^{-\lambda v_1^2}<1+2\int_0^{\infty}\mathrm{e}^{-\lambda t^2}\mathrm{d}t=1+\sqrt{\frac{\pi}{\lambda}}$$

$$\sum_{v_2=N_2+1}^{\infty}\mathrm{e}^{-\mu v_2^2}<\int_{N_2}^{\infty}\mathrm{e}^{-\mu x^2}\mathrm{d}x<\int_{N_2}^{\infty}\mathrm{e}^{-\mu N_2 x}\mathrm{d}x=\frac{1}{\mu N_2}\mathrm{e}^{-\mu N_2^2}$$

按(7.16)可得

$$|R_1(f,k)|\leqslant 4|D|\times\left[\left(1+\sqrt{\frac{\pi}{\lambda}}\right)\frac{\mathrm{e}^{-\mu N_2^2}}{\mu N_2}+\left(1+\sqrt{\frac{\pi}{\mu}}\right)\frac{\mathrm{e}^{-\lambda N_1^2}}{\lambda N_1}\right]\qquad(7.17)$$

综合(7.15),(7.12)和(7.17)可得

$$H(f,k)=\begin{cases}1+\zeta, & \text{当}(f,k)\in D_{\text{内}}\\ \zeta', & \text{当}(f,k)\in D_{\text{外}}\end{cases}$$

其中 $|\zeta|$ 和 $|\zeta'|$ 都不超过

$$\zeta_0=\frac{2}{\sqrt{\pi}}\left[\frac{\mathrm{e}^{-\pi^2\delta_1^2/\lambda}}{\sqrt{\pi^2\delta_1^2/\lambda}}+\frac{\mathrm{e}^{-\pi^2\delta_2^2/\mu}}{\sqrt{\pi^2\delta_2^2/\mu}}\right]+4|D|\times\left[\left(1+\sqrt{\frac{\pi}{\mu}}\right)\frac{\mathrm{e}^{-\lambda N_1^2}}{\lambda N_1}+\left(1+\sqrt{\frac{\pi}{\lambda}}\right)\frac{\mathrm{e}^{-\mu N_2^2}}{\mu N_2}\right]$$

8. 两组信号之间相似性的衡量

这个问题来自地震勘探的断层对比. 为了避免过多的地震术语和概念,我们先讨论数学问题,最后再对地震勘探上的应用作一说明.

(1) 数学问题.

设有两组信号

$$I:x_i(t),i=1,2,\cdots,n,\quad t=1,2,\cdots,T$$
$$J:y_j(t),j=1,2,\cdots,m,\quad t=1,2,\cdots,T$$

问题是:如何给出一个标准,以判别或衡量 I 与 J 两组信号之间的相似性或差

异. 下面我们讨论解决这个问题的两种方法.

(2) 概率统计方法.

在这种方法中可从两个角度讨论.

① 多元分析法.

假设 I 组的信号 $x_i(t) = (x_i(1), x_i(2), \cdots, x_i(T))$ 服从多元正态分布 $N(\mu_1, \sum)$, J 组的信号 $y_j(t) = (y_j(1), y_j(2), \cdots, y_j(T))$ 服从多元正态分布 $N(\mu_2, \sum)$, 其中 $\mu_1 = (\mu_{11}, \mu_{12}, \cdots, \mu_{1T})$, $\mu_2 = (\mu_{21}, \mu_{22}, \cdots, \mu_{2T})$, $\sum$ 为协方差阵.

所谓判别 I 与 J 两组信号是否相似, 就是判别 $\mu_1 = \mu_2$ 是否成立, 按照数量统计多元分析理论, 这个问题的检验步骤如下.

首先计算:

平均数

$$\left.\begin{aligned} \bar{x}(t) &= \frac{1}{n}\sum_{i=1}^{n} x_i(t) \\ \bar{y}(t) &= \frac{1}{m}\sum_{j=1}^{m} y_j(t) \end{aligned}\right\} \tag{8.1}$$

协方差

$$\bar{\sigma}_{kl} = \frac{1}{n+m-2}\Big[\sum_{i=1}^{n}(x_i(k) - \bar{x}(k))(x_i(l) - \bar{x}(l)) + \sum_{j=1}^{m}(y_j(k) - \bar{y}(k))(y_j(l) - \bar{y}(l))\Big]$$

协方差矩阵

$$\sum = \begin{pmatrix} \bar{\sigma}_{11} & \bar{\sigma}_{12} & \cdots & \bar{\sigma}_{1T} \\ \bar{\sigma}_{21} & \bar{\sigma}_{22} & \cdots & \bar{\sigma}_{2T} \\ \vdots & \vdots & & \vdots \\ \bar{\sigma}_{T1} & \bar{\sigma}_{T2} & \cdots & \bar{\sigma}_{TT} \end{pmatrix}$$

第二步是选取统计量

$$U = \frac{nm}{n+m} \cdot \frac{q-T+1}{qT}(\bar{x} - \bar{y})' \sum{}^{-1} (\bar{x} - \bar{y}) \tag{8.2}$$

其中

$$q = n + m - 2$$

$$\bar{x} = \begin{pmatrix} \bar{x}(1) \\ \vdots \\ \bar{x}(T) \end{pmatrix}, \quad \bar{y} = \begin{pmatrix} \bar{y}(1) \\ \vdots \\ \bar{y}(T) \end{pmatrix}$$

上面的统计量(8.2) 服从 F 分布, 第一个自由度为 T, 第二个自由度为

$q-T+1$.

第三步是,给出显著性水平 α,由 F 分布表查出临界值 λ,计算(8.2) 的值. 若这个值小于 λ,则认为 I 组与 J 组信号相似,否则,认为不相似.

② 最优判决函数法.

关于 I 组信号 $x_i(t)$ 与 J 组信号 $y_j(t)$ 的假设与 ① 相同. 设

$$D=(\bar{x}-\bar{y})'\sum^{-1}(\bar{x}-\bar{y}) \tag{8.3}$$

按照统计判决理论(可参看[2]),I 组与 J 组相似的概率(其实为某种判决函数)为

$$P(I,J)=\frac{2}{\sqrt{2\pi}}\int_{\sqrt{D}/2}^{+\infty}\mathrm{e}^{-z^2/2}\mathrm{d}z \tag{8.4}$$

我们指出,在地震勘探中所得到的两组信号来自不同的地方,它们总有一些差异,即 μ_1 与 μ_2 总是有一定差异的. 因此,由(8.2) 算出的 U 值往往要大于临界值 λ,或者由(8.4) 算出的概率往往不会很大,这样就失去了概率估计的意义. 所以,作为衡量两组信号相似性的一种度量. 我们直接取(8.2) 或(8.3) 就行了. 因(8.3) 比(8.2) 简单,我们就取(8.3) 式作为相似性的一种度量.

(3) 几何方法.

这种方法的主要思想是:把 $x_i(t)$ 或 $y_j(t)$ 作为 T 维空间中的一个点,然后给出一种标准来衡量 $x_i(t)$ 与 $y_j(t)$ 的差异,这种标准可以是各种距离,也可以是差的平方和,或其他量,最后得到一个衡量两组点之间差异的量. 下面给出一种衡量标准.

两个信号 $x_i(t)$ 与 $y_j(t)$ 的差异量 $L(x_i,y_j)$ 我们规定为

$$L(x_i,y_j)=\sum_{t=1}^{T}q(t)[x_i(t)-y_j(t)]^2 \tag{8.5}$$

其中 $q(t)\geqslant 0$,为加权系数.

两组信号 I 与 J 之间的差异量我们规定为

$$L(I,J)=\frac{1}{nm}\sum_{i=1}^{n}\sum_{j=1}^{m}L(x_i,y_j)=\sum_{i=1}^{T}\left[\frac{1}{nm}\sum_{i=1}^{n}\sum_{j=1}^{m}[x_i(t)-y_j(t)]^2\right]q(t) \tag{8.6}$$

设 $\bar{x}(t)$、$\bar{y}(t)$ 由(8.1) 确定. 因为

$$\sum_{j=1}^{m}[x_i(t)-y_j(t)]^2=\sum_{j=1}^{m}[x_i(t)-\bar{y}(t)+\bar{y}(t)-y_j(t)]^2=$$

$$m[x_i(t)-\bar{y}(t)]^2+\sum_{j=1}^{m}[\bar{y}(t)-y_j(t)]^2$$

$$\sum_{i=1}^{n}[x_i(t)-\bar{y}(t)]^2=\sum_{i=1}^{n}[x_i(t)-\bar{x}(t)+\bar{x}(t)-\bar{y}(t)]^2=$$

$$\sum_{i=1}^{n}[x_i(t)-\bar{x}(t)]^2+n[\bar{x}(t)-\bar{y}(t)]^2$$

所以

$$\frac{1}{nm}\sum_{i=1}^{n}\sum_{j=1}^{m}[x_i(t)-y_j(t)]^2=\frac{1}{n}\sum_{i=1}^{n}[x_i(t)-\bar{x}(t)]^2+\frac{1}{m}\sum_{j=1}^{m}[y_j(t)-\bar{y}(t)]^2+[\bar{x}(t)-\bar{y}(t)]^2$$

由(8.6)可得

$$L(I,J)=\sum_{i=1}^{T}\Big[\frac{1}{n}\sum_{i=1}^{n}[x_i(t)-\bar{x}(t)]^2\Big]q(t)+\sum_{i=1}^{T}\Big[\frac{1}{m}\sum_{j=1}^{m}[y'_j(t)-\bar{y}(t)]^2\Big]q(t)+\sum_{t=1}^{T}[\bar{x}(t)-\bar{y}(t)]^2q(t) \tag{8.7}$$

在(8.7)右端三项中,前两项是由每组内部信号之间的差异引起的,第三项是由两组平均信号的差异引起的.因为我们考虑的是两组信号之间的总体差异,所以差异量 $L(I,J)$ 要包含这三项内容.当然,还可给前两项以权 $p_1(n)$,$p_1(m)$,第三项以权 $p_2(n,m)$.

一般情况下,我们取加权系数 $q(t)\equiv 1$.在特殊情况下,要根据具体情况确定 $q(t)$.

(4) 在断层对比应用的几个问题.

① 信号参数的确定.

反映信号的 T 个参数 $x_i(1),x_i(2),\cdots,x_i(T)$ 或 $y_j(1),y_j(2),\cdots,y_j(T)$ 在地震勘探处理中是如何确定的呢?从某一地层反射的地震波为一振动曲线 $S(t)$,为了刻画这种地震波,有两种办法:一是选取特殊的参数,例如波峰和波谷的振幅值,两个零点之间的距离,等等,文献[2]就是这样做的;二是直接选取一段时间上的信号 $S(t)$ 作为信号参数.前一种方法对波形要求严,且要进行大量的计算(如寻找0点),后一种方法简便易行,在对一段时间上信号 $S(t)$ 的能量归一化后,直接把信号的值作为参数.

② 断层对比.

在中断地带两边分左区与右区,左区有 I_N 层,右区有 J_M 层.对于左区的 I 层有一组信号 $x_i(t),i=1,2,\cdots,n$,对于右区的 J 层有一组信号 $y_j(t),j=1,2,\cdots,m$.为了衡量 I 层与 J 层是否在地质上属于同一层,我们计算 $D(I,J)$ 或 $L(I,J)$,对于所有的 I 与 J,可得一张表(以 $L(I,J)$ 为例):

$$\begin{pmatrix} L(1,1) & L(1,2) & \cdots & L(1,J_M) \\ L(2,1) & L(2,2) & \cdots & L(2,J_M) \\ \vdots & \vdots & & \vdots \\ L(I_N,1) & L(I_N,2) & \cdots & L(I_N,J_M) \end{pmatrix}.$$

以第二行为例,在 $L(2,1)$,$L(2,2)$,…,$L(2,J_M)$ 中,若 $L(2,3)$ 最小,再找第三列,若 $L(2,3)$ 仍为最小,则认为左第二层与右第三层属于同一地质层可能性大.

参 考 书 目

[1] 燃料化学工业部石油地球物理勘探局计算中心站,北京大学数力系等编. 地震勘探数字技术,第二册[M]. 北京:科学出版社,1974.

[2] BOIS P. Correlation a Distance, Geophysical Prospecting[M]. 19:4, 592-611.

闵嗣鹤主要论著目录

一九三三年

1. 根式与代数数及代数函数. 师大月刊,1933(3):85-98.

一九三四年

2. 行列式之推广(译). 数学季刊,1934,2(1):Ⅰ-5.
3. 函数方程式之解法和应用. 数学季刊,1934,2(1):Ⅰ-98.

一九三五年

4. 函数方程解法举例. 师大月刊,1935(19):61-86.

一九四〇年

5. 相合式解数之渐近公式及应用此理以讨论奇异级数. 科学,1940,24(8):591-607.

一九四一年

6. On the number of solutions of certain congruences(合作者:华罗庚). *Sci. Rep. of Nat. Tsinghua Univ.* ,*Ser. A*,1941,4(2-3):113-134.

一九四二年

7. On a double exponential sum(合作者:华罗庚). *Science Record*,1942,1(1-2):23-25.

8. An analogue of Tarry's problem(合作者:华罗庚). *Science Record*,1942,1(1-2):26-29.

一九四四年

9. On the distribution of quadratic non-residues and the Euclidean algorithm in real quadratic fields. Ⅱ(合作者:华罗庚). *Trans. of Amer. Math. Soc.* ,1944,56(3):547-569.

10. Non-analytic functions. *Amer, Math. Monthly*, 1944, 51(9): 510-516.

一九四五年

11. A generalized theory of vectorial modular forms of positive dimensions. *Science Record*, 1945, 1(3-4): 313-318.

一九四七年

12. On a system of congruences. *J. London Math. Soc.*, 1947(22): 47-53.

13. On the Euclidean algorithm in real quadratic fields. *J. London Math. Soc.*, 1947(22): 88-90.

14. On a generalized hyperbolic geometry. *J. London Math. Soc.*, 1947(22): 153-160.

15. On a double exponential sum(合作者; 华罗庚). *Sci. Rep. of Nat. Tsinghua Univ.*, *Ser. A*, 1947, 4(4-6): 484-518.

16. On systems of algebraic equations and certain multiple exponential sums. *Quart. J. Math. Oxford*, 1947, 18(71): 133-142.

一九四八年

17. Euclidean algorithm in real quadratic fields. *Sci. Rep. of Nat. Tsinghua Univ. Ser. A*. 1948, 5(2-3): 190-225.

一九四九年

18. On the order of $\zeta(1/2+it)$. *Trans. of Amer. Math. Soc.*, 1949, 65(3): 448-472.

一九五〇年

19. On the zeros of the Riemann Zeta function. *Sci. Rep. of Nat. Tsinghua Univ.*, *Ser. A*, 1950, 5(4): 379-401.

一九五一年

20. On a generalization of the Stieltjes integral and its application to the generalized harmonic analysis. *Science Record*, 1951, 4(2): 109-118.

一九五三年

21. 北京大学数学分析教研组第一次全系性试教. 数学通报, 1953(7):

35-48.

一九五四年

22. 谈一个求极限的问题. 数学学报,1954,4(4):381-385.

23. 不等式. 数学通报,1954(11):1-8.

一九五五年

24. 数论在中国的发展情况. 数学进展,1955,1(2):397-402.

25. 黎曼 ζ 函数的一种推广——Ⅰ. $Z_{n,k}(s)$ 的全面解析开拓. 数学学报,1955,5(3):285-294.

26. 谈一个制造处处不可微的连续函数的方法. 数学通报,1955(7):10-13.

一九五六年

27. 黎曼 ζ 函数的一种推广——Ⅱ. $Z_{n,k}(s)$ 的阶. 数学学报,1956,6(1):1-11.

28. 黎曼 ζ 函数的一种推广——Ⅲ. $Z_{n,k}(s)$ 的均值公式. 数学学报,1956,6(3):347-362.

29. 二元半纯函数的局部展开式(合作者:董怀允). 北京大学学报,1956,2(1):25-38.

30. 论黎曼 ζ 函数的非明显零点. 北京大学学报,1956,2(2):165-189.

31. 谈 $\pi(x)$ 与 $\zeta(s)$. 北京大学学报,1956,2(3):297-302.

一九五七年

32. 初等数论(合作者:严士健). 北京:高等教育出版社,1957.

一九五八年

33. 关于 $Z_{n,k}(s)$ 的均值公式(合作者:尹文霖). 北京大学学报,1958,4(1):41-50.

34. 数论的方法(上册). 北京:科学出版社,1958.

一九五九年

35. 关于多重积分的近似计算. 北京大学学报,1959,5(2):127-130.

36. 关于定积分及重积分的近似计算. 北京大学学报,1959,5(3):203-208.

37. On the numerical integration of double and multiple integerals. *Science Record*,1959,3(11):531-533.

38. 十年来的中国数学(1949-1959)(合作者:柯召). 北京:科学出版社,1959,55-75.

一九六二年

39. $Z_{n,k}(s)$ 与一个格点问题(合作者:尹文霖). 北京大学学报,1962,8(2):81-89.

40. 从北京市中学 1962 年数学竞赛试题谈起. 数学通报,1962(6):36-40.

一九六三年

41. 广义解析函数论的具体化与一般化. 北京大学学报,1963,9(1):1-12.

42. On concrete examples and the abstract theory of the generalized analytic functions. *Scientia Sinica*,1963,12(9):1270-1283.

43. 关于 Лаврентаев 微分方程的一个简单处理方法(合作者:华罗庚). 未发表.

一九六四年

44. 广义 Selberg 不等式与 Tauber 型定理. 未发表.

45. 谈一类 Tauber 型定理. 未发表.

46. 关于黎曼 ζ 函数零点分布的均匀性(合作者:李忠). 北京:中国数学会数论专业学术会议论文摘要,1964.

47. 格点和面积. 北京:人民教育出版社,1964.

48. 北京市 1964 年中学生数学竞争试题解答(合作者:越民义等). 数学通报,1964(6):21-25.

一九七三年

49. 地震勘探数字技术,(第一册合作编著). 北京:科学出版社,1973.

一九七四年

50. 关于数值滤波. 物探数字技术,1974(1):32-43.

51. 关于数值滤波(续). 物探数字技术,1974(2):113-138.

52. 地震勘探数字技术(第二册合作编著). 北京:科学出版社,1974.

一九七五年

53. 独立自主发展石油地震数字处理(笔名:宏油兵,舒立华). 数学学报,1975,18(4):231-246.

一九七六年

54. 独立自主发展石油地震数字处理(续完)(笔名:宏油兵,舒立华). 数学学报,1976,18(1):64-72.

一九八一年

55. 数论的方法下册. 北京:科学出版社,1981.

◎ 附 录

附录一　北京大学数学分析教研组第一次全系性试教

闵嗣鹤

教　案

时间：一九五三年五月二十一日下午讲演第一节 2:30 ~ 3:15；第二节 3:20 ~ 4:05；讨论 4:20 ~ 5:45.

试教目的：1. 对教案的制订交换意见.

2. 交流课堂教学经验.

3. 交流对苏联教材的体会.

教材内容：有序变量　无穷小量　$\varepsilon - N$说法　无穷小量的和（孙译斯米尔诺夫高等数学教程第一分册 42-46）

试教教案：

Ⅰ. 教学目的

在学生具有变量、变量范围、函数概念等知识后，开始引进极限概念，从直观入手，逐步引导到无穷小量的定义. 通过例题，使学生能初步认识无穷小量的实质.

有序变量的引进目的在统一编号与非编号变量的极限理论，讲演重点是在编号变量，使学生认识了编号变量的极限理论后，能够自己独立解决非编号变量的问题.

$\varepsilon-N$方法的引进要使学生了解怎样用无穷小量的定义来判断一个变量是否是无穷小量. 通过例题，从给定的 ε 求 N，使学生对无穷小量的意义有比较深刻的认识，不再停留在直观与笼统的阶段.

“有限个无穷小量的和是无穷小量” 这一性质的引进，在使学生能体会抽象出来的一般性质可以用来解决具体的问题，就是从已知的无穷小量来得到或判断新的无穷小量.

Ⅱ. 开始部分

1）回忆前阶段：提出从常数到变量是数学上从静到动的一个显著的进展，因为变量是变动的，所以我们要讨论它的变化范围.

2）引入本阶段，并指出本阶段的目的：为了要进一步研究变量的变化情形，除了以前讨论过的变量的变化范围以外，我们现在要讨论变量的变化顺序与它的变化趋势，本单元要讨论的有序变量就是在研究变量的变化顺序. 本单元要讨论的无穷小量就是在研究变量的变化趋势.

Ⅲ. 中间部分

1）由实例引入有序变量

① 庄子天下篇，一尺之锤，日取其半，万世不竭.

② 一变量随时间而变，其所取值与时间成反比.

2）分别编号与非编号变量.

3）从变化趋势引出无穷小量.

4）通过例题熟悉 $\varepsilon-N$ 说法.

例 1. $$x=\frac{1}{t}$$

例 2. $$x=\frac{1}{2^n}$$

5）引理与无穷小量的和.

Ⅳ. 结尾部分

1）总结本单元.

2）布置思考题.

① 把引理在非编号的情形下叙述出来.

② 证明非编号无穷小量的和是无穷小量（两个变量的情形）

Ⅴ. 习题课的配合

1）补充习题（占 15 分钟）. 为了使学生巩固并进一步认识有序变量与无穷

小量的意义,必须给以丰富的具体例子,习题课应结合讲课,补充各种形式的有序变量与无穷小量的例子.

2) 布置讨论(占 15 ~ 30 分钟). 理论部分的讲课从能解决问题为原则,但学生初学极限理论,必须充分估计他们的困难,在一些关键性的问题上,布置一些讨论题,分别叫学生口头回答,教员把学生的答案记录在黑板上,让全体学生讨论是否正确,然后教员做总结,布置讨论以前先要了解学生上课后的学习情况,然后针对疑难处出讨论题.

3) 作题(占45 ~ 65 分钟). 习题的布置要联系过去的教材并有意识地配合下一次的讲演,作下次讲课的准备. 例如在习题中对非编号变量可出这样的问题:设 y 是一个非编号变量,它与时间 t 的关系是 $y=\frac{1}{2^t}$,问当时间无限继续时,这个变量是否是无穷小量. 用 $\varepsilon-T$ 的方法,加以证明!作 $y=\frac{1}{2^t}$ 的曲线,从图形上加以说明. 这就是配合了以前指数函数的作图. 又可出如下的习题:利用引理证明一个常量乘无穷小量仍是无穷小量(顺便把乘的意义交代一下). 这就结合了下一单元.

讲　稿

Ⅰ. 开始部分

今天是第二阶段,第一单元,开始讲书的第二章 §1. 我们从 42 页讲到 46 页前半,同时还要讲 47 页的一部分,今天要学的主要内容已经写在黑板上,就是有序变量、无穷小量、$\varepsilon-N$ 说法及无穷小量的和.

我们在第一阶段已经学过常量及变量,知道了变量的引进是高等数学与初等数学的分界点,所以变量的研究是非常重要的事. 关于变量我们提出三个问题:

甲　在哪里变化 —— 变化范围.

乙　怎样变化 —— 变化顺序.

丙　趋势如何 —— 变化趋势.

在第一阶段已经讲过什么叫变化范围,例如 x 在(0,1) 区间内变化,就说 x 的变化范围是(0,1) 这个开区间. 但在实际应用上,不仅要知道变化范围,还要讨论到变化顺序,例如不仅要知道 x 在(0,1) 内变化,还要问到底 x 从 0 变向 1,还是从 1 变向 0. 还有,不仅要知道变化顺序,还要讨论变化的趋势.

例如:在苏联或中国的工业建设中,生产量是逐渐增加,这是一个变量,工厂里工作的效率也逐渐提高,这也是一个变量. 但有些东西(例如钢铁) 的生产量，虽然不如资本主义的国家那样多，我们并不因此而气馁，因为根据变化的趋势讲，我们的生产量最终要超过他们. 这说明了变化趋势的重要性. 下面要举两个更具体的例子，来说明变化的顺序及趋势.

Ⅱ. 由实例引入有序变量

例甲　大约两三千年以前，中国的一个哲学家庄周在他的书里（庄子天下篇），引到那时候的雄辩家惠施的话："一尺之棰，日取其半，万世不竭." 所谓"棰" 就是一根木头做的杖，所谓"竭" 就是尽的意思，一尺的木杖，每天取一半，两天就取完了，为什么"万世不竭呢"？他的意思是第一天取一半剩一半；第二天所取的是第一天所剩的一半，也就是原来的$\frac{1}{4}$；第三天所取的是第二天所剩的一半，也就是原来的$\frac{1}{4}\times\frac{1}{2}=\frac{1}{8}$. 这样每天取一半，每天总要剩一半，到明天总还有可取的，所以他说万世不竭.

如果用 x 代表所剩下的长度，那么 x 就是一个变量. 第一天 x 的值是$\frac{1}{2}$，第二天是$\frac{1}{4}=\frac{1}{2^2}$，第三天是$\frac{1}{8}=\frac{1}{2^3}$，…，第 n 天 x 的值是$\frac{1}{2^n}$，x 依次所取的值是$\frac{1}{2}$，$\frac{1}{2^2}$，$\frac{1}{2^3}$，…，$\frac{1}{2^n}$，…，这就是所谓"有序变量" 的一个例.

例乙　另外的一个例是这样：变量 x 随时间 t 而改变，永与时间成反比. 因此，可以写成 $x=\frac{k}{t}$，其中 k 是一个常量. 为简单起见，今设 $k=1$. 假定时间从 1 点钟开始变下去，以至无穷，则 x 的值最初是 1，后来越来越小，但永远没有是 0 的时间. 这是"有序变量" 的另一个例子.

讲到这里，我们要问：到底一个变量在什么情况下才叫做有序变量呢？从以上两个例来看，我们说应该适合下面两个条件：

1）取值要有先后，就是说先取哪个值，后取哪个值要有规定.

2）没有最后的值，什么叫没有最后的值呢？就是说，取了任何一个值以后，还要有值可取，例如在例甲里面，取了$\frac{1}{16}$，还有$\frac{1}{32}$，取了$\frac{1}{32}$，还有$\frac{1}{64}$，等等.

本来，有了第一个条件，似乎就够了，为什么还要第二个条件呢？这因为我们要研究变化趋势，所以希望它永在变化过程之中，没有终止的时候.

Ⅲ. 分别编号变量与非编号变量

上面两个例虽然都是有序变量，但他们之间是有很大分别的. 例甲里面，变量 x 所取的值，可以按照次序去编号. 第一次所取的值是$\frac{1}{2}$，这可以编成第一号，第二次所取的值是$\frac{1}{4}$，这个可以编成第二号，…，第 n 次所取的值是$\frac{1}{2^n}$，这可以编成第 n 号，如下表：

号码	1,	2,	…,	n
值	$\frac{1}{2}$,	$\frac{1}{4}$,	…,	$\frac{1}{2^n}$

这样的变量叫做编号变量，一个编号变量依次所取的值，称为组成一个序列.

例乙虽然也是有序变量，但不能依次编号，譬如把 1 编作第一号，那么就不能说出哪个值该编第二号. 如果说是$\frac{1}{2}$该编第二号，就不合理，因为 x 从 1 变到$\frac{1}{2}$之前还取过$\frac{3}{4}$这个值. 总之任何值都不能编成第二号. 因为这个例所代表的不是编号变量，而是非编号变量.

总结起来，有序变量可以分成两类如下：

有序变量 $\begin{cases}\text{编号变量：所取的值可以依次编号，组成一个序列.}\\ \text{非编号变量：所取的值不能依次编号.}\end{cases}$

现在试问编号变量的一般情形，是不是可以表出来？若 x 是编号变量，它总有第一次取的值，也就是编成第一号的值，我们可以用 x_1 代表它；它也总有第二次所取的值，也就是编成第二号的值，我们用 x_2 代表它；…，它总有第 n 次取的值，也就是编成第 n 号的值，我们用 x_n 代表它，…，这样，在一般情形之下，编号变量所取的值总可以依次写成

$$x_1, x_2, \cdots, x_n, \cdots$$

除编号变量以外，当然一切有序变量都是非编号变量，但是我们所要讲的非编号变量，仅限于像例乙那样的随时间变化的变量. 这种变量 x 都可以表成 t 的函数

$$x = f(t)$$

Ⅳ. 从变化趋势引出无穷小量

现在让我们多举一些例子，通过他们来观察变量的变化趋势.

编号变量的例：前面说过一般的编号变量的值，可以依次表出如下：

$$x_1, x_2, x_3, x_4, \cdots, x_n, \cdots$$

最简单的一个例子是 x 依次取下面的值：

例 1　　$1, 2, 3, 4, \cdots, n, \cdots$

当然前面举的庄子的例也是一个好例.

例 2　　$\frac{1}{2}, \frac{1}{2^2}, \frac{1}{2^3}, \frac{1}{2^4}, \cdots, \frac{1}{2^n}, \cdots$

把 x 依次所取的值逐一变号就得到：

例 3 $$-\frac{1}{2},-\frac{1}{2^2},-\frac{1}{2^3},-\frac{1}{2^4},\cdots,-\frac{1}{2^n},\cdots$$

如果只变更 x 在第奇数次所取值的号,而保留偶数次所取值的号. 就得到:

例 4 $$-\frac{1}{2},-\frac{1}{2^2},-\frac{1}{2^3},-\frac{1}{2^4},\cdots,(-1)^n\frac{1}{2^n},\cdots$$

如果把例 2 里面,x 在第偶数次所取的值都换成 0,就得:

例 5 $$\frac{1}{2},0,\frac{1}{2^3},0,\cdots$$

$$x_n=\begin{cases}\frac{1}{2^n},\text{当 } n \text{ 是奇数}\\0,\text{当 } n \text{ 是偶数}\end{cases}$$

从以上几个例可以看到,有序变量所取的值,并不一定按大小排列,也不一定完全不相同,又在例 2 内,x 所取的值可以写成:

$$2^{-1},2^{-2},2^{-3},2^{-4},\cdots,2^{-n},\cdots$$

如果把第偶数次所取的值的指数,改成正数,就得:

例 6 $$2^{-1},2^2,2^{-3},2^4,\cdots,2^{(-1)^n},\cdots$$

如果把例 2 中每一个都加$\frac{1}{1\ 000}$,就得到

例 7 $$\frac{1}{2}+\frac{1}{1\ 000},\frac{1}{2^2}+\frac{1}{1\ 000},\frac{1}{2^3}+\frac{1}{1\ 000},\cdots,\frac{1}{2^n}+\frac{1}{1\ 000},\cdots$$

如不加$\frac{1}{1\ 000}$,而用正数 M 去乘例 2 内各值,即得

例 8 $$\frac{M}{2},\frac{M}{2^2},\frac{M}{2^3},\frac{M}{2^4},\cdots,\frac{M}{2^n},\cdots(M>0)$$

把例 8 和例 4 内对应的值加起来,即得

例 9 $$\frac{M-1}{2},\frac{M+1}{2^2},\frac{M-1}{2^3},\frac{M+1}{2^4},\cdots,\frac{M+(-1)^n}{2^n},\cdots$$

最后还要举一个最简单的例,就是 x 顺次所取的值都是 0.

例 10 $$0,0,0,0,\cdots,0,\cdots$$

如果一个骰子的六面都是 0,那么依次掷出来的数,就永远是 0.

非编号变量的例:

例 11 $x=\frac{1}{t}(1\leqslant t<+\infty)$

例 12 $x=\frac{1}{2^t}(1\leqslant t<+\infty)$

我们已经举了够多的例子,让我们来观察一下,各例里面的变量是怎样变化的?

有的是越变越大的,例 1 及例 3 即是. 有的是越变越小的,如例 2、例 7 及

例8. 有的是忽大忽小的,如例4、例5及例6.

在这些例子当中,有一部分的例(如例2),和其他的例不同,这种例的变化趋势比较容易看出来. 虽然惠施说得不错"一尺之锤,日取其半,万世不竭". 但是它的长度越来越短,可以说是趋向0.

例3也是一样,不过x趋向0的方向与例2相反,不是从正的方面越来越小,趋向于0,而是从负的方面越来越大,趋向于0.

例4里面,x也趋向0,但不是从一个方向趋向它.

例5里,x也趋向于0,但是离0忽远忽近.

例11里,时间越过得多,x越小,虽然永不为0,但是可以无限制地变小,所以也可以说趋向0. 考虑了这么多的例,我们要问:到底在什么情形下,x才算是趋向0呢?

(1) 我们很容易回答:"当x所取的值越来越离0近时,就可以叫做趋向0."但这是错的,因为例5是趋向0的,但所取的值并非越来越离0近;另一方面例7里面的值,例是越来越离0近,但总保持一段距离$\frac{1}{1\ 000}$,这又不能算是趋向0.

(2) 也许你会说:x要能任意地接近0,才算趋向0,这是对的,但还不够,如在例6中,第奇数个值越来越小,而且可以任意地接近于0,但第偶数个值就越来越大,所以并不是趋向0.

(3) 所以你应该说:不仅能任意接近于0,还要能保持任意的接近于0才成. 但是这句话还有缺点,因为一个趋向0的变量,并不是从头起就能保持任意接近于0的,如例2,第一值是$\frac{1}{2}$,并离0不很近. 所以这句话还要修正成:

"x到后来,要能保持任意地接近于0,才算趋向0."这句话已经是正确的了,但是还嫌太空洞不够具体.

第一,怎样叫任意地接近于0呢?

所谓"任意地接近于0",就是"对于无论多么小的区间(但须以0为中心),x的值都有钻进去的时候". 例如,两条黄线夹住一个小区间(简称黄区间),x_3就在他里面,两条红线夹住一个更小的区间(简称红区间),x_4就在它里面,绿线所夹的区间(绿区间)更小,x_5就在它里面.

第二,怎样叫到后来呢?

具体地说,就是x取过了某一个值X之后.

第三,怎样叫能保持呢?

就是代表x的点,永远不出那个区间. 例如当x取过$x_2=\frac{1}{4}$之后,代表x的点($x_3, x_4, \cdots$) 就永远不出黄区间了. 当 x 取过 $x_3 = \frac{1}{8}$ 之后代表 x 的点(x_4, $x_5, \cdots$), 就永远不出红区间了. 当 x 取过 $x_4 = \frac{1}{16}$ 之后, 代表 x 的点($x_5, x_6, \cdots$) 就永远不出绿区间了.

(4) 总结起来, 我们就得到 x 趋向 0 的几何定义:

若对于无论多么小的区间(但须以 0 为中心), 当 x 取过某一个值 X 之后, 代表 x 的点就永远跑不出那个区间, 则我们说 x 趋向 0.

这个定义是正确的, 但是我们还要脱离几何的说法, 纯粹用分析的语言表达这个定义.

(5) 习惯上在这里我们要引用一个希腊字母 ε, 这是第五个希腊字母, 前四个是($\alpha, \beta, \gamma, \delta$). 我们要用 2ε 专门表示前面所说区间的长度.

现在试问: 在什么情形之下, 代表 x 的点才在长度是 2ε 的区间内呢? 显然只要那点离原点 0 的距离小于 ε, 就超不出那个区间了, 但 x 点离 0 的距离是什么呢? 我们知道是 $|x|$. 因此, "代表 x 的点在那个区间内" 这句话就可以用

$$|x| < \varepsilon$$

来代替. 另一方面, 所谓区间无论多么小, 就是长度无论多么小也就是 ε(他的长度的一半) 无论多么小(注意 ε 必须是正的). 因此, 上面几何的说法就可以改成:

任给	都可以找到	使当	永远有
$\varepsilon > 0$	x 的一个值 X	x 取过 X 之后	$\|x\| < \varepsilon$

这已经是标准的定义了. 但是我们还可以分开编号与非编号两种情形, 把定义说得更简明些.

先讨论编号变量的情形, 就例 4 而论, 我们可以说 x 取过 $x_2 = \frac{1}{4}$ 这个值之后, 代表 x 的点($x_3, x_4, \cdots$) 就不再跑出黄的区间了. 但更明确的说法是当号码 n 大于 2 时, x_n 就不再跑出黄区间. 同样地, 与其说当 x 取过 $-\frac{1}{8}$ 就不出红区间, 不如说当号码 n 大于 5 时, x_n 就不出红区间, 还有, 我们最好说: 当号码 $n > 4$ 时, x_n 就不出绿区间. 因此, 在编号情形下, 可以把趋向 0 的定义改写成下面的形式:

任给	都可以找到	使当	永远有
$\varepsilon > 0$	号码 N	$n > N$	$\|x_n\| < \varepsilon$

又当 x 是随时间 t 变的非编号变量

$$x = f(t)$$

时,我们与其说 x 取过某一个值 X 之后,不如说,当时间大于某一个时刻 T 之后(这里的时刻 T 相当于前面的号码 N),因此,趋向 0 的定义可以改写成

任给	都可以找到	使当	永远有
$\varepsilon > 0$	T	$t > T$	$\vert f(t)\vert < \varepsilon$

以上三个定义可以用第二个(即编号变量的情形)作代表,叫做 $\varepsilon - N$ 说法. 这种说法在分析里面很有用,希望大家逐渐能够掌握它.

如果 x 趋向 0,我们就说 x 是一个无穷小量. 记作

$$x \to 0$$

或

$$\lim x = 0$$

应该注意,无穷小量即是趋向 0 的有序变量,与很小的量不能混为一谈. 例如 $\frac{1}{1\ 000}$ 很小,并非无穷小量,又如 $\frac{1}{1\ 000^{1\ 000}}$ 更是小得厉害,也不是无穷小量.

另一方面,例 10 里的变量是无穷小量,因为它合乎我们的定义:任给 $\varepsilon > 0$,永远有

$$|x_n| = 0 < \varepsilon$$

V. **通过例题熟悉 $\varepsilon - N$ 说法**

前面从几个例出发,一步一步推出了无穷小量的分析定义. 现在反过来看,是否那些例都合乎无穷小量的定义呢?还有,怎样根据定义判断一个有序变量是不是无穷小量呢?我们先看:

例乙 $$x = \frac{1}{t}(1 \leqslant t < +\infty)$$

任给	可找到	使当	永远有
$\varepsilon = \frac{1}{100}$	$T = 100$	$t > T$	$\left\vert\frac{1}{t}\right\vert < \frac{1}{100}$
$\varepsilon = \frac{1}{1\ 000}$	$T = 1\ 000$	$t > T$	$\left\vert\frac{1}{t}\right\vert < \frac{1}{1\ 000}$
$\varepsilon > 0$	$T = \frac{1}{\varepsilon}$ (即 $\frac{1}{T} = \varepsilon$)	$t > T$	$\left\vert\frac{1}{t}\right\vert < \varepsilon$

应该注意:我们仅仅知道 $\varepsilon = \frac{1}{100}$ 时可以找到 T,是不够的,即使知道当 $\varepsilon = \frac{1}{1\ 000^{1\ 000}}$ 时,可以找到 T 也不能断定 x 是无穷小量 x,必须对于任给的 $\varepsilon > 0$ 都能找到 T,才能确定 x 是无穷小量.

其次看:

例甲　x 顺次取$\frac{1}{2},\frac{1}{2^2},\cdots,\frac{1}{2^n},\cdots$,即 $x_n = \frac{1}{2^n}$,问题是:

任给	都可以找到	使当	永远有
(一)　$\varepsilon = \frac{1}{100}$	$N = ?$	$n > N$	$\left\|\frac{1}{2^n}\right\| < \frac{1}{100}$
(二)　$\varepsilon > 0$	$N = ?$	$n > N$	$\left\|\frac{1}{2^n}\right\| < \varepsilon$

先讨论(一),问题是当 $n > ?$时可以得到$\frac{1}{2^n} < \frac{1}{100}$.

这只要 $2^n > 100$ 也就是要(两边取对数)$n \log_{10}2 > 2$ 即 $n > \frac{2}{\log_{10}2}$.

我们不能取 $N = \frac{2}{\log_{10}2}$,因为$\frac{2}{\log_{10}}$不是正整数,不能作为号码. 现在引用一个记号$[a]$. 这表示 a 的整数部分. 例如$[\pi] = 3$,$[\sqrt{2}] = 1$,$[0] = 0$. 引用这个记号就可以取

$$N = \left[\frac{2}{\log_{10}2}\right]$$

为什么呢?因为 n 是正整数,所以当 n 大于$\frac{2}{\log_{10}}$的整数部分时,必然就大于$\frac{2}{\log_{10}2}$.

其次讨论(二). 要解决的问题是:当 $n > ?$时$\frac{1}{2^n} < \varepsilon$,即$\frac{1}{2^n} < \frac{\varepsilon}{1}$. 这只是 $2^n > \frac{1}{\varepsilon}$. 也就是只要(两边取对数)$n\log_{10}2 > \log_{10}\frac{1}{\varepsilon}$,即$n > \frac{\log_{10}\frac{1}{\varepsilon}}{\log_{10}2}$. 当$\varepsilon \geqslant \frac{1}{2}$时,$\frac{\log_{10}\frac{1}{\varepsilon}}{\log_{10}2} \geqslant 1$,我们可以取 $N = \left[\frac{\log_{10}\frac{1}{\varepsilon}}{\log_{10}2}\right]$. 但当$\varepsilon > \frac{1}{2}$时,我们要取 $N = 1$,这因为当 $n > 1$ 时 $|x| > \frac{1}{2}$.

Ⅵ. 一个引理及无穷小量的和

从上面的例,我们看到怎样根据无穷小量的定义,去判断一个有序变量是不是无穷小量. 在平常并不直接从定义去判断,而利用一些更容易引用的定理去证明. 例如想证明例 8 代表无穷小量,就不必直接去证明,因为我们已经证明例 2 里的变量 $x \to 0$,但例 8 里的变量就是例 2 里变量的 M 倍,即 Mx,所以我们只要证明当 $x \to 0$ 时,一定要 $Mx \to 0$ 就行了. 现在以编号变量为例,先证"若

$x \to 0$ 则 $3x \to 0$”.

因为 $x \to 0$,所以

任给	都可以找到	使当	永远有
$\varepsilon > 0$	N	$n > N$	$\lvert x_n \rvert < \varepsilon$
$\frac{\varepsilon}{3} > 0$	N	$n > N$	$\lvert x_n \rvert < \frac{\varepsilon}{3}$

但给 $\frac{\varepsilon}{3} > 0$ 与给 $\varepsilon > 0$ 是一样的,所以

任给	都可以找到	使当	永远有
$\varepsilon > 0$	N	$n > N$	$\lvert x_n \rvert < \frac{\varepsilon}{3}$

既然若把 3 换成 5 或 $\frac{5}{2}$,都可以得到同样的结果. 普遍地说,就得下面的引理:

引理 若 $x \to 0$,则

任给	都可以找到	使当	永远有
$\varepsilon > 0$ $M > 0$	N	$n > N$	$\lvert x_n \rvert < \frac{\varepsilon}{M}$

由此得 $\lvert Mx_n \rvert < \varepsilon$. 这表明 $Mx \to 0$.

从上面的引理可以判断例 8 是无穷小量. 现在讨论例 9. 这个例是把例 8 与例 4 里面相当的值相加而得到的. 因此我们先要讨论无穷小量的代数和:

(1) 编号变量的代数和. 设

x 依次取 $x_1, \quad x_2, \quad \cdots, \quad x_n, \quad \cdots$ 各值

y 依次取 $y_1, \quad y_2, \quad \cdots, \quad y_n, \quad \cdots$ 各值

z 依次取 $z_1, \quad z_2, \quad \cdots, \quad z_n, \quad \cdots$ 各值

又设

w 依次取 $w_1, \quad w_2, \quad \cdots, \quad w_n, \quad \cdots$ 各值

而 $w_1 = x_1 + y_1 - z_1, w_2 = x_2 + y_2 - z_2, \cdots, w_n = x_n + y_n - z_n, \cdots$

则称 w 为 x,y,z 的代数和,写作

$$w = x + y - z$$

当变量个数不是 3,显然可以仿此给代数和下定义.

(2) 非编号变量的代数和. 设 $x = f(t), y = \varphi(t), z = \psi(t)$,而

$$w = f(t) + \varphi(t) - \psi(t)$$

则称 w 是 x,y 与 z 的代数和,并写作 $w = x + y - z$.

要注意的是，只有同类型的有序变量才能求和，或者都可以编号，或者都随时间变化才可以求和. 一个编号变量与一个非编号变量是不能求和的.

现在我们要以编号变量为例，证明：

有限个无穷小量的代数和仍然是无穷小量.

证 仍以 $w = x + y - z$ 为例. 问题是：

任给	要找	使当	永远有
$\varepsilon > 0$	N	$n > N$	$\lvert w_n \rvert < \varepsilon$

因为

$$\lvert w_n \rvert = \lvert x_n + y_n - z_n \rvert \leqslant \lvert x_n \rvert + \lvert y_n \rvert + \lvert z_n \rvert$$

要想使上式右边小于 ε，只要使右边三项各小于 $\frac{\varepsilon}{3}$，因为 $x \to 0$，所以可以找到 N_1，使

$$\text{当}\ n > N_1\ \text{时}, \lvert x_n \rvert < \frac{\varepsilon}{3}$$

又因为 $y \to 0$，所以又可以找到 N_2（可能与 N_1 不相同）使

$$\text{当}\ n > N_2\ \text{时}, \lvert y_n \rvert < \frac{\varepsilon}{3}$$

最后，因为 $z \to 0$，所以又可以找到 N_3，使当 $n > N_3$ 时，$\lvert z_n \rvert < \frac{\varepsilon}{3}$.

设 N_1, N_2, N_3 中最大的一个是 N（上表中 N_2，最大，当然也可能 N_1 或 N_3 最大），则当 $n > N$ 时

$$\lvert x_n \rvert < \frac{\varepsilon}{3}, \quad \lvert y_n \rvert < \frac{\varepsilon}{3}, \quad \lvert z_n \rvert < \frac{\varepsilon}{3}$$

即当 $n > N$ 时，$\lvert w_n \rvert < \frac{\varepsilon}{3} + \frac{\varepsilon}{3} + \frac{\varepsilon}{3} = \varepsilon$. 这证明 w 是无穷小量.

根据上面的定理，可以断定例 9 是无穷小量.

Ⅶ. 总结

今天就讲到这里，总结起来有下面各项：

有序变量 —— 取值有先后，没有最后值.

{编号变量 —— 所取值可以依次编号，作成一个序列.
非编号变量 —— 所取值不能依次编号.

无穷小量 —— 有几何定义，$\varepsilon - X$ 说法，$\varepsilon - N$ 说法及 $\varepsilon - T$ 说法. 有限个无穷小量的和仍为无穷小量.

附录二　数论在中国的发展情况[①]

闵嗣鹤

（北京大学）

在中国，数论的发展是有着极其悠久的历史的，远在纪元以前，孙子所建立的中国除数定理和距今约七百年前秦九韶所发明的解一次不定方程的方法，都是比较突出的例子. 到了近代，数论方面的发展更由于早期向苏联学习而有了长足的进步. 谈到近代数论，必须要提起数学研究所所长华罗庚在这方面所作过的许多优秀的贡献.

华罗庚的数学研究有很多方面，我现在只能简单地介绍他在数论方面的一些贡献. 还是在 1935 年的时候，华罗庚开始学习苏联维诺格拉多夫（Виноградов）院士的新方法，掌握了它的原理原则，而创造性地予以灵活运用，因而获得了一系列值得称道的结果.

首先应该提起他在华林问题方面的成就. 设 $r(N)$ 表示不定方程

$$N = x_1^k + \cdots + x_s^k,\quad k, s \text{ 正整数}; N \text{ 整数}$$

的非负整数解的个数，他证明：当 $s \geqslant 2^k + 1$ 时

$$r(N) = \frac{\Gamma^s\left(1 + \frac{1}{k}\right)}{\Gamma\left(\frac{s}{k}\right)} \mathfrak{G}(N)^{\frac{k}{s}-1} + O\left(N^{\frac{s}{k}-1-s}\right)$$

其中 $\delta = 2^{1-k}s - 2 - \varepsilon$，而 $\varepsilon > 0$，又 $\mathfrak{G}(N)$ 表示所谓奇异级数. 这个结果优于哈代（Hardy）与李托伍德（Littlewood）的结果，而在 $k < 14$ 时，就优于维诺格拉多夫的结果. 他又推广华林问题到把 N 表成整数值多项式之和的问题，例如他曾证明每一个大的整数可以表成 8 个（满足必要的同余条件的）三次多项式之和. 我们必须提到，在中国最早研究三次多项式的华林问题的是杨武之. 他用初等方法证明了：任一正整数是 9 个三角垛数之和，他的方法后来被很多人用来研究其他的三次多项式的华林问题. 对于哥德巴赫问题，华罗庚也曾加以推广，

---

① 本文系1954年闵嗣鹤先生在欢迎德意志民主共和国洪堡大学第一数学研究所所长格雷耳博士教授大会上的讲稿.

他证明了每一个充分大的奇数 n 是两个素数与一个素数的 k 方之和,几乎所有适合必要的同余条件的正整数皆是一个素数与一个素数的 k 方之和.

在塔利问题方面,他有下述结果:设 $M(k)$ 表示能使下列不定方程组有解的 s 的最小值:

$$x_1^k + \cdots + x_s^k = y_1^k + \cdots + y_s^k, \quad 1 \leqslant h \leqslant k$$
$$x_1^{k+1} + \cdots + x_s^{k+1} \neq y_1^{k+1} + \cdots y_s^{k+1}$$

则

$$M(k) \leqslant (k+1)\left(\left[\frac{\log \frac{1}{2}(k+2)}{\log\left(1+\frac{1}{k}\right)}\right]+1\right) \sim k^2 \log k$$

这结果优于瑞特(Wright)的结果 $M(k) = O(k^4)$. 他又证明:当 $s > s_0$(其中 s_0 也是一个 k 的函数,适合 $s_0 \sim 3k^2 \log k$)时,可以得到上列方程组的解数的渐进公式.

在堆垒数论里常常要用到下列形式的三角和:

$$\sum_{x=1}^{q} \mathrm{e}^{2\pi i f(x)/q}$$

其中 $f(x) = a_k x^k + \cdots + a_1 x + a_0((a_k, \cdots, a_1) = 1)$ 是整系数的多项式. 华罗庚利用很精致的方法证明:当 $\varepsilon > 0$ 时

$$\sum_{x=1}^{q} \mathrm{e}^{2\pi i f(x)/q} = O(q^{1-\frac{1}{k}+\varepsilon})$$

此处 O 中所含的常数只与 ε 及 k 有关. 他又把这一结果推广到代数数域,这里研究代数数域的华林问题不可少的工具.

他在苏联出版了《堆垒素数论》一书,这本书是当时维诺格拉多夫的研究方法和他自己的研究方法的一个良好的总结,书里面给予维诺格拉多夫的中值定理以显著的中心地位,并且改进了它. 书中把华林问题与哥德巴赫问题的研究方法结合起来,把华林问题一方面推广到每一加数是整系数多项式的情形,一方面限制变数仅取素数值. 书中把塔利问题也加上了变数只取素数的限制,同时又讨论到更广一些的素未知数的不定方程组:

$$p_1^k + \cdots + p_s^k = N_K,$$
$$\cdots$$
$$p_1 + \cdots + p_s = N_1$$

他在这些问题中,当 k 大时都得到了相当于维诺格拉多夫对华林问题的结果.

在几何数论方面,他对于圆内格点问题保持了良好的结果. 设 $R(x)$ 表圆 $W^2 + V^2 \leqslant x$ 内格点数. 他证明:

$$R(x) = \pi x + O(x^{\frac{13}{40}} + \varepsilon), \quad \varepsilon > 0$$

这优于梯其玛什(Titchmatsh)的结果.又如以 $R_1(x)$ 表球 $u^2+v^2+w^2\leqslant x^2$ 内格点的数目,在1940年,他曾证明

$$R_1(x)=\frac{4}{3}\pi x^3+O(x^{1.4-\frac{1}{203}})$$

(注:原华所得结果 O 项为 $x^{4/3}$,后经检验原证,应改为上述形式).

在数论的其他方面,必须在这里提出的是:他对于素数是小元根的估计.设 $g(p)$ 表素数 p 是最小元根.他曾证明:

$$g(p)\leqslant 2^{m+d}p^{\frac{1}{2}}$$

其中 $d=0$ 或1视 $p\equiv 1$ 或 $3(\mathrm{mod}\ 4)$ 而定,而 m 表 $p-1$ 的不同的素因子的个数.这结果优于维诺格拉多夫的结果 $g(p)=O(2mp^{1/2}\log\log p)$.在证明此结果时,他运用了他关于特征和数的平均估值,这一方法有不少其他应用:例如对于佩尔(Pell)氏方程的最小解他得到了优于秀尔(Schur)所曾得到的结果.

华罗庚又曾对一整数分成两两不相同的数之和的分法个数导出了一个表示式.以上不过概括地介绍了华罗庚在数论研究上的主要工作,这当然并不是很完全的.对于其他中国数学家在数论方面的贡献(除了我自己的工作以外),由于手边材料不足的缘故,只能更简略地介绍一下.

现在仅就我所知来谈一下柯召在数论方面的贡献.我们知道,在虚二次数城 $k(\sqrt{m})(m<0)$ 中只有5个欧几里得域(即存在着欧几里得算法的数域),这5个数域就是 $k\sqrt{m}$,$m=-1,-2,-3,-7,-11$.要想定出所有实二次欧几里得域是比较困难的问题.但当 $m\equiv 2$ 或 $3(\mathrm{mod}\ 4)$ 时容易证明只有有限个实二次数域是欧几里得域,因此,当 $m\equiv 1(\mathrm{mod}\ 4)$ 时,要问是否也只有有限个欧几里得域就是一个核心问题,这问题已经在1938年由柯召、爱尔特希(Erdös)与海尔伯朗(Heilbronn)三位数学家予以肯定的回答.华罗庚和我自己都在这方面作过一些工作,曾经先后定出:当 $k(\sqrt{m})$ 是欧几里得数域时,整数 m 的一些上限.在我1948年所发表的一篇文章里(实际写完是在1945年以前)也说过这问题离解决不远.不过到1949年问题即为H·达文波特(Davenport)奥恰特兰德(Chatland)全部解决.他们证明了在所有实二次数域 $k(\sqrt{m})$ 中恰好有17个实二次数域是欧几里得域,即相当于 $m=2,3,5,6,7,11,13,17,19,21,29,33,37,41,57,73,97$ 的情形.

柯召另一方面的主要贡献是在二次型方面.他研究过行列式为1的正二次型的类数问题,不可分正二次型和二次型的平方和问题,讨论过包含6个、7个及8个变数的情形,作了一系列的文章.在他的指挥下,朱福祖及王绥旃皆曾做出一定的结果.

习惯上我们常把关于黎曼 ζ 函数的研究看成分析数论的一部分,在这方面

已故的王福春作过不少工作. 他曾证明下列形式的中值公式:

$$\int_1^T |\zeta(\sigma + \mathrm{i}t)|^2 \mathrm{d}f = T\zeta(2\sigma) + (2\pi)^{2\sigma-1} \frac{\zeta(2-2\sigma)}{2-2\sigma} T^{2-2\sigma} + O(T^{\frac{5}{6}(1-\sigma)}) \tag{A}$$

$$\int_1^T \frac{\log|\zeta(\frac{1}{2}+\mathrm{i}t)}{t^2}\mathrm{d}t = \tag{B}$$

$$2\sum_{r=1}^{\infty} \frac{\beta_r}{|\rho_w|^2} + \int_0^{x/2} R\left\{\mathrm{e}^{-\mathrm{i}\theta}\log\zeta(\frac{1}{2}+\mathrm{i}\mathrm{e}^{\mathrm{i}\theta})\right\}\mathrm{d}\theta + O\left(\frac{\log T}{T}\right)$$

其中 $P_w = \beta_r + \mathrm{i}\gamma_w$ 是 $\zeta(s)$ 满足 $\beta_w \geqslant 0$ 的零点,因而改进了培来与维纳(Paley Wiener) 的一个定理,原来培来与维纳只证明,上式左边是 $O(\log T)$.

当 $\sigma > \frac{1}{2}$ 时

$$\frac{1}{T}\int_0^T |\zeta(\sigma+\mathrm{i}t)|^2 \log|\zeta(\sigma+\mathrm{i}t)|\,\mathrm{d}t \sim \zeta(2\sigma)\log\zeta(2\sigma) \tag{C}$$

这和寻常中值公式

$$\frac{1}{T}\int_0^T |\zeta|\,(\sigma+\mathrm{i}t)|^2\mathrm{d}t \sim \zeta(2\sigma)$$

形成一个有趣的对比.

王福春对于黎曼 ζ 函数的零点个数也作过一些估计,他相信黎曼关于 ζ 函数的假设是不对的,极力想反证它. 在他故去之前还一直在研究这一个问题,可惜没能完成他的愿望.

现在略微谈一下我自己在数论方面的工作. 我在黎曼 ζ 函数方面的工作是这样:设用 $N(T)$ 表示 $\zeta\left(\frac{1}{2}+\mathrm{i}t\right)$ 在 $0 \leqslant t \leqslant T$ 这个区间内的零点个数,塞尔伯格(Sellberg) 曾证明有一个常数 A 存在,使得

$$N(T) > \frac{AT\log T}{2\pi} \tag{1}$$

及当 $u > T^{1/2+\varepsilon}(\varepsilon > 0)$ 时

$$N(T+u) - N(T) > \frac{Au\log T}{2\pi} \tag{2}$$

由(2) 可以推出(1). 我曾简化了(2) 的证明,并证明(1) 中的常数 A 可以取 $\frac{1}{60\,000}$ 这个值,另一方面我曾证明:

$$\zeta\left(\frac{1}{2}+\mathrm{i}t\right) = O(t^{\frac{15}{92}+\varepsilon}), \quad \varepsilon > 0 \tag{3}$$

这优于梯其玛什的结果. 证明(3) 的方法还可用到狄利克雷的除数问题,这件

工作已由迟宗陶完成. 他曾证明:

$$\sum_{m\leqslant x} d(n) = x\log x + (2\gamma - 1)x + O(x^{\frac{15}{46}+\varepsilon}), \quad \varepsilon > 0 \tag{4}$$

其中 $d(n)$ 表 n 的除数个数,这优于范德尔古璧(Van der corput) 的结果.

最近我发现函数

$$Z_{n,k}(s) = \sum_{x_1=-\infty}^{\infty}\cdots\sum_{x_k=-\infty}^{\infty}\frac{1}{(x_1^n+\cdots+x_k^n)^t} = \sum_{m=1}^{\infty}\frac{B(m)}{m^t}$$

$$B(m) = \sum_{x_1=-\infty}^{\infty}\cdots\sum_{x_k=-\infty}^{\infty}{}'1$$

$$x_1^n + \cdots x_k^n = m$$

(式中“1”表 $x_1,\cdots,x_k$ 不同时为零,n 为偶数) 像 $\zeta(s)$ 一样除只有一个简单极点外,可以开拓到全平面去,它也有类似的中值公式.

接着让我谈一下过去和华罗庚合作的文章. 我们曾经把莫德尔(Mordell) 的定理

$$\sum_{x=0}^{p-1} \mathrm{e}^{2\pi i f(x)/p} = O(p^{1-\frac{1}{k}})$$

式中 p 是素数,$f(x) = a_0x^k + \cdots + a_k, a_0 \not\equiv 0(\bmod p)$,推广到二重三角和的情形.

$$\sum_{x=0}^{p-1}\sum_{y=0}^{p-1} \mathrm{e}^{2\pi i f(x,y)/p} = O(p^{2-(1-\frac{1}{k})})$$

其中 $f(x,y)$ 是满足适当条件的 k 次多项式. 这个定理曾由我自己推到 n 个变数的情形,至于我和华罗庚合作的另外一些文章,例如关于类似塔利问题的一个问题的解决等,就不在这里细说了.

在密率论方面,周伯壎考虑了高斯整数的密率问题有一定的结果,张德馨关于连续素数的结果以及叶彦谦对于凸域上的圆柱内的格点所得的结果也应当提及.

越民义最近曾应用维诺格拉多夫的方法研究含素未知数的不等式的可解问题.

在分析数论方面,还有董光昌在除数问题方面做了不少工作. 他考虑

$$D_k(x) = \sum_{n\leqslant x} d_k(n)$$

其中 $d_k(n)$ 是把 x 分解成 k 个因数乘积的方法数. 仿照(4) 我们有下列形式的公式:

$$D_k(x) = (a_{k,0} + a_{k,1}\log x + \cdots + a_{k,k-1}\log^{k-1}x)x + \Delta_k(x) \tag{5}$$

其中 $a_{k,0},\cdots,a_{k,k-1}$ 是适当的常数, 而 $\Delta_k(x)$ 是误差项, 典型的简单结果是 $\Delta_k(x) = O(T^{\frac{k-1}{k+2}} + \varepsilon)(\varepsilon > 0)$. 董光昌对于 $\Delta_k(x)$ 给予了比前人更好的估计. 他

在这方面还有许多其他的工作未曾发表.

以上只是粗略地介绍了我国近年来在数论方面发展的情况,由于时间仓促和手边材料不足,很难作出较全面的报告;所有遗漏及详略不很恰当的地方希予指正.

附录三　不等式①

闵嗣鹤

1. 在数学的各分支里面,尤其是在数学分析里面,我们不可避免地都要用到不等式. 我们知道极限概念是数学分析的最重要的基础,一切其他上层建筑,如微商(或导数)、积分等都要建立在极限概念上面. 但是极限概念本身的建立,又完全依靠在一组不等式上,因此我们可以说,不等式是在数学分析最深处的一块基石. 也就是由于这个缘故,在数学分析全部理论的建立过程中,不断地出现不等式,不断地通过不等式获得最后的等式. 必须牢固地掌握不等式的重要性质,并且能够灵活地运用它,才有条件彻底地了解和真正地掌握数学分析的理论与应用.

但是一般在讲授大学一年级数学分析的过程中,最先感到必须为学生补充的预备知识,就是关于不等式的若干简单而又重要的性质. 事实上,这些性质是应该在中学里讲授的,这就说明在中学里面,一般对于不等式是不够重视的. 若能克服这一个缺点,充分地提起中学生对于不等式的注意,那么,对于他们以后在大学里面的学习,就会减少许多不必要的困难.

2. 不等式的基本性质. 在人民教育出版社出版的高级中学课本《代数》里面,第四章的主题就是不等式. 在那章里面,罗列了不等式的七条基本性质如下:

(1) 若 $a > b$,则 $b < a$;

(2) 若 $a > b$, $b > c$, 则 $a > c$;

(3) 若 $a > b$, $c = d$, 则 $a + c > b + d$;

(4) 若 $a > b$, $c > d$, 则 $a + c > b + d$;

(5) 若 $a > b$, $c > d$, 则 $a - c > b - d$;若 $a < b$, $c > d$, 则 $a - c < b - d$;

(6) 若 $a > b, m > 0$, 则 $am > bm$, $\frac{a}{m} > \frac{b}{m}$;

(7) 若 $a > b, m < 0$, 则 $am < bm$, $\frac{a}{m} < \frac{b}{m}$.

除此以外,我们还可以加一条:

---

① 本文系北京大学闵嗣鹤教授在中国数学会北京市分会主办的中学数学讲习会上的讲稿.

(8) 在下面三个式子 $a = b, a > b, a < b$ 之中,必有一样成立.

事实上,以上各条可以由很少的几个性质推出来. 为了这个目的,我们首先要肯定 $a > 0$ 的意义是已知的,并且规定 $a > b$ 的意义就是 $a - b > 0$, $a < b$ 的意义就是 $b > a$. 有了这一些规定,就可以将以上八条性质,从以下三条性质推出来:

Ⅰ. $a = 0$, $a > 0$, $a < 0$ 三者恰好有一样成立.

Ⅱ. 若 $a > 0$, $b > 0$, 则 $a + b > 0$.

Ⅲ. 若 $a > 0$, $b > 0$, 则 $ab > 0$.

(1) 的证明. 根据定义就可以得到所需要的结果.

(2) 的证明. 若 $a > b$, $b > c$, 则 $a - b > 0$, $b - c > 0$. 故由(Ⅱ)得 $(a - b) + (b - c) > 0$,即 $a - c > 0$,故 $a > c$.

(3) 的证明. 若 $a > b$, $c = d$, 则 $a - b > 0$, $c - d = 0$. 故 $(a + c) - (b + d) = (a - b) + (c - d) = a - b = 0$,即 $a + c > b + d$.

(4) 的证明. 若 $a > b$, $c > d$, 则 $a - b > 0$, $c - d > 0$. 故由(Ⅱ)$(a - b) + (c - d) > 0$,即 $(a + c) - (b + d) > 0$,即 $a + c > b + d$.

(5) 的证明. 若 $a > b$, $c < d$, 则 $a - b > 0$, $d - c > 0$. 故由(Ⅱ)$(a - b) + (d - c) > 0$,即 $(a - c) - (b - d) > 0$,故 $a - c > b - d$. 仿此可证(5)的后半.

(6) 的证明. 若 $a > b$, $m > 0$, 则 $a - b > 0$, $m > 0$. 故由(Ⅱ),$(a - b)m > 0$ 即 $am - bm > 0$ 即 $am > bm$. 又用反证法可证 $\frac{a}{m} > \frac{b}{m}$.

(7) 的证明. 若 $a > b$, $m < 0$, 则 $a - b > 0$, $-m > 0$. 故由(Ⅱ),$(a - b)(-m) > 0$,即 $-am + bm > 0$,故 $bm > am$,即 $am < bm$.

(8) 的证明. (8) 的意义就是 $a - b = 0$, $a - b > 0$, $a - b < 0$ 三式之中恰好有一样成立,这显然可以由 Ⅰ 推出来.

由此可见,不等式的8条基本性质可以由 Ⅰ、Ⅱ、Ⅲ 三条性质推出来. 这件事实对于我们了解不等式来说是有它的意义的. 但这并不等于说,实际在中学教学之中,也要作这些推理. 虽然这些证明是很简单的,然而对于中学生来说,他们还不一定能够真正领会这些推理的作用,所以只能作教师的参考. 另一方面,在以上的证明中把不等式的性质化为正负数性质的方法,却在推证不等式时非常有用,以后还要看到更多的例.

3. 证不等式与解不等式. 为方便起见,我们现在把不等式分成两种,一种姑且把它叫做绝对不等式,另一种姑且把它叫做条件不等式. 所谓条件不等式,就是要在适当条件之下才成立的不等式,像上节所说,不等式的前 7 条基本性质都可以作为条件不等式的例子. 另一方面也有所谓绝对不等式,就是对于一切实数都无条件地成立的不等式，举个最简单的例来看，如 $x^2+1>0$. 下面再举一个比较有意思但仍然非常简单的例子：

例 1 $2ab\leqslant a^2+b^2$.

要证明它，只要证明 $a^2+b^2-2ab\geqslant 0$ 即 $(a-b)^2\geqslant 0$.

但最后一式显然成立，故 $2ab\leqslant a^2+b^2$.

又只有当 $a=b$ 时，才得 $(a-b)^2=0$，故只有当 $a=b$ 时，才得 $2ab=a^2+b^2$.

以上的证明虽然简单，但它告诉我们两个常用的方法．其一是要证 $A\geqslant B$，有时变成 $A-B\geqslant 0$ 去证明，比较方便．其二是要证一式大于等于0，可以设法把它表成一个平方，或者更广泛一些，把它表成若干个平方之和．为了说明这个方法，再举一个关于条件不等式的例子如下：

例 2 设 $b^2-4ac<0$，则(1) 当 $a<0$ 时，$ax^2+bx+c<0$；(2) 当 $a>0$ 时，$ax^2+bx+c>0$.

证 在两种情形下都得到

$$ax^2+bx+c=a\left(x^2+\frac{b}{a}x+\frac{c}{a}\right)=a\left[\left(x+\frac{b}{2a}\right)^2+\frac{4ac-b^2}{4a^2}\right]$$

要证明的条件不等式显然可以从此推出来.

又当 $b^2-4ac=0$ 时，上式右端可以是零$\left(\text{即当 } x+\frac{b}{2a}=0\text{ 时}\right)$，所以要把结果略为改变一下，得到：

(1) 当 $a<0$ 时，$ax^2+bx+c\leqslant 0$；

(2) 当 $a>0$ 时，$ax^2+bx+c\geqslant 0$.

不管 $b^2-4ac<0$ 还是 $b^2-4ac=0$，我们看到 ax^2+bx+c 除可能是0外，符号总是不变的，换句话说，符号是不随 x 的改变而改变的．但当 $b^2-4ac>0$ 时，情形就不同，这时 ax^2+bx+c 的符号要因 x 的值不同而改变．在这种情形下，我们平常不给出条件去证明不等式，而是问 x 在什么条件之下 $ax^2+bx+c>0$，又在什么条件下 $ax^2+bx+c<0$. 这就产生了解不等式的问题．换句话说，所谓解不等式的问题，就是替条件不等式补足所缺条件的问题.

关于解一次不等式的问题（即问在什么条件下 $ax+b>0$），应该早为大家所熟知．现在为完全起见，仍然以解二次不等式为例来谈一下．当 $b^2-4ac>0$ 而 $a\neq 0$ 时，$ax^2+bx+c=0$ 有两个相异的实根 x_1 及 x_2，并设 $x_1<x_2$，则

$$ax^2+bx+c=a(x-x_1)(x-x_2)$$

在这里，我们只要记住一个最简单的原则，就可以解决问题，那就是“奇数个负数相乘是负的，偶数个负数相乘是正的”．例如当 $x_1<x<x_2$ 时，$x-x_1$ 是正的而 $x-x_2$ 是负的，故 ax^2+bx+c 的符号与 a 相反．从此我们可以把结果列成一

个表：

$a>0$	$x<x_1$	$ax^2+bx+c>0$
	$x_1<x<x_2$	$ax^2+bx+c<0$
	$x_2<x$	$ax^2+bx+c>0$
$a<0$	$x<x_1$	$ax^2+bx+c<0$
	$x_1<x<x_2$	$ax^2+bx+c>0$
	$x_2<x$	$ax^2+bx+c<0$

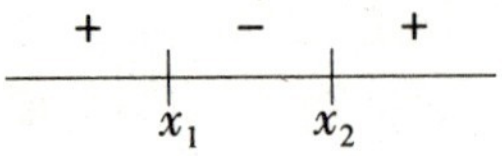

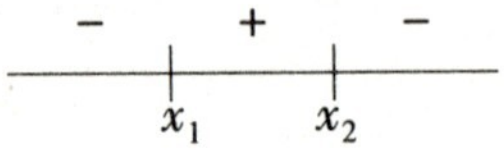

以上所述的原则可以用来解较高次不等式，如解$(x-1)(x-2)(x-3)>0$.

又如结合例 1 后面所述方法，可以解$(x^2+x+1)(x^2+x-1)>0$.

最后，特别在这里说明一下，条件不等式的概念对于学习数学分析来说是非常重要的．如果中学生在这方面能够充分地理解和熟悉，不知道对于以后学习分析会有多么大的方便．解不等式，就是理解条件不等式的一个最好的途径. 平常对于等式，总感觉是很完美的一样东西，对于绝对不等式也会觉得还整齐有趣，唯独对于条件不等式总难免觉得很累赘．但是为了以后学习的需要，我们要尽量使中学生理解条件不等式．理解怎样解不等式，怎样从不等式推出不等式.

还要附带在这里提起一下，绝对值的意义，也有很多中学生弄不清楚．尤其需要注意的是，含有绝对值的不等式的意义．例如$|x-a|<r\ (r>0)$ 的意义是

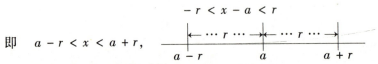

$$-r<x-a<r$$

即 $a-r<x<a+r$,

在讲不等式的时候，最好提到这一点.

4. 不等式与最大最小问题. 利用不等式可以求一个函数$f(x)$ 的最大值或最小值．理由是这样：如果k是一个常数，如果我们能证明下面两件事，就可以说$f(x)$ 的最小值(或最大值) 是k.

(1)$f(x)\geqslant k$(或$f(x)\leqslant k$)；

(2) 可以找到x_0，使$f(x_0)=k$.

反之，如果知道k是$f(x)$ 的最小值，即得不等式$f(x)\geqslant k$. 因此证不等式与求最大最小值的问题是密切相关的．现在仍然以二次函数$f(x)=ax^2+bx+c$为例. 前已证

$$ax^2+bx+c=a\left[\left(x+\frac{b}{2a}\right)^2+\frac{4ac-b^2}{4a^2}\right]$$

因此：

（1）当 $a>0$ 时，$ax^2+bx+c\geqslant\frac{4ac-b^2}{4a}$；

（2）当 $a<0$ 时，$ax^2+bx+c\leqslant\frac{4ac-b^2}{4a}$.

但当 $x=-\frac{b}{2a}$ 时，$ax^2+bx+c=\frac{4ac-b^2}{4a}$，所以$\frac{4ac-b^2}{4a}$是$f(x)=ax^2+bx+c$的最小值或最大值，视 $a>0$ 或 $a<0$ 而定. 又由

$$ax^2+bx+c=a\left[\left(x+\frac{b}{2a}\right)^2+\frac{4ac-b^2}{4a^2}\right]$$

可知，若 $a>0$ 则当 $x>\frac{b}{2a}$ 时，x 越大，上式右边也越大，并且没有上界，所以说 ax^2+bx+c 没有最大值．仿此可证，当 $a<0$ 时，ax^2+bx+c 没有最小值.

为清楚起见，我们可以分别情形画出函数 $y=ax^2+bx+c$ 的图形如下：

下面再举一个比较复杂的例．我们把它写成定理的形式

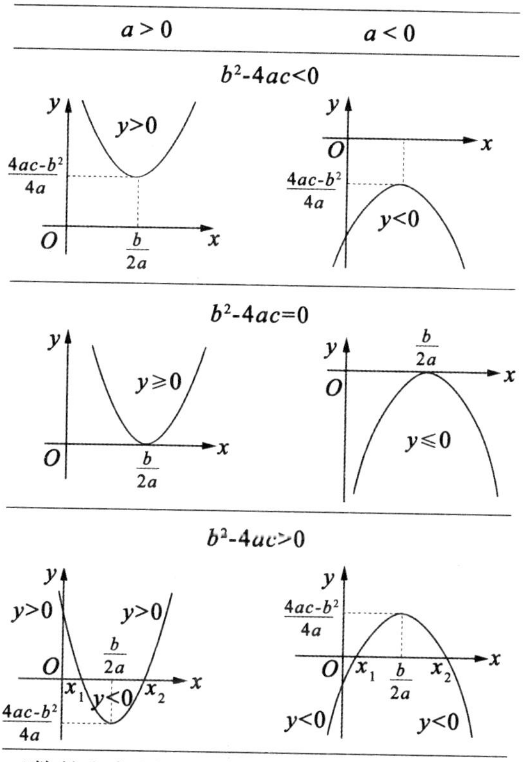

定理 1　n 个正数的积如果是 1，则其和最小是 n，且只当 n 个数彼此相等时

其和才是 n.

证 (1) 显然当 n 个正数 $x_1, x_2, \cdots, x_n$ 彼此相等其积为1时，一定都等于1，因此其和为 n. 今将用归纳法证明当 $x_1, x_2, \cdots, x_n$ 不全相同时，$x_1, x_2 + \cdots + x_n > n$.

(2) 设 $n = 2$，并设两数为 x 与 $\frac{1}{x}$. 今将证，当 $x \neq 1$ 时

$$x + \frac{1}{x} > 2$$

我们知道当 $a \neq b$ 时

$$a^2 + b^2 > 2ab$$

令 $a = \sqrt{x}$, $b = \frac{1}{\sqrt{x}}$，则因 $x \neq 1$，故 $a \neq b$，故 $x + \frac{1}{x} > 2$.

(3) 设当 $n = k$ 时，定理成立. 换言之，若 $x'_1, x'_2, \cdots, x'_n$ 都是正数且不全相等，又若 $x'_1 x'_2 \cdots x'_k = 1$，则

$$x'_1 + x'_2 + \cdots + x'_k > k$$

今将证当 $x_1, x_2, \cdots, x_{k+1}$ 是不全相等的正数而 $x_1 x_2 \cdots x_{k+1} = 1$ 时

$$x_1 + x_2 + \cdots + x_{k+1} > k + 1$$

由

$$x_1 x_2 \cdots x_{k+1} = 1$$

容易推出

$$x_1^{k+1} < 1 < x_{k+1}^{k+1}$$

若 $x_1 \geqslant 1$ 则 $x_1^{k+1} \geqslant 1$. 这不可能. 故 $x_1 < 1$. 仿此可证 $x_{k+1} > 1$. 我们可以把 $x_1 x_2 \cdots x_k x_{k+1} = 1$ 写成

$$(x_1 x_{k+1}) x_2 x_3 \cdots x_k = 1$$

令 $y_1 = x_1 x_{k+1}$，则得

$$y_1 x_2 x_3 \cdots x_k = 1$$

上式左边只有 k 个因数，故由归纳法的假设得

$$y_1 + x_2 + x_3 + \cdots + x_k \geqq k$$

因 $y_1 = x_1 x_{k+1}$，故

$$x_1 x_{k+1} + x_2 + x_3 + \cdots + x_k \geqq k$$

两边加上 $x_1 - x_1 x_{k+1} + x_{k+1}$，即得

$$x_1 + x_2 + x_3 + \cdots + x_k + x_{k+1} \geqq k + x_1 - x_1 x_{k+1} + x_{k+1} = k + 1 + (x_{k+1} - 1)(1 - x_1) > k + 1$$

最后一步由于 $x_1 < 1 < x_{k+1}$. 定理随之成立.

例3 当 x 为锐角时

$$\sin x + \csc x \geqq 2,\ \cos x + \sec x \geqq 2,\ \tan x + \cot x \geqslant 2$$

以上三式只当 $x = \frac{\pi}{4}$ 时才能用“=”号.

例 4 若 a,b,c 为正数,则 $\frac{b}{a}+\frac{c}{b}+\frac{a}{c}\geqslant 3$.

上式中只当 a,b,c 全相等时才能用"="号.

5. 三个著名的不等式. 本节介绍三个最常用的著名不等式.

所谓 n 个数 $x_1,x_2,\cdots,x_n$ 的算术平均就是 $\frac{x_1+x_2+\cdots+x_n}{n}$,又所谓 n 个数 $x_1,x_2,\cdots,x_n$ 的几何平均就是 $\sqrt[n]{x_1x_2\cdots x_n}$.

关于算术平均与几何平均有下面的重要定理.

定理 2 n 个正数的几何平均不大于它们的算术平均,即

$$\sqrt[n]{x_1x_2\cdots x_n}\leqslant\frac{x_1+x_2+\cdots+x_n}{n}$$

又上式中只有当 $x_1=x_2=\cdots=x_n$ 时,才能用"="号.

证 设

$$g=\sqrt[n]{x_1x_2\cdots x_n}$$

则
$$\frac{x_1}{g}\cdot\frac{x_2}{g}\cdot\cdots\cdot\frac{x_n}{g}=\frac{x_1x_2\cdots x_n}{g^n}=\frac{g^n}{g^n}=1$$

故由上节的定理,

$$\frac{x_1}{g}+\frac{x_2}{g}+\cdots+\frac{x_n}{g}\geqslant n$$

且上式中的等号,只有当左边各项相等(即 $x_1=x_2=\cdots=x_n$)时才成立. 用 $\frac{g}{n}$ 乘上式两端,即得所需要的结果.

例 5 设长方体的长宽高之和一定,则当长方体成正方体(即立方体)时,体积最大.

证 设长宽高分别是 a,b,c,而其和是一定的数 k. 又设体积是 V,则 $V=abc$.

由定理 2,

$$\sqrt[3]{V}\geqq\frac{a+b+c}{3}$$

即
$$V=abc\geqq\left(\frac{a+b+c}{3}\right)^3=\left(\frac{k}{3}\right)^3$$

上面的等号只有当 $a=b=c=\frac{k}{3}$ 时才成立,定理随之证明.

定理 3(Буняковский - Schwarz 不等式) 设 $a_1,a_2,\cdots,a_n$ 和 $b_1,b_2,\cdots,b_n$ 都是正数,则

$$(a_1b_1+a_2b_2+\cdots+a_nb_n)^2\leqslant(a_1^2+a_2^2+\cdots+a_n^2)(b_1^2+b_2^2+\cdots+b_n^2)$$

证 显然

$$(a_1x+b_1)^2+(a_2x+b_2)^2+\cdots+(a_nx+b_n)^2\geqslant 0$$

即

$$Ax^2+Bx+C\geqslant 0$$

其中

$$A=a_1^2+a_2^2+\cdots+a_n^2, B=2(a_1b_1+a_2b_2+\cdots+a_nb_n)$$

$$C=b_1^2+b_2^2+\cdots+b_n^2$$

只有当 $B^2-4AC\leqslant 0$ 时，Ax^2+Bx+C 才能保持同一符号（除有时等于0以外）．因此 $B^2\leqslant 4AC$，即

$$(a_1b_1+a_2b_2+\cdots+a_nb_n)^2\leqslant(a_1^2+a_2^2+\cdots+a_n^2)(b_1^2+b_2^2+\cdots+b_n^2)$$

当 $n=2$ 时，这个不等式有它的几何意义．设两个矢量的分量分别是 a_1,a_2 及 b_1,b_2，则二矢量的内乘是 $a_1b_1+a_2b_2$，而其长分别为 $\sqrt{a_1^2+a_2^2}$ 及 $\sqrt{b_1^2+b_2^2}$．定理3的几何意义是：两矢量的内乘不大于两矢量的长之积．

这个定理可以推广成下面的形式（Hölder 不等式）．在定理3的假定下，若又知 $p>0$，$q>0$ 且 $\frac{1}{p}+\frac{1}{q}=1$，则

$$a_1b_1+a_2b_2+\cdots+a_nb_n\leqslant(a_1^p+a_2^p+\cdots+a_n^p)^{\frac{1}{p}}(b_1^q+b_2^q+\cdots+b_n^q)^{\frac{1}{q}}$$

这个定理的证明较长，不在这里叙述了．

定理4 若 $a_1,a_2,\cdots,a_n$，和 $b_1,b_2,\cdots,b_n$ 都是正数，则

$$\sqrt{(a_1+b_1)^2+(a_2+b_2)^2+\cdots+(a_n+b_n)^2}\leqq \sqrt{a_1^2+a_2^2+\cdots+a_n^2}+\sqrt{b_1^2+b_2^2+\cdots+b_n^2}$$

证

$$\begin{aligned}&(a_1+b_1)^2+(a_2+b_2)^2+\cdots+(a_n+b_n)^2=\\&a_1(a_1+b_1)+a_2(a_2+b_2)+\cdots+a_n(a_n+b_n)+\\&b_1(a_1+b_1)+b_2(a_2+b_2)+\cdots+b_n(a_n+b_n)\leqslant\\&(a_1^2+a_2^2+\cdots+a_n^2)^{\frac{1}{2}}[(a_1+b_1)^2+(a_2+b_2)^2+\cdots+(a_n+b_n)^2]^{\frac{1}{2}}+\\&(b_1^2+b_2^2+\cdots+b_n^2)^{\frac{1}{2}}[(a_1+b_1)^2+(a_2+b_2)^2+\cdots+(a_n+b_n)^2]^{\frac{1}{2}}\end{aligned}$$

最后的不等式系由定理3得出．用 $[(a_1+b_1)^2+(a_2+b_2)^2+\cdots+(a_n+b_n)^2]^{\frac{1}{2}}$ 除两边即得所求证的不等式．

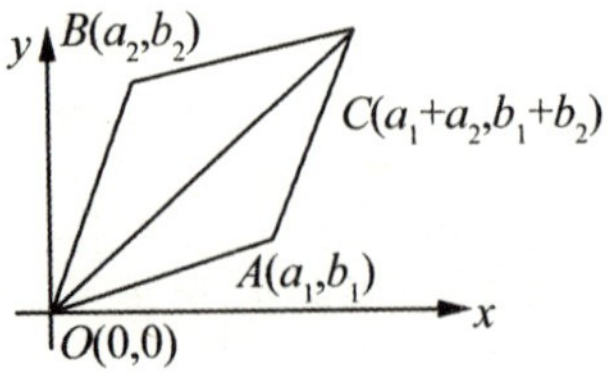

当 $n=2$ 时，上面的不等式有它的几何意义．如右图 $OACB$ 是一平行四边形，其顶点的坐标已在图中写出．上面的不等式就等于说

$$\overline{OC}\leqslant\overline{OA}+\overline{AC}$$

这个不等式也可以推广如下（Minkowski 不等式）：设 $p>1$，则

$$[(a_1+b_1)^p+(a_2+b_2)^p+\cdots+(a_n+b_n)^p]^{\frac{1}{p}}\leqslant$$

$$(a_1^p + a_2^p + \cdots + a_n^p)^{\frac{1}{p}} + (b_1^p + b_2^p + \cdots + b_n^p)^{\frac{1}{p}}$$

这个不等式可以仿照上定理的证明方法从 Hölder 不等式推出来.

现在就以介绍这三个在数学上最常用的著名不等式作为本文的结束．读者如果想得到更多的关于不等式的知识,可以阅读以下几本书:

1. 科罗夫琴著,许霖译:不等式.
2. Chrystal 著:Algebra 第 XXIV 章.
3. Hardy, Littlewood, Polya 著:Inequalities.

编后记

“树欲静而风不止，子欲养而亲不在。”1973年10月家父去世时我们五兄妹中，最大的也只有20岁出头。按理做子女的本应尽些孝心，但在父亲的晚年，他身边的子女不过是一群十几岁不懂事的孩子。后来“上山下乡”，哥哥和我天各一方，一个去了内蒙古呼伦贝尔盟的农村插队，一个到了内蒙古的生产建设兵团，大妹则进了北大的仪器厂，两个小妹还在上中学。我记得当年为父亲做过能算上孝道的事，也就是在“文化大革命”期间父亲在北大被隔离时，为他送过衣物；再就是父亲身体不好时曾在下雪天为他去西苑医院取过中药。而当我们子女们逐渐长大成人，懂些事理且有能力、有时间为他尽孝心时，家父却早已远去。

家父这一生很不容易。他发奋读书，兼课教学养家糊口；他走南闯北，游学海外；他教书、著述，淡泊名利；他提携后学，在数论和培养人才方面颇有建树。同时他又经历了诸多的磨难，特别是“文化大革命”的浩劫。记得那时父亲作为“资产阶级反动学术权威”被抄家、被批斗。父亲痛苦与无助的眼神，一直在我脑海里挥之不去。在“文化大革命”最压抑的时期，父亲不停地写检查，后来被派到印刷厂“劳动改造”。在命运未卜的年代，他甚至想好以后干脆就做个印刷厂的工人，我想这或许是因为他喜欢读书、喜欢书页上散发出的油墨芳香。

不过，现实要比他想象的好些。“文化大革命”风暴的间隙，他在接受工人阶级再教育中，似乎也多少找到了数学家真实的自我。他跑到城里的技术工人家里去辅导数学；他到河北徐水石油地球物理勘探局和工程技术人员研究数字勘探技术；他登上小艇到渤海湾与工程师们采集数据、研究算法；他为学校的训练班和工农兵学员讲课；他和不约而至的陈景润等后学在家中探讨数论问题；他甚至偷闲在蜗居中仅有的一张书桌上摊开纸笔演算起他心中的数学猜想，并哼出了京剧小曲。这短暂的几年，大概是这位数学家生前最后的快慰时光。然而，父亲生命的时钟却戛然而止，病逝时年仅60岁。父亲的突然离去，可以说令学界、令亲友和我们全家扼腕叹息。

父亲生前并没有给子女们留下什么财产，但他给子女留下的精神财富，他对子女有形无形的影响，至今仍难以忘怀。这次哈尔滨工业大学出版社的刘培杰编辑要出版一套中国著名数论家的文集，父亲被列入其中。我想这是一种对学者、对逝者的敬重与缅怀，也是对父亲一种最好的纪念。我有时在想，即便父亲头脑中有再多的智慧，不都随他而去了吗？能有机会看到父亲身后留下的文论结集出版，这不是做子女的莫大荣幸吗？对此我们心中充满了感动与感激。

我是个在小学就被老师批评的“怎么数学家的儿子数学学得那么差”的一个，而且至今仍然是个缺少数学细胞的人。不过我感觉还是可以为编辑出版父亲的《文集》尽一点力，因为我毕竟做了十多年的出版，毕竟还有些闲暇时间，更何况始终有一颗对父亲的敬仰与感恩之心。

这本《文集》是在20年前北京大学出版社出版的《闵嗣鹤论文选集》基础上编辑而成的，当年周培源先生亲自作序，潘承彪、戚鸣皋先生等为编辑出版颇费辛劳。这次在原有论文的基础上，增加了家父的演讲稿及几篇文章等，新增了几篇“手稿”、“书信”的原件，此外附上了仅存的几张家父不同时期的照片。我想这样的一本文集会更接近一个比较真实和比较丰满的家父形象，也会使读者在感受他的学术思想和建树的同时，更好地感受一个人。

惠泉　执笔2010年金秋十月

编辑手记

对闵先生的认识从笔者中学时代开始，初中时读过徐迟先生的报告文学《哥德巴赫猜想》，感觉到闵先生是一位厉害程度不亚于陈先生的人物，因为他能审阅那篇让国人倍感骄傲的论文.

笔者的高中阶段是上世纪 80 年代，笔者的父亲当时有逛书店的习惯，经常给笔者买一些小册子看，其中就有闵先生所写的《格点与面积》，虽是初版于 1964 年但在 20 世纪 80 年代又重印了. 读后眼界大开，诸如毕克定理、闵可夫斯基定理今天想起来还记忆犹新，而且在数学竞赛辅导讲座中还能信手拈来，讲给现在的学生听. 当年海伦 · 凯勒读完《圣经》后，体会到深远的慰藉，她写道："有形的东西是短暂的，无形的才能永垂不朽."

闵先生虽然早已离我们而去，但他留下的数学精神还在. 本来在组织这套中国数论名家著作选时，首先考虑的是闵先生 1958 年由科学出版社出版的《数论的方法》（上、下册）（这本书笔者曾试图研读过，但终因学力不逮而中途放弃），但在联系过程中得知科学出版社即将出版，便改选了目前这本文集，并在其子闵乐泉、闵惠泉先生和潘承彪先生的大力支持下最终完成.本书最早是由北京大学出版社出版的.1998年笔者曾到北京大学出版社去买,但早已没有了.因为仅印了区区800册.后笔者给当时该书责编刘勇先生打电话,刘勇先生从家里找到一本骑自行车送到笔者手中.今天重版此书想起13年前的情景颇有感慨.有人曾感叹道"数卷残书,半窗寒烛,冷落荒斋里",这就是中年.不知不觉中,笔者已近中年,难免心灰意冷.但看到赵慈庚为闵先生所写的小传又颇受鼓舞,赵先生说:

"(闵先生)前半生里,他每有一点进展,便遭遇一次灾难.刚入大学便死了祖母与父亲;毕业后刚能谋生又死了祖父;在昆明他学术上初露头角,次妹死于车祸.这些坎坷都被他的坚强意志抗过去了.以后的不幸却都逼向他本身.1946年博士学位在望,又有人生烦恼降临,以致神志失常,不得已而接受基督教洗礼.1954年业术具见峥嵘,而高血压病魔缠来,时常忍着眩晕讲授繁重的基础课.从1966年夏季起,又在'旧知识分子'行列中泅渡'文化大革命'的骇浪.多少年往事蹉跎,使他长期苦闷……两年之后发现了冠心病."

闵先生年仅60岁就逝世了.他的祖父曾在弥留之际牵着他的手说:"你的前程不能太好,也不会很坏."果然一语成谶.

闵先生的人生信条写在1935年《毕业同学录》中,他说:"能受苦方为志士,肯吃亏不是痴人."今天国学盛行就是社会上肯受苦、肯吃亏的人太少了而产生的一种自我校正.这方面其实我们多学学老一辈学者比读那些所谓国学宝典有用得多.

一位著名历史学家说道:探索知识的人与"粗俗的从业人士"完全不同,他们是社会中"仅存"的圣徒,他们对知识的执著热爱"绝不会受到不良动机的玷污".《大学的观念》作者G·斯丹利·霍尔(G. Stanley Hall)曾经说过,一颗爱好探索的心灵"需要完全放弃自我",研究者是"追求真理的圣灵骑士",理想的研究者"必须具有天赋,心中藏有天火".

还是毛主席那句话用在评价闵先生时最贴切,他是一个纯粹的人,一个高尚的人,一个脱离了低级趣味的人.闵先生自己总结一生说:"一生经历,点滴无愧——发肤之痛可以忍,民族正气不能亏.要坚守旧志,用学术为祖国服务,要继续努力."用今天的人眼光看,闵先生40年的学术生涯一直都在"取"与"舍"之间,舍小我成就"大我",舍自己成就事业.

我国著名哲学家、文学家徐訏(1908—1980)爱书如命,但又随世事变迁多次遗失.故以佛学自释:

"人在这个世上,都有所'执',佛所教我们的是'无执'.但是人而无执,这短短数十年也就更加空虚.想到人生的无常,能‘执’也应该准备能‘舍’.‘舍’是一种英雄的行为,对于我们这种凡人是不容易的.这因为‘执’是一种累积的得,‘舍’则是一种突兀的失.”(钟敬文,张岱年,邓九平.灯下书影[M].北京:中国广播电视出版社,1997年.)

今天的图书市场多见珠光宝气的影视明星自传记和踌躇满志的企业家的豪言壮语.老一代数学家逐渐淡出了人们的视线.我们重版闵先生的文集是为了这忘却的纪念.

在写这篇编辑手记的前两天,笔者刚去过北京,从潘家园旧书市场的书商手中高价买到了一本北平厂甸师大附中算学业刻社印行的(中华民国26年1月印)的由闵先生和朗好常编译的,傅种孙、程廷熙参校的《高中解析几何教科书(下卷)》,手拂旧卷,感慨万千.回望历史感叹烟云,叹数学出版事业由盛到衰,由朱门绮窗到斜阳衰草,写到最后,除了一声叹息,似没再剩下什么.

刘培杰

2011年3月31日于哈工大

哈尔滨工业大学出版社刘培杰数学工作室已出版(即将出版)图书目录

书　　名	出版时间	定　价	编号
新编中学数学解题方法全书(高中版)上卷	2007－09	38.00	7
新编中学数学解题方法全书(高中版)中卷	2007－09	48.00	8
新编中学数学解题方法全书(高中版)下卷(一)	2007－09	42.00	17
新编中学数学解题方法全书(高中版)下卷(二)	2007－09	38.00	18
新编中学数学解题方法全书(高中版)下卷(三)	2010－06	58.00	73
新编中学数学解题方法全书(初中版)上卷	2008－01	28.00	29
新编中学数学解题方法全书(初中版)中卷	2010－07	38.00	75
新编平面解析几何解题方法全书(专题讲座卷)	2010－01	18.00	61

数学眼光透视	2008－01	38.00	24
数学思想领悟	2008－01	38.00	25
数学应用展观	2008－01	38.00	26
数学建模导引	2008－01	28.00	23
数学方法溯源	2008－01	38.00	27
数学史话览胜	2008－01	28.00	28

从毕达哥拉斯到怀尔斯	2007－10	48.00	9
从迪利克雷到维斯卡尔迪	2008－01	48.00	21
从哥德巴赫到陈景润	2008－05	98.00	35
从庞加莱到佩雷尔曼	即将出版	98.00	

数学解题中的物理方法	2011－03	28.00	114
数学解题的特殊方法	即将出版	38.00	115
中学数学计算技巧	即将出版	38.00	116
中学数学证明方法	即将出版	48.00	117

历届 IMO 试题集(1959—2005)	2006－05	58.00	5
历届 CMO 试题集	2008－09	28.00	40
全国大学生数学夏令营数学竞赛试题及解答	2007－03	28.00	15
历届美国大学生数学竞赛试题集	2009－03	88.00	43
历届俄罗斯大学生数学竞赛试题及解答	即将出版	68.00	

哈尔滨工业大学出版社刘培杰数学工作室已出版(即将出版)图书目录

书　名	出版时间	定　价	编号
数学奥林匹克与数学文化(第一辑)	2006－05	48.00	4
数学奥林匹克与数学文化(第二辑)(竞赛卷)	2008－01	48.00	19
数学奥林匹克与数学文化(第二辑)(文化卷)	2008－07	58.00	36
数学奥林匹克与数学文化(第三辑)(竞赛卷)	2010－01	48.00	59
数学奥林匹克与数学文化(第四辑)(竞赛卷)	2011－03	48.00	87
发展空间想象力	2010－01	38.00	57
走向国际数学奥林匹克的平面几何试题诠释(上、下)(第2版)	2010－02	98.00	63,64
平面几何证明方法全书	2007－08	35.00	1
平面几何证明方法全书习题解答(第2版)	2006－12	18.00	10
最新世界各国数学奥林匹克中的平面几何试题	2007－09	38.00	14
数学竞赛平面几何典型题及新颖解	2010－07	48.00	74
初等数学复习及研究(平面几何)	2008－09	58.00	38
初等数学复习及研究(立体几何)	2010－06	38.00	71
初等数学复习及研究(平面几何)习题解答	2009－01	48.00	42
世界著名平面几何经典著作钩沉——几何作图专题卷(上)	2009－06	48.00	49
世界著名平面几何经典著作钩沉——几何作图专题卷(下)	2011－01	88.00	80
世界著名平面几何经典著作钩沉(民国平面几何老课本)	2011－03	38.00	113
世界著名数学经典著作钩沉——立体几何卷	2011－02	28.00	88
世界著名三角学经典著作钩沉(平面三角卷Ⅰ)	2010－06	28.00	69
世界著名三角学经典著作钩沉(平面三角卷Ⅱ)	2011－01	28.00	78
几何学教程(平面几何卷)	2011－03	78.00	90
几何变换与几何证题	2010－06	88.00	70
几何瑰宝——平面几何500名题暨1000条定理(上、下)	2010－07	138.00	76,77
三角形的五心	2009－06	28.00	51
俄罗斯平面几何问题集	2009－08	88.00	55
俄罗斯平面几何5000题	2011－03	48.00	89
500个最新世界著名数学智力趣题	2008－06	48.00	3
400个最新世界著名数学最值问题	2008－09	48.00	36
500个世界著名数学征解问题	2009－06	48.00	52
400个中国最佳初等数学征解老问题	2010－01	48.00	60
500个俄罗斯数学经典老题	2011－01	28.00	81

哈尔滨工业大学出版社刘培杰数学工作室已出版(即将出版)图书目录

书　　名	出版时间	定　价	编号
超越吉米多维奇——数列的极限	2009－11	48.00	58
初等数论难题集(第一卷)	2009－05	68.00	44
初等数论难题集(第二卷)(上、下)	2011－02	128.00	82,83
谈谈素数	2011－03	18.00	91
平方和	2011－03	18.00	92
数论概貌	2011－03	18.00	93
代数数论	2011－03	48.00	94
初等数论的知识与问题	2011－02	28.00	95
超越数论基础	2011－03	38.00	96
数论初等教程	2011－03	28.00	97
数论基础	2011－03	18.00	98
数论入门	2011－03	28.00	99
解析数论引论	2011－03	48.00	100
基础数论	2011－03	28.00	101
超越数	2011－03	18.00	109
三角和方法	2011－03	18.00	112

俄罗斯函数问题集	2011－03	38.00	103
俄罗斯组合分析问题集	2011－01	48.00	79
博弈论精粹	2008－03	58.00	30
多项式和无理数	2008－01	68.00	22
模糊数据统计学	2008－03	48.00	31
解析不等式新论	2009－06	68.00	48
建立不等式的方法	2011－03	98.00	104
数学奥林匹克不等式研究	2009－08	68.00	56
初等数学研究(Ⅰ)	2008－09	68.00	37
初等数学研究(Ⅱ)(上、下)	2009－05	118.00	46,47
中国初等数学研究　2009卷(第1辑)	2009－05	20.00	45
中国初等数学研究　2010卷(第2辑)	2010－05	30.00	68
数学奥林匹克超级题库(初中卷上)	2010－01	58.00	66

哈尔滨工业大学出版社刘培杰数学工作室 已出版（即将出版）图书目录

书　　名	出版时间	定　价	编号
中等数学英语阅读文选	2006－12	38.00	13
统计学专业英语	2007－03	28.00	16
数学 我爱你	2008－01	28.00	20
精神的圣徒　别样的人生——60位中国数学家成长的历程	2008－09	48.00	39
数学史概论	2009－06	78.00	50
斐波那契数列	2010－02	28.00	65
数学拼盘和斐波那契魔方	2010－07	38.00	72
数学的创造	2011－02	48.00	85
数学中的美	2011－02	38.00	84
最新全国及各省市高考数学试卷解法研究及点拨评析	2009－02	38.00	41
高考数学的理论与实践	2009－08	38.00	53
中考数学专题总复习	2007－04	28.00	6
向量法巧解数学高考题	2009－08	28.00	54
新编中学数学解题方法全书（高考复习卷）	2010－01	48.00	67
新编中学数学解题方法全书（高考真题卷）	2010－01	38.00	62
高考数学核心题型解题方法与技巧	2010－01	28.00	86
方程式论	2011－03	28.00	105
初级方程式论	2011－03	28.00	106
Galois 理论	2011－03	18.00	107
代数方程的根式解及伽罗华理论	2011－03	28.00	108
线性偏微分方程	2011－03	18.00	110
N 体问题周期解	2011－03	38.00	111
闵嗣鹤文集	2011－03	98.00	102
吴从炘数学活动三十年（1951～1980）	2010－07	99.00	32

联系地址：哈尔滨市南岗区复华四道街10号哈尔滨工业大学出版社刘培杰数学工作室
邮　　编：150006
联系电话：0451－86281378　　13904613167
E-mail：lpj1378@yahoo.com.cn